REDISCOVERY
OF SHAMANIC HERITAGE

Bibliotheca Shamanistica

Edited by
Mihály Hoppál

International Society for Shamanistic Research

EDITORIAL COMMITTEE

Volume 11

A series of books on the advances in the studies of shamanism

Published for the
INTERNATIONAL SOCIETY FOR SHAMANISTIC RESEARCH

REDISCOVERY
OF SHAMANIC HERITAGE

Edited by

Mihály Hoppál and Gábor Kósa

Akadémiai Kiadó, Budapest

This publication has been sponsored by

the Korean National Commission for UNESCO

and the Hungarian National Commission for UNESCO

This volume is the result of a symposium of comparative studies
in East and West, for the promotion of intercultural dialogue.
The symposium was organized
by the Korean National Commission for UNESCO,
the European Folklore Institute,
and the International Society for Shamanistic Research.

Front cover picture:
Picture made by Mihály Hoppál at the Korean shamanic ritual,
which was performed at the conference.
(3 April, 2000, Budapest)

Revised by
Clifford Sather and Louise Klemperer
Barbara Tedlock
Joan B. Townsend

ISBN 963 05 80853
HU ISSN 1218-988X

Published by Akadémiai Kiadó
Prielle Kornélia u. 19/D.
H–1117 Budapest, Hungary
www.akkrt.hu

Technical editor
Krisztina Ádám

CONTENTS

Notes on Contributors vii

Introduction
MIHÁLY HOPPÁL
    Shamanic Traditions as Intangible Cultural Heritage of Mankind 1

Part I. Shamanism and Mythology
HUNG-YOUN CHO
    An Archetypal Myth and Its Reality in Korean Shamanism 21
ELVIRA EEVR DJALTCHINOVA-MALETS
    Shamanic Tradition in Mythosophy of Kalmyks 37
GÁBOR KÓSA
    Mythology and Shamanism in the Ancient Chinese State of Chu 45
PÉTER SIMONCSICS
    Shaman as the Hero of a Kamassian Tale: a Riddle in Narration 109
KATALIN URAY-KŐHALMI
    The Myth of Nishan Shaman 113

Part II. Traditional Roles
DAGMAR EIGNER
    Tamang Healing Rituals and Psychotherapy: a Comparison 125
ULLA JOHANSEN
    Ecstasy and Possession: a Short Contribution to a
    Lengthy Discussion 135
CLIFFORD SATHER
    The Shaman as Preserver and Undoer of Life:
    The Role of the Shaman in Saribas Iban Death Rituals 153
DÁVID SOMFAI KARA
    Living Epic Tradition among Inner Asian Nomads 179

Part III. Local Traditions

EUGENE HELIMSKI
Nganasan Shamanistic Tradition: Observations and Hypotheses 195
MIHÁLY HOPPÁL
Shamans in Buryat Sacrificial Rituals 211
DILMURAT OMAR
Modern Kazakh Shamanism... 227
BARBARA WILHELMI
The Prophetic Performance and the Shamanic Ritual:
Shamanism in the Bible 241
YEE-HEUM YOON
The Diversity and Continuity of Shamanism in
Korean Religious History 255

Part IV. Shamanism and the Modern World

MAJAN GARLINSKI
Video-Ethnography and Shamanic Rituals 267
SEONG-NAE KIM
Korean Shamanic Heritage in Cyber Culture 279
BARBARA TEDLOCK
Recognizing & Celebrating the Feminine in Shamanic Heritage.......... 297
JOAN B. TOWNSEND
Western Core and Neo-Shamanism: Trends and Relations with
Indigenous Societies 317
DANIÈLE VAZEILLES
Revival of Lakota Sioux Shamanism 335

Index 355

CONTRIBUTORS

DAGMAR EIGNER studied psychology, physiology, philosophy, and ethnology at the University of Vienna, and music at the Conservatory of Vienna (1983, Dr. Phil., 2000 habilitation for medical anthropology). Psychotherapist, health psychologist, and clinical psychologist; lecturer at the University of Vienna and at the University of Koblenz-Landau, Germany. Fieldworks in Nepal, India, Indonesia, and Thailand. Major research areas: altered states of consciousness, changes of the demarcation of the Ego in therapeutic processes, the role of spirit possession in shamanic healing rituals.

MAJAN GARLINSKI studied social cultural anthropology at Zurich University, he actively participated in the production of various video films, especially in the Nepal region. Since 1999 he works as the curator of Visual Anthropology at the Ethnographic Museum in Geneva.

EUGENE HELIMSKI studied linguistics in Moscow. Cand. Sc. (Finno-Ugric Languages), Tartu 1979, Dr. Sc. (Finno-Ugric Languages), Tartu 1988. Researcher at the Academy of Sciences, Moscow (1978–1997), Professor at the Russian State University of the Humanities (1992–1998), guest professorships at the ELTE Budapest (1994–1995), at the Free University Berlin (1995), at the Humboldt University Berlin and at the Yagellonian University Cracow (1997–1998). Since 1998 Professor and Director of the Institute for Finno-Ugric (Uralic) Studies at the University Hamburg.

MIHÁLY HOPPÁL (Ph.D.) was born in Hungary (1942). He is the director of the Ethnographic Institute of the Hungarian Academy of Sciences, and the European Folklore Institute (Budapest). He is publishing extensively on comparative mythology (especially Finno-Ugric) and shamanism. He did fieldwork in Siberia, Korea, Manchuria, and China. He published the book on the visual history of Eurasian shamanism (*Shamans and Shamanism*) in

Hungarian, in German, in Japanese and in Chinese. He is the acting president (1991–2003) of the International Society for Shamanistic Research.

ULLA JOHANSEN (born in Estonia) is now the retires director and professor of the Institute of Ethnology at the University of Cologne. She was carrying out ethnographic fieldwork among South-eastern Anatolian nomads in 1956–57, followed by several more researches between 1964–1995. She was working in Russia and Central Asia as an employee of the Soviet Academy of Sciences in 1959–1961. The subject of her current ethnographic work is the culture of Turkic-speaking peoples and Estonians. Besides shamanism, she is generally interested in comparative studies of religions and ethnohistory.

SEONG-NAE KIM is an associate professor of anthropology of religion and Korean religions at the Department of Religious Studies, Sogang University, Seoul. She has written several articles on shamanic religious traditions on Cheju Island (Korea), and also a historical review on Korean shamanism studies in the last hundred years. Her publications include Chronicles of violence, ritual of mourning: Cheju shamanism in Korea, Dances and songs of exorcism in Cheju shamanism, Iconic power of modernity: reading a Cheju shaman's life history and initiation dream, and Mourning Korean modernity in the memory of the Cheju April Third Incident of 1948.

GÁBOR KÓSA is a teacher of classical Chinese language at the Gate of Dharma Buddhist University of Budapest, Ph.D. student of ELTE University. Research Areas: shamanism, alchemy, Manichaeism, and mythology in China.

DILMURAT OMAR studied in Beijing, Alma Ata (Kazakhstan), Bishkek (Kyrgyzstan), Kyushu University (Japan), and Cologne University (Germany). He finished his Ph.D. in 1991 at Beijing Academy of Social Sciences. He is now professor for Cultural Anthropology and director of the Institute for Cultural Anthropology at the Xinjiang University in Urumchi. Since 1986, he has been carrying out fieldwork among Kazakh, Kyrgyz and the Uyghur shamans every year.

CLIFFORD SATHER, (Ph.D.) (Harvard University), is currently Professorial Fellow in the Department of Social and Cultural Anthropology, University of Helsinki. He is editor of the *Borneo Research Bulletin* and the author of several books, including *The Bajau Laut* (Oxford, 1997) and *Seeds of Play, Words of Power: An Ethnographic Study of Iban Shamanic Chants* (Tun Jugah Foundation and the Borneo Research Council, 2001) and is co-editor with James J. Fox of *Origins, Ancestors and Alliance* (ANU, 1996).

PÉTER SIMONCSICS graduated from the University of Szeged (Hungary) in 1969 (Doctor Universitatis [1972, Szeged], Ph.D. [1996, Szeged], Dr. habil. [Pécs, Hungary, 2001]). He was teaching Hungarian language and linguistics in Indiana University (USA) in 1973–74, Turku University (Finland) in 1976–81, Aarhus University (Denmark) in 1988–1992. and worked as a researcher in Uralic studies from 1971 until 2003. His major fields of interest: language of folklore (shamanism) in Samoyedic and Finno-Ugric languages, Hungarian linguistics, history of linguistics.

DÁVID SOMFAI KARA is presently finishing his PhD studies at the Department of Inner Asian Studies, ELTE University, Budapest. He was conducting fieldworks in Kazakstan (1992, 1995/97), Kyrgyzstan (1995/99/01/02), Siberia (1995/97/98/01/02), Mongolia (1996/97/00), Volga-Ural Region (1996), Turkmenistan (1998) and Tajikistan (2001). He collected material between the Turkic speaking Kazak, Kyrgyz, Tyba, Tofa, Altai, Abakan (Khakas), Sakha (Yakut) groups, mostly folksongs, epic tradition, shamanism and other popular believes. His main research field is comparative studies of Siberian, Central Asian and Mongolian nomadic cultures.

BARBARA TEDLOCK is Distinguished Professor and Chair of Anthropology at the State University of New York at Buffalo. She has done extensive field work among shamans, diviners, dream interpreters, and other religious healers in North America, Meso-America, and Africa. Her books include *Time and the Highland Maya, Dreaming: Anthropological and Psychological Interpretations,* and *The Beautiful and the Dangerous: Dialogues with Zuni Indians.*

JOAN B. TOWNSEND (Anthropology, BA 1959, Ph.D. 1965 University of California, Los Angeles) was teaching at the Department of Anthropology: University of Manitoba Winnipeg, Manitoba., Canada, now retired as full professor and received special award as Professor Emerita. Research Fields: historic and prehistoric archaeology, traditional shamanism (Nepal), theoretical aspects of shamanism; Core shamanism and Neo-shamanism, non-allopathic healing.

KATALIN URAY-KŐHALMI was studying under the guidance of LAJOS LIGETI and GYULA NÉMETH (Ph.D. in 1968). Teaching at Bonn, Vienna, Szeged and Budapest, since 1987 formally retired. Research fields: role and history of weapons in nomadic cultures; folklore, mythology and religious traditions of the Mongolian, (south Siberian) Turkish and Tungus people.

DANIÈLE VAZEILLES is a professor of Social Anthropology at the Université Paul Valéry – Montpellier. She has done fieldworks among reservation and urban Indians of North America, especially the Lakota Sioux from South Dakota. Her main themes of interests are religious studies (from traditional shamanism to neo-shamanism and New Age) and intercultural studies, with fieldworks both in France and in the USA. She is now involved in Ethno-archeological researches. She wrote several articles and books on these subjects: *Le Cercle et le Calumet*; *Les Chamanes, Maîtres de l'Univers*; *Chamanes et visionnaires sioux*.

BARBARA WILHELMI studied theology, history of culture, psychology and art at Bielefeld and Tübingen, teaching at Institut für Kirchenbau und Kunst der Gegenwart, and Philips-Universität Marburg, Deutschland. She organizes exhibitions and performances since 1980. Major topics include prophetic ritual as performance, theology and shamanism, healing practices in the Bible, art and therapy, and intercultural theology

MIHÁLY HOPPÁL

Shamanic Traditions as
Intangible Cultural Heritage of Mankind

This volume is based on a conference that took place at Hungarian Culture Foundation, Budapest in April 2000. For financial support we are grateful to the Korean and Hungarian National Commissions for UNESCO. We are also indebted to Barbara Tedlock, Joan B. Townsend, and Clifford Sather and his wife, who proofread and polished the style of the articles.

Originally a meeting of scholars from East and West was planned within the frames of a UNESCO program called *Dialogue between Cultures*. This project proclaims the importance of the protection of the world cultural tangible and intangible heritage as a common ground for the promotion of mutual understanding among cultures and civilizations. UNESCO has adopted a decision which proclaims 2002 as the United Nations Year for Cultural Heritage. Shamanic traditions, however deeply rooted in different ethnic folklores, are truly belong to the common cultural heritage of mankind. Thus, let us make the International Year for Cultural Heritage more significant by presenting the papers of our conference.

"The celebration of the United Nations Year for Cultural Heritage gives us an exceptional opportunity to ensure that the public authorities, the private sector, civil society as a whole, and young people in particular have a better understanding of the fact that the cultural heritage is simultaneously, an instrument for peace, reconciliation and mutual understanding, and a factor in development. For this reason it is suggested that activities to commemorate this United Nations Year for Cultural Heritage be based on the two main themes of dialogue and development.

Dialogue, so that instead of being targeted as a mark of identity, the heritage becomes the symbol of a plural heritage and a shared future—as is the case today in Afghanistan and Cambodia. Development, because, as numerous examples show, a new approach to the management of the cultural heritage can promote economic growth by creating employment opportunities for local populations, whether through crafts, cultural tourism and the emergence of new trades, or new forms of creativity."— Let us continue quoting the letter by Koïchiro Matsuura, Director-General of UNESCO. "All peoples gain a sense of identity and cohesion from their heritage. At the same time the origins of this heritage are multifarious and its history marked by many different influences. A people that is aware of its roots is better able to build peaceful relations with other peoples, to pursue what is often an age-old dialogue and to forge its future."—These are important statements for further considerations.

In this context, in 1998 the Korean National Commission for UNESCO launched a medium-term project on shamanism heritage entitled "Discovery of Shamanic Heritage". As the first step an International Symposium was held, in cooperation with the Korea Performing Arts Center in Seoul, Korea. Over 20 scholars and experts from China, England, Japan, Nepal, U.S.A. and Korea gathered to discuss the cultural values of shamanic heritage, especially focusing on its performance aspects. Through the opening speech, Dr. Kwon Tai-joon, the Secretary General of the Korean National Commission for UNESCO, conveyed the significance of the symposium, as follows: "This symposium is not to glorify or celebrate shamanism. This is to provide a forum for unbiased and sincere inquiries and discussions on the cultural meaning and significance of shamanism."

In 2000, the Korean National Commission for UNESCO and its Hungarian counterpart, together with the International Society for Shamanistic Research decided to organize the second symposium of the project on shamanic heritage in Budapest, Hungary.

For the four day symposium, which was organized by the professional staff of the European Folklore Institute some two dozens of experts came together from Korea, U.S.A., Russia, France, Germany, Austria, Belgium and Hungary. The meeting was a success in terms of scholarly debates and genuine presentations including some film documents on shamanic rituals from different cultures. In the course of discussions, the cultural value of shamanism has been re-evaluated as the heritage of humanity, the important source of performing arts, and a reservoire of traditional knowledge.

As it usually happens, some of the invited guests were not able to attend the symposium, but they have sent their contributions, some others presented their paper, but failed to provide a final version of it. Anyhow, the present volume will provide a fairly rich material with full of details and fine theoretical insights for those who wants to know more about shamanic heritage.

For the sake of difference, we have modified the original title of our symposium, therefore here we use Rediscovery (in the title of this book) which is more appropriate to signify the most recent tendencies in the development of shamanistic research. In order to place the present volume in a more wider context, let me present a short outline of the recent publications on shamanic cultural heritage.

By the early seventies, a whole series of changes had taken place in anthropological studies of shamanism in both theory and practice. The incredible proliferation of books dealing with shamanism is characteristic of the last ten years, or, to be precise, of the nineties. In November 2001, the Royal Anthropological Institute in London had records of 386 books on the subject of shamanism, of which 240 (or over 60%) were written in the 1990s and quite a number in this century (KIM HOGARTH 2003: 51). The reason for this is on the one hand, the flourishing of anthropological research, the interest shown in the subject by young researchers doing field work, since, influenced by their teachers, they had chosen precisely this subject. On the other hand, however, it is also true that the establishment of an international group of researchers, the *International Society for Shamanistic Research* (1991), the bi-annual conferences, the regular appearance of the Society's journal (*Shaman*, edited by ÁDÁM MOLNÁR and MIHÁLY HOPPÁL, honorary editor in chief: ÅKE HULTKRANTZ), and of a series of books (*Bibliotheca Shamanistica*, Akadémiai Kiadó [the publisher of the Hungarian Academy of Sciences], Budapest, series editor: MIHÁLY HOPPÁL), has also contributed enormously to the development of this part of the field of the comparative science of religion.

From 1991, the *International Society for Shamanistic Research* (ISSR), held a conference every two years. Shorter or longer accounts of these and the reports of the general assemblies of the society have been regularly published in the official journal of the society *(Shaman)*. Unfortunately, only some of the papers given at these conferences have been published, as in the case of the first two conferences, held in Seoul in 1991 and in Budapest in 1993 (HOPPÁL – HOWARD [eds.] 1993; HOPPÁL – PÁRICSY [eds.] 1993; KIM – HOPPÁL [eds.] 1995). Only the papers of the fourth ISSR conference appeared, with few exceptions, in their entirety. The volume entitled *La politique des esprits* (AIGLE et alii. [eds.] 2000), is a collection of papers in French (with the exception of two Russian authors), which divides the material into three large thematic chapters. In the first, the writers examine the co-existence of shamanism and Buddhism in Asia; in the second, the mutual influence of Christianity and the native cultures of Latin America and in the third, the mutual influence of Islam and shamanism is explored.

In connection with the books of conference papers, I must mention the regional conference on the science of religion, which was organised in Helsinki in 1990 by the International Association for the History of Religion (IAHR) and its Finnish branch. Part of the material appeared in the volume entitled *"Shamanism and Northern Ecology"* (PENTIKÄINEN [ed.] 1996). The rest of the papers had been published earlier under the title *"Northern Religions and Shamanism"* (HOPPÁL – PENTIKÄINEN [eds.] 1992), as the third volume in the series *Ethnologica Uralica*, brought out by Akadémiai Kiadó in Budapest. Papers on the subject of mythology are to be found in the first half of the book, while the second part contains papers dealing with the shamanic traditions of Northern peoples (Sami, Inuit, Finns, Udmurt and other Finno-Ugric peoples).

In the last ten years, a serious debate has started about whether pictograms (rock art) and cave paintings have some kind of connection with shamanism; in other words, whether the creators of pictures, illustrations and drawings were the shamans of ancient times. What were the ritual or trance conditions under which these depictions were made? And many other questions arise which are hardly possible to be answered. Researchers have split into two camps. One camp feels that it is perhaps possible that the Palaeolithic depictions can be connected with the beginnings of art, the activities of the first artist-shamans, with the beginning of the conscious use of signs and symbols in the cognitive development of mankind. The other camp fiercely rejects such speculations. An example of the former is the work of the South African DAVID LEWIS-WILLIAMS and the Frenchman JEAN CLOTTES. Their work was severely criticized by the participants of the ISSR conference held in Chantilly, near Paris (FRANCFORT – HAMAYON [eds.] 2001). An American researcher, DANIEL NOEL, joined the critical mood recently (2003). In an earlier book he had already referred to the most successful writers of neo-shaman literature (ELIADE, HARNER, CASTANEDA) with scathing criticism (NOEL 1997).

At the same time, there are numerous researchers who do not speak in tones of fierce rejection, but look for (and find) methodological points of reference, in order to understand the pictographic art of ancient times. With full knowledge of data from Central Asia and Siberia (which are for the most part unknown to Western researchers, with due respect to the exceptions), it is primarily the Russian and Polish researchers who tend to see the figure of the shaman among the simple signs and symbols engraved in the cliffs. A good example of this opinion is a volume of essays which appeared in Poznan in 2002 (ROZWADOWSKI – KOŚKO [eds.] 2002), in which archaeologists and ethnographers examine Siberian pictographic art and its possible mythological and ritual context. The present writer tries to understand the secrets of ancient, enigmatic depictions with the help of semiotic analysis (HOPPÁL 2002a: 42–47; 2003), just as certain Russian researchers use ethnological and mythological facts to explain pictograms (DEVLET 1997, 2000, 2001; DEVLET – DEVLET 2002).

In 1992, GLORIA FLAHERTY published her excellent summary of how the word *shaman* and the expression shamanism appeared in the European mind. She based her analyses on the accounts of 18th century travellers (FLAHERTY 1992). The early French, German, later the Russian and English travellers, explorers, missionaries and other adventurers first brought news and authentic descriptions of the activities of the shamans. Thus, in Diderot's *French Encyclopaedia*, the headword *shaman* appeared as early as 1765, surprisingly, with a fairly accurate description (cf. FLAHERTY 1992: 123). Following this, the American scholar examined the influence of the activities of the shaman on 18th–19th century writers, artists and works of art, such as Herder, Mozart, and Goethe's Faust.

At least as interesting is a work by ANDREI A. ZNAMENSKI, in which he describes the history of the conjunction of shamanism and Christianity. Between 1820 and 1917, the early romantic wide-eyed wonder is gradually replaced in the 19th century by contempt and persecution of the shamans (ZNAMENSKI 1999). From the 1920s onwards, this persecution, in all its political entirety, unfolds ever more tragically in the 20th century (KEHOE 2000: 16–19; GLAVATSKAYA 2001; REID 2002). Since the secret or closed archives in the ex-Soviet Union were only recently opened, many new details about the early persecution of the shamans can be discovered in these documents. Thus, for example, the Hantis living in the Kazym region, led by their shamans, organised a rebellion in the early 1930s against the abuses and atrocities of the Russian authorities (LEETE 1998). Naturally, the rebellion was put down and those involved were executed or taken away to gulags, which was almost synonymous with death.

These years were sad chapters in the history of Siberian shamanism, but they still have to be examined, even if they bring back painful memories. We must report these details or facts, because the persecution of the shamans meant genocide in many cases. The old battle against religion appeared disguised as the class struggle and basically, even if in a milder form, lasted till the end of the 20th century. There are in general, numerous different misunderstandings and prejudices surrounding the way the shamans are judged. Certain writers are trying to dispel these and clear up misinterpretations (KEHOE 2000).

Naturally, there are popularising works, whose writers simply summarize the lessons of earlier works, giving extracts from them (STUTLEY 2003), and we are fortunate if they state some kind of individual viewpoint. For example, among German writers, the psychological attitude dominates, which says that shamanism is to be considered a spiritual technique to cure and improve one's personal quality of life (ZUMSTEIN 2001). Another approach regards the role of dreams as the most important condition for understanding shamanism (ELSENSOHN 2000).

Another such characteristic and basic principle for introducing material is to present the manifestations of shamanism in terms of a world of signs and symbols. This is evident to those who deal not only with the manifestations of shamanism, but also with its meaning, since nearly everything, every object and every movement in Siberian shamanism has a ritual and symbolic meaning (LAR 1998; SEM 1999; KNÖDEL – JOHANSEN 2000; HOPPÁL 2002a). This is especially true of the shaman worldview, the symbolic construction of the cosmos (LAR 1998, MASTROMATTEI – RIGOPOULOS [eds.] 1999; HOPPÁL 2002b). This is also true of the figures in symbolic myths and the totemistic personification of animal ancestors, (BALDICK 2000, and PENTIKÄINEN et alii [eds.] 2001).

The presentation of relics of shamanism in the last decade has opened a new chapter. Earlier, only one or two smaller exhibitions (e.g. in the Ethnographic Museum in Budapest, on the occasion of the second ISSR conference in 1993) had been dedicated to shamanism. In the last decade of the 20th century, however, especially with the opening up of the Soviet borders, large-scale and extensive exhibitions of shaman objects kept in Russian museums, were organised one after the other in European cities. Series of exhibitions were opened by the Chamber of Art in St. Petersburg, but no catalogue was published. On the other hand, when the material was shown in Tampere in 1998, a catalogue with very rich contents appeared, illustrated by many pictures and containing excellent dissertations, (PENTIKÄINEN et alii. [eds.] 1998). The Russian Ethnographic Museum gave a flavour of the shaman material it holds at the Tropen Museum in Amsterdam, (ROSENBOHM [ed.] 1997, in German, 1999). The material from the museum at Kizil was exhibited in the Antwerp Museum and a catalogue full of excellent dissertations was also published (VAN ALPEN [ed.] 1997).

In 2002, three exhibitions opened in three European cities. The first in Helsinki at the Museum of Culture *(Siberia – Life in the Taiga and the Tundra)* was open for a good year and a half. As the sub-title of the publication or catalogue indicates, the intention of the exhibition was not only to present the way of life in characteristic northern (forest) conditions, but also to show Even, Evenski, Hakas, Selkup, Hanti and Mansi, Yakut and shaman drums and other ritual objects. The organisers praised the exemplary professionalism of the Hungarian ILDIKÓ LEHTINEN, who also edited the accompanying volume (LEHTINEN [ed.] 2002). In mid-October, an exhibition on Yakut shamanism and folk belief systems opened in the Polish town of Poznan, which was combined with a limited international conference. Since the greatest experts on shamanistic researches took part in the discussions and in the debates after the presentation of papers, it can be said that this symposium was very successful and was outstanding. The publication of the papers is expected soon. A Polish language explanatory brochure has already appeared (KOŚKO 2002).

The *Museo Nazionale delle Arti e Tradizioni Popolari* in Rome (the local ethnographic museum), organised a very tastefully arranged exhibition entitled *The Flight of the Shaman – Symbols and Art of Siberian Cultures*, and published a large format catalogue of valuable material under the same title (MASSARI – MOZZOLENI [cura.] 2002). There were five complete sets of shaman clothes to be seen at the exhibition, as well as many shaman accessories which count as rarities from the rich collection of the Russian Ethnographic Museum in St. Petersburg.

The doyen of Eurasian research in shamanism, ÅKE HULTKRANTZ has written several articles in recent years on the history of research in Siberian shamanism (HULTKRANTZ 1998). He also summarized his opinion on the use of drugs by Eurasian shamans (HULTKRANTZ 2003), mentioning the ancient Lapps (Sami) and Samoyed and Central-Asian data. According to his conclusions, if the acquisition of shaman knowledge requires the ability to enter a trance, then the use of drugs is only an extra, local feature, because in many cultures this altered state of consciousness can be reached without them (HULTKRANTZ 2003: 14).

The turn of the century was the time of great summaries. It is true that no work similar to MIRCEA ELIADE's one, written around fifty years earlier, was born (or at least it was not published), but two publishers felt that the "reader" giving a comprehensive picture was much needed. This was important as the works regarded as classics had long since disappeared from the shelves of bookshops since they had been sold-out. This is why J. NARBY and FR. HUXLEY decided that a few older works should be re-published. Their book is perhaps still the best selection dedicated to the historical developments of shamanism and to its historical understanding (NARBY – HUXLEY [eds.] 2001). The selection of abbreviated texts covering the period from the oldest data to shamanism today is very successful. Another volume also brings us up to date. Everything in shaman activities can be found in it: the various aspects of shamanism, initiation, ceremonies, aesthetics, from the social context and the cosmic to local protection of the environment (HARVEY [ed.] 2003).

The leading figure in French research and university teaching on shamanism, ROBERTE N. HAMAYON, started his career as a Mongolist. He published his enormous summarizing work in 1990, and its objective was to lay the theoretical foundations of Siberian shamanism (HAMAYON 1990). In this work of more than five hundred pages, he elucidates the concept, among others, that shamans enter into sexual relationships with the helping spirits and that this is how they ensure the continuing procreation of animals for the hunt and thus of the human community. He is also among those who no longer consider today's forms of manifestation of shamanism as a subject for ethnological examination and he denies that trance or ecstasy are definitive elements of Siberian shamanism. It is interesting, however, that he undertook the writing of the text for a book of poetically beautiful photographs, entitled *Taiga: Land of the Shamans*, which contains superb photographs of a famous Evenki shaman mother and a young Yakut shaman (GARANGER – HAMAYON 1997).

Research into shamanism in China was really revived in the last years of the past century, (accounts of this appeared in turn in the pages of *Shaman*, SHI 1993, KÓSA 2001). I regard it as my personal good fortune that I could be an eye witness of this development, the political and ideological reasons for which are, of course, not worth denying. Chinese communism became more and more open and as it became economically stronger, it allowed more and more freedom in the field of research into minorities and, within this, into ancient customs and beliefs, among them shamanism. Thus, when I first went to China in 1991, I had to meet an elderly shaman virtually in secret; a few years later, I was able to meet him openly and in 2001 and 2003, I was allowed to shoot video film with full cooperation and help. It is true that meanwhile quite a number of works had appeared, which give a picture of life and death—in the strictest sense of the words—about the shamans of minorities (Evenki, Dahur, Hezhe or Nanay, Manchu, Mongol and other nations) living in north-eastern China (MENG 2000; GUO – WANG [eds.] 2001). The book by the woman researcher living in Beijing contains 90 pictures, while the book by the two writers contains 300. This is a breakthrough in the history of Chinese publications, which were hitherto not illustrated.

The latter book is the first extensive illustrated monograph published in China. Moreover, it was the first time that the writers gave a picture of the shamans of small nations living on the fringes of Chinese culture. In fact, there is very little information to be read about the shamanism of the peoples living in China, or about the figure of the *sa-men* (the village wizard) in Chinese culture, which according to the assumptions of certain scholars, was probably the origin of the Tunguz *šaman* figure. The volume by colleagues in Changchun (GUO – WANG [eds.] 2001), is a source book, which will be much quoted in the coming decades by the researchers who deal with the comparative investigation of shamanism. And even more people will turn its pages for the sake of the colour pictures. These pictures are very valuable because they are authentic! They are not set up photographs, but snapshots which show folk customs faithfully; the photographers have made the movements and gestures of their subjects immortal. Thus, the photographs, with the help of the arrested moment, hand over the past to the future generation for safe keeping. And for the foreign observer arriving from a distant culture, these pictures of the shamanism of minorities living in modern China, truly recall classical descriptions and pictures of conditions at the turn of the century, that is the early 20th century. These are pictures of classical shamanism, which are hardly to be found any more in Siberia today. Researchers of Eurasian shamanism can be especially grateful for this book and its authors, because they can find in it inexhaustible parallel material. Thus, for example, the authors describe flat copper mirrors and their function of keeping evil at bay and protecting the heart (Buryat and Tuva shamans still use these important shaman emblems "sent from heaven"). The role of sacrificial trees is of central significance and we discover that in the rites of the Manchu shamans the cosmic tree reaches the sky, and also that in the shaman worldview, the sky has nine floors. The ritual role of shamans was important in animal sacrifices, for example, among the Manchu, it was they who cleaned the horse before a sacrifice. With nearly every Eurasian people (including the Finno-Ugrians of the Volga!), one element of the rites is that the sacrificial animal (be it a cock, a pig, a lamb or an ox) has alcohol poured into its ear and if it shakes itself, that is a sign that the deity has accepted the sacrifice. We ascertain on the basis of the writers' descriptions and pictures that without a sacrifice and a communal meal to follow, there is essentially no shaman religious ceremony—this too shows that shamanic religious ceremonies were ritual occasions for the togetherness of the community. At the same time, it is also clear that honouring their forefathers is one of the most important aspects of shamanism. Naturally, it was the great heroes and brave warriors who became the outstanding figures of the shaman pantheon (e.g. the Manchu *Baturu Mani*). Shamans with special capabilities were also respected, for example shamans who walked on fire. (I note that these excellent pictures could have done with more detailed and longer explanatory captions!)

The foreign reader picks up this book with justifiable curiosity and therefore expects much more from the ancient Chinese sources, wider quotations of texts from these sources, which are difficult to access, where shamans, or religious specialists fulfilling a similar social function, are mentioned. The unearthing and quoting of these texts is the task of Chinese scholars. As is the selection of representations pertaining to the early history of shamanism, from material contained in books publishing pictograms, which increase in number every day. In the case of such a valuable source publication, it would be (it would have been!) important to note precisely when and where every single photograph was taken. Naturally, we know that the pictures were taken in the 80s and 90s by and large, that is to say the volume is the result of twenty years' work by the writers.

Besides the work of the Chinese writers, many valuable dissertations on the shamanism of the Chinese nations have appeared in the journal *Shaman*, for example on the various groups of Sibo shamans (PANG 1994), on the "shaman handbook" used by them (QI 1997), the characteristics of the Manchu shaman dance (SONG 1997) and the shamanic elements in Yugur folk tales (ZHONG 1995). A separate monograph appeared on the shamanism of the Oroch people (GUAN – WANG 1998), with many pictures taken in the 90s of the still living customs and shaman religious ceremonies. Of the north-eastern ethnic groups, perhaps it is the Dahur we did not know much about right up to 1996, when an excellent monograph appeared, containing discussions between a Dahur emigré and a British woman anthropologist, as well as commentaries and explanations on the recollections of an elderly informant (HUMPHREY – ONON 1996). In the early nineties, a seventy-year-old Dahur man recorded conditions typical of the forties in his stories, that is pre-communist conditions which were still guided by tradition. It is no accident that, when describing the details of local shaman identity, he uses the expression *shamanship*, and not the meaningless category *shamanism* (see fuller account of this debate in HOPPÁL 2002a: 11–13). It is interesting that the *ominan* "remembrance of the spirits" ritual, reported in detail by URGUNGE ONON, was still practised in the 90s among the Dahur living in the Hailar region (cf. GUO – WANG 2001: 29–34).

The Chinese researchers dealt not only with the shamanic culture of north eastern minorities, but also with that of the south Chinese nations. The way the historic Naxi shamans organized the research and elaboration of the *Dongba* traditions is exemplary (BAI – YANG [ed.] 1998). Just as the volume on Naxi ethnography published by the Völkerkunde Museum in Zurich is of the highest standard (OPPITZ – HSU [ed.] 1998). Of the south Chinese nations, the Naxi minority is the best organized, since they have their own research institute in Lijiang city, which is incidentally part of the World Heritage. Better and better ethnographic descriptions, full of interesting details are being written on the Naxi *Dongba* traditions (GUO 1999), which are really shaman-like, special religious features, fulfilling the role of leading ceremonies. In the territory of Sichuan, among the Giang (ZEVIK 2001), and the Yi nations, these leaders of rituals and healers, who make up a wandering priesthood, fulfil an important role in the life of the small, local communities (BAMO AYI 2003). A very important characteristic of this social group is that their sense of responsibility towards the community is very strong; they feel a moral responsibility not only towards each other within the group, (since the craft of 'shamanship' or *bimo-ship* is inherited within the family), but their behaviour and their example also set an ethical standard for simple people.

Research into Korean shaman tradition has developed enormously since the nineties. This is largely due to the fact that South Korea has become one of the world's leading industrial powers and (even at the time of the military dictatorship) attached and assigned great significance to tradition. One of the important characteristics of Korean culture, wanting to distinguish its individual features from Chinese and Japanese culture, is the individual shamanism (*musok* in Korean). Over the centuries this has established a specific system of religious ceremonies that last several hours and are almost like theatrical performances. We compare them to theatre because, during the service consisting of several acts, the leading figure changes clothes several times and every part (or "act") has a dramatic climax (an excellent analysis of this topic is provided by KISTER 1997). Singing, knowledge of dance, text improvisation, humour and the ability to concentrate, are needed for the ceremony, which lasts several hours, sometimes a whole day. It is no accident that a long process of learning is necessary for shaman candidates to acquire the many layers of knowledge. Earlier they studied individually with one or two of the more famous shaman women (*mudang*), but more recently and currently, they study in groups, organized by the official shaman association. This association has over forty thousand registered members and its name (*Tachan Suggong Kyongshin Yönhaphoe*, Korean Spirit Worshippers' Association for Victory over Communism) contains the hope of victory against communism (KIM HOGARTH 2003: 57).

The research into Korean shamanism was always closely related to a kind of cultural nationalism (KIM HOGARTH 1999), which basically only meant a very conscious safekeeping of traditions and the collection of folklore. Thus, the songs of shaman women and a precise description of religious ceremonies have appeared in several volumes. This work was carried out in Korea by the first president KIM TAEGON (1937–1996) of the ISSR (International Society for Shamanistic Research).

From the eighties onwards, excellent ethnographic descriptions appeared. These were written by foreign researchers (KENDALL 1985, 1988; KIM HOGARTH 1999) and Korean researchers who had studied abroad (KIM 1989; KIM HOGARTH 1999). The English language collection of KIM TAEGON'S essays is illuminating (KIM 1998), and it reports on the basic religious and ideological concepts of early shamanism. Even more interesting is the work that uncovers for us the syncretism of Korean shamanism and Buddhism, in the cultural context of a modern city way of life in Korea today (KIM HOGARTH 2002).

MERETE DEMANT JAKOBSEN, a Danish researcher (who received her Ph.D. in Oxford), published the results of her research in 1999 in the form of a book. She was essentially exploring two subjects: one was the memories of shamanism of the Innuit of Greenland in the writings of Danish missionaries of old, and the other is her examination of the manifestations of shamanism in the city today, observed from inside by taking part as a participant observant. She too was a pioneer among anthropologists in regarding neo-shamanism as a subject worthy of research (JAKOBSEN 1999, 2003). The tone of ROBERT J. WALLIS' articles represents an accommodation of new attitudes in the world of European universities. Briefly, this means that it is no longer shameful among researchers to refer to the works of M. HARNER, C. CASTANEDA or others. This is because on the one hand, these writers were the first to say something new about altered states of consciousness, on the other, the development of urban or neo-shamanism influenced by them has grown into a real cultural movement, and as such, can be investigated by anthropological methods (WALLIS 1999, 2000, 2001). This relates particularly to the "new pagan" movements, which are not a fashion, but whose time has now come. These are not simply short-lived 'new-age' fashions, but the revival of pagan cults that look to the past, search for their cultural roots and respect nature (BLAIN – WALLIS 2000; WALLIS 2003).

All these above reviewed works are of great importance for a better understanding of various shamanic traditions as an important form of intangible cultural heritage of mankind.

REFERENCES

AIGLE, D. et alii (eds.)
   2000   *La politique des esprits. Chamanisme et religions universalistes.* Nanterre: Société d'ethnologie.
BALDICK JULIAN
   2000   *Animal and Shaman: Ancient Religions of Central Asia.* London – New York: I. B. Tauris Publishers.
BAMO AYI
   2004   The Religious Practitioner *Bimo* in Yi Society of Lingshan Sonthwest China Today. *Shaman* vol. 13. (in print)
BAI GENGSHENG – YANG FUQUAN (eds.)
   1998   *Guoji dongba wenhua yanjiu jicui* (International Studies on Dongba Culture) Kunming: Yunnan renmin chubanshe.
BIRTALAN ÁGNES
   1995   Some Animal Representations in Mongolian Shaman Invocations and Folklore. *Shaman* 3: 2: 99–111.
   1996   A Lineage of Tuvinian Shamans in Western Mongolia. In STARY, G. (ed.) *Proceedings of the 38th Permanent International Altaistic Conference (PIAC) Kawasaki, Japan* 85–105. Wiesbaden: O. Harrassowitz.
   2001   The Tibetan Weather-Magic Ritual of Mongolian Shaman. *Shaman* 9: 2: 119– 142.
BLAIN, J. – WALLIS, R. J.
   2000   The 'Ergi' Seidman: Contestation of Gender, Shamanism and Sexuality in Northern Religion Past and Present. *Journal of Contemporary Religion* 15: 3: 395– 411.
DEVLET, M. A.
   1997   Ancient Sanctuaries in Tuva and the Origin of Shamanism. In J. van ALPHEN (ed.) *Spellbound by the Shaman.* Antwerpen: Etnografisch Museum, 37–51.
DEVLET, E. G.
   2000   X-ray style, anthropomorphic rock art images and the mythological subject of obtaining the gift of shamanizing. *Archeology Ethnology and Anthropology of Eurasia* 2: 88–95. (Novosibirsk).
   2001   Rock art and the material culture of Siberian and Central Asian shamanism. In PRICE, N. (ed.) *The Archeology of Shamanism.* London: Routledge, 43–55.
DEVLET, E. G. – DEVLET, M. A.
   2002   Siberian Shamanistic Rock Art. In ROZWADOWSKI, A. – KOŚKO, M. (eds.) *Spirits and Stones: Shamanism and Rock Art in Central Asia and Siberia.* Poznan: Instytut Wschodni UAM, 120–136.
DIÓSZEGI VILMOS
   1974   Shamanism. In *Encyclopaedia Britannica* (15th edition). London: Macmillan, 16: 638–641.
   1998   *Shamanism. Selected Writings of Vilmos Diószegi.* Edited by MIHÁLY HOPPÁL. Budapest: Akadémiai Kiadó. (Bibliotheca Shamanistica, vol. 6.)

DIÓSZEGI, V. – HOPPÁL, M. (eds.)
 1996a *Shamanism in Siberia* (Selected Reprints) Budapest: Akadémiai Kiadó
 (Bibliotheca Shamanistica, vol. 2.)
 1996b *Folk Beliefs and Shamanistic Traditions.* (Selected Reprints). Budapest: Akadémiai
 Kiadó. (Bibliotheca Shamanistica, vol. 3.)
ELSENSOHN, SUSANNE
 2000 *Schamanismus und Traum.* Kreuzlingen – München: Hugendubel Verlag.
FLAHERTY, GLORIA
 1999 *Shamanism and the Eighteenth Century.* Princeton, N.J.: Princeton University
 Press.
FRANCFORT, HENRI-PAUL – HAMAYON, ROBERTE N. (eds.)
 2001 *The Concept of Shamanism: Uses and Abuses.* Budapest: Akadémiai Kiadó
 (Bibliotheca Shamanistica, vol. 10.).
GARANGER, MARC (photographies) – HAMAYON, ROBERTE H. (text)
 1997 *Taïga: terre de chamans.* Paris: Imprimerie Nationale Editions.
GLAVATSKAYA, ELENA
 2001 The Russian State and Shamanhood: The Brief History of Confrontation. In
 PENTIKÄNEN, J. et alii (eds.) *Shamanhood, Symbolism and Epic.* Budapest:
 Akadémiai Kiadó, 237–247 (Bibliotheca Shamanistica, vol. 9.).
GOODMAN, F. D.
 1972 *Speaking in Tongues: A Cross-Cultural Study of Glossolalia.* Chicago: Chicago
 University Press.
 1980 Hungarian Shamanism in Cross-Cultural Perspective. *Ural-Altaische Jahrbücher
 / Ural-Altaic Yearbook* 52: 32–41.
 1988 *Ecstasy, Ritual, and Alternate Reality: Religion in a Pluralistic World.* Bloomington –
 Indianapolis: Indiana University Press.
GOODMAN, F. D. – HENNEY, J. H. – PRESSEL, E.
 1982 *Trance, Healing and Hallucination – Three Field Studies in Religious Experience.*
 Malabar, Florida: Krieger.
GUO DALIE
 1999 *Naxi Nationality and Dongba Culture* (in English and in Chinese) Kunming:
 Junnan Social Science Academy.
GUO SHUYUN – WANG HONGGANG (eds.)
 2001 *Living Shamans: Shamanism in China.* (in English and in Chinese) Shenyang:
 Liaoning People's Publishing House.
GUAN XIAOYUN – WANG HONGGANG
 1998 *Elunchunzu samanjiao tiaocha* (Research on Oroqen Shamanism) Shenyang:
 Liaoming Peoples' Press.
HARVEY, Gr. (ed.)
 2003 *Shamanism: a Reader.* London – New York: Routledge.
HOPPÁL, M. – HOWARD, D. K. (eds.)
 1993 *Shamans and Culture.* Budapest – Los Angeles: Fullerton (ISTOR Books).
HOPPÁL, M. – PENTIKÄINEN, J. (eds.)
 1992 *Northern Religions and Shamanism.* Budapest – Helsinki: Akadémiai Kiadó –
 Finnish Literature Society (Ethnologica Uralica, vol. 3.).

HOPPÁL MIHÁLY
    1993   Studies on Eurasian Shamanism. In HOPPÁL, M. – HOWARD, D. K. (eds.)
           Shamans and Culture. Budapest – Los Angeles: Fullerton, 258–288 (ISTOR
           Books).
    1994   *Shamanen und Schamanismus*. Augsburg: Pattloch.
    1998   Vilmos Diószegi: Life and Works. *Shaman* 6: 2: 117–149.
    2000a *Shaman Traditions in Transition*. Budapest: International Society for Shamanistic
           Research.
    2000b *Studies on Mythology and Uralic Shamanism*. Budapest: Akadémiai Kiadó
           (Ethnologica Uralica, vol. 4).
    2002a *Das Buch der Schamanen: Europa und Asien*. Berlin Ullstein.
    2002b *Teatro Cosmico: Simboli e miti degli sciamani Siberiani*. Milano: Contemporanea –
           Budapest: International Society for Shamanistic Research.
    2003   Signs and Symbols in Siberian Rock Art. In TARKKA, L. (ed.) *Dynamics of
           Tradition. Perspectives on Oral Poetry and Folk Beliefs*, 171–183.
HULTKRANTZ, ÅKE
    1998   On the history of research in shamanism. In PENTIKÄINEN, J. et alii (eds.)
           Shamans. Tampere: Tampere Museums' Publ., 51–70.
    2003   Thoughts on Drugs in Eurasian Shamanism. *Shaman* 11: 1–2: 9–16.
HUMPHREY, CAROLINA – URGUNGE ONON
    1996   *Shamans and Elders: Experience, Knowledge, and Power among the Dawi Mongols*.
           Oxford: Clarendon Press.
JAKOBSEN, MERETE DEMANT
    1999   *Shamanism. Traditional and Contemporary Approaches to the Mastery of Spirits and
           Healing*. New York – Oxford: Berghahn Books.
    2003   Researcher or Searcher: Studying Shamanic Behaviour in the New
           Millennium. *Shaman* 11: 1–2: 17–28.
JOHANSEN, ULLA
    1999   Further Thoughts on the History of Shamanism. *Shaman* 7: 1: 40–58.
    2003   Shamanistic Philosophy: Soul-A Changing Concept in Tyva. *Shaman* 11: 1–2:
           29–50.
KEHOE, A. B.
    2000   *Shamans and Religion. An Anthropological Exploration in Critical Thinking*. Prospect
           Heights, Illinois: Waveland Press.
KENDALL, LAUREL
    1985   *Shamans, Housewives and Other Restless Spirits*. Honolulu: University of Hawaii
           Press.
    1988   *The Life and Hard Times of a Korean Shaman*. Honolulu: University of Hawaii
           Press.
KIM, SEONG-NAE
    1989   *Chronicle of Violence, Ritual of Mourning: Cheju Shamanism in Korea*. (Ph. Diss.)
           University of Michigan.
KIM, TAE-GON
    1998   *Korean Shamanism-Muism*. (Trans. And edited by CHANG, SOO-KYUNG) Seoul:
           Jimoondang.

KIM, TAE-GON – HOPPÁL MIHÁLY (eds.)
  1995 *Shamanism in Performing Arts*. Budapest: Akadémiai Kiadó (Bibliotheca Shamanistica, vol. 1.)

KIM HOGARTH, HYUN-KEY
  1998 *Kut: Happiness Through Reciprocity*. Budapest: Akadémiai Kiadó (Bibliotheca Shamanistica, vol. 7.).
  1999 *Korean Shamanism and Cultural Nationalism*. Seoul: Jimoondang.
  2002 *Syncretism of Buddhism and Shamanism in Korea*. Seoul: Jimoondang.
  2003 Inspiration or Instruction Shaman-training Institutes in Contemporary Korea. *Shaman* 11: 1–2: 51–67.

KNÖDEL, S. – JOHANSEN, U.
  2000 *Symbolik der tibetischen Religionen und des Schamanismus*. (Tafelband) Stuttgart: Anton Hiersemann Verlag (Symbolik der Religionen XXIII.)

KÓSA GÁBOR
  2000 Shamanism in China before the Tang Dynasty. (Part One) *Shaman* 8: 2: 131– 179. (Part Two) *Shaman* 9: 2: 169–197.
  2001 Some Recent Chinese Works on Shamanism. *Shaman* 9: 1: 77–81.

KOŚKO, M. M.
  2002 *Szamanizm: Teatr jednego aktora*. Poznan: Muzeum Narodowe.

KUPER, MICHAEL (hrsg.)
  1991 *Hungrige geister und rastlose seelen – Texte zur Schamanismusforschung*. Berlin: D. Reimer Verlag.

KÜRTI LÁSZLÓ
  1994 Language, Symbol and Dance: An Analysis of Historicity in Movement and ˇ Meaning. *Shaman* 2: 1: 3–60.

LAR, LEONID
  1998 *Samani i bogi* (Shamans and Gods – Foreword in English p. 3–6.) Tyumen: Institut Problem Osvoyeniya Severa.

LEETE, ART
  1998 The Kazym Uprising: The West Siberian Peoples' Struggle for Freedom in the 1930s. *Shaman* 6: 2: 171–178.

LEHTINEN, ILDIKÓ (ed.)
  2002 *Siberia: Life on the Taiga and Tundra*. Helsinki: National Board of Antiquities.

MASSARI, ST. – MAZZOLENI, G. (cura di)
  2002 *Il volo dello Sciamano: Simboli ed arte delle culture siberiano*. Roma: De Luca Editoni d'Arte.

MASTROMATTEI, R. – RIGOPOULOS, A. (eds.)
  1999 *Shamanic Cosmos – From India to the North Pole Star*. Venice: Venetian Academy of Indian Studies – New Delhi: D.K. Printworld.

MENG, HUI-JING
  2000 *Zhong guo bei fang minzu samanjiao*. (Shamanism among the Northern Minorities in China) Beijing: Social Science Publishing House.

NARBY, J. – HUXLEY, FR. (eds.)
  2001 *Shamans Through Time: 500 years on the Path to Knowledge*. New York: J. P. Tarcher/Putnam.

NOEL, D. C.
  1997 *The Soul of Shamanism: Western Fantasies, Imaginal Realities.* New York: Continuum.
  2003 Neuro-shamanology in the Ice-Age Caves: A Case of Methodological Promise and Modern Projection. *Shaman* 11: 1–2: 85–111.
OPPITZ, MICHAEL – HSU, ELISABETH (eds.)
  1998 *Naxi and Moso Ethnography: Kin, Rites, Pictographs.* Zurich: Völkerkunde-museum.
PANG, T. A.
  1994 A "Classification" of the Xibe Shamans. *Shaman* 2: 1: 61–66.
PENTIKÄINEN, J. et alii (eds.)
  1996 *Shamanism and Northern Ecology.* Berlin – New York: Mouton de Gruyter.
  1998 *Shamans.* Tampere: Tampere Museums.
  2001 *Shamanhood, Symbolism and Epic.* Budapest: Akadémiai Kiadó (Bibliotheca Shamanistica vol. 9).
QI CHESAN
  1997 Contemporary Shamans and the "Shamans' Handbook" of the Sibe. *Shaman* 5: 1: 69–90.
REID, ANNA
  2002 *The Shaman's Coat: A Native History of Siberia.* London: Weidenfeld – Nicolson.
ROSENBOHM, ALEXANDRA (red.)
  1997 *Wat bezielt de sjamaan.* Amsterdam: Koninklijk Instituut voor de Tropen.
  1998 *Schamanen zwischen Mythos und Moderne.* Lepzig: Militzke Verlag.
SEM, T. I.
  1999 Schamanische Symbole und Rituale in Sibirien und dem Fernen Osten. In ROSENBOHM, A. (hrsg.) *Schamanen zwischen Mythos und Moderne.* Leipzig: Militzke Verlag, 10–40.
SHI, KUN
  1993 Shamanistic Studies in China: A Preliminary Survey of the Last Decade. *Shaman* 1: 1: 47–57.
SONG, HEPING
  1997 The Dances of Manchu Shamans. *Shaman* 5: 2: 143–154.
STUTLEY, MARGARET
  2003 *Shamanism: An Introduction.* London – New York: Routledge.
VAN ALPHEN, JAN (ed.)
  1997 *Spellbound by the Shaman – Shamanism in Tuva.* Antwerpen: Etnografisch Museum.
WALLIS, R. J.
  1999 Altered States, Conflicting Cultures: Shamans, Neo-shamans and Academics. *Anthropology of Consciousness* 10: 2: 41–49.
  2000 Queer shamans: autoarcheology and neo-shamanism. *World Archeology* 32: 2: 252–262.
  2001 Waking ancestor spirits: Neo-shamanic engagements with archeology. In PRICE, N. (ed.) *The Archeology of Shamanism* 213–230. London – New York: Routledge.

2003   *Shamans/Neo-Shamans: Ecstasy, alternative archeologies and contemporary Pagans.* London – New York: Routledge.

ZEVIK, EMMA

2001   Beizhi Neuer Had a *Gaigva. Shaman* 9: 1: 61–76.

ZHONG, JINWEN

1995   Shamanism in Yughur Folk Tales. *Shaman* 3: 1: 55–66.

ZNAMENSKI, A. A.

1999   *Shamanism and Christianity. Native Encounters with Russian Orthodox Missions in Siberia and Alaska, 1820–1917.* Westport, Connecticut – London: Greenwood Press.

ZUMSTEIN, CARLO

2001   *Schamanismus: Begegnungen mit der Kraft.* Kreuzlingen – München: Hugendubel.

Part I.

SHAMANISM AND MYTHOLOGY

HUNG-YOUN CHO

An Archetypal Myth and Its Reality in Korean Shamanism

I.

Sondog of Shilla (r. 632–647) was Korea's first queen. In the twelfth year of her reign Girimsa Temple was built on Mt. Hamwol. Until early Chosŏn, the temple at Girimsa directed sixty branch temples including the Bulguksa temple. Due to road difficulties and the restoration of Bulguksa, however, Girimsa was scaled back to become a branch of Bulguksa. I visited the legendary temple in the summer of 1999.

In the "Chronicle of the Girimsa Temple," it is recorded that Bŏmmara country's Imjŏngsa's Gwang-yu the Sacred, with his five hundred disciples practiced the maintenance of a flower hill. Hearing that King Sarasu of the Sŏchon Nation was generous and enjoyed almsgiving, Gwang-yu the Sacred sent a Brahman to obtain someone from that area to participate in the maintenance of the flower hill. The King selected eight ladies out of many and sent them over.

The Sacred resends his disciple to Sŏchon with a message stating that the King should participate in the flower hill maintenance. The King hesitates and Queen Wŏnang says she will join. The three head towards Imjŏngsa.

The pregnant Queen hurts her foot and can no longer continue the journey. Upon consulting with the King she decides to sell the soon-to-be-born baby and herself as slaves to Jugrim country's Elder Jahyŏn. The King names the unborn child Allaggug and departs with Brahman. The Queen sings "Verses on Departure for Paradise" (Wangsaeng-ge) to the King and asks him to recite it always. While performing his duty of watering the flower hill at Imjŏngsa, the King often recites these verses.

Elder Jahyŏn inflicts all kinds of hardship on the Queen and her son because she refuses to go to bed with him. They survive with the help of heavenly beings. Once Allaggug becomes a young man, he begs his mother for the identity and whereabouts of his father; then he tries to escape. The first attempt fails when he is captured by the Elder's men. In his second attempt he comes to a river, crosses safely, and arrives at Imjŏngsa. When father and son finally meet, they weep.

When Allaggug meets the Sacred he tells him that his mother has been killed by the Elder and gives him five flowers to resurrect her. On his way back, near the house, he learns through the song of shepherds that his mother has been chopped into three parts and thrown into a bamboo garden. In the midst of his sorrow, he recovers his mother's body and brings her back to life with the flowers.

Heaven and earth shake and rain pours forcing mother and son to escape and spend the night on top of a tree. At this moment, Amida Buddha and Bodhisattvas of all the heavens ride down on a dragon vessel to Imjŏngsa and joyfully hold a Buddhist service. Elder Jahyŏn falls into Hell. It has become clear that Gwang-yu the Sacred is Śākyamuni Buddha, King Sarasu is Amitābha, the Queen and her son are Mahāsthāmaprāpta, and the messenger Brahman is Mañjuśrī and the five hundred arhats.

II.

This Girimsa epic legend, which is known as the "Chronicle of Crown Prince Allaggug" (Allaggug-taeja-jŏn), has been alluded to in the shaman songs of Cheju Island. I have discovered 18 versions of the text. Moreover, if Japan's "Buddhist Picture of King Sarasu" (Seizan Bunkō Museum's Sarasu-taeng) is added, it would make a total of 19 versions. Among them, five are in Chinese characters, nine in Korean, and four are in the form of shaman songs. Since there is no other myth or epic that has been passed down in so many different forms it gives evidence of its deep historical roots in Korea's religious culture.

It is difficult to understand the text only as a Buddhist theme. Concepts such as flower-hill maintenance for the afterlife by calling for a person in the current life, as well as reincarnation performed through flowers, are unfamiliar in Korean Buddhism. This type of myth does not appear anywhere in the Sūtra. Rather, these are concepts and themes that we frequently see and hear in the world of Korean shamanism.

The Girimsa epic is not a Buddhist myth. Although it does have Buddhist embellishments with Buddha's and Brahman's appearance and Allag in Allaggug meaning "Pureland." However, they remain mere insertions of proper nouns which do not carry much importance in mythologies. As we will see the structure and contents of the story is typical of Korean shamanism.

It is generally known that Korean shamanism started wearing the robes of Buddhism in the 7th century when it first began to be established in Korea. This myth, embedded in Korean shamanism, was transmitted as a shaman song. On the other hand, it seems that it was formed as a Girimsa's epic myth into the "Chronicle of Crown Prince Allaggug." It was edited into Sŏgbosangjŏl in 1449 and Wŏrinsŏgbo in 1485, and in private hands it became Allaggug-jŏn, the novel, as well as Buddhist novels.

Although Allaggug's role in the myth is important the central character is Queen Wŏnang. Professor Minn, Young-gyu, entitled the story "The Myth of Lady Wŏnang's Departure for Paradise" (Wŏnang-buin-gŭgnag-wangsaeng-yŏn). Its name should undoubtedly be "The Myth of the Provenance of Lady Wŏnang" (Wŏnang-buin-bonpuri). In the new era it is important to firmly establish a myth about a woman.

III.

The Korean copy of "Allaggug-jŏn" offers a different version from the Girimsa version. Gwang-yu the Sacred appears as a Buddha and raises all kinds of Udambarahwa and treasures of lotus flowers, with 3,000 disciples at Sŏchŏn country. These flowers wither under tortuous drought that lasts for seven years. Along with the flowers, Sejon's face also withers. He swims in a pool of sadness. In order to find someone to restore the flower hill a Brahman is sent to King Sarasu of Taewon country in Kangnam region. After the testimony of slaves who see Allaggug and his reincarnated mother going to Paradise, the Elder orders their immediate arrest. As the slaves leave heaven and earth shake, lightning strikes the Elder's house, and it disappears into thin air.

"The Myth of the Provenance of Lady Wŏnang" begins with the flower hill. Gwang-yu the Sacred is directing the repair of the hill which faces a crisis because of a seven-year drought. The withering flowers reflect the withering face of the Buddha protecting the hill. Both symbolize the decline of the righteous order of the cosmos which signifies the end of the world. To solve the crisis a saint seeks someone from this world who can repair the flower hill. Interest in the idea of the flower hill becomes problematic in that giving water to the hill signifies humans' nurturing an imaginary idea.

It is appropriate to examine Korean shamanism's world structure within this realm of imagination. The sensual realm is composed of King Sarasu's

Sŏchŏn nation, Jahyŏn's Jugrim country, and the world of the imagination in Bŏmmara country. The sensual realm is the human realm while the realm of the imagination is god's realm. Between them a river flows dividing and connecting the two realms. In Korean shamanism's ritual for the dead, "Princess Bari" also has a river that divides this world from the nether world. The concept of a river dividing the two worlds also appears in Siberian shamanism.

The realm of the imagination and the sensual realm are in a mutually dependent relationship. One cannot exist without the other and each gives the other reasons for existence. Allaggug revives his mother with a flower from the realm of the imagination and the flower hill sustains its life through the water given it by eight ladies and King Sarasu of the sensual realm. We also need to pay attention to the fact that Lady Wŏnang's verses on departure for paradise breathed life into King Sarasu, the superintendent of the flower hill, and to the realm of the imagination's flower hill itself. MICHAEL ENDE's *Die Unendliche Geschichte* (1979) discusses this relationship and makes clear relationships between the other world and this world. In the world view of Korean shamanism, the flower hill of the imagination thrives on human prayer and care, whereas the sensual realm thrives on earning salvation from the realm of the imagination's flowers.

IV.

The crisis of the withering flower hill is temporarily solved by the eight ladies and King Sarasu. In the myth two other kinds of world-end crisis unfold: one is the demise of Jugrim country, represented by Jahyŏn the Elder, and the other is the end of Lady Wŏnang. The Elder is a powerful figure similar to a governor with many slaves, wealth, and power. His country is struck by lightning and disappears. The Elder falls into hell. Since lightning-struck deaths are heaven's will, his disregard for the realm of the imagination, brought about his death..

Lady Wŏnang's death is mythical. Originally fated never to enter the realm of the imagination she nevertheless helped to revive the flower hill by teaching her husband the shaman songs. She also instructed her son about the path to the realm of the imagination, allowing him to traverse between the other world and this world. That she already knew these songs and that she was able to teach them to someone else gives rise to speculation that she may possibly be an Earth Mother figure.

For these reasons her death should not be viewed as personal. Her body is cut up into three parts by the Elder who represents the secular world.

This may signify a division of the three spheres: Heaven, Earth, and the Human sphere. It may also mark the end of the Past, Present, and the Future. Her body, abandoned in a bamboo forest, is dismantled. Her son puts together the bones and flesh, finally reviving her with the flowers the Sacred had given him.

A special meaning is embedded in the fact that her bones were dismantled then put back together. In Siberian shamanic initiation some candidates experience dismemberment of their flesh and bones. The gods return life by joining the bones again. Since they have gone through such a religious experience, the candidates earn the right to perform shamanic rituals.

In comparing Siberian and Korean shamans' experiences, the Korean version has the uniqueness of automatic bone dismemberment and the fact that in the realm of the imagination a son reincarnates his mother through flowers. Future shamans who are reduced to skeletons, as ELIADE pointed out, undergo a mystical death that enables them to return to the inexhaustible fountain of cosmic life. The skeleton is brought back to life by being given new flesh. Novice shamans are not born again; they are "revivified."

In the Old Testament the prophet Ezekiel gives life to dried-out bones and experiences the scene of reincarnation: "O ye dry bones . . . I will lay sinews upon you, and will bring up flesh upon you, and cover you with skin, and put breath in you, and ye shall live" (Ezekiel 37: 4-6). The element that connects the sinews, or gives flesh in Korean shamanism, is the flower. Lady Wŏnang becomes the first shaman who is invested with the authority to travel to the otherworld, lead the dead to the flower hill, and instil life into humans. Her demise was a necessary step in establishing her as the first shaman.

V.

We have so far examined Lady Wŏnang's initiation and death. But let us also examine her actions in a larger context as part of rite of passage. She did not need to accompany her husband on his journey but she abandons her life of luxury and departs. Moreover, she was pregnant. Her self-imposed hardship draws a sharp contrast with the passive hardship inflicted on Princess Bari because she was the seventh princess. This is not an isolated event but one of mythical proportions that describes a person with the precious status of a Queen, infinitely denigrated to a slave, preparing for her death.

Jesus has taught: "unless a grain of wheat drops into the earth and dies, it remains single, but if it dies, it produces a rich yield" (John 12:24). This is why Lady Wŏnang dies and is reborn through the flower. She is no longer herself. As the one who has seen and experienced the secrets of the flower of reincarnation, she possesses the power and the authority to lead the people to the flower hill.

The "Myth of the Provenance of Lady Wŏnang" demonstrates the three kinds of world end possible within the cosmos. The realm of the imagination of the flower hill, the sensual realm's Jugrim country, and the human realm are intertwined horizontally unfolding as a cosmic concerto. When Lady Wŏnang rises from the dead, rain pours down making the mother and her son spend the night at the top of a tree. (This passage is reminiscent of the Biblical Deluge.) This myth revolves around the polarity between the sensual realm and the realm of the imagination. Lady Wŏnang's micro-cosmos connects with the flower hill's macro-cosmos through the "Verses on Departure for Paradise." Her death and resurrection shakes the entire realm of the imagination and covers it with jubilation. It is similar to viewing Jungjung-mujin (mutual-reflective ad infinitum) of Hwa-om philosophy, or DNA as a double-spiral structure.

End without salvation is in vain. Judeo-Christianity's linear eschatology revolves around keeping an eye on the Millennium Kingdom's paradise as salvation. Korean shamanism exhibits two distinctive traits that cannot be found in other religions. Korean salvation, instead of being vertical, is accomplished horizontally. In Christianity, Jesus rises to Heaven and salvation comes down from Heaven. In Buddhism the dragon ship comes down from heaven. But in Korean shamanism the realm of the imagination is only a river away from the sensual realm. The fact that the flower of the realm of the imagination is the saviour is the other uniqueness. In Korean shamanism it is not salvation but reincarnation or revivification that is reached through the flower hill.

VI.

In Korean mythology there are many mythemes but the flower hill is the most important. In Girimsa's epic the Sacred with his five hundred disciples attends to the maintenance of the flower hill. When Allaggug meets with the Sacred he gives him flowers of five different colours to revive his mother.

That flower hill disappears in the "Wŏrinsŏgbo, the eighth." In the Sangŏl part, the Sacred sends his disciple Brahman to King Sarasu to obtain a woman who will water the hill then asks the king to become the watering manager. In Sarasu-taeng, the situation goes a little further producing a picture of a jewel-tree of the Pureland. The "Chronicle of Crown Prince Allaggug" contains a more concrete portrait. Sŏggamoni in the Buddhist seminary raises all kinds of lotuses along with Udambarahwa. But due to the drought Sŏggamoni's face, along with the flowers, withers. The eight ladies and the king repair the hill by carrying water. They give Allaggug three flowers—white, red, and blue lotuses—and instruct him to revive his mother and bring her back.

In Chejudo's shaman song "Igong-bonpuri," this process is recorded in some detail. Hallaggung-I's father Kim Jin-guk is commanded by the Supreme Being of Sŏchŏn to become the superintendent of the flower hill. When looking for his father, Hallaggung-i finds young girls watering the garden. His father answers each of his questions by telling him in detail that the flowers have the ability to raise the dead. One of the flowers is for laughter and another is for destruction. After cutting one of each Hallaggung-i returns to this world and with the flowers and kills everyone in the Elder's house. Then with flowers that give muscles, life to bones, blood, and organs he revives his mother. He then returns to Sŏchŏn's hill with his mother. His father becomes the King of Sŏchŏn hill and he becomes its superintendent.

The flower hill's existence and its character became quite clear in the Girimsa version. It is the realm of the imagination, full of flowers that revive life. In the Allaggug-jŏn the flowers take on the proper nouns and nouns of Buddhism but it still contains the same characteristics of the Girimsa version. Another important fact is that Sŏggamoni has the characteristic of the flower: as flowers wither, so does his face. Korean shamanism's realm of the imagination rests within the flower hill.

The flower hill disappears in "Wŏrinsŏgbo, the eighth," which gives some reason for alarm. The story's structure remains the same but instead of the flower hill there is Buddhism's paradise of Pureland in the West. On the other hand, there are two changes in the Igong-bonouri that has been handed down among shaman folks. With the flower, revenge sometimes plays out in a grand scale. The other change is in relation to the flower hill, the hierarchical chain of management seems to have escalated. There is a flower hill king and underneath there is the superintendent of the garden who rules over flower attendants. The actual watering is done by girls. While the flower hill seems full of prosperity, it also reflects the organization of this world. Because the human mind has become evil flowers can be used to kill.

The flower hill does not only make its appearance in "Wŏnang-buin-bonpuri." Princess Bari also displays the instinctive characteristics of the flower hill. With a shaman song performed as a part of the "Saenam-gut," Princess Bari goes to the otherworld to save her parents who are suffering under a deadly disease. Although the otherworld here exhibits both Buddhist and Taoist colours, it stays familiar to most Koreans because it looks like the mountainside village where Princess Bari lived with Musangsŏn in the otherworld. On her way back from the otherworld she meets with the funeral procession of her parents and returns them to life with the flowers she has brought.

I have touched upon this issue of the flower hill of the realm of the imagination in a paper entitled *"Study on Korean Hell – Otherworld in Shamanism."* I quote a passage here: "Our sister Princess Bari became a Shaman because she travelled to the otherworld to seek medicine. She sings here today "Princess Bari", the song of a shaman. It is to revive our parents. The place that she revives or recreates is none other than the ancestral home of Korea, the flower hill. It is a place where our parents will be buried, where the parents of our parents have returned to rest and live. It is said that our ancestor Tan'gun retired and became a mountain god, that mountain is ancestral home to where he returned."

This flower hill, the ancestral home, is not a physical location. It exists anywhere and everywhere in the myths of our hearts. The ancestral home lives within our minds. Princess Bari revives our parents as our ancestors within the flower hill of our hearts. That is why Koreans have rituals for the dead and shamans perform shaman rituals, or Kut. Myth's "illud tempus" is vivid here.

Thus we realize that the realm of the imagination's flower hill in the "Myth of the Provenance of Lady Wŏnang" is actually the ancestral home. The ancestral home differs from a hometown in that it carries a much more fundamental essence. We can understand the reason behind the careful inlay of the character of the flower hill rather than the display of all the intimate details. It is the source and the symbol of that source. It is only visible to those who know and seek the myths of Korean shamanism.

Koreans share an unusual love of flowers. From Kim Sowŏl's "Jindallae" (the azalea) to children's songs celebrating "gardens father and I have built," flow inside the heart of Koreans. "My home was a mountain village with flowers blossoming," must be sung with the pathos for that home. When people die, Koreans say "they have returned." It signifies a return to that ancestral home. Within the floral funeral bier, the dead return home. To me, the Korean folk song, "Arirang" tells of that longing for home beyond the hills.

VII.

It is difficult to find flower hills within western mythologies. Virgil's *Aeneid* provides a rare exception. The underground world Aeneas visits with Cumae's shaman Sibyl is Elysium or Elysian Fields. It is a holy place where the spirits of those blessed dead may enter after the final judgment. It is a place of eternal spring with fruits lovingly hanging from the trees and fragrant flowers smiling with their full blossom. The spirits earn youth and eternal rest here. Elysian Fields exude a different atmosphere from our flower hill, but it is a hill nevertheless. The flower hill is a place that raises and produces future life.

This flower hill becomes Limbo in Dante's *Inferno*. Limbo, Hell Number One, is surrounded by light and beautiful streams with fresh green grass but there are no flowers. In Homer we find at the end of the earth, Oceanus the land of happiness, which goes underground with Virgil, but in Dante it is transformed into hell's Limbo. The flower hill is separated and taken to Paradise. This indicates the alienation of the flower hill in accordance with the development and selection of paradise. We can also call it the forfeit of the flower hill.

In the world of flower hills in East Asia, we must consider the ones in Taoism and Buddhism. Buddhism's Pureland can be seen as a type of a flower hill. It exists in abundance in Amitābha's Pureland of the West and others. The flower hills of Taoism, along with those of Buddhism, have influenced Korean shamanism's realm of the imagination but they have not altered and could not alter Korea's fundamental flower hill. As was the case in Western mythology, these religions also show flower-hill alienation. Building and expanding flower hills becomes an artificial background as Hell and Paradise become specialized. In comparison, shamanism's ancestral flower hill is a permanent staple *an sich* with its root deep inside Korean hearts and mountainside villages.

VIII.

I came to know Shaman Yi, Young-hŭi about four years ago when he was studying with the master shaman of Seoul Saenam-gut, Kim, You-gam. At first, I vaguely knew him as a peculiar shaman who worshipped the Fire-god General and Queen Sŏndŏg. Fire-god General has burned Yi's house on no less than three occasions. In early 1999 in the midst of gathering material for Wŏnang-buin-bonpuri, it occurred to me that other gods might also be with him since he serves Queen Sŏndŏg. I discovered that they were but before I explained this to him, he did not know who these gods might be.

Yi is blessed with many gods. Among the deities there are four related to Wŏnang-buin-bonpuri: King Narasu, Lady Bichwi, Narag and eight fairies. The eight fairies as a group are construed as one god. King Narasu is King Sarasu in our myth and his wife, Lady Bichwi, is our Lady Wŏnang. Allaggug is called Narag as King Narasu's son.

In Korean shamanism the gods are usually worshipped by means of a picture of the god on the shaman's altar. Besides the picture of the eight fairies Yi also gives the gods flowers. King Narasu, as the flower of Prunus Mume, and Lady Bichwi, as Magnolia, are each placed in their vases in front of the portrait of Queen Sŏndŏg. Narag, as a lotus, is kept in a pot in front of the eight fairies portrait. It is not common for these gods to be worshipped in the form of flowers. While Yi has done this in accordance with the god's instructions, we already know the meaning behind these flowers. They are directly linked with the gods of the ancestral flower hill. Yi is a master of not only Seoul Saenam-gut but also a superb craftsman of paper flowers. It is magical to watch him make his flowers bloom.

These gods appear on the left wall of his shrine and in front of it. Queen Sŏndŏg and the eight fairies' portraits are side by side and the flowers for Lady Bichwi and King Narasu are in front of the Queen. The flower for Narag rests in front of the fairies. One can guess at the deep relationship between the gods of Wŏnang-buin-bonpuri and Queen Sŏndŏg. It may be possible that she is the historical Lady Wŏnang of Korea.

For MIRCEA ELIADE mythology is the primal world of eternally revolving archetypes. It was his endeavour to research the way in which myths evolved and were transmitted from ancient times. He pursued this from a religious historical perspective in which archaic techniques of the shamanic world are centred on the archetype of ecstasy. While he viewed shamanism as a body of myth he failed to realize that it is also a mythological religion. Shamanic performances are mythic happenings where gods appear with the shaman's arbitration. We saw this in the "Myth of the Provenance of Lady Wŏnang" and also the world of the shaman Yi.

There are major differences in understanding shamanism between ELIADE and myself. I wonder if he was not too keen on the idea of the archetype. It also bothers me that he did not conduct field research on shamanism. Along with that, I would also like to point out his error in criticizing Korean shamanism's deteriorative form based only a single work by C. HENTZE (who conducted comparative research on Kyŏngju's Gŭmgwan-chŏng).

IX.

Shilla has shared a profound relationship with the Buddha. A Buddhist monk by the name of Jajang arrived at Mt. Wutai and heard Mañjuśrī Bodhisattva explaining the meaning behind the sacred images ·of the Buddha. Śākyamuni Buddha and Kāśyapa Buddha originally lectured at Hwangryongsa Temple, where the stones they sat on still remain. The gold that Chŏnchug's (India) King Ayuk sent rests in that temple as a gilt bronze image of Buddha from 1,300 years ago. It is claimed these are due to the fact that the temple stands on a piece of soil that had a special linkage with the Buddha. Jajang is commanded by a heavenly being to raise a nine-storey pagoda. If he does so, it is predicted that many nations in the East Sea will surrender to Shilla. Taking on Jajang's suggestion, Queen Sŏndŏg builds the pagoda.

Many historians interpret this Shilla-Buddha country theory as a scheme to strengthen the royal authority in relation to Shilla's national and international political situation at the time. It was also claimed that it was created by some old priests: to them religion must appear as mere ideology and the nation's denizens as fools. However, these critics do not pay attention to how Buddhism in Shilla was formed on the basis of unique religious and cultural traditions. There is no understanding or effort to comprehend the cultural world of the imagination that served as the background for Buddhism.

Queen Sŏndŏg is said to have had foreknowledge of three things. The Tang dynasty Emperor Taizong sent a picture of peonies of three different colours along with three packages of seeds. She predicted that the flowers would not have scent and this proved to be true. Because of her second prediction she sent troops to Yŏgŭn-gog Valley and defeated the troops of the enemy. Finally, she predicted the day of her own death and asked to be buried in Dori-chŏn, south of Mt. Nang. She died on the day predicted and was laid to rest on a sunny spot on Mt. Nang. Ten years later, King Munmu raised the Sachŏnwangsa Temple under the tomb and her cabinet then realized how wondrous and holy she really was. In Buddhist mythology Dori-chŏn is on the peak of Mt. Sumi.

The three stories of Queen Sŏndŏg have almost no relevance to Buddhism. In the third story while Buddhist myth appears it is Shilla's realm of the imagination that took over the Buddhist myth. These stories elaborate on the queen's brilliant ability to observe an object, and see its essence, and predict the future. This kind of acuity can only be found in a great shaman who has had a spiritual experience. It is a good indication that she was a shaman. She also personally conducted the rites after her coronation at the Palace of the Gods (Sin-gung). In the same year she built Chŏmsŏngdae Observatory that embellished Mt. Sumi.

Kim Dae-mun's Hwarang-segi bears a record of same worldview. Duke Yangdo and Boryang shared the same mother but were siblings of different fathers. When Princess Yangmyŏng tried to marry the two, with the permission of the Emperor, Yangdo opposed the marriage. But he finally relented and married in accordance with his parent's wishes. At this moment his mother hugged him and said, "The Sin-gug has its ways, how can we allow ourselves to follow the old way of China?" This passage should be read to mean, "Shilla is god's nation and has its own set of proprieties." The people of Shilla knew their land was a nation of gods.

The opening passage of the foreword begins, "Our nation with respect to the Palace of gods offers our Great Worship to Heaven." Great Worship to Heaven means the ritual of the heavenly gods. That Ancient Korean society organized these Chŏnju gatherings every spring and fall through Koguryŏ, Buyŏ, and Ye societies has been pointed out as a unique feature of the religious tradition. Many scholars, myself included, have demonstrated that these are traditional rituals of Korean Shamanism have been ceaselessly transmitted into the village rituals of today.

The ceremony of heavenly gods, which was performed in Sijomyo the ancestral shrine for the nation's progenitor, began with the second King Namhae-chachaung. Both he and his sister Aro were shamans. This tradition continued until King Soji's 9th year (487) when the place of worship changed to the Palace of the Gods. With the rising number of patrons the palace was enlarged and became the nation's most holy site of worship. The construction of the palace at the site of the progenitor's birthplace foreshadowed Shilla's identity crisis after the nation imported Confucianism, Buddhism, and Taoism into Korea. In time these religions had ideological and cultural conflicts among themselves and with Korea's traditional worldview. Therefore, it became necessary for the nation to strengthen and re-establish its ancient cultural identity.

X.

Queen Sŏndŏg was buried at Dori-chŏn after her death. For the people of Shilla their realm of the imagination stops there. For them, heaven was not a far-off place but on their own soil, Sin-gug. Queen Sŏndŏg believed in shamanism and strove arduously to revive the ancestral home, the realm of the imagination of shamanism. Buddhism was wide-spread enough at the time to even wield a formidable power within her administration. The withering flower hill at Imjŏngsa and its immediate need for repair reflect the turbulence of the period. Realizing this, the Queen embarks on reviving the realm of the imagination. Shamanism and Buddhism are not separate realms of the imagination. Shamanism retains its original principles and structure and adds only the outer layers and colours of Buddhism.

Korea's belief in Pureland is not much different. In *Yuma-gyŏng*'s Bulgug-pum chapter, Saribul pointedly says that what he sees on earth are filthy and sinful things. Hearing this, the Buddha touches the earth with his toes and the entire cosmos turns into Pureland decorated with unbelievable treasures and mankind bows in admiration. When the Buddha lifts his toes, the world turns back into its original form.

Samgug-yusa's Sabog-burŏn tells a different story. When Sabog's mother dies he carries her corpse to a mountainside with the famous monk Wŏnhyo. He also forms the verses for her burial and pulls out a weed after finishing his words. Under the weed he sees a joyous world which he goes into. The chasm closes after he enters it with the corpse. There is in fact no fundamental difference between the Pureland Sabog shows and the one in *Yuma-gyŏng*. But Sabog's is one that is close to home, one that lies in our backyard.

The image of Buddha in Kyŏngju's Sŏggul-am is regarded as one of the finest treasures of religious history in the world. From *Yuma-gyŏng*'s perspective, the image is of the Śākyamuni Buddha. His hands are in the form of a ground-touching mudrā. I place a particular importance on his touching the ground. He touches the ground with his toes in *Yuma-gyŏng* but his touching the ground with his toes while sitting with his legs crossed is not right. The place he pointed to with his fingers is none other than Shilla's ancestral home, the Pureland. He teaches that the ancestral home is of this world and heaven is its meaning. Subtly, he tells us that in the ancestral home the earth hugs the sky, drawing a sharp contrast with Christianity's "pressing on the upward way."

SUGGESTED READINGS

AKAMAZU – AKIBA TAKASHI
    1937   *Chosen-fusoku-no-kenkyu* (Study on Korean Shamanism). Vol. 1. Tokyo – Seoul: Osaka-okugou-shoten.

AN, JIN-HO (ed.)
    1936   *Sogga-yorae-sibji-haengrog* (Records of Sakyamuni's Works in Ten Places). Seoul: Man-sanghoe Co.

CHONG, CHAE-YONG

   1997 *Allaggug-taeja-gyong-byonsangdo* (The Sutra-picture of the Allaggug Sutra).
        (Munhon-gwa haesog, Documents and Interpretation, Vol. 1.) Seoul:
        Taehagsa.

CHO, HUNG-YOUN

   1992 *Mugyo-sasangsa* (Ideological History of Shamanism). (Han-gug-jong-gyo-
        sasangsa, Ideological History of Korean Religions. Vol. 4.) Seoul: Yonsei
        University Press.

   1995 *Hwarang-ui jong-gyo-munhwa* (Religious Culture of Hwarang). (Hwarang-
        munhwa-ui sin-yon-gu, New Studies on the Hwarang Culture) Seoul:
        Mundogsa.

   1999a *Han-gug-ji-ok yon-gu — mu-ui josung* (Study on Korean Hell — Otherworld
        in Shamanism). (Syamonijum yon-gu, Studies on Shamanism. Vol. 1.)
        Seoul: Han-gug-syamonijum-haghoe.

   1999b *Han-gug-ui syamonijom* (Shamanism in Korea). Seoul: Seoul National
        University Press.

CHO, TONG-IL

   1997 *Tong-asia gubi-sosasi-ui yangsang-gwa byonchon* (The Aspects and Transition
        of Oral Epics in East-Asia). Seoul: Munhag-gwa-jisongsa.

DURAND, GILBERT

   1996 *Introduction la Mythodologie.* Paris: Albin Michel.

ELIADE, MIRCEA

   1968 *Myth and Reality.* New York – Evanston: Harper & Row Publishers.

   1970 *Shamanism: Archaic Techniques of Ecstasy.* (Bollingen Series LXXVI.) New
        York: Pantheon Books.

   1971 *The Myth of the Eternal Return.* (Bollingen Series XLVI.) Princeton:
        Princeton University Press.

   1975 *Rites and Symbols of Initiation.* New York – London: Harper & Row
        Publishers.

ENDE, MICHAEL

   1979 *Die unendliche Geschichte.* Stuttgart: K. Thienemanns Verlag.

HWANG, PAE-GANG

   1975 *Shilla-bulgyo-solhwa-yon-gu* (A Study on Shilla Buddhist Fables). Seoul:
        Ilsisa.

KIM, DAE-MUN

   1999 *Hwarang-segi* (The Genealogical Records on Hwarang) (Trans. Yi Chong-
        ug) Seoul: Sonamu.

KUMAGAE NOBUO

   1969 "Seizan-bunko-jang Allaggug-taeja-gyong-byonsang (The Sutra-picture
        of the Prince Allaggug Sutra in the Collection of Seizan-bunko
        Museum)." In: *Kim-chaewon-bagsa-hoegab-ginyom-nonchong* (Collection of
        Articles for the Commemoration of the 60th Birthday Anniversary of
        Dr. Kim Chae-won). Seoul.

KWON, SANG-NO (ed.)
  1979 *Han-gug-sachal-jonso* (A Complete Book of the Korean Buddhist Temples). Vol. 1. Seoul: Dong-gug University Press.
LEACH, EDMUND
  1985 *Structuralist Interpretations of Biblical Myth.* Cambridge: Cambridge University Press.
MINN, YOUNG-GYU
  1955 *Worin-sokbo je-chil je-pal yong-in-gaeje* (A Bibliographical Introduction of the Volume 7 and 8 of Worin-sogbo). (Guggo-chong-gan) Vol. 5. Dongbanghag-yon-guso. Seoul: Yonsei University.
NAKAMURA HAJIME et al. (trans.)
  1990 *Joudo-sanbu-kyo* (Three Sutras of Pureland) 2 vols. Tokyo: Iwanami-shoten.
ONO GEMMYÔ
  1993 *Bukkyo-sinwa* (Buddhist Myth). Tokyo: Daito-shuppansha.
SA, CHAE-DONG
  1977 *Bulgyo-gye-gugmun-sosol-ui hyongsong-gwajong yon-gu* (Study on the Formation of the Buddhist Novels in Korea). Seoul: Asea-munhwasa.
SIN, CHONG-WON
  1998 *Shilla choecho-ui gosung-dul* (The First High Priests of Shilla Buddhism). Seoul: Minjogsa.
TURNER, ALICE K.
  1993 *The History of Hell.* New York – San Diego – London: Harcourt Brace & Co.
VIRGIL
  1982 *The Aeneid of Virgil.* (Trans. A. Manselbaum) Berkeley – Los Angeles: University of California Press.
YU, TONG-SIK
  1975 *Han-gug-mugyo-ui yogsa-wa gujo* (The History and Structure of Korean Shamanism). Seoul: Yonsei University Press.
ZIMMER, HEINRICH
  1946 *Myths and Symbols in Asian Art and Civilization.* (Ed. by JOSEPH CAMPBELL) (Bollingen Series VI.) Princeton: Princeton University Press.

ELVIRA EEVR DJALTCHINOVA-MALETS

Shamanic Tradition in Mythosophy of Kalmyks

INTRODUCTION

The Kalmyk culture arose in Central Asia. The best mythosophical[1] ideas were brought to the new fatherland in Eastern Europe, where Oirads (old name of Kalmyks) looked for a better place to live. Between the Volga, the Don, and the North Caucasus a unique culture was coming into existence since the 17th century. The new fatherland was not *"Bumbin orn"*[2] (like "the promised land"). Dramatic periods of Kalmyk history—the exodus of more than half the population from the Volga to Jungaria in the 18th century, the bloody establishing of Soviet power in the Kalmyk steppe, the 15 years in Siberia, where all Kalmyks were deported by Stalin's regime put the culture on trial.

Almost all evidence of the old culture disappeared without a trace. People (shamans, Buddhist monks and others), who kept traditional values, were tortured and exterminated. More than half of the Kalmyks died in Soviet concentration camps. In all of the history of Kalmyk culture, nothing is so surprising or so difficult to account for as the sudden rise of shamanic tradition today. Of this important fact almost nothing was known officially until "Perestroika". The conceptions of life and the world that we call "shamanism" still exist (in a new form) in recent Kalmyk culture, hidden under Buddhist and other cultural covers. The studying of this phenomenon is the topic of this article.

It is very important to support all aspects of Kalmyk culture, because there is very little alive, and so many traditions and evidences of culture are

---

[1] The term "mythosophy" is suitable for denoting the world-outlook of shamans. Mythosophy is the union of mythological and philosophical thinking in the stage of cultural development when philosophy is still mythological and mythology starts to be philosophical.

[2] "Place, where death is not known. Country of happy people"—from the Kalmyk Epic poem "Jangr".

going to die. It is not true that we are witnesses the revival[3] of Kalmyk culture, because it never died, even during times when Kalmyks were being exterminated. But if the political and economical situation does not change, the unique culture of Kalmyks will disappear. The second most dangerous enemy is the recent strong Western influence on Kalmyks' civilization.

Kalmyks, like other Mongols, had shamans before the spread of Buddhism. They were respected as shamans even during Buddhist indoctrination and for a long time afterwards. When Buddhism became the state religion in the seventeenth and eighteenth centuries, shamans were punished, but shamanic mythosophy was assimilated into Buddhism (BAKAEVA 1994). Even times of strong socialist propaganda did not break or interrupt the shamanic worldview, which was one of the important characteristics of people's existence. Kalmyks, first of all, believed in Sky Justice – *Teŋr*, in the power of the Lord of Underworld and magical knowledge – *Erklg Nomn Khan*. They also believed in the Lord of time and space, the Lord of the year – *Delkan Cayan Öbyn*, who was the guardian of all Kalmyks, and in a huge army of large and small, good and evil, calm and nervous spirits, etc. There are a few holy days and special days which were important because of their order in the Universe. Because of their importance for Kalmyk traditions they were strongly assimilated into Buddhist doctrine: New Year Holy days: *Ĵul, Jilin Eĵn* – (Holy day of the Lord of the Year), *Cayan Sar*,[4] *Ürs Sar* (Summer Holy day). Rituals, which were used in celebrating holy days, were – *Usn arshan* (the blessing of water), *Usn täklyn* (the offerings to water), *yal täklyn* (the offerings to fire), and *Oba täklyn* (the Ova offerings).

In fact, "*Udhn*" or "*böö*" – words, which meant "shaman" in *sensu stricto* – have disappeared from the modern Kalmyk language[5] as well as "*jadč*" ("the man who call the rains"), "*juryač*" (astrologists), "*kelmrč*" (fablers), "*tärnč*" (magician, sorceress), "*esč*" (the seer, the clairvoyant), who were not shamans. Their importance in Kalmyk mythosophy, however, is unquestionable, because like shamans they create and keep order in the Universe. Nevertheless, in modern Kalmyk language we meet with terms which were assimilated from other languages like "healer", "bioenergotherapist", "extrasense" (very popular in recent times) or even "gelung" (from tib. gelong), which belongs to people, who are respected as

---

[3] The etymology of "revival" suggests that something must be dead before rebirth.

[4] There is no reason to discuss which holy day was primarily the New Year. Probably in the past some of ethnic groups celebrated the Autumn New Year, others the winter.

[5] According to the decision of UNESCO, the Kalmyk language has been treated as a "dying language" which should be protected from disappearance and must be revitalized.

shamans. We should emphasize that *"Udhn"* or *"böö"* were used by shamans themselves rather seldom; needless to say that should be used carefully.

YAMAN ERGĴANA

From fragmentary evidence that survived, we can reconstruct some important moments of the shamans' life. Tradition tells us about the beginning of "shamanic illness", which is called *"Yaman ergĵana"* ("to be twisted by a goat"). The chosen person usually (about 7 or 9 years old) had a lot of visions and dreams in which the White Old Man or Erklg Nomn Khan (they possess the ability to change appearance) give signs of having chosen this person. These are some of them: White Old Man or Erklg Nomn Khan gives a goat: white or black, sometimes both, which will guide the chosen person. The goat suggests how the person must behave. These suggestions are unquestionable, but the character of them is more than unusual, so the chosen person looks mentally ill. Needless to say, guardians are invisible to the unenlightened.

A modern shaman (DJALTCHINOVA-MALETS 1986–1991/1) told me his story: "It happened near a small village *Güdg,*[6] when he was seven years old. He was looking after horses with cousin one night. Suddenly a big Old Man with hair of snakes had appeared on the horizon riding a white horse. He was angry and lashed the boy's horses. The boy was frightened. White Old Man promised to come back and then disappeared. A black goat was given to the boy. The cousin did not see it, because he slept and because he could not. After that night one horse died. The goat was very whimsical and malicious. He spoke the people's language. The goat persecuted the boy all day and night. Nobody believed his story. After a few days the situation was repeated. White Old Man appeared on the horizon and attacked the boy. He tied the boy to a horse tail and dragged him everywhere all night. When he stopped, he ordered the boy to obey the goat. In the early morning the boy's body was heavily bruised. Like other chosen people, he was recognized as mentally ill and sent to the hospital. There was only one real *böö* – Namka (DJALTCHINOVA-MALETS 1986–1991/2), who "adopted" and taught the young man, who was now 28 years old.

---

[6] Kalmykia, region of Jashalta. Old buzava kalmyks report that it was the shamans' place before the Second World War.

A woman who was also chosen told another story. When she was 9 years old, she saw the White Old Man for the first time. He was very kind to her. A kind white goat twisted her for a long time. Namka told his story too, before his death. The first meeting with the guardians happened when he was seven. He was picking up cow dung (*kijäk*), when the tempest had begun. Suddenly the earth opened and Erklg Nomn Khan appeared with the White Old Man. They gave him white and black goats. He came back home the next day and the shaman illness began. He started to practice very early, when he was 14 years old. At the beginning, the goats swore at each other and ordered him in contradictory ways, but later they became real guardians and helped him (even in Siberia) to avoid dangerous situations. Old Kalmyks told other very similar stories (DJALTCHINOVA-MALETS 1986–1991/3).

The shamanic illness is a very undesirable state of mind. When it happens, people respect it with fear. There are very dramatic events that happened in the Kalmyk's lives when they were returning from Siberia. These were known as the "shamanic epidemic". Old people, who witnessed it, said that the White Old Man attacked whole villages. Armies of angry ghosts and unhappy souls of dead begged him to create peace with them and the villagers. Nobody wanted to be a shaman; they searched for a solution in alcohol and in suicide, but there is no way to escape from fate. There was not a person who knew what to do (DJALTCHINOVA-MALETS 1986–1991/4).

There are many instances of "shamanic epidemic" events which happened in the 1970s and 1980s, when chosen people were sent to psychiatric hospitals and were

Picture 1. White Old Man

treated as schizophrenics. Young chosen people did not know whom they should ask for help.

Many shamans' dynasties were interrupted, as was the transmission of traditional knowledge. Mythosophical reality for new adherents looked strange. There were only a few real *böö* who could help them, but they practiced in secret and sometimes did not want to help.

Kalmyks believed that guardians sought only one person in one generation of a family, but sometimes a mistake was made and guardian ghosts gave signs for more than one person to be chosen. If this happened, the family asked the *böö* who must be the shaman. Then a ceremony "of sucking out" took place. *Böö* contacted the guardians and if the guardians allowed him, they took away the goat from the mistaken chosen person. Usually everything was concentrated in one person in any family. Kalmyks believed in the hereditary character of the chosen.

JANΓRIN ĴEG

When old *böö* accepts a young person, the dress should be prepared for initiation (DJALTCHINOVA-MALETS 1986–1991/5). Old women from the mother's side have to make the dress with ornaments, which are called "*Janyrin jeg*". For 9 days women make the dress and recite prayers all the time. The texts of the prayers were strongly influenced by Buddhism; some words come from the Tibetan language. I found "pure" shamans' prayers. These are some of them:

> *Minyn jēbä dersen Janyrin je*
> *Rimbu Čimbu Bambu Jambuyan*
> *Qanǎn kēbä jüüji Junkba*
> *Luúɲ örgbä Solban solbande*

> *Dēdin ik oln burqd*
> *Delkän eɲn cayan öbüyün*
> *Tüyjä Jänj orula jeg*
> *Janyrin jeglän caqcalu*

There is no single version of "*Janyrin jeg*" ornaments. As we know (DJALTCHINOVA-MALETS 1986–1991/6), one usually used "*yana bügü*". It may be translated as "Khan's bracelet". Sometimes ornaments used zoomorphic motifs. For example, some buzava Kalmyks used "*yana bügü*" ideograms of animals that are totem signs of kin. The names of some buzava Kalmyk's kin are *šar merkid* – yellow eagle, *čön omgllyn* – proud wolf, *bogšurgya* – sparrow, and so on. Old *böö* also decided what color the dress must be. It depends on the color of the goat. There is no evidence to support the suggestion that a specific color means a specific kind of shaman ("white" or "black"). In comparison with other Mongols, we can discern two kinds. Ornamentation on a dress is very important, because it symbolized the length and quality of the future shaman's life. Consequently everything must be made very neatly, without unnecessary knots. It was thought that interrupting the ornamentation might cause the early death of the shaman. On the 9th night the dress must be given to the old *böö*. During the night he asks the guardians to bless the dress. Old women should recite prayers too. The next night, immediately after sunset, the chosen person visits the *böö*, who dresses him. The old shaman smears the lips and the crown of the head of the initiated person with goat's blood, which should be prepared beforehand. I suppose that a ceremony of symbolic revival (transformation) takes place here. After that the chosen person becomes a shaman. People call him *Janrin je*. After the ceremony the goat's skin must hang on long sticks behind the village near a crossroads. It is an offering for the guardians. Old and new shamans eat the raw heart and liver. The meat should be prepared for the old women who made the dress. All the bones and the remains of the goat must be buried. Kalmyks believed that in another world the goat would live. Goats were used as offerings for different occasions: for the Lord of the Water, for Erklg Nomin Khan, for the Lord of the Earth etc. (DUSHAN 1973).

JANΓRIN ĴE

Janyr is the name of the hero of Kalmyk epics. *Ĵe* means "daughter's children". As we know, *Janyr* possessed the magical knowledge and abilities to go through all three worlds. According to the epics, which were built on a base of archaic myths, *Janyr* survived *Qoyr*—another hero of epics, from the underworld. He revived him in a way that is used by shamans in modern times. Briefly speaking, the name "*Janyrin ĵe*" connects shamans with the old shamanistic root. They wanted to belong to *Janyr*, because the shaman's power depends on the root. Between the 1920s and 1948 there was a shaman called *Dūta* (his name may be translated as "famous" or "the man, who sings"), who used a "*mörinyür*" (small instrument from wood, with two strings and small horse head sculpture on a head of instrument) for his practice. Witnesses (DJALTCHINOVA-MALETS 1986–1991/6) testify that he obtained connections with Jangar by singing. Dūta never used a drum, only his *"mörinyür"*. He used his instrument when he healed people. His *je* (*Dūtn Ĵe*) is a shaman too. Dūtn Ĵe used a guitar in his shaman practice.

The mythosophical point of view is very much alive among Kalmyks. When they were in Siberia, they believed that one day in the future the real *Janyrin Ĵe* would come and repair their whole world.

REFERENCES

BAKAEVA, E. P.
   1994 *Buddizm w Kalmykii* [Buddhism in Kalmykia] Elista: Kalmyskoye Knizhnoye Izdatelstvo.
DJALTCHINOVA-MALETS, ELVIRA E.
   1986–1991 *Interviews with informers in Kalmykia:*
      /1. Informer: Dūtn Ĵe, Gierasimienko 43, Elista, Kalmykia.
      /2. Informer: Namka Kichikov, Zalivnoy, Kalmykia
      /3. Informer: Badmash Chimidova, Sladkoye, Kalmykia
      /4. Informer: Ulumji Ivanova, 4 mkr. 29/52, Elista, Kalmykia.
      /5. Informer: Siaha Antonova, Gudg, Kalmykia.
      /6. Informer: Dukhar Utashova, Gierasimienko 43, Elista, Kalmykia.
DUSHAN, U. D.
   1973 Istoriko-etnograficheskie zamietki ob Erketienovskom ulusie Kalmyckoi ASSR [Historical and ethnographical remarks about Erketenovsk region in Kalmyk Republic]. *Etnograficheskie vesti* Vol.3.

GÁBOR KÓSA

Mythology and Shamanism in the Ancient Chinese State of Chu

INTRODUCTION

Chinese shamanism, as well as Chinese mythology, is a rather debated area of Sinology; thus, the relationship between the two, inevitably, became one of the major problematic topics of sinological studies. In this presentation, I endeavour to summarize the basic hypotheses and conclusions of leading sinologists on the shamanism and the mythology in the ancient Chinese state of *Chu*, which was a dominant political, cultural and religious power in south China between the 7th–3rd century B.C. In my study, besides the original Chinese sources, I will heavily rely on and amply quote from the works of sinologists who touched upon this rather elusive subject.

SHAMANISM IN THE STATE OF *CHU*

Within the history of the Eastern *Zhou*[1] dynasty (8th–3rd c. B.C.), just like in the whole history of Chinese shamanism, the state of *Chu* has enjoyed an exceptional status. This ancient state was, now it seems, the center *par excellence* of shamanic phenomena, the former "possessors" of which were probably the *Shang*, "the inheritors", as the majority of scholars think, being the Taoist priests.[2] This southern state covering modern *Henan*, *Hunan*, *Hubei* and *Anhui* was in its heydays especially in the Eastern *Zhou* period

---

[1] Both in my own text and in the quotations I have given all Chinese words in *pinyin* transcription and in italics.

[2] On a general history of Chinese shamanism see KÓSA 2000, 2001; MATHIEU 1987; THIEL 1968.

(770–221. B.C.).[3] The state of *Chu* made several major contributions to Chinese culture—a distinctive art differing largely from the other regions and ages of China, a monumental poet (*QU YUAN*), several mythological and philosophical works (*Shanhaijing, Zhuangzi, Huainanzi*), and an influential school of religious Taoism (*Shangqing*). Before analyzing these products of *Chu* culture in detail, however, I present the wider context (i.e. the north-south opposition), in which *Chu*, according to the Chinese tradition and some modern scholars, represents the southern side.[4]

Shamanism in the Context of North and South

The essence of the north-south opposition can be summarized in the following, slightly simplified way: the roots of what would become the two major intellectual, spiritual and religious movements of ancient China can be traced to two areas of Warring States China. Confucianism can mostly be linked to the intellectual sphere of the northern state of *Lu*,[5] where its major representatives (CONFUCIUS and MENCIUS) were born. On the other hand, Taoism originated from and developed in the rather different religious context of the southern state of *Chu*, where two of its major originators (*LAOZI* and *ZHUANGZI*)[6] came from.[7] The topographical

---

[3]   On *Chu* generally see BARNARD – FRASER 1972; BLAKELEY 1985–87; COOK – MAJOR 1999; LAWTON 1991; MAJOR 1978.

[4]   The following part on *Chu* shamanism, on the *Chuci* and the *Shanhaijing* is a significantly enlarged version of the *Chu* chapter in KÓSA 2000.

[5]   On the original intellectual characteristics of *Lu* as a background for the later Confucian concepts see e.g. M. E. LEWIS' opinion: "A relatively small state of little political importance, it was best known for its preservation of the Western *Zhou* cultural heritage, particularly music and rites" (LEWIS 2000: 364).

[6]   "*Laozi* was a native of the hamlet of *Quren* in the village of *Li* in *Hu* County of [the state of] *Chu*" (*Shiji* 63: 2139; NIENHAUSER et al. 1994: 21). Furthermore, there is another person whom *SIMA QIAN* identifies with *Laozi*. Interestingly, this person can be also linked to the state of *Chu*. "Some say [*Laozi*] was *Lao Laizi*, also a man of *Chu*. He composed a book in fifteen sections which spoke of the ideas of Taoism and was contemporary of Confucius" (*Shiji* 63: 2141; NIENHAUSER et al. 1994: 22). Moreover, whatever the traditional (Confucian) interpretations and the usual translations claim, the name of the famous guardian (*guan ling yin xi*), who at the frontier asks *Laozi* to summarize his wisdom, also implies some kind of hidden reference to *Chu*. "This is odd, since *lingyin* was the state of *Chu*'s equivalent to prime minister..." (NIENHAUSER et al. 1994: 22. n.11.) *Lingyin* was not a general term, but "a title unique to *Chu*" (BLAKELEY 1999: 56). The alleged author of the *Zhuangzi* (which is in fact true for the first seven chapters) was *Zhuang Zhou* who was "a native of *Meng*. (...) There was nothing on which his teachings did not touch, but in their essentials they went back to the words of *Laozi*" (*Shiji* 63: 2143; NIENHAUSER et al. 1994: 23). On *Meng* as a

indebtedness of these two influential traditions, however, are only consequences of a wider dissimilarity in the mentality of the two regions. Despite being challanged by some, this discrepancy between the two ways of thinking has been clearly expressed by several authors. M. LOEWE, the top expert on *Han* society and culture expressed this idea as follows: "There is the evidence of a natural, romantic and free tradition, sometimes associated with the south, and that of a formal, classical and inhibited tradition, sometimes associated with the north."[8]

The written documents of the *Zhou* and *Han* dynasty and the northern tradition in general regarded the South as barbaric and uncivilized.[9] This

recipient of *Chu* see V. MAIR's opinion: "*Meng* was very close to the border with the powerful state of *Chu* and consequently strongly influenced by southern culture" (MAIR 1998: xxxi). *Zhuang Zhou* was so much appreciated and deemed by the king of *Chu* that he "sent a messenger with lavish gifts to induce him to come and promised him the position of prime minister" (NIENHAUSER et al. 1994: 24). The episode, which naturally resulted in *Zhuang Zhou*'s rejecting the offer, is recorded both in the *Shiji* and the *Zhuangzi* (*Shiji* 63: 2145; *Zhuangzi* 10: 12a–b).

[7] This fundamental opinion is shared by YU WEICHAO, who adds Legalism to Taoism and Confucianism, claiming that this basically political tradition can also be defined locally. Accordingly, Legalism was born in the intellectual sphere of the three *Jin* states and the state of *Qin*, the latter becoming the leading political force at the end of the 3rd century B.C. (*Yu* 1995: 132). The connection between Taoism and *Chu* culture, especially *Chu* shamanism was also emphasized by FUNG YU-LAN (1952: 175–176) and IZUTSU TOSHIHIKO (1967. Vol. 2: 18–19). A well-known example from the complex relationship between Taoism and *Chu* culture is *Chisongzi*, one of the most popular Taoist heroes, who is first encountered in the *Chuci* and the *Huainanzi*, both, as will be demonstrated later, closely connected with *Chu* culture. In a passage of the *Liexianzhuan*, a *Han* dynasty collection of the immortals' biographies, *Chisongzi* appears in the company of several other figures and motifs (e.g. *Xiwangmu, Yandi, Kunlun*, Master of Rain) which we will later identify as typical *Chu* heritage (MATHIEU 1989: 205–206). (On Master of Rain (*Yushi*) as a *Chu* spirit, see ZHANG 1996: 296). On the other hand, N. J. GIRARDOT convincingly warns that, although "there is, no doubt, a good deal of truth in this observation", it can be also seen as an oversimplification, especially if the origins of *Chu* culture are not taken into account (GIRARDOT 1983: 170–171). "Some scholars (e.g. GIRARDOT 1925, ELIADE 1964, Welch 1965) feel it (Taoism, G. K.) inherited certain aspects of Chinese shamanism" (CARR 1992: 140). On these and other opinions see n.11.

[8] LOEWE 1994: 38. On the other hand, this kind of dichotomy can be justly seen as an oversimplification, especially if considered as an "attempt to validitate the traditional self-image of Confucianism as the purest manifestation of Chinese culture" (GIRARDOT 1983: 175).

[9] ZHENG 1963: 237; FUNG 1952: 175–176. "The *Chu* people were perceived by their northern neighbors as "barbarians", that is, ethnically and/or culturally distinctive. (...) The *Chu* on occasion described themselves as *Man Yi* barbarians. The *Chu* people were regarded by their contemporaries as being remarkably religious and having a religion dominated by shamanism. The early portions of the *Chuci* give ample testimony to *Chu*

idea of difference between north and south, for which further examples could be amply quoted from Chinese history, was clearly articulated and expressed in 20th century China. In 1904 *LIU SHIPEI* published an essay which asserts that the northern culture of China is based on the reverence for reality, therefore, it aimed at an accurate description of factual events and everyday life; in contrast, the southern way of thinking (*Chuci, Laozi, Zhuangzi*) is closer to the supernatural world of illusion, dreams and visions. Later on the literary aspect of this difference can be seen in the different styles of the two major poem collections (*QU YUAN*'s *Chuci* and the *Shijing*). *WANG GUOWEI* further elaborated on the problem, writing that the northern imperial China was aristocratic, mundane and strongly inclined towards politics, while the southern regions lay emphasis on the common people and imagination. *GUO YINTIAN* is also of the same opinion when claiming that the north is conservative, utilitarian, rational and realistic, while the south is characterised by an innovative, destructive, imaginative and romantic spirituality.[10] The contributors of the most authoritative summary of *Chu* culture use the term 'Northern Bias' to denote the

---

shamanism, while the geographical treatise of the *Han Shu* gives a clear record of contemporary opinion" (MAJOR 1978: 228). The *Zhou* state was definitely distinct from the state of *Chu*, therefore it cannot be excluded that their culture was, to a certain extent, different. Sometimes it is assumed that the collapse of the *Zhou* might be, partly at least, attributed precisely to the *Zhou*'s attempt to conquer the *Chu* territories: "Successful as this northern campaign obviously was, an attempt made shortly thereafter by King *Kang*'s son and successor, King *Zhao* (r. 977/75–957 B.C.), to expand *Zhou* control southwards resulted in the *Zhou* court's first military setback. It was a crushing defeat, and one that was to have lasting and far-reaching repercussions. Only hinted at in the traditional historical record, a campaign or campaigns led by King *Zhao* against the southern state of *Chu* is commemorated by so many inscribed vessels that we may be justified in assuming that it began with high hopes. The *Zhushu jinian* is again our best source of what happened [...] Thus, according to this recors, not only did King *Zhao* lose his own life in the campaign, but the main force of the royal army was also destroyed. As we will see, the *Zhou* state never really recovered from this loss" (SHAUGHNESSY 1999: 322–323). Moreover, the description in a later document (*Santian neijing*) also implies that the state of *Chu* simply does not belong to China, i.e. it is a totally different country (KOHN 1995: 15).

[10] On these and other opinions see SCHNEIDER 1980: 94–109. The difference between north and south was apparent in various areas of culture, like, for example, in calligraphy. "In addition to this northern tradition there existed in southern China explicitly ornamental inscriptions on bronze vessels and weapons which were often playfully enriched by the integration of small images of birds' heads into the characters. They gave rise to the name 'bird script' (*niaoshu*). Such stylistic forms, which were obviously intended to create a decorative effect, are expressions of the material and cultural wealth of the south-eastern area, especially the state of *Chu*" (GOEPPER 1996: 279–280).

northern attitude toward the southern *Chu* (COOK – BLAKELEY 1999: 1–2). Therefore, we can claim that there is a general, though slightly oversimplified, opinion both in the Chinese tradition and in Sinology which distinguishes between a northern and a southern tradition from which later the Confucian state religion and the more shamanic, Taoist tradition evolved respectively.[11]

On the other hand, it is to be noted that, if no further meticulous analysis is applied, this general cultural distinction between the north and the south would result in an oversimplified vision of ancient Chinese culture. It can be very useful at the beginning but it might lead to historical distortions unless we realise that a more convincing, though still simplified, picture can emerge if we conceive all the states during the Eastern *Zhou* period (770–221 B.C.) as possessing distinctive cultural and religious features and, at the same time, sharing some common concepts and beliefs of their time. The culture of all the states (especially *Lu, Qin, Qi* and *Chu*) had a distinctive intellectual atmosphere, which became more and more evident during the Warring States period. With the *Qin* and *Han* unification, however, as more emphasis was laid on the shared knowledge and less on the differences, these specific "intellectual dialects" disappeared, or, in other words, contributed to form what later became "the Chinese culture". This general process seems to be valid in the case of religion and mythology as well. In sum, first of all, the religious characteristics of the state of *Chu* are to be investigated; shamanism, in some form at least, was

---

[11] H. MASPERO asserts that Taoist meditation is derived directly from shaman ecstasy (MASPERO 1971: 42), while R. MATHIEU states that esoteric (i.e. religious) Taoism has incorporated a great variety of shamanic methods (MATHIEU 1987: 23). M. ELIADE also remarks that Taoism has, to a greater extent than yoga or Buddhism, assimilated "archaic techniques of ecstasy" (ELIADE 1989: 453). This kind of similarity can be, perhaps, attributed to the fact that Taoism and shamanism, or certain of their layers at least, stem from and developed in the south, in the state of *Chu.* "Throughout the early Taoist texts there are a number of specific characteristics suggestive of shamanism and especially *Chu* tradition" (GIRARDOT 1983: 82). Furthermore, P. J. THIEL (1968: 165) was convinced that shamanic techniques of ecstasy were transformed into Taoist "techniques of enstasy." K. SCHIPPER, an expert on Taoism, states that "for the religion of the common people, from antiquity up until the present, I often make use of the term shamanism. (...) It should be seen, I think, as being the substratum of Taoism" (SCHIPPER 1993: 6). Also see L. KOHN's opinion: "Many of their (Taoists, G. K.) powers are similar to the abilities of shamans. Taoist immortals heal the sick, exorcise demons or beasts, make rain or stop it, foretell the future, prevent disasters, call upon wild animals as helpers, and remain unharmed by water and fire, heat and cold. Control over the body, a subtle harmony with the forces of nature, as well as an easy relationship with gods and spirits, ghosts and demons are equally characteristics of successful shamans as of the immortals of Tao" (KOHN 1993: 280).

probably part of the religious life of all the states in ancient China, but *Chu* seems to excel in adopting more of its features than usual, even at a courtly level.

Shamanism and the Origin of *Chu* Culture

As for the source and origin of *Chu* culture, in his stimulating article, J. S. MAJOR discussed nine hypotheses, which can be, of course, supported by various data of different kinds: "1. The dominant inhabitants of *Chu* were not indigenous to the region but were a northern group ethnically distinct from the *Shang* Chinese and related to the inhabitants of the Mongolian steppe and northeast Asia, who, for reasons not clearly understood, migrated south around the end of the second millennium B.C." 2. The belief system of the early *Chu* people was a variant of the pan-European Grand Origin Myth, transmitted to them by the proto-Indo-European inhabitants of the south Siberian steppe and in turn transmitted by them to the *Shang* Chinese; the cosmological mythology of ancient China was essentially a *Chu* phenomenon and survived most strongly and coherently in *Chu* in the *Zhou* period.[12] 3. The religious tradition of *Chu* was indeed strongly characterized by shamanism and was directly related to the shamanistic cultures of north and northeast Asia. 4. The state of *Qi* also had, to perhaps a lesser extent, a shamanistic religious culture, with elements in common with that of *Chu*. 5. Taoism and the *yin-yang*/Five-

---

[12] The novelty of MAJOR's ideas is more conspicuous if considered in the light of the former suggestions on the relationship between the *Chu* and the *Shang* tradition. "The traditional ideas of the *Chu* people as recorded in the *Chu* Silk Manuscript show that they still followed the ways of *Shang*" (RAO 1972: 122). "The *Chu* culture preserves some *Shang* lore and legends not found in *Zhou* works" (HO 1975: 316–317). HAYASHI mentions "the preservation and the development of *Shang* culture which had entered the *Chu* territory", and cites the *Chu* survival of *Shang* official titles, bronze decor, and bronze bell types as evidence (HAYASHI 1972: 177). RAO ZONGYI, HE BINGDI and HAYASHI Minao all assume that the pro-*Chu* civilisation was the recipient of the *Shang* culture, which is not completely approved by MAJOR, who exchanges the roles. MAJOR, however, also admitted that "there is some agreement that the *Chu* culture in part represents a survival and/or revival of *Shang* culture" (MAJOR 1978: 228). The hypothesis that *Chu*, in a certain sense at least, gained possession of the cultural heritage of the *Shang* can be further supported by the fact that the so-called *Huai*-style (700–300 B.C.) bronze vessels of the *Chu* state resuscitated motifs which became extinct by 950 B.C. (KARLGREN 1941). The close connection between *Chu* and *Shang* is also approved by the leading Chinese archaeologist, *Zheng Dekun* (ZHENG 1963: 12), and several leading experts on the topic (COOK – MAJOR 1999: 1, 9, 24, 43, 124, 131, 137).

Phase School of Naturalism were in large part derived from the *Qi* and *Chu* element of the religious-intellectual heritage of *Shang* and *Zhou*. 6. A belief in immortality and in ecstatic spirit-journeys was both a characteristic and a consequence of the distinctive religious cosmology of *Qi* and *Chu* and its expression in shamanistic practices. 7. Burial practices in *Chu* differed significantly in form and intent from those of the Middle States. The purpose of burial in *Chu* was not so much to adhere to a semisecular cult of ancestor worship as to prepare the deceased for a spirit-journey to paradise. 8. The *Qin-Han* political unification of China resulted in the gradual destruction of a distinctive *Chu* culture, but also in the increased dissemination of *Chu* beliefs and practices throughout China. 9. Local cults reflecting *Chu* beliefs and practices survived in the *Huai*-Yangtse region at least into the *Tang* period" (MAJOR 1978: 231).

If these hypotheses prove to be correct, they would explain several unclear aspects of *Chu* culture, especially the strong shamanic component. However, even if only some of them are valid, the incorrect ones would not disqualify the rest, which means that the different hypotheses are not interdependent either in the positive or the negative way.

Shamanism and the Major Characteristics of *Chu* Culture

In a recently published collection of scholarly summaries on all the fundamental aspects of *Chu* culture, J. S. MAJOR, one of the most influential Western experts on *Chu* religion, was invited to summarize the main characteristics of *Chu* religion and thinking (MAJOR 1999).

"I would propose that *Chu* religion is characterized by at least the following special features that define its regional distinctiveness as compared with the mainstream religious tradition(s) of the Central Plains states: A special emphasis on spatial orientation and directionality in the definition of a religious cosmology; this feature is shared with "mainstream" ancient Chinese religion but accorded unusual importance in *Chu* • Belief in, and rites directed at, gods of directions and months depicted as being masked, monstrous, or otherwise extraordinary in appearance • An emphasis in religious iconography on a small and consistent set of animal images, most importantly snakes, dragons, predatory birds, and tigers (in part a legacy evolved from *Shang* dynasty motifs) • Religious use of iconic and probably apotropaic figures depicted as having protruding tongues, bulging eyes, and (usually) antlers • An unusual emphasis on hunting as an aspect of ritual behavior, and on hunting scenes as part of the decor of ritual bronze vessels • Shamanism, mediumism, and other manifestations of spirit possession in a state of trance, together with • A belief in the capacity of the temporarily disembodied human soul to undertake spirit journeys through time and space" (MAJOR 1999: 124).

Everything mentioned above on the nature of the hypotheses concerning the origin of *Chu* culture is also valid for this general overview of the major traits of *Chu* culture.[13]

Shamanism in the Religious Practice of *Chu*

As it is evident from his articles written in 1978 and 1999, the leading scholar on *Chu* religion, J. S. MAJOR stressed the presence of shamanism in the culture of *Chu*.[14] "I would argue that shamanism was a key part of early Chinese religion and especially of the religious culture of *Chu*. (...) The evidence for a shamanistic component of *Chu* religion is strong and diverse

---

[13] It is interesting to contrast the two lists to show that despite the gap of 21 years MAJOR's perception of *Chu* culture has remained rather consistent.

[14] Naturally, one might argue that sinologists are not always on good terms with the complex issue of shamanism, therefore a religious phenomenon that a sinologist labels as shamanic or shamanistic would not necessarily be accepted by an expert on shamanism. Nevertheless, the fact itself that shamanism was used to ·describe phenomena which were first recorded in details only in the 17th century Siberia already reveals the obvious complications when applying it to phenomena of 4th c. B.C. China. Furthermore, the plethora of definitions offered by experts on shamanism makes the whole question even more complicated. Still, we may assert that for the majority of Western sinologists shamanic features roughly mean the following complex system of religious phenomena: conscious ecstatic journey to solve some problems, direct communication with the spiritual world, a more intimate relation with the world of nature, and specific skills (divination, healing, etc.). Although these characteristics are not sufficient to define shamanism, they are specific enough to separate them from other ancient Chinese religious movements. In sum, as a hypothesis we can accept that the sinological usage of the word 'shamanism' is specific enough to define a tradition in ancient China; later on, however, the notion of Chinese shamanism needs to be more subtly articulated. A first step towards this definition is probably the sound assessment of the earlier usage of the word; therefore, I am preparing an article on the usage of the word 'shaman', 'shamanic', 'shamanistic' and 'shamanism' in the works of Western Sinologists (J. J. M. GROOT, A. WALEY, D. HAWKES, K. C. CHANG, R. MATHIEU, D. N. KEIGHTLEY, M. GIRARDOT, H. MASPERO, S. ALLAN, L. KOHN, I. ROBINET, K. SCHIPPER, J. S. MAJOR, L. VON FALKENHAUSEN, H. PETERS, etc), which would investigate the underlying notions and the articulated opinions of sinologists writing on shamanism.

enough to be quite persuasive."[15] He emphasizes that *Chu* shamanism can be regarded as a proven fact, as all historical data support this idea.[16] Let's quote some examples. The sources, for instance, refer to a king of *Chu* who, in case of emergency, danced exactly as shamans do.[17] In 531 B.C. Marquis *Wu* of *Qi* summoned a shaman called *Wei* from *Chu* because he needed help to get in contact with (the spirits of) the five legendary emperors. Duke *Zhao* of *Chu* (515–489 B.C.) had an official with sacerdotal functions who, in order to help the state, „could contact the deities above and the spirits below".[18] There is a document from the *Han* period which attests to the strong southern presence of shamanism.

"*Ban Gu*, author of the *Han Shu* (Book of *Han*), added to *SIMA QIAN*'s already negative view of the south. *Ban Gu* claimed that in the *Jiangnan* region, the region he understood to be *Chu*, the people employed shamans in the worship of 'ghosts and spirits' (*guishen*) and placed weight on *yinsi* (excessive, or lewd, rites) (...) These regional practice involved great expenditures, dancing and singing, animal sacrifices, and the use of shamans, exorcism, or prayers to local gods."[19]

ZHANG ZHENGMIN (1996: 114) emphasizes that shamans in *Chu* held much higher positions than in any other parts of China. What is more, even from a much later period (the *Song* dynasty) we have some evidence that this southern people occasionally gathered to perform ceremonies which

---

[15] MAJOR 1999: 136. Also see SUKHU's opinion: "By the late Warring States period, however, *Chu* was one of the states singled out as a place where belief in shamans and ghosts were common" (SUKHU 1999: 149).

[16] "Regarding the third hypothesis, there is no dispute that the religion of *Chu* was shamanistic, this being amply attested by contemporary accounts and by modern studies alike. Waley and HAWKES have studied the shamanism of the *Chuci*, while HAYASHI has examined the *Chu* Silk Manuscript from that point of view, concluding that the peripheral figures of the manuscript have little relationship to the various tribe of fabulous beings mentioned in the *Shanhaijing*, the *Huainanzi*, etc., but are clearly related to the divine shamans named in the same sources. What is less clear is the exact nature of *Chu* shamanism and its relationship to other shamanistic cultures, particularly those of northern Asia. The most persuasive evidence for such a connection is derived from the antler-bearing, long-tongued wooden cult images, demonic in form and presumably apotropaic in intent, that have been found in *Chu* tombs and the antler headdresses associated with shamanism in the Siberian steppe" (MAJOR 1978: 236).

[17] EICHHORN 1973: 60. The king reigned between 540–529 B.C.

[18] *Guoyu Chuyu* 2: 7 (EICHHORN 1973: 94).

[19] COOK – BLAKELEY 1999: 3. "Historians of the Later *Han* considered shamanistic rites the salient barbarian characteristic of *Chu*. The term "*yin*" (excessive), which, as we have seen, was used for the *Chu* rites, was also applied to Emperor *Wu*'s rites. In the case of rites involving a ritual love relationship between the shaman and the invoked spirit, the word "*yin*" also carried the meaning "lewd" (SUKHU 1999: 157; also see ZHANG 1996: 115–116).

involved drumming, dancing and singing. The same source reveals that they never applied official doctors and medicaments; instead, they used a special kind of divination to cure diseases (EICHHORN 1973: 95). Furthermore, as we will show, the two major literary products of *Chu* (the *Chuci* and the *Shanhaijing*), the representatives of Taoism (especially *Zhuangzi* and the *Huainanzi*), a religious movement often associated with *Chu* (the *Shangqing*[20] movement), as well as the artistic finds of this region are full of references to a special *Chu* version of shamanism.

Shamanism and the Art of *Chu*

During the last decades numerous statues, strikingly different from the better-known, classical northern Chinese art, were unearthed from tombs all situated within the territory of the former state of *Chu*.[21] The difference between the northern Yellow river artefacts and the southern *Yangzi* artifacts is expressed by J. RAWSON, a leading expert on Chinese art, in the following way: "The contrasts between objects from the Yellow river and *Yangzi* river areas suggest that we should be on the look out for such contrasts at later times also. The beliefs and practices attributed to CONFUCIUS were some of the principal descendants of the early cultures of the Yellow river, while the images of a much more varied spirit world, seen most specially on the chariot fitting and on the hill censers, were in large measure adopted to express beliefs more typical of the south and eastern regions of the *Yangzi* river" (RAWSON 1998: 45).

One of the features of *Chu* art is the abundant use of wood,[22] bronze mirrors[23] (dissimilar from those used in the north),[24] large bells[25] and

---

[20] *Shangqing* (or *Maoshan*) sect was one of the most important religious Taoist movements with a clear southern shamanic background, especially evidenced by its various techniques of ecstatic journeys into the astral realms of divinities. On the *Shangqing* sect generally see ROBINET 2000; on ecstatic techniques see e.g. ROBINET 1993: 171–225.

[21] On *Chu* art see LAWTON 1991; MACKENZIE 1987; So 1999.

[22] See e.g. MACKENZIE 1987. J. RAWSON remarks that "one of the reasons why this sculpture [a large wooden bird with antlers in the tomb of the Marquis *Yi* of *Zeng*] has turned up in a southern tomb may have been the predilection of peoples in the area for wood carving. It is even possible that among the different southern cultures a wooden sculptural tradition of some sort had existed in much earlier times, even in the centuries contemporary with the *Shang*. Out of this general southern interest in sculpture may have arisen both the strange figures at *Sanxingdui* and the later, Eastern *Zhou* period (771–256 BC) sculpture of the state of *Chu*" (RAWSON 1996a: 44–45).

[23] "In *Chu*, the bronze mirror industry was highly developed, especially in the area of present-day *Hunan* province, which for a time was the industry's most important

lacquerwares.[26] The artifacts found at some *Chu* burial sites bear antlers and have a long protruded tongue,[27] which have no analogy in "northern" Chinese art.[28] The history of their controversial interpretations deserves a brief summary. A. SALMONY, the first scholar to investigate these strange figures traced their origin to India (SALMONY 1954), while HAYASHI MINAO identified them with the figure of *Jiangliang* appearing in the *Shanhaijing*. MIZUNO and *WANG RUIMING* think that they represent mountain spirits (*shanshen*), PENG HAO claims that they are three-dimensional representations of dragons, while CHEN YAOJUN and YUAN WENQI were convinced that the statues represent *Tubo*, the Lord of the Underworld (DEMATTÉ 1994: 332). E. CHILDS-JOHNSON thinks that these antlered statues are representations of *Bo Feng*, and descendants of the *Shang* dynasty *taotie* motif.[29] The latest interpretation suggests that the antler refers to longevity, immortality, and ascension to Heaven, while the protruded tongue is the symbol of desire for new life, for rejuvenation and resurrection (DEMATTÉ 1994). The diverseness of explanations offered clearly demonstrate that *Chu* art is resistant to decipherment on the basis of classical (northern) art history. Numerous further examples could be quoted as examples of a distinctive *Chu* art, especially during the 5th–3rd

---

centre. The use of bronze mirrors was very widespread in *Chu*, and it became customary to include them in tomb burials" (CHEN 1997: 90).

24 Bronze mirrors have also been discovered in the north, but "the overall compositional structure [of these northern bronzes] is quite different from that of the *Chu* mirrors" (CHEN 1997: 92). Similarly, mirrors excavated in the north-western state of *Qin* (which eventually conquered *Chu*) were "thick and heavy, and roughly cast" (CHEN 1997: 93).

25 On large bells as the defining artifact of a distinctive *Yangzi* bronze industry see KANE 1974–75; SHAUGHNESSY 1999: 209–210.

26 On a specific lacquerware type, painted in red and black, which were dominantly found in the southern region see So 1997. On a fifth century example of pictorial representation on a lacquer box, which seems to possess several of the characteristics labelled by J. S. MAJOR (1999: 124) as distinctive *Chu* features see HEARN 2000.

27 "There is, however, evidence to suggest that the protruding tongue depicted frontally was originally a southern motif" (MACKENZIE 1987: 89).

28 "No representations of faces with protruding tongues are known in North China until the *Han* Dynasty and no archaeological remains of fantastic animals with two horns have come to light" (CHANG 1972: 33, 35). "These apotropaic antler-and-tongue figures in their concrete manifestations are specific to *Chu* culture and thus fit into the *Han* view of *Chu* as 'barbarian' and 'other'" (MAJOR 1999: 132).

29 "Their [i.e. Ku's (the Music Master's) and the Dark Woman's, G. K.] child was *Bo Feng*, a pig who caused the state of *Kui* to be wiped out and their ancestral rites ended. It is possible that the famous antlered tomb or guardian monsters found in *Chu* tombs were physical representations of this demon/god and as such likely iconographic descendants of the 'gluttonous' *Shang taotie*" (with a reference to CHILDS-JOHNSON's conference paper from 1993 – COOK 1994: 14.n.70).

centuries B.C.[30] The author of the present article thinks that the former interpretations have not given full explanation of these, as well as other unusual, artistic products of *Chu* culture, so these odd statues need further clarifications, especially in the context of shamanism,[31] as, for example, J. F. SO suggests: "Figures resembling the deities on the Sackler manuscript appear in other contexts, such as the lacquered inner coffin of *Zeng Hou Yi* (...) Flanking portal-like openings on the sides of the coffin are two rows of bird-man figures, armed with menacing weapons, presumably to ward off unwanted intruders to the marquis' sanctuary. They could be protective deities or shamans in professional gear. (...) Birds, snakes, and deer (often symbolized by just their antlers), together with quasi-human or feline figures, are the main protagonists in these *Chu* representations. Crane-like birds often join with felines to form drumstands; some of them display fancy antlers on their heads. The small lacquered wooden screen from Tomb 1 at *Wangshan* combines bird, snake, and deer in an ornamental

---

[30] On the *Shang* roots of this distinctive art see, for example, R. Bagley's opinion who thinks that, contemporenous with the northern *Anyang* industries, there was a "self-assured local industry" in what was to become later the central *Chu* territory (BAGLEY 1999: 210). Let's quote some of his conclusions: "On the evidence of material culture the most sophisticated contemporaries of the *Anyang* [northern, *Shang*] civilization were located in the middle and lower *Yangzi* region. Despite variation within it, this region had an overarching cultural unity that manifests itself in the archaeological record in finds of large bells. [...] Examples from the south are large and lavishly decorated. [...] Typical of *Anyang nao* are the five found in *Fu Hao*'s tomb, the largest of which is 14 cm high and weighs 600 grams. Bells from the south belong to another world. the largest so far reported, from *Ningxiang* in northern *Hunan* weighs 220 kg. [...] In technical quality southern castings yield nothing to bronzes from *Anyang*, and they are often significantly larger than their *Anyang* counterparts. [...] Animals were favorite motifs in the south, not the formalized imaginary animals of *Anyang* bronzes but real animals treated with affectionate naturalism. [...] Find contexts, the repertoire of typres, extravagant size, eccentrities of shape and decoration—in all these features southern bronzes advertise a civilization sharply different from that of *Anyang*. The narrow range of types, dominated by large bells, must signify important differences of ritual" (BAGLEY 1999: 208–210). It is to be noted, however, that the question of whether the roots of *Chu* are to be searched for in the Warring States area of *Chu* or somewhere else is still open to scholarly debates. Furthermore it is to be noted that art in other southern cultures (like ancient *Sichuan*, as the *Sanxingdui* finds reveal) were also different from the art of the contemporaneous Yellow River culture: "The bronzes of *Sanxingdui* are the means to realize the supernatural, and are therefore very different from the repertory of animal motifs found on *Shang* bronze vessels and other utensils" (RAWSON 1996a: 43).

[31] J. RAWSON, for instance, correlates shamanism with certain *Chu* figures: "The wearing of antlers seems to have been significant in these shamanistic rituals. It seems probable that carved wooden figures with such antlers represent the shamans or their powers" (RAWSON 1980: 166). Also see MIYAKAWA – KOLLAUTZ 1966.

composition (...) Intertwining snakes form the walls of an egg-shaped box from *Yutaishan*. The similarity of these images with those on the marquis' coffin and the Sackler manuscript suggests that their popularity was deeply rooted in *Chu* mythology. Snakes and other serpentine creatures also interact with shaman-like figures, portrayed as wearing long robes and fancy headdresses" (So 1999: 45).

Although of slightly later origin, the *Mawangdui* finds near modern *Changsha* were obviously greatly influenced by *Chu* culture.[32] S. ALLAN emphasizes the fact that *Mawangdui* is situated within the boundaries of the former state of *Chu* (ALLAN 1991: 30), while M. LOEWE maintains that the finds discovered can be easily explained if placed in the context of representative *Chu* works like the *Chuci* or the *Shanhaijing*, and if further evidence is furnished from the southern shamanic practice.[33]

"Both from the text that is under consideration and the unique silk manuscript it is possible to trace features that are generally and almost universally associated with shamanistic practice; for example, assimilation with an animal's garb or guise; utterances in the tongues of animals or birds; and dependence on trees for ascent to or descent from another world. This last feature may be seen clearly, and somewhat regularly, at the corners of the silk manuscript" (LOEWE 1994: 45).

Some of the Chinese scholars also seem to agree on this issue. "It has been suggested by *Gao Zhixi* that the contents of tombs at *Mawangdui* illustrate a conscious revival of *Chu* practices and styles" (RAWSON 1989: 98. n.10). The twelve strange figures of the famous *Chu* Silk Manuscript from another site (*Zidanku, Changsha*), as HAYASHI Minao and M. LOEWE convincingly suggests, may represent deified shamans (LOEWE 1994: 42), also featuring in the *Shanhaijing* and the *Huainanzi*. "The twelve figures of the silk manuscript, including some hybrids, may thus perhaps be taken to represent twelve spirits, or twelve shamans able to contact them and to drive away evil influences" (LOEWE 1994: 45). Thus, the *Mawangdui* and the *Zidanku* finds seem to bear evidence of the surviving *Chu* culture in the subsequent *Han* period. Moreover, the *Han* survival of the *Chu* legacy is not confined to the realm of art, it can be clearly demonstrated in the case of various other cultural motifs as well.[34] It can be assumed that the reason of

---

[32] See MAJOR's ninth hypothesis as well as Chang's view: "This powerful state (*Chu*, G. K.) was overthrown by the *Qin* Dynasty in 223 B.C., but the people and the culture maintained their distinct identity into the *Han* Dynasty" (CHANG 1968: 396).

[33] On the painting found in the tomb No.1. at *Mawangdui* see LOEWE 1994a: 17–59.

[34] MAJOR 1999: 140–143; SO 1999: 37–38; SUKHU 1999.

this survival and spread is, paradoxically, due to the *Qin* defeat of *Chu*.[35] As it will be important later on, we must assert that *Chu* culture, including its shamanic and mythological aspects, was highly esteemed and appreciated in the first century of the *Han* dynasty.[36]

---

[35] "Political unification gave the *Qin* and the *Han* emperors an opportunity to assimilate systematically practices and beliefs from many parts of the area we today call China, but which, in the fourth and third centuries B.C., had been parts of independent political entities. What resulted was not only a new political, social and economic order, but also, it now seems, a new religious or ideological outlook" (RAWSON 1999: 7). We know several previous examples of assimilation of mythological material and religious concepts into a new context as a result of dynastic change. AKATSUKA KIYOSHI, for example, "has shown that many of the chief diviners in the early records came from allied cities in the *Shang* confederation, that several early kings in the royal genealogy originated in allied tribes and settlements, and that many of the gods sacrificed to by the *Shang* were originally the local gods of allied cities. The pre-dynastic *Zhou* similarly incorporated *Shang* ancestors into *their* pantheon [...] Groups who subsequently fell under *Shang* domination were drawn into new state through the adoption of their leaders as diviners and the addition of their gods to the *Shang* pantheon" (LEWIS 2000: 360).

[36] "*Chu* state was the home of *Liu Bang*, who founded the fortunes of the *Han* to become Emperor *Gao* (r. 206–94 BCE) and introduced at court further objects, as well as cusoms and beliefs, from *Chu*" (RAWSON 1998: 37). "The *Han* founders were natives of *Chu*, and the influence of this region's cultural life was especially strong during the early years of the dynasty. These facts doubtless explain the noticeable shamanistic element in *Han* ritual and the popularity of the *Chuci* during these years..." (HARTMAN 1986a: 63). An illustrative example is *Han Wudi*'s (r. 141–87 B.C.) performing the *feng* and *shan* sacrifices, the roots of which can be, partly at least, traced back to shamanic spirit travels: "A final element in our analysis of the *feng* and *shan* sacrifices is the literary *topos* of the spirit journey around the four quarters of the earth. [...] These tales and poems of spirit travel derive from *Qi* and *Chu* variants of what is loosely called shamanism, and they all provide liturgical images of travel as a mode of power. [...] Royal processions— reviously the actual medium of political control and then re-imagined as rituals of the ruler's potent virtue—were superimposed upon the map afforded by the sacred geography of the five directional mountains. These same processions were also charged with a spiritual power through evoking a range of 'shamanic' practices which in the Warring States period had been drawn into the political realm through the re-writing of divinities as ancient rulers, the re-ceartion of the spirit realm as a political administration, and the literary co-optation of shamanic spirit travel as a mode of speaking about human government" (LEWIS 1999: 63–64). During the second half of the *Han* dynasty, however, with the increasing power of Confucianism, the shamanic component becomes gradually rejected, so much so that "shamans were at some point prohibited from holding office because in the *Hou Han Shu* (History of the Later *Han* Dynasty) a man cites the fact that he is from a shaman family for his inappropriateness for serving at court" (SUKHU 1999: 161).

THE SOURCES OF *CHU* MYTHOLOGY
(Tianwen, Shanhaijing, Huainanzi, Zhuangzi, and other sources)

For a long time China was described as a basically secular[37] society, almost completely lacking mythology similar to that of other classical cultures. This view can be, partly at least, attributed to the fact that, unlike in the Greece of Homer or Hesiod, in China no systematic written summary of oral mythic narratives was composed, which resulted in a literary, philosophical and religious corpus that frequently alludes to but almost never dwells upon mythological topics.[38] Therefore, the researcher of Chinese mythology must be prepared to search for the various elements of the same myth in sources of different kinds. A. BIRRELL, for example, collected the three hundred mythic narratives of her seminal book from more than one hundred classical texts (BIRRELL 1993: 1).

Chinese mythology,[39] as outlined above, comes to us in a rather fragmented way; four works, however, are exceptions in this respect, as they contain extremely abundant information on Chinese mythic topics. Interestingly enough, all these works come from the state of *Chu,* which, thus, could gain the reputation of being the center *par excellence* of Chinese mythology.

QU YUAN: **Chuci (Tianwen)**

This collection of poems has been paid so much scholarly attention that just a few citations from the relevant studies can be sufficient. The *Chuci* is

---

[37] See e.g. FINGARETTE 1972.
[38] Although at a first glance it seems to be a shortcoming, it can be interpreted as an advantage as well, as, unlike in the Greek or the Roman tradition, the usual literary adaptations do not dim the original contents of these mythic narratives which thus preserved their rather archaic nature (BIRRELL 1994: 382).
[39] On Chinese mythology generally see BIRRELL 1993; BODDE 1961; CHEN-YANG 1995; CHRISTIE 1983; DING 1992; KARLGREN 1946; KECSKÉS 1988; MA 1994; MACKENZIE 1994; MASPERO 1924; MATHIEU 1989; WERNER 1986; YUAN 1993. On a sound assessment of these ad other works see BIRRELL 1994, 1994a.

usually considered to be the most prominent evidence of southern[40] shamanism.[41]

"It was the poetry of South alone (...) that preserved the legacy of the distinct shamanistic cult of nature in the *Chuci* 'Songs of *Chu*' (principality in modern *Hunan-Hubei* region) toward the end of *Zhou*-period. In most grandiose form we meet it in the poetry of *QU YUAN* (about 340–278 B.C.), the greatest poet of classical China. The poems expressing his cosmic-size sorrow and longing to get off the place of his exile deep in the south, represent the best source of ancient Chinese shamanistic practice and technique."[42]

QU YUAN, the alleged author of most of the poems, was born in *Chu*, had a successful official career; due to his enemies' malicious slander at the court, however, he was exiled. From that time on, he lived in the countryside, writing poems. Later, as the mythical narrative in the *Shiji* says, he was so desperate that he committed suicide by jumping into the river *Mile*. People of the countryside cherished his memory by choosing the date of his suicide (the fifth of the fifth month) to be his memorial day.[43] Basically, *QU YUAN*'s purpose was, it now seems, to rewrite the shamanic songs of this area in a more refined manner, as *WANG YI*'s preface attests.

"In former times the people living in the area lying between the *Yuan* and *Xiang* rivers south of *Nanying* were superstitious and much given to the

---

[40] Its southern features are stressed by L. P. VAN SLYKE who asserts that *QU YUAN* "spoke in a characteristically 'southern' idiom: extravagant language, passionate emotional tone, a richly inhabited spirit world complete with seductive shaman goddesses, transparent sensuality, lush images of plants as metaphors" (SLYKE's opinion quoted by CHILDS – JOHNSON – SULLIVAN 1996: 55).

[41] On *Chuci* generally see CHAN 1962; CHEN 1986; HAWKES 1959, 1967; SCHENEIDER 1980; WALEY 1955. The shamanic influence is a commonplace in the sinological literature. "All the earlier *Chuci* poems (i.e., those traditionally attributed to *QU YUAN* or his disciple *Song Yu*) are often influenced by or connected with the beliefs and practices of shamanism. Some (*Jiuge*, *Zhaohun*, *Dazhao*) are explicitly concerned with these practices; but even in those which are not, the supernatural world of the shamans makes intermittent appearances" (HAWKES 1993: 51).

[42] ECSEDY 1984: 108–109. "Whether traditional shaman songs or examples of a new secular poetry which developed out of them, they [the *Chu* Texts] all in one way or another, have their origins in *Chu* shamanism" (HAWKES 1985: 39).

[43] *QU YUAN* was not the only person with shamanic gifts who died on this very day. "*Cao Xu*, the *Zhejiang* shaman who was drowned in AD 143 while going out in a boat to seek the river god met his death on the fifth day of the fifth month, the day of the Dragon Boat Festival, whose great antiquity has been demonstrated by *Wen Yiduo*" (HAWKES 1974: 74–75). Thus, it can be inferred that at that time *QU YUAN* was deemed as a mythical, and not as a historical, figure.

worship of spirits.[44] In their service of the gods they would sing, play, drum, and dance to do them pleasure.[45] It was in this area that QU YUAN concealed himself after his banishment. Full of grief and bitterness and in a greatly disturbed state of mind, he would go out to watch the sacrificial rites of the local inhabitants and witness the singing and dancing which accompanied them. Finding the words of their songs crude and barbarous, he composed the Nine Songs to replace them.[46] In his work he both sings the praises of the gods and at the same time uses the hymns as a vehicle for expressing his own resentments."[47]

While analyzing the different layers of *Chuci*, D. HAWKES classified the poems of the *Chuci* collection as follows: "Apart from the explicitly shamanistic poems (*Jiuge*, the 'Summons' poems, and the unclassifiable *Tianwen*) the content of the *Chuci* poems is classifiable into two main categories: one, which I shall designate *tristia*, expresses the poet's sorrows, his resentments, his complaints against a deluded prince, a cruel fate, a corrupt, malicious and uncomprehending society; the other, which I shall

---

44 In his subcommentary to WANG YI's commentary, HONG XINGZU (1099–1155) adds that "the *Hanshu* says: 'In *Chu*, the people believe in sorceresses and prize lewd sacrifices.' The *Suishu* says: 'In *Jingzhou* [*Chu*] they especially prize sacrifices.' QU YUAN's creation of the Nine Elegies probably originated from this" (Waters 1985: 31).

45 The different wording of another translation stresses more strongly the shamanic component: "In the area of the southern capital city *Ying* of the former state of *Chu*, between the rivers *Yuan* and *Xiang*, the people believed in spirits and sacrifices. During the sacrifice they had to sing and to dance ecstatically, in order to please the different gods" (RAWSON 1996: 141).

46 ZHU XI (1130–1200), the most famous philosopher of the *Song* period, also wrote a commentary on the *Jiuge*. He explains the origin of the poems as follows: "Their [people of the *Chu* region] sacrifices required male and female sorcerers to make music, sing and dance in order to give pleasure to the Spirits. The vulgar phrases of the barbarous people of *Jingzhou* [*Chu*] were crude, and in their intermediacy between *Yin* and *Yang*, man and ghost, they were unable to avoid the confusion of profanity and licentiousness. QU YUAN had been banished. Because he saw their sacrifices and was moved, he emended their words somewhat" (WATERS 1985: 33). ZHU XI's last sentence implies that the difference between the original and the reworked version was not that significant.

47 From WANG YI's introduction to *Jiuge* (HAWKES 1967: 73.n.5). D. HAWKES uses this particular part of the introduction to prove that the poems of the *Chuci* are, actually, the secularised versions of an originally oral and religious tradition (HAWKES 1967: 73). The same attitude is echoed in the words of *Liu Yuxi*'s (772–842): "Of old, when QU YUAN was living in the region of *Yuan* and *Xiang* [rivers], the people of those parts summoned the spirits in crude and rustic language; he then wrote the Nine Songs, and even today they sing and dance them in *Chu*" (SCHNEIDER 1980: 66). The adjectives used to describe the original poetry of *Chu* is, of course, to be understood in comparison with the standards of the more refined and, at the same time, more secular poetry of the North.

designate *itineraria*, describes the poet's journeys, occasionally real ones, but more often the imaginary, supernatural journeys to which I have just referred."[48]

The underlying shamanic substratum of the *Chuci* is approved by all sinologists, see for example its summary in the most authoritative history of Chinese literature: "The unique rhythms of the *Chuci* are certainly related to the anthology's origins in the state of *Chu* and that state's practice of institutionalized shamanism. Much of the vocabulary and imagery of the *Chuci* texts derives from shaman rituals, and there is much evidence to suggest that *QU YUAN* (...) was a shaman in the service of the king of *Chu*. Nevertheless, in the commentary of *WANG YI*, the shaman motifs were systematically allegorized to stand for Confucian values, and traditional readers understood the texts in this way" (HARTMAN 1986: 348).

In the Nine Songs, for example, "male and female shamans—it is not always clear which—having first purified and perfumed themselves and dress up in gorgeous costumes, sing and dance to the accompaniment of music, driving the gods down from heaven in a sort of divine courtship. The religion of which these songs are the liturgy is a frankly erotic one. The relationship of the worshipper to the god reminds one of the *épouses célestes* of Siberian shamans."[49] In the *Lisao* poems the poet himself, desolated and exiled, leaves for a shaman journey, while in the *Zhaohun* poem a wandering soul is addressed and prayed for to return.[50] The invoker is, without doubt, a shaman, who gives a detailed description of the dangers of the realm beyond awaiting the departed soul.[51]

The mythologically most relevant part of the *Chuci* is the *Tianwen* ('Asking the Heaven').[52] "Written in about the fourth century B.C., it presents a systematic account of the main myths of ancient *Chu* in its 186

---

[48] HAWKES 1967: 82. The *tristia* and *itineraria* poems made some scholars think that the *Chuci* can not be regarded as shamanic because the purpose of the poet is not to help his fellowmen but to escape from the world as a consequence of his personal sorrow (PETERS 1983: 126–133).

[49] HAWKES 1959: 35. See, for example, the poem.

[50] It should be noted that *SIMA QIAN*, *LIU XING* and *WANG YI* all believed that the *Zhaohun* was written for a living person, not for the dead (HAWKES 1985: 221–222). On the ceremony of retrieving the errant souls of the sick see YÜ 1987.

[51] "The 'Li sao' and the 'Nine Songs', and similar poems of the *Chuci* have long been seen by scholars as literary treatments of genuine experiences of shamanistic spirit possession and arguments against that view have not been convincing" (MAJOR 1999: 136).

[52] On the *Tianwen* see ERKES – CONRADY 1931; FIELD 1986, 1992.

verses."[53] This rather neglected text of the *Chuci* collection could be one of the most important sources of information (HAWKES 1983: 2) on *Chu* (and Chinese) mythology if studied with thorough scholarly care. The *Tianwen* consists of a series of questions concerning a great variety of myths and mythic figures, without providing any answer.[54] In many instances, it was the *Tianwen* that preserved the only material on certain deities or mythic narratives, which makes it rather difficult to interpret.

Shanhaijing

Besides the *Tianwen* part of *Chuci*, the only document that preserved much of the ancient Chinese pantheon is "The Classic of the Mountains and the Seas" (*Shanhaijing*).[55] According to several scholars[56] the *Shanhaijing*, alternatively called "the book of shamanism"[57] or "a shamanic text"[58], was composed in *Chu*.[59] *Yuan Ke* and others even assumed that "the text was partly derived from the pictures of supernatural beings used by shaman in

---

[53] BIRRELL 1993: 26. On the other hand, it is to be noted that this opinion on the *Chu* roots of *Tianwen* is not shared by everyone; St. Field, for example, states that the *Tianwen* was originally more syncretistic in nature (FIELD 1986: xv).

[54] This feature of the *Tianwen* is rare in ancient Chinese literature, the only stylistic parallel being another *Chu* work, the *Zhuangzi*. "The format of the poem, a rapid succession of enigmatic questions or riddles, is almost unique in the annals of ancient Chinese literature. Still, one remarkably similar poem exists in a roughly contemporeneous work, the philosophical text known as the *Zhuangzi*" (FIELD 1986: xi). Despite the fact that this poem is in the "Outer Chapters" of the extant version, which is believed to date from a later period, originally it was, as A. C. Graham has shown, in the authentic 2nd chapter (FIELD 1986: xii).

[55] On the *Shanhaijing* see BIRRELL 1999, FINSTERBUSCH 1952; FRACASSO 1996; JANSINOJ 1977; MÄNCHEN-HELFEN 1924; MATHIEU 1983; THEERN et al. 1985. The text itself is usually believed to have several layers: the first 5 chapters were composed during the 3rd c. B.C., the 6–13th chapters during the 2nd–1st c. B.C., the 14–17th chapters in the 1st c. A.D., while the last 18th chapters was probably written during the 2nd c. A.D. (BIRRELL 1994: 387). Although the majority of the chapters were composed during the *Han* dynasty, it is believed to contain much earlier and archaic mythic material. In this case it is worth considering the phenomenon, already referred to above, that the *Chu* heritage spread throughout China only during the *Han* dynasty.

[56] These scholars include *LU KANRU, HOU RENZHI, MENG WENTONG, SHI QINGCHEN, YUAN KE* (FRACASSO 1993: 360).

[57] *YUAN XINGPEI*'s opinion from 1979 (CHANG 1983: 114).

[58] *LU XUN*'s expression, quoted in FRACASSO 1993: 359.

[59] "The *Shanhaijing*, or *Classic of the Mountains and the Lakes*, is a text which reflects the southern tradition" (LOEWE 1994: 40).

Chu."[60] It contains twenty three references to *wu* shamans, moreover, a description of the mountains where "the shamanistic ascent was to take place."[61] The *Shanhaijing* is a "*catalogus rerum*", or, rather, a "*descriptio mundi*", a detailed, and, seemingly at least, monotonous enumeration of mountains and rivers, plants and animals, stones and minerals, strange peoples with their even stranger customs, and, in addition, deeds of gods and goddesses. Everything mentioned above is described in a simple and objective tone, presenting all its odd contents in a realistic manner.

In the text the reader may often encounter shamans who seem to be primarily engaged in and responsible for the communication between Heaven and Earth. They usually dwell at places (most often mountains) where this kind of ascent and descent is possible. "The Country of Shaman Whole (*Wu Xian*, G. K.) lies north of the country of Girl Deuce. In his right hand Shaman Whole holds a green snake.[62] In his left hand he holds a scarlet snake. His land lies near Mountain Climbscreen. The land of shaman Whole is the place from which crowds of shamans make their ascension and descend from the mountain."[63] *Wu Xian*, according to other sources, seems to be a major figure in Chinese shamanism. He lives in the north, invented (more precisely, used for the first time) yarrow stalk divination, and was sent by Emperor *Taimou* to invoke the spirits of mountains and rivers. R. MATHIEU thinks that *Wu Xian* actually refers to a people practicing shamanism.[64]

In the 15th chapter we read about the Shaman mountain, which seems to be closely connected with some kind of purification process. "To its west are the yellow bird and the great god's drugs for the Eight Purification Rites."[65] R. MATHIEU, relying on *He Yixing*'s commentary, concludes that the mountain in question was situated on the borderland of modern *Sichuan*

---

[60] FRACASSO 1993: 362. "*Shanhaijing* has been commonly assigned to the *Chu* literary reader and compared to the rather mysterious poetic work '*Tianwen*'. Recently YUAN KE has added some lexical evidence to other arguments that the *Shanhaijing* in fact was produced in the southern Chinese region of *Chu*" (NIENHAUSER 1986: 671).

[61] CHANG 1983: 48. The cult of mountains stems from the most archaic layers of Chinese religions and, thus, seems to constitute an integral part of all Chinese religions, either Confucian, Taoist or Buddhist (See NAQUIN – CHÜN 1992).

[62] The *Shanhaijing* abounds with figures who hold snakes on different parts of their bodies. Irrespective of these snakes being used in an apotropaic way or somehow else, the fact remains that snake is "the *Chu* emblem of evil spirits" (RAWSON 1998: 39), and "the obsessive *Chu* decor on lacquerware and bronzes" (COOK 1994: 7).

[63] *Shanhaijing* 7:3b (BIRRELL 1999: 116).

[64] *Huainanzi* 4:8b; *Lüshichunqiu* 17:10b; MATHIEU 1983: 402.n.1. (Also see later on *Wu Xian* as a prominent *Chu* figure)

[65] *Shanhaijing* 15:2a (BIRRELL 1999: 167).

and *Hubei*. This assumption would be merely of geographical interest if we ignored the fact that this region once belonged to the territory of the state of *Chu*.[66]

The *Shanhaijing*, furthermore, specifies the names of some shamans. Two lists of names were recorded in two different chapters, the first consisting of six, the second of ten names. "East of the Openbright there are Shaman Robust, Shaman Pushaway, Shaman Sunny, Shaman Shoe, Shaman Every, and Shaman Aide. They are all on each side of the corpse of Notch Flaw and they hold the neverdie drug to ward off decay."[67] The second list contains some names common with the first one. "In the middle of the Great Wilderness there is a mountain. Its name is Mount Fertilesoak-jadegate. There is where the Sun and the moon set. There is Mount Divinepower[68] (*Ling*, G. K.). This is where Shaman Whole, Shaman Reach, Shaman Share, Shaman Robust, Shaman Motherinlaw, Shaman Real, Shaman Rite, Shaman Pushaway, Shaman Takeleave and Shaman Birdnet ascend to the sky and come down from Mount Divinepower. This is where the hundred drugs are to be found."[69] It is to be noted that both passages include explicit references to some kind of healing process.

The Huainanzi and the Zhuangzi

A great variety of mythic material comes from the *Huainanzi*[70] compiled by the Prince LIU AN (175–122 B.C.) and his courtly guests, the magicians (*fangshi*).[71] All this happened in *Huainan*, a small kingdom within the boundaries of *Chu*;[72] therefore, it is not too far-fetched to assume that LIU AN and his work, the *Huainanzi* was greatly influenced by the *Chu* culture.

---

[66] MATHIEU 1983: 455.n.7.

[67] *Shanhaijing* 11: 6a. The original Chinese names are as follows: shaman *Peng, Di, Yang, Li, Fan* and *Xiang*.

[68] EICHHORN (1973: 72) thinks that this mountain lies in modern *Henan*. *Wen Yiduo*, furthermore, asserts that most of the Shaman mountains are to be found in the state of *Chu*.

[69] *Shanhaijing* 16: 3a. The original list of the shamans' names runs as follows: shaman *Xian, Yi, Fen, Peng, Gu, Zhen, Li, Di, Xie* and *Luo*.

[70] "*Huainanzi* comes close to being a comprehensive synthetic handbook of Chinese mythic history" (GIRARDOT 1987: 298).

[71] These magicians came from the state of *Qi* where a tradition rather similar to that of *Chu* prevailed (see MAJOR's 4th–6th hypotheses).

[72] "A century or so after the lifetime of *Zou Yan*, an academy at *Huainan* (in the northeastern part of the former state of *Chu*) under the patronage of LIU AN, king of *Huainan*, maintained and extended the *Jixia* tradition. The most famous product of this academy was the book now known as the *Huainanzi*" (MAJOR 1993: 2).

"In discussing the survival and compilation of *Chuci*, DAVID HAWKES has pointed out that *Chu* poetry and presumably other *Chu* customs were fostered by LIU AN, the Prince of *Huainan*" (RAWSON 1989: 98). The similarities between the *Huainanzi* and the *Chuci* are so conspicuous that "some Chinese scholars have attributed the authorship of *Lisao*, one of the most important *Chuci* poems, to LIU AN."[73]

"Many of the original and idiosyncratical features of *Huainanzi*, ideas as well as style, reflect the peculiarities of *Chu* culture. The early commentaries of *Huainanzi* by XU SHEN (30–124) and GAO YOU (205–212) already felt the need to explain many expressions particular to the cultural area of *Chu* and unintelligible to Northerners. The many poetic passages of *Huainanzi* are couched in a language closely akin to some songs of *Chuci* (the Songs of *Chu*). Recent research by Chinese linguists has also revealed the similarity of the rhyme system of *Huainanzi* with that of other earlier or contemporary *Chu* writings. The great importance given to the self-transformative aspect of Taoism in *Huainanzi*, especially the themes of 'mystical flight' and 'return to the beginning', may at least in part be rooted in the shamanistic traditions of *Chu*" (LE BLANC 1985: 7–8).

The famous Taoist work, the *Zhuangzi* is another storehouse of mythic materials. Although the present text of *Zhuangzi* contains numerous mythological references, it can be assumed that originally it had been an even richer treasure-trove of myths. This reduction in myth can be attributed to the radical recension by GUO XIANG who "reduced the text by about 30%, removing passages that he could not comprehend and those which resembled other works such as the *Shanhaijing* and the *Huainanzi*" (ROTH 1993: 58). This work with exceptional literary qualities can also be associated with the southern culture of *Chu*,[74] which relation might also be

---

[73] LE BLANC 1985: 7.n.12. *Huainanzi* seems to contain myths that are definitely different from those of the northern *Zhou* house. "It [the *Huainanzi*] seems to preserve legends and tales of non-*Zhou* minorities in souther and eastern China, and we may find *Shang* materials here that have not been distorted by *Zhou* editors" (HENRICKS 1996: 272).

[74] As VICTOR H. MAIR, an expert on *Zhuangzi* remarks: "Born around the year 369 B.C.E., *Zhuang Zhou* was from *Meng*, a district of the northern state of *Song*. (...) Although *Song* was considered to be a northern state, *Meng* was very close to the border with the powerful state of *Chu* and consequently strongly influenced by southern culture. (...) Not much is known of *Zhuang Zhou*'s life except that he seems to have spent some time in *Chu* ..." (MAIR 1998: xxxi). ZHANG ZHENGMING also stresses that the distance between the *Laozi*'s and *Zhuang Zhou*'s place of birth was only 60 kilometers. He also asserts that the *Zhuangzi* is strongly imbued with the spirit of *Chu* (ZHANG 1996: 256). It is also to be noted that *Song* was the state where the *Shang* religious and mythological tradition could most easily survive after the *Zhou* conquest. "The *Shang* kings were established in the city [i.e. city-state, G. K.] of *Song*, in order to maintain the sacrifices to the potent shades of the diseased kings" (LEWIS 2000: 361).

reflected in its *Tang* title "The True Book of the Flourishing South."[75] The *Huainanzi* and the *Zhuangzi* have much in common, especially as far as their *Chu* features are concerned. "The close affinity on many essential points between *Huainanzi* and *Zhuangzi* is best explained, it would seem, by their common indebtedness to the transcendental spirit of the poets of *Chu*" (LE BLANC 1985: 8). Interestingly, the similarities of the two texts are so striking that a recent study by H. ROTH ascribes the compilation of *Zhuangzi* to Prince LIU AN, the author of the *Huainanzi*.[76]

OTHER SOURCES
(*Chu* Silk Manuscript, Mawangdui, Leigudun, Baoshan, Guodian, Wangjiatai)

Recent decades have witnessed a revolution in Chinese archaeology which has in many aspects changed our concepts on the Chinese past. Finds from different parts and different periods of China have been unearthed; one of the most abundant material, however, comes from the ancient state of *Chu*. It goes without saying that these products can be a major aid to reconstruct the mythological world of the *Chu* population.

One of the first archaeological finds from *Chu* was the Silk Manuscript,[77] already mentioned, which was unearthed at a tomb of *Zidanku, Changsha*. As an introduction let's quote the words of an authority on the topic:[78]

"The *Chu* Silk Manuscript is the only published and complete manuscript among several discovered in 1942 by tomb robbers in *Zidanku, Changsha, Hunan*. (...) The manuscript dates to about 300 BCE and was buried with a man approximately forty years old (...) the man was not an important official. (...) The *Chu* Silk Manuscript consists of both illustrations and texts; it is designed to resemble a divination board (...), which is itself a model of the cosmos" (LI – COOK 1999: 171–172).

Another major *Chu* discovery was the *Mawangdui*[79] finds where a great number of manuscripts have been discovered. These written materials

---

[75] MAIR 1998: xxxi. The practice of using this alternative title (*Nanhua zhenjing*) originated in an imperial edict of 742 A.D., though it cannot be excluded that the title had some earlier roots.

[76] ROTH 1992. "For all these reasons I think it likely that the text of the *Zhuangzi* was compiled at the court of LIU AN" (ROTH 1991: 120).

[77] On the *Chu* Silk Manuscript see BARNARD 1973; LI 1985; LI – COOK 1999.

[78] LI LING's introduction is summarized by C. A. COOK.

[79] On *Mawangdui* generally see e.g. FU – CHEN 1992; WU 1992. On its relationship to *Huang-Lao* Taoism see DU 1979.

centered around various subjects, like medicine, sexual arts or philosophy.[80] As mentioned earlier, the tomb was sealed in 168 B.C. (*Han* dynasty) when the state of *Chu* did not exist any more. However, the concepts it represents definitely correlate with *Chu* notions. The famous Silk Banner for example could be one of the most crucial clue to our understanding of *Chu* mythology if properly deciphered.[81]

At *Leigudun, Hubei* province the decorated tomb of Marquis *Yi* of *Zeng*[82] has been discovered in 1978. The various figures on the wooden coffin, though challenged by some, represent typical *Chu* religious notions. The contents of three further tombs are important in the reconstruction of *Chu* mythology. Two relatively recent sites are the *Guodian*[83] and the *Baoshan*[84] burials, rather close to each other geographically; in several aspects they display intriguing similarities.[85] Most scholars claim that the *Guodian* sites (discovered in 1993) were the burials of the *Chu* ruling families (BOLTZ 1999: 590). The *Baoshan* complex of burials was discovered in 1986. The largest tomb (No. 2) yielded 278 inscribed bamboo strips.[86] Both the *Guodian* and the *Baoshan* tomb date to the 4th c. B.C.[87] Another recent (1993) discovery was a tomb belonging to a *Qin* period diviner or archivist at *Wangjiatai* near the former *Chu* metropolis (*Jiangling, Hubei*).[88] The

---

[80] On a brief introduction to the contents of the tomb see NIENHAUSER et al. 1986: 614–617.

[81] On the most thorough interpretation see LOEWE 1994a: 17–59.

[82] On the *Leigudun* finds see *Hubeisheng bowuguan* 1991.

[83] On the *Guodian* finds see BOLTZ 1999; *Jingmen shi bowuguan* 1998. "The *Guodian* 'Tomb Complex' is one of twenty tomb complexes that have been identified in the area of the *Jishan* mountains in *Hubei* province, nine kilometers north of the site of the ancient *Chu* capital of *Ying*, near the modern city of *Jingmen*. (...) It is assumed that most of these tombs are burials of the *Chu* ruling families. (...) Among the artifacts retrieved from the tomb were significant pottery, bronze, and lacquer-ware items, a wooden seven-string *qin* ('cithara'), a jade belt hook, and a bronze styles and designs typical of Warring States-period *Chu* material culture" (BOLTZ 1999: 590).

[84] On the *Baoshan* finds see CHEN 1996.

[85] "But the tomb [at *Guodian*] is very similar in its structure and contents to the *Baoshan* tomb about two kilometers away" (BOLTZ 1999: 590). "The characters [of the *Guodian* manuscripts] themselves are written in a stereotypically *Chu* orthography, matching the orthography of the *Baoshan* strips closely" (BOLTZ 1999: 592).

[86] WELD 1999: 77. At *Baoshan* 278 strips were unearthed which contained 12,472 characters. This was "the largest find of *Chujian* (*Chu* bamboo script). Excavated from tomb 2 in 1986 and 1987. The texts date from 323–292 B.C. They are among the earliest yet discovered and include records of events, legal works, divinatory texts and lists of burial articles" (WILKINSON 1998: 445).

[87] It is to be noted that the earliest version of the *Daodejing* comes from the *Guodian* site (BUMBACHER 1998).

[88] On the *Wangjiatai* find see COOK 1998; *Jingzhou dichu bowuguan* 1995.

Wangjiatai finds contain a rather strange version (*Guizang*) of the well-known "Book of Changes" (*Zhouyi*).[89]

MAJOR MYTHOLOGICAL FIGURES IN *CHU*

The picture that emerges from the previous pages is an image of a southern state with rather distinctive features, especially if compared to the literary, artistic and religious characteristics of the northern states.[90] This distinctive nature in art, literature and religion encourages the researcher to assume that the mythology, which evidently provides the underlying substratum for the artistic, literary and religious concepts, must also contain idiosyncratic features. Therefore in the following analysis, the local roots of Chinese mythology, which became universal after the unification of China in 221 B.C., are being investigated to demonstrate that certain myths were more popular in *Chu*; according to some scholars this popularity was precisely due to their originating from the local traditions of this southern state. The southern presence and, in several instances, the shamanic background, of these myths is easy to prove in some cases, while in others it is more or less only hypothetical. We assume that the mythic figures and narratives which are mentioned in several southern sources, either the major (*Chuci, Shanhaijing, Huainanzi, Zhuangzi*), or the minor ones (*Guoyu, Mawangdui, Baoshan, Guodian, Chu* Silk Manuscript, *Wangjiatai, Daodejing*), constituted an integral part of the intellectual tradition of *Chu*. Moreover, it will be stressed that the figures appearing in both northern and southern sources are, as a the result of the different mentality, always linked with definitely specific roles in the different sources. It will be demonstrated that in these cases the northern versions most often distort the figures to place them in a historical and ethical perspective, while the southern material preserved

---

[89] On its indebtedness to the southern culture see COOK's (2000: 3) opinion: "Besides songs using natural and cosmic imagery, the *Guizang* preserves fragments from myth cycles that appear in texts more closely associated with Daoist traditions, such as the *Chuci*, and in the *Shanhaijing*, than with the *Ru* [Confucian, G.K.] traditions, such as the *Shijing* and the *Zhouyi*." In many instances, the *Guizang* contains references to ecstatic flights in a mythic context (COOK 2000: 4).

[90] As the articles of C. A. COOK – J. S. MAJOR's recent book (1999) reveal, this kind of difference becomes especially conspicuous during the last centuries of *Chu*, when *Chu* has to a great extent assimilated the local traditions of the newly conquered regions. Therefore, we might even risk the hypothesis that *Chu*, unlike the northern states, was specific in its willing to assimilate local features, and not, as always stated, in its literary, artistic and religious products, which, seen in this perspective, are only the consequence of this kind of receptive attitude.

the original mythic nature of these narratives. Moreover, as one of the dominant religious components of *Chu* was, beyond doubt, shamanism, it is not too far-fetched to assume that some of the mythic figures whose origin can be traced to this southern state preserved, to some extent at least, their shamanic heritage. Thus, leaving the peripheral figures aside,[91] I will concentrate on the major members of the Chinese mythic pantheon whose homeland is to be searched for in southern China.

The Myth of *Zhong* and *Li*

As far as the specific pantheon of *Chu* is concerned, SIMA QIAN, who visited this southern state personally, gives a good overview of the ancestors of the *Chu* royal house. "The ancestors of *Chu* originate from *Zhuan Xu Gaoyang. Gaoyang* was the grandson of *Huang Di*, and the son of *Chang Yi. Gaoyang* begat *Cheng. Cheng* begat *Juan Zhang. Juan Zhang* begat *Zhong Li. Zhong Li* occupied the office of Governor of Fire for *Di Ku Gao Xin* and had very great accomplishments. He was able to light and warm [*rong*] the world. *Di Ku* named him *Zhu Rong*. When *Gong Gong* rebelled, *Di Ku* sent *Zhong Li* to punish him but he [*Zhong Li*] did not complete the mission."[92] As it is clear from the passage above, in the official history, although placed in a historical, moral and bureaucratic context, *Zhong Li* is mentioned in clear association with the *Chu* royal house.

As this *Shiji* passage proves, the *Chu* people traced their origin back to *Huangdi*'s grandson, the mythical emperor *Zhuanxu*.[93] If the assumption of

---

91 Though probably not of southern origin, the myth of *Chiyou*'s battle with *Xuanyuan* is, as M. LOEWE suggests, a mythic equivalent of the so-called *juedi* games, which probably originates in the shamanism of Inner Asia. The *juedi* game is a kind of bull game: "According to some scholars the *juedi* involved a dance in which the performers used a mask which was adorned with bulls' horns; and it has been suggested that the act may have derived from contests that were staged between live bulls" (LOEWE 1994: 238). This Chinese performance must have had a deep impressions on the barbarians of Inner Asia, as a memorial from the 2nd century B.C, mentions it as one of the spectacles that could be used for luring the Huns (*xiongnu*) from their homeland (LOEWE 1994: 236).

92 COOK – MAJOR 1999: 211. On the four versions of the *Chu* genealogy see COOK 1994: 1.

93 On *Zhuan Xu* see ALLAN 1991: 67–69; BIRRELL 1993: 95–97. The 16th chapter of the *Shanhaijing* also mentions *Zhuanxu*, as the father of *Laotong* and the grandfather of *Zhong* and *Li. Lao Tong* (Old Lad) appears in two lists of *Chu* genealogies, and it cannot be excluded that his figure has contributed to the concept of the cosmic, deified *Laozi*, becoming the central figure of Taoism from the *Han* on, see COOK's opinion: "There is no mythological information on *Lao Tong*. We know only that his ancestors were

the interrelatedness of *Chu* shamanism and mythology is valid, one can expect that *Zhuanxu* appears in a major myth which has a close relationship with shamanism. The myth of *Zhong* and *Li* seems adequate to meet this criterion. The most detailed description of this myth is preserved in the *Guoyu* ('Discourses of the States'), which is, according to *Wei Juxian*'s meticulous analysis, a product of *Chu* (CHANG – BOLTZ – LOEWE 1993: 264). The book, containing historical descriptions and discourses from various states (*Zhou, Lu, Qi, Jin, Zheng, Chu, Wu, Yue*), has a relatively longer chapter on *Chu* (*Chuyu*) which belongs to the oldest layer of the whole text and can be dated in 431 B.C. (CHANG – BOLTZ – LOEWE 1993: 264).

"King *Zhao* (of *Chu*, 515–489 B.C.) asked *Guan Shefu*, "Is it really true as the History of the *Zhou* says that *Zhong* and *Li* caused Heaven and earth to be kept apart? If they had not done that, the people would be still be able to ascend to Heaven, wouldn't they?" He replied, "No, it wasn't like that. In ancient times gods and humans did not intermingle. But among the people there were some who were gifted with clear vision, who were single-minded, and who possessed the power of absolute reverence and authority. Such was their knowledge that they could correlate the affairs of the world on high and the world below. Such was their wisdom that they could illuminate the remote and reveal what was clear (...) Therefore the shining gods descended to the people, to the males known as *xi*-shamans and to the females known as *wu*-shamans. It was they who arranged the positions of the gods and their due sequence at ceremonies (...) Thus the offices in charge of the functions of Heaven and earth, and of gods and humans, were named the Five Offices (...) Humans and gods were treated as separate entities (...) Therefore the gods sent down their blessings on humans, and they received their offerings, and no calamities were visited upon them. When it came to the period of decline under *Shao Hao*, the Nine *Li* disrupted the cosmic powers, and gods and humans intermingled and became indistinguishable, and it became impossible to determine who were mortal creatures. Everyone performed the sacrifices with offerings as if they were shaman officials, and they lost their essential sincerity of faith. (...) Blessings no longer came down to them and calamities were visited upon them. *Zhuan Xu* succeeded him [*Shao Hao*], and then he ordered *Zhong*, the Principal of the South, to control Heaven in order to assemble the gods in their proper place, and he ordered *Li*, the Fire Principal, to control earth in order to assemble the people in their proper places. He

---

associated with the regulation of time and the birth of cosmos" (COOK 1994: 1). Although *Zhuanxu*'s affinity to *Chu* is clear, it is to be noted that "many genealogies lead up to *Zhuanxu*" (EBERHARD 1968: 67).

made them go back to old established customs and not usurp powers or commit sacrilege. This was termed to "sever the links between earth and Heaven." Later the *San Miao* repeated the disruption of the cosmic powers as the Nine *Li* had done. Therefore *Yao* protected the descendants of *Zhong* and *Li*, who had not forgotten the old ways, and ordered them supervise them. Right up until the era of the *Xia* and the *Shang*, therefore, the descendants of *Zhong* and *Li* arranged Heaven and earth in their due spheres and kept their functions and sovereigns separate."[94]

It is probably not accidental that the *Chu* people considered *Zhong – Li*, and *Zhuan Xu* as their ancestors. They regarded themselves as the inheritors of this specific (shamanic) relationship with heavenly affairs.[95] Moreover, it has to be noted that in Chinese mythology this is not one of the many myths relating this rather important event closely linked with shamanism, but seems to be the only one of this genre in China.[96] The figures of *Zhong* and *Li*, as W. EBERHARD also emphasizes, are certainly deeply rooted in *Chu* civilization.

"I have already indicated (...) that the much-discussed *Zhongli* myth must hang together with these world-egg myths. I cannot repeat the material which was presented there, but I shall make some remarks. First, it has never been doubted that this is a southern myth connected with the ancient state of *Chu*. In the *Guoyu* (*Zhengyu*) *Zhongli* is made the ancestor of *Jing* (usually equal to *Chu*), and he is equated with *Zhu Rong*, the fire-god of *Chu* (see also commentary to *Hou Hanshu* 89.8b). *Zhongli* is buried at the *Hengshan* in *Hubei*. At the time of king *Ling* of *Chu* his grave was broken open, and magic maps were found in it (...). The *Hengshan* is an old cult center of the southern peoples" (EBERHARD 1968: 443–444).

The uniqueness and prominent importance of this *Guoyu* excerpt from the 4th c. B.C., which R. MATHIEU considers to derive from *Chu* (MATHIEU 1989: 31. n.1), was also emphasized by K. C. CHANG, one of the leading expert on Chinese archaeology and ancient shamanism: "This myth is the most important textual reference to shamanism in ancient China, and it provides a crucial clue to our understanding the central role of shamanism in ancient Chinese politics."[97]

---

[94] *Guoyu, Chuyu* 18: 1a–3a (BIRRELL 1993: 94–95).
[95] On the relationship between this myth and shamanism see KEIGHTLEY 1989.
[96] On other variants of the same myth in the world see THOMPSON 1955: 128–129; NUMAZAWA 1984.
[97] Chang 1983: 45. Also see RAO ZONGYI's (1972: 121) opinion: "The idea of 'non-communication between heaven and earth' (*juedi tongtian*) would seem to be a concept traditional to the *Chu* kingdom."

Xiwangmu

Xiwangmu is one of the most controversial figures of Chinese mythology. Probably to no other member of the Chinese pantheon has been paid as much scholarly attention as to her.[98] As for her origin, opinions vary, but the sources unanimously attest to her central role in the southern region, especially in the state of *Chu*. "*Xiwangmu* certainly was a significant cult figure in *Chu*, as can be seen from her prominence in the *Shanhaijing*, from her position enthroned between the sun and the moon at the apex of the silk banner from *Mawangdui* tomb 1, and from the elaborate description of her realm, the *Kunlun* Mountains, in the *Huainanzi* chapter 4. National interest in her cult, as exemplified by official devotions instituted under *Wuti*, thus probably represents another instance of the influence of the *fangshi* of *Qi* and an extension of *Chu* beliefs to the Middle States."[99]

---

[98] On *XIWANGMU* generally see BIRRELL 1993: 171–174; CAHILL 1993; DUBS 1942; FRACASSO 1988; GILES 1905; JAMES 1995; LOEWE 1994A: 86–126; MACKENZIE 1994: 137–139; TOKAREV 1988: 407–408; WERNER 1986: 136–138; WU 1987; YUAN 1985: 154–155.

[99] MAJOR 1978: 241. A further proof of her southern origin is that the religious Taoist sect, the Highest Clarity (*Shanqing*) (the sacred texts of which were revealed to the families of the southern aristocrats and which was greatly influenced by the southern traditions) preserved *Xiwangmu* as a goddess in its pantheon (ROBINET 2000: 213–214). The myth of the *Kunlun* mountain, the residence of *Xiwangmu* (and some shamans), also seems to reveal some southern affinity, as its most detailed description comes from the *Shanhaijing*, while other early passages all come up in other southern writings (*Chuci, Huainanzi*; further, HONG XINGZU's and GAO YOU's commentaries to these works. On the exact references see HENRICKS 1994: 87). It can be assumed that the word *Kunlun* is etymologically related to *hundun*, a word and concept with a similar southern affiliation. "In pre-*Han* times, according to the Rites of *Zhou*, the word "*kun*" was pronounced as "*hun*"; hence "*kunlun*" sounded as "*hunlun*", a homophone or synonym of "*hundun*" (chaos). This bit of etymological information indicates that in ancient China the meaning of chaos was connected with both the belief in a mythological mountain where people return to their origin and the belief in a mythical progenitor. According to Schafer, both the words "*kunlun*" and "*hunlun*" belonged to a family of words "whose members have such meanings as 'vault', 'cavern', 'canopy', 'dome', 'roof', 'cage', 'chamber', 'rainbow' and the like." This means that words such as "*Kunlun*" and "*hundun*" share a common motif of being something like an enclosure which does not have an opening but is the source of all openings. The *Kunlun* Mountains conveys the idea of returning to chaos, the primordial condition of the world" (YU 1986: 14). Moreover, there are suggestions which connect *Kunlun* with another *Chu* motif, *Gun* (on *Gun* as a *Chu* hero see III.6.): "The flora of *Kunlun* are also suggestive of a relationship with the *Gun* myths. [...] *Kunlun* (...) is thus contextually related to *Gun*. [...] Percussion instruments also figure in the imagery connecting *Gun* and *Kunlun*. [...] This, in addition to the many images shared by both myths, raises the possibility that the proper names *Kunlun* and *Gun* refer to the same [celestial, G. K.]

J. S. MAJOR also shares this opinion: "I would suggest that the cult of *Xiwangmu*, Queen Mother of the West (...) is a clear example of *Chu* influence on China as a whole. The earliest literary references to *Xiwangmu* occur in these texts that may be identified as southern and *Huang-Lao*. Her manifestation as it is described in these texts may represent a long evolution from diverse sources, reflecting the ethnic diversity of *Chu* itself. (...) In other respects *Xiwangmu* and her eastern counterpart, *Dongwang gong*, may descend from deities that, by the Warring States period at least, were accepted by the *Chu* royal house as representing the founding deities of their state" (MAJOR 1999: 143).

Being a prominent *Chu* goddess, *Xiwangmu* must naturally be deeply embedded in the specific shamanic context of the region both in her attributes and in her place of dwelling.

"The description of the Queen Mother of the West in the *Classic of Mountains and Seas* suggests a shamanistic deity. (...) The Queen Mother is linked with the native southern shamanism of early China in the songs of the *Chuci* (Elegies of *Chu*) anthology in which she also figures. Her special headdress, leopard's tail, and tiger's teeth are reminiscent of costumes worn by Chinese shamans. The shaman's hair becomes disheveled in ecstatic communion. The connection with a world mountain and with stars is likewise shamanistic. Shamans travel back and forth to the heavens by climbing up and down world mountains and other pillars of heaven such as divine trees (both linked with the Queen Mother). They may summon deities by whistling or by roaring like a tiger. The shaman flies through the heavens on a quest for deities, often traveling to stars, where deities reside. The goddess's cult in medieval and modern times definitely has strong shamanistic overtones. During the Warring States period, works by philosophers and geographers show familiarity with the Queen Mother of the West as a mountain deity who dwelt in the exotic west, where she controlled immortality and heavenly asterisms. She was a revered teacher who occasionally taught special human men, such as sage-emperors or shamans. As a powerful shaman, she joined human and divine realms in communication" (CAHILL 1993: 17).

The description of *Xiwangmu* in the *Shanhaijing* mentioned at the beginning of the excerpt runs as follows: "As for the mountain of the serpent shamans, on top of it is a person brandishing a cup as she stands facing east. One source calls it the Tortoise Mountain. The Queen Mother

---

place, via two different linguistic forms. [...] *Kunlun* Mountain represents a variant concretization of the cosmogonic concept of *Gun*" (PORKERT 1996: 82–85). On the *Kunlun* generally see TOKAREV 1988: 418; MÜNKE 1976: 210–219; BIRRELL 1993: 183–185, on its relationship with *Xiwangmu* see PORKERT 1996: 91–98.

of the West leans on a stool; moreover, she wears a *sheng* and carries a staff. To the south are three blue birds who take food for the Queen Mother of the West, north of the *Kunlun* barrens."[100]

All her attributes can be identified as Chinese shamanic paraphernalia. "The stool, headdress, and staff—still part of the shaman's paraphernalia in Taiwan today—reflect her shamanistic side" (CAHILL 1993: 19). Being a major goddess, she was revered throughout the country; her cult seems to be especially influential at the beginning of our era when some major movements of obviously ecstatic nature began.

"In the firth of the fourth year of the Establishing Peace Reign period [3 B.C.], the population was running around in a state of alarm, each person carrying a manikin of straw or hemp. People exchanged these emblems with one another, saying that they were carrying out the advent procession. Large numbers of persons, amounting to thousands, met in this way on the roadsides, some with disheveled hair or going barefoot. One of them broke down the barriers of gates by night; some clambered over walls to make their way into houses; some harnessed teams of horses to carriages and rode at full gallop, setting up relay stations so as to convey the tokens. They passed through twenty-six commanderies and kingdoms until they reached the capital city. That summer the people came together in meetings in the capital city and in the commanderies and kingdoms. In the village settlements, the lanes, and paths across the fields, they held services and set up gaming boards for a lucky throw; and they sang and danced in worship of the Queen Mother of the West. They also passed around a written message, saying: 'The Mother tells the people that those who wear the talisman will not die; let those who do not believe her words look below the pivots of their gates, and there will be white hairs there to show that this is true."[101]

As can be expected, the elements of her followers' behavior indicate that ecstatic practice was also involved in her cult, probably not without precedent in her homeland.[102]

"Her followers' behavior recalls the shamanistic aspects of her cult suggested by the *Classic of Mountains and Seas*. People moving in a collective trance, with disheveled hair and bare feet, dancing and playing games of chance, all suggest shamanistic behavior. Manikins, emblems, tokens, and talismans are paraphernalia of shamans. And the shaman's job is to

---

[100] *Shanhaijing* 12:1a.

[101] *Hanshu* 27C:22a; CAHILL 1993: 21–22.

[102] In A.D. 25 the rebellion of the Red Eyebrows was led by a shaman who was drumming in ecstasy (KAGAN 1980: 12).

transmit a message to the faithful such as the one preserved in the *Book of Han*" (CAHILL 1993: 23).

In sum, *Xiwangmu*, later becoming a prominent goddess in Taoism, is most likely of southern provenance, equipped with some shamanic attributes, and, not surprisingly, her cult also involved ecstasy and trance.

Fuxi and Nüwa[103]

Although *Fuxi* and *Nüwa* (or *Nügua*) became a couple only in the *Han* times, there might have been something common in them before that era. It cannot be excluded that both deities are basically derived from the southern region of *Chu* or the neighboring *Ba* culture in modern *Sichuan*, which shared many cultural features with *Chu*.[104] LÜ SIMIAN collected all the materials concerning *Fuxi*, who later underwent the process of what D. BODDE (1961: 372) called "reverse euhemerization", and concluded that *Fuxi* originated in the southern state of *Chu*.[105] The figure of *Nüwa*, according to W. MÜNKE and W. EBERHARD, was born in the neighboring state of *Chu*, in the *Ba* culture (TOKAREV 1988: 387).

From the *Han* dynasty on, the figure of *Fuxi* and *Nüwa* are linked, and on the pictorial representations they appear as a couple with intertwined serpentine bodies.[106] This kind of hybrid representation of divine figures is, as J. S. MAJOR (1999: 131) has stressed, a recurrent motif of mythical figures with a southern (most often *Chu*) provenance. According to several scholars, this type of iconography is closely related to the *Shang* imagery.[107] The motif of hybrid creatures, which became a constant element of Chinese culture only during the *Qin* and *Han* dynasty (MAJOR 1999: 127–

---

103 On *Fuxi* and *Nüwa* generally see LE BLANC 1985: 167–170; BIRRELL 1993: 33–35, 44–47, 69–72, 163–165, 203–204. BIRRELL 1997: 221–228, Keller 1992.

104 The inhabitants of the state of *Ba* "were intimately related—both racially and culturally—with the people of *Chu*" (Fracaso 1988: 16).

105 *Lü Simian, Gushibian* 7B: 350–52 (quoted in LE BLANC 1985: 157.n.148.)

106 Moreover, these *Han* representations probably have earlier roots. "With regard to *Nügua*, WEN YIDUO and GIRARDOT have shown that this mythic figure was related to the ancient practice of marriage rituals performed at the time of equinoxes. Other evidence leads to the conclusion that these deities were originally consanguineous, animallike gods (especially of serpent form) associated with water and thunder. (...) Such hints as to the true animal ancestor nature of *Fuxi* and *Nügua* are further corroborated by the *Han* iconographical depictions of them as half-human creatures with intertwined, caduceuslike, serpent tails" (GIRARDOT 1993: 203).

107 The close relationship between the *Shang* and the *Chu* culture was, as mentionde earlier, emphasized by numerous researchers (J. S. MAJOR, S. ALLAN, HAYASHI MINAO, ZHENG DEKUN, HE BINGDI, RAO ZONGYI, etc.).

131), is one of the most salient features of *Chu* culture, as can be attested in its numerous products: *Shanhaijing, Chu* Silk Manuscript, *Zheng Hou Yi's* coffin, *Chuci, Mawangdui*, etc. (POO 1998: 94–96).

Fuxi, appearing in the *Guizang* of *Wangjiatai* and in a cosmogonic myth of the *Chu* Silk Manuscript (COOK 1994: 2), was a legendary cultural hero, allegedly reigning between 2953–2838 B.C. He is reputed for being the inventor of the nets for hunting and fishing, discoverer of melody and music, inventor of musical instruments and the Eight Trigrams divination. His courtesy name was *Tai Hao*, who was, according to the *Shanhaijing*, the founder of *Ba* people who were, as mentioned before, geographically and culturally rather close to the people of *Chu*.[108] WANG YI (A.D. 89–158), coming from the state of *Chu*, was the compiler, editor and commentator of the earliest version of the *Chuci*. He, just like R. MATHIEU (1989: 72. n.2), saw an intimate relationship between some divine melodies associated with *Fuxi* and *Chu* music.

"*Fu Xi* was an ancient king. He ordered the creation of the zither instrument. The '*Jiabian*' and '*Laoshang*' are the names of the tunes. It is said that *Fu Xi* made the zither and composed the '*Jiabian*' tune. Someone from *Chu* state composed the '*Laoshang*', based on the '*Laoshang*' tune. They are divine pieces of music, a delight to listen to. Some people say that the '*Fu Xi*' and the '*Jiabian*' are divine song tunes" (BIRRELL 1993: 46–47).

Nüwa (or *Nü Gua*) has a more complex and elaborated mythology. She is the protagonist of a creation myth in which she, similarly to the Greek, Old Testament or Norse equivalents, creates human beings from the yellow earth and mud.[109] The first references to *Nüwa* can be found in the

---

[108] BIRRELL 1993: 44–45; FRACASSO 1988: 16.

[109] BIRRELL 1993: 34. The detailed description of this myth can be read in a later work: "Some people say that when Heaven and earth opened and unfolded, humankind did not yet exist. *Nü Gua* kneaded yellow earth and fashioned human beings. Though she worked feverishly, she did not have enough strength to finish her task, so she drew her cord in a furrow through the mud and lifted it out to make human beings. That is why rich aristocrats are the human beings made from yellow earth, while ordinary poor commoners are the human beings made from the cord's furrow" (*Fengsu tongyi* 1: 83; BIRRELL 1993: 164). The more popular creation myth associated with *Pan Gu*, probably of southern origin as well, survived in two versions: "Heaven and earth were in chaos like a chicken's egg, and *Pan Gu* was born in the middle of it. In eighteen thousand years Heaven and earth opened and unfolded. The limpid that was *Yang* became the heavens, the turbid that was *Yin* became the earth. Each day the heavens rose ten feet higher, each day the earth grew ten feet thicker, and each day *Pan Gu* grew ten feet taller. And so it was that in eighteen thousand years the heavens reached their fullest height, earth reached its lowest depth, and *Pan Gu* became fully grown. Afterward, there were the Three Sovereign Divinities. Numbers began with one, were established to three, perfected by five, multiplied with seven, and fixed with nine. That

Tianwen, the *Shanhaijing*, the *Chu* Silk Manuscript[110] and the *Huainanzi*.[111] Besides being a creator of mankind, she also appears as the protector of the world when repairing the damaged cosmos, as related in the *Huainanzi*.[112] One of the four flood traditions features *Nüwa* as a protagonist;[113] while the only description of this myth derives from the *Huainanzi*.[114] As natural in

---

is why Heaven is ninety thousand leagues from earth" (*Sanwuliji*, cited in *Yiwenleiju* 1:2a; BIRRELL 1993: 33). "When the firstborn, *Pan Gu*, was approaching death, his body was transformed. His breath became the wind and clouds; his voice became peals of thunder. His left eye became the sun; his right eye became the moon. His four limbs and five extremities became the four cardinal points and the five peaks. His blood and semen became water and rivers. His muscles and veins became the earth's arteries; his flesh became fields and land. His hair and beard became the stars; his bodily hair became plants and trees. His teeth and bones became metal and rock; his vital marrow became pearls and jade. His sweat and bodily fluids became streaming rain. All the mites on his body were touched by the wind and were turned into black-haired people" (*Wuyun linnianji*, cited in *Yishi*; BIRRELL 1993: 33). Interestingly, the expression "transformation" also appears in the case of *Nü Gua*. According to the *Huainanzi*, *Nü Gua* made "seventy transformations" (BIRRELL 1993: 164). On Chinese creation myths see ERKES 1931, 1942; GIRARDOT 1976; KALTENMARK 1959.

[110] COOK 1994: 2. "The text begins with *Fuxi* residing in the unformed dark cosmos of wind and rain. He takes as wife 'the child of XX's child (XX *zi zhi zi*)', who was called *Nü Huang* (= *Nü Gua*), who then gives birth to the four spirits of the seasons, thus initiating the regulation of time and the cosmos. These are the same four spirits that *Yan Di* commanded *Zhu Rong* to bring down to continue with the regulation of the motion of astral bodies and the Nine Heavens. The birth mother of the cosmos and of the *Chu* opeople (descendants of the fire god, *Zhu Rong*) was *Nü Gua*" (COOK 1994: 5).

[111] BIRRELL 1993: 33. As can be seen on later representation, she had the tail of a snake. Probably, it is her very feature which the *Tianwen* alludes to when asking: "Who shaped the body of *Nü Gua*?" (*Tianwen* 3: 20b; BIRRELL 1993: 35). Obviously in connection with her strange body, the *Shanhaijing* mentions "ten spirits whose name is 'the bowels of *Nü Gua*'" (BIRRELL 1993: 164).

[112] "In remote antiquity, the four poles collapsed. The Nine Regions split up. Heaven could not cover all things uniformly, and earth could carry everything at once. Fires raged fiercely and could not be extinguished. Water rose in vast floods without abating. Fierce beasts devoured the people of *Zhuan*. Violent birds seized the old and weak in their talons. Then *Nü Gua* smelted five-color stones to mend the blue sky. She severed the feet of a giant sea turtle to support the four poles and killed a black dragon to save the region of *Ji*. And she piled up the ashes from burned reeds to dam the surging waters. The blue sky was mended. The four poles were set right. The surging waters dried up. The region of *Ji* was under control. Fierce beasts died and the people of *Zhuan* lived. They bore earth's square area on their back and embraced the round sky" (*Huainanzi* 6: 7b; BIRRELL 1993: 71).

[113] Later folkloric materials indicate a southern affinity. "A final assessment of the evidence leads to the conclusion that the closest analogue to the Chinese primordial couple lore [*Fuxi* and *Nüwa*] is seen in the deluge cycle of legends rekated to the local folklore of south China" (GIRARDOT 1993: 205).

[114] *Huainanzi* 6: 7a–8a. (BIRRELL 1993: 221–228).

the southern shamanic context, both *Nü Gua* and *Fuxi* ascended to Heaven.[115]

Kui[116]

The first Chinese etymological dictionary, the *Shuowen* (compiled A.D. 100) defines *Kui* as a kind of "divine spirit that looks like a dragon with a single foot" (CHANG 1983: 57). It is supposed to live in the southern mountains of *Shu* (modern *Sichuan*, neighboring state of *Chu*), or on the *Minshan* of *Ba* culture, where according to the legends Emperor *Yu* was born.[117] It is to be noted that both the *Shu* and the *Ba* cultures were racially and culturally intimately related to *Chu* (FRACASSO 1988: 16–18). During the *Jin* period a *Kui* was captured in the *Shangyang* district of *Chu* (modern *Hubei*).[118] W. EBERHARD stresses his close relationship with *Chu* culture.[119] The shamanic features of this southern mythological figure can be supported by a citation from the *Shanhaijing*: "It looks like a bull, black, hornless, with a single foot. When it enters into and emerges from the water, there will be a windstorm. It shines like the sun and moon and its voice sounds like thunder (...) The Yellow Emperor once captured one. He used its skin to make a drum and beat the drum with the bone of a thunder beast. The sound could be heard beyond five hundred *li*."[120]

---

[115] *Huainanzi* 6:11b; 2:12a. (LE BLANC 1985: 167).

[116] On *Kui* generally see BIRRELL 1993: 134–135; EBERHARD 1968: 57–58; GIRARDOT 1959: 311–313, 506–509; SANTILLANA–DECHEND 1995: 110–111; TOKAREV 1988: 417; *YUAN* 1985: 451–452.

[117] EBERHARD 1942: 329–330. Besides the place of birth and the single foot, which is a special characteristic of the *Yu*-dance, there is another link between *Kui* and Emperor *Yu*, i.e. *Kui* helped *Yu* to control the flood (*Taipingyulan* 882:5a).

[118] *Taipingyulan* 898:1b (EBERHARD 1942: 329).

[119] "*Kui* (...) was a relative of the ruling families of *Chu* and *Yue* (*Guoyu, Zhengyu* and *Shuijingzhu* 34: VI.18). (...) *Kui*, the monkey, just as *Kui*, the buffalo, belonged to southwest *Hubei* and east *Sichuan*. (...) *Kui* being a monkey and ancestor of *Chu* makes intelligible the fact that certain people in *Chu* observed a monkey taboo" (EBERHARD 1968: 58).

[120] *Shanhaijing* 14: 6b. (CHANG 1983: 57). Another southern reference can be found in the *Zhuangzi* (BIRRELL 1993: 134). On *Kui*'s appearance in the *Yaodian* chapter of the *Shujing* see Lo's opinion: "This [*Shanhaijing*, G. K.] version of the *Kui* story represents a form which, characterized by its primitive crudeness, is obviously prior to the '*Yaodian*' one in which *Kui* appears as a talented musician who is able to make all the animals dance by knocking on the stone. [...] As might have been expected, the fact that *Kui* was one-legged is deliberately withheld in the '*Yaodian*'." What Confucius and *Wang Chong* have laboured to uphold must be this '*Yaodian*' tradition, in which *Kui* has been turned into a fully historical figure. The rationalization of myth, it may certainly be

Being the ruler of natural forces associated with the drum,[121] *Kui* might have some relationship with shamanism. Interestingly enough, other sources mention a *Kui* who was associated with teaching dance during the mythical reign of *Yao*, and being the master of music under the reign of *Shun*.[122] According to certain works, he was not simply the master but the discoverer of music.[123] His shamanic feature can be further supported by the fact that besides being the master of dance and music, he was the master of the blacksmiths as well (SANTILLANA – DECHEND 1995: 112). These two mythological figures (the one-legged master of natural forces associated with the drum and the master of music, dance and the blacksmiths) step by step became amalgamated (EBERHARD 1942: 331), eventually resulting in a shamanic figure. Considering the apparent contradiction that a one-legged[124] person is the master of dance, one has to conclude that this kind of dance must have had a magical rather than an aesthetic function. The same aspect is stressed by the fact that the shamanic *Yu*-dance (*Yubu*),[125] later becoming rather popular with the Taoists, was also performed by a supposedly lame dancer.[126]

---

said, is an effective means to reinforce and complement the process of historization"
(LO 1995: 194–195).

[121] The *Xuanzhongji* (cited in the *Taipingyulan* 887:6a) describes *Kui* as a mountain spirits that lookes like a drum and has one leg (EBERHARD 1968: 57).

[122] *Hanshu* 22:4b. The similarity between *Kui* and *Kuang*, the famous master of music is stressed by W. EBERHARD (1968: 66).

[123] *Xunzi* 21; *Liji* 2:1.

[124] Shamanism and the feature of single leg must have something very important in common as the mythical one-legged *Shangyang* bird of the *Qi* state could make rain, which is a shamanic activity *par excellence* in China (see SCHAFER 1951; COHEN 1978).

[125] "The Taoist *bugang* appears as a further development of certain forms of shamanistic dances attested for the period of the late Warring States. An ancient term for these dances is *Yubu*, "Steps of *Yu*" (ANDERSEN 1989–90: 16). Also see *Yang Xiong*'s (53 B.C.–18 A.D.) comment: "Formerly *Sishi* (i.e., *Yu*) regulated the waters and the earth, and the steps of shamans in many cases are those of *Yu*" (ANDERSEN 1989–90: 16). In addition, W. EBERHARD also stressed the shamanic character of the *Yubu*. "I have shown (...) that, up to the present time, the modern female shamans of south *Zhejiang* practiced the dance of *Yu* on one leg. During the dance the face was covered with a kerchief until the woman was in trance and a spirit spoke out of her" (EBERHARD 1968: 74). With some additional remarks, D. HARPER approves M. GIRARDOT's opinion on the shamanic origin of *Yubu*. "Marcel GIRARDOT argued that the Daoist Pace of *Yu* went back to ancient shamanistic traditions. GIRARDOT pointed to accounts of *Yu*'s lameness in Warring States philosophical texts as indirect evidence of an original shamanic trance-indulging limp like the one described in the *Baopuzi*. Occurences of the Pace of *Yu* in both the *Shuihudi* and *Fangmatan* almanacs concern travel, but the Pace of *Yu* is employed seven times in the *Mawangdui Wushier bingfang* as part of the magical strategy for exorcising demons blamed for ailments. GIRARDOT is surely correct about its shamanic origins. However, the excavated manuscripts show

The Ten Suns on the Mulberry Tree[127]

Several mythological narratives mention a certain *Kongsang* tree, i.e. the Hollow Mulberry. This tree seems to function as an *axis mundi*.[128]

"The Hollow Mulberry (...) is often mentioned in early texts as a dwelling place of the gods or cosmic tree which served as an *axis mundi* between heaven and earth. (...) The *Guizang* describes it thus: 'The Hollow Mulberry, luxuriant and vast, extends to the eight extremes (of the world). There is *Xihe* who controls the comings and goings of the sun and moon to make light and darkness.' The *Guizang* also records that '*Chi You* attacked the Hollow Mulberry in which *Di* lived.' *Di* in this case must be understood as *Huangdi*, the Yellow Emperor, since another fragment of the *Guizang* tell of *Huang Di* killing *Chi You. Di Shao Hao* and *Di Zhuan Xu* also lived at Hollow Mulberry, according to other texts. And in the legend of later times, Confucius (...) was born at Hollow Mulberry after his mother dreamed of *Xuan Di*, the 'Black Emperor'" (ALLAN 1991: 44–45).

The southern works depict this Mulberry Tree in similar ways. "The references to the Mulberry Tree tradition in the *Shanhaijing, Huainanzi* and

---

that in the third century B.C., the Pace of *Yu* had already become part of the fund of magico-religious knowledge regularly employed by the elite. It was probably in this more popular milieu that the Pace of *Yu* found its way into religious Daoism" (HARPER 1999: 873). Moreover, a Chinese scholar even hypothesized an intimate connection between the *Yubu* rituals and the shamanism of the *Chu* culture: "The very archaic character of these rituals supports DU DISHENG's assertion of a connection with the rites of ancient shamans, *wu*, of the state of *Chu*" (ANDERSEN 1989–90: 20).

126 SCHIPPER 1993: 85. Also see GIRARDOT's opinion on *Yu*. "The story of *Yu* stresses not the actual flood, or its causes, but the necessary methods of ordering the human world in a way that maintains a harmonious relationship with the secret structure of the cosmos. It is said that *Yu* assumed the form of an animal, limped from the titanic labors (the so-called 'step' or dance of *Yu*), received the sacred *Luoshu* (*Luo* River Writing) and *Hetu* (Yellow River Chart) cosmic diagrams, and cast the nine *ding* cauldrons; these are all symbolic details that suggest *Yu*'s shamanic function and his use of an esoteric methodology" (GIRARDOT 1987: 302). The *Chu* popularity of the *Yubu* is best evidenced by the discovery of two manuscripts (from *Mawangdui* and *Shuihudi*, both in the territory of ancient *Chu*), which contain the earliest descriptions of *Yu*'s steps (ANDERSEN 1989–90: 16).

127 On these myths generally see ALLAN 1991; BIRRELL 1993: 38, 68, 77–78; KARLGREN 1946: 267–270; YUAN 1985: 4, 303–304; MATHIEU 1983: 440.n.3.

128 On the *Kongsang* and the *Fusang* trees see HENRICKS 1994. R. G. HENRICKS thinks that these seemingly similar tress derive from two distinct traditions: "I think the evidence shows that *Kongsang*, as a significant place or thing in early mythology, has its provenance in southern traditions that were originally distinct from the 'mulberry tradition' of the *Shang/Yin* people in which the *Fusang* tree played such a prominent role" (HENRICKS 1994: 82).

Chuci are generally in accordance, with only minor discrepancies" (ALLAN 1991: 27). ALLAN's statement is corroborated by the appearance of the *Fuxi* tree in the *Guizang* mansunscript of *Wangjiatai*. In many instances, the Mulberry Tree is the dwelling place of the ten suns,[129] the myth of which can be linked to the origin myth of the *Shang* dynasty and at the same time to the mythology of the *Chu* state.

"The prevalence of this myth [of the ten suns, G.K.] in the *Chuci* and, to a lesser extent, in the *Huainanzi* indicates an association between the ten-sun tradition and southern China. It might be argued that this was not a *Shang* tradition retained in the south during the *Zhou*, but one which originated in the state of *Chu*. However, an association between *Shang* and *Chu* culture has long been conjectured and this hypothesis has recently been confirmed by archaeological excavation."[130]

As some sources relate, the ten suns, which normally appear in the sky one by one, during the reign of *Yao* appeared together, causing a great calamity in the world. *Yi*, the famous archer was charged to eliminate the imminent danger. As the myth of the Mulberry tree and the related myth of

---

[129] See the following three references to the ten sun tradition from the *Shanhaijing*. "Above the *Tang* Valley is the *Fu Sang*. [The Valley] is wherein the ten suns bathe. It is north of the Black Tooth Tribe. In the swirling water is a great tree, Nine suns dwell on its lower branches; one sun on its uppermost branch" (*Shanhaijing* 9:3a–b.; ALLAN 1991: 28). "On the top of a mountain named *Nieyaojundi* is the *Fu* Tree. Although its trunk is three hundred *li*, its leaves are like those of mustard. The valley there is called, its leaves are like those of mustard. The valley there is called the Warm Springs Valley. Above the Tang Valley is the *Fu* Tree. When one sun reaches it, another sun goes out; all of them are carried by birds" (*Shanhaijing* 14: 5a–b.; ALLAN 1991: 28). "Beyond the South-eastern Sea amidst the Sweet waters is the Tribe *Xihe*. There is a woman named *Xihe* who regularly bathes the suns in the Sweet Springs. *Xihe* is the wife of *Dijun*. It is she who gave birth to the ten suns" (*Shanhaijing* 15: 7b ; ALLAN 1991: 33).

[130] ALLAN 1991: 26. The *Chu* influence, as mentioned before, extended into the *Han* period; therefore, it is not surprising that the tradition of the ten suns can be found at *Han* dynasty burial sites of the former *Chu* state: "*Han* tomb murals most frequently include one sun and one moon, but there are some examples in which the Mulberry Tree and its many suns are depicted. One example is the funerary pendant excavated in 1972 from *Han* tomb number one at *Mawangdui* near *Changsha* in *Hunan* Province—formerly within the boundaries of the state of *Chu*. The tomb dates to the early Western *Han* Dynasty. Here nine suns are depicted on the branches of a ·tree, the twisting trunk of which is consistent with the form of a mulberry" (ALLAN 1991: 30). The missing tenth sun is obviously that of the deceased person. "The prevalence of the Mulberry Tree tradition in the *Chuci* and to a lesser extent in the *Huainanzi*, as well as the portrayal of the nine suns on the Mulberry Tree in the *Mawangdui* painting, indicate an association in *Zhou* and *Han* times with Southern China, but as discussed above, *Shang* influence had extended into what became a semi-independent state of *Chu* in *Zhou* times" (ALLAN 1991: 38).

the ten suns was, without doubt, widely known in the southern region, it cannot be excluded that the myth of shooting the ten (actually nine) suns was probably also popular in *Chu*,[131] which can be further evidenced by the fact that the best description derives from a southern work, the *Huainanzi*.[132]

"When it came to the era of *Yao*, the ten suns all rose at once, scorching the sheaves of grain and killing plants and trees, so that the people were without food. And the *Zhayu* Dragon-Headed beast, the Giant-Gale bird, the *Fengxi* wild boar, and the Giant-Head long-snake all plagued the people. So *Yao* ordered *Yi* to execute the Chisel-Tusk beast in the wilds of *Chou Hua*, to slaughter the Nine-Gullet beast near *Xiong* River, to shoot down with his corded arrows the Giant-Gale at *Qingqiu* Marsh. He ordered him to shoot the ten suns up above and to kill the *Zhayu* Dragon-Head beast below, to behead the Giant-Head *long*-snake at *Dongting*, and to capture the *Fengxi* wild boar at Mulberry Forest. The myriad people were overjoyed and decided on *Yao* as their Son of Heaven. And so for the first time in the whole world, there were roads and signposts in the broadlands and in the

---

[131] The *Wangjiatai* bamboo texts also mention him (COOK 1998: 137). Furthermore, S. ALLAN suggests that "the myth [of *Yi*] may have been particularly important in *Chu*, a theory given some support by its mention in the *Tianwen* section of the *Chuci*" (MACKENZIE 1993: 145.n.20). Myths similar to that of *Yi* are especially widespread in southern China: "The story of *Yi*'s shooting the suns is clearly an example of the 'myth of the superfluous suns', which *He Tingrui* has documented for the native peoples of *Taiwan*, for the Lolo and *Miao* minorities in southern China, and among various groups in South-East Asia and Indonesia" (HENRICKS 1996: 273). On the other hand, the general opinion on *Yi*'s cultural origin is that *Yi*'s myth, which was probably an integral part of *Shang* mythology, originated from among the Eastern *Yi*, "an ethnic group on the east coast of China out of which, we think, the *Shang* people developed" (HENRICKS 1996: 274). On the other hand, S. ALLAN (1981) claims that the myth of Archer *Yi* was invented by the *Zhou*. D. HAWKES, similarly to other scholars mentioned above, also suggests that the name of *Yi* (*Yi Yi*) implies that this figure was originated among the eastern (*Yi*) tribes (HAWKES 1983: 8–9). The Chinese concepts of directions, however, would give a plausible explanation for this phenomenon. The cardinal directions in the Chinese culture were the north and the south, while the east and west were subordinated to them. Accordingly, the barbarians of the four directions were often contracted as north-and-west (*rongdi*) and south-and-eastern (*manyi*) barbarians and the two components within *rongdi* and *manyi* were often interchangeable (ECSEDY 1980: 253). The *Chu* population, for example, was often labelled as *manyi*, *yi* being the same character as in *Yi Yi* (COOK – BLAKELEY 1999: 2). A further illustration could be the southern *Ba* culture which was known as *Ba Yi* or *Ba Man* (FRACASSO 1988: 16. n.38).

[132] "The most explicit early reference to this myth [Archer *Yi*] is in the *Huainanzi*" (ALLAN 1991: 36).

narrow defiles, in the deep places and on level ground both far and wide."[133]

Gun[134]

According to the *Shanhaijing*, *Gun* was the son of *Gaoyang* mentioned in *SIMA QIAN*'s description of the *Chu* royal house.[135] As A. BIRRELL has demonstrated, the mythical traditions related to *Gun* differ in several aspects (BIRRELL 1997: 235). The southern works (*Tianwen*, *Shanhaijing*)[136] are the older and the more genuine, while the northern source (*Shujing*) interprets *Gun*'s figure historically, thus distorting the original mythic material (BIRRELL 1997: 240). A. BIRRELL, who is one of the most prominent experts on Chinese mythology, emphasizes that the figure of *Gun* is inextricably linked with *Chu* culture,[137] and assumes that the myth of this *Chu* figure was consciously altered to fit the northern narrative of *Yu*, his successor in controlling the flood.[138] "It might be further hypothesized

---

[133] *Huainanzi* 8: 5b–6a. (BIRRELL 1993: 141.) The *Shanhaijing* also refers to the archer's courageous deed. "*Di Jun* presented *Yi* with a vermilion bow and plain-colored arrows with silk cords in order that he should bring assistance to the land below. So *Yi* was the first to bring merciful relief to the world below from all its hardships" (*Shanhaijing* 18:7b; BIRRELL 1993: 78). On *Di Jun* as the mythic source of the historical *Shun* see Lo 1995: 199.

[134] On *Gun* generally see TOKAREV 1988: 417–418; BIRRELL 1993: 79–82, 121–122; CHANG 1983: 10, 25, 131; YUAN 1985: 430–431; GIRARDOT 1959: 238–376; MA 1994.II. 200–222. On his successor, *Yu* and the Flood Myth generally see MATHIEU 1992; BIRRELL 1997; BOLTZ 1981; TEISER 1985–86.

[135] "*Gun*, father of the demiurge *Yu*, who is regarded as the founder of the *Xia* line, was supposed to be the son of *Gaoyang*" (HAWKES 1983: 6). It is evident that D. HAWKES sees some kind of connection between the state of *Chu* and the *Xia* dynasty as he cites two stories on the *Xia* from the *Zuozhuan*, which were both told by *Wu Zixu*, an exiled nobleman from *Chu*. He also claims that "*Chu* aristocracy believed that they and the *Xia* kings had a common ancestor in *Gaoyang*" (HAWKES 1983: 9. n.4). According to HAWKES "the southern colonies of *Xia* culture in *Chu* and *Yue* are likely to have been pre-*Shang* ones. The exceptional level of interest in *Xia* legends shown by *Qu Yuan* in his poems has often been remarked on and may not inconceivably be connected with this fact" (HAWKES 1983: 21).

[136] In a disguised manner, the *Zhuangzi* might also contain reference to *Gun* as *Su Xuelin*, on a phonetic basis, associated *Gun* with the *Kun* fish, appearing in the first part of the first chapter of the *Zhuangzi* (PORKERT 1996: 79).

[137] BIRRELL 1997: 238, 242, 252.

[138] Despite contrary opinions, flood myths do exist in China. As an example of this silent contrary opinions we might refer to A. DUNDES'S anthology which completely ignores the early Chinese flood myth traditions (DUNDES 1988).

that the process of degrading the myth of the popular *Chu* hero, *Gun,* was a prerequisite to establishing the orthodoxy of the figure of *Yu* in Chinese culture."[139]

The difference between the southern and the northern tradition can be further exemplified by the myth of *Yu,* who after *Gun's* failure succeeded in controlling the flood.[140] *Yu,* as portrayed in the mythical southern *Tianwen, Shanhaijing* and *Huainanzi,* uses some kind of magical soil (*xirang*) to save the world, while the northern tradition (*Mengzi, Shizi, Shujing*) lays the emphasis on *Yu's* moral qualities and technical knowledge (BIRRELL 1997: 241–251). This kind of difference suggests, as already mentioned, a general difference between the Confucian and the Taoist interpretation of ancient myths.

"A fundamental difference between a Confucian and Taoist consciousness consequently hinges on their respective emphasis on either a 'historical' or a 'primordial' memory. In Confucianism, knowledge starts with and depends on historical or civilizational origins. In Taoism, on the other hand, history is only the human continuation of a more ancient, more mythic, story of life. To remember the connection between myth and history in Taoism is to remember or rearticulate the 'original' human nature, to reassemble the body of the primordial giant (*Pangu*) who was dismembered in the creation of the world. Analogously, it is a closing of the holes of face bored into Emperor *Hundun.* Having a comprehensive and undifferentiated insight into the parts of his body and the world, a Taoist knows the Many and the One simultaneously. In this way, history (whether personal or social) is not an end in itself but only another path back to time, condition, or knowledge that was not historically ordered.

---

[139] BIRRELL 1997: 242. R. G. HENRICKS (1996: 276) also agrees that *Yu* was a divinity and hero of the *Zhou. Shun,* who was "largely a Confucian creation" (HENRICKS 1996: 268), considered these mythic figures, whom we associated with the south, as enemies. His attitude is apparent when "he banishes *Gonggong* to *Youzhou,* and kills *Gun* on *Xushan*" (HENRICKS 1996: 280).

[140] "Floodwater swelled up to the sky. *Gun* stole God's breathing-soil so as to stop up the flooding waters. But he did not wait for God's official permission. God ordered *Zhu Yong* to kill *Gun* on the approaches to Feather Mountain. Then commanded *Yu* in the end to spread out the (breathing-) soil so as to restore order in the Nine Provinces" (*Shanhaijing* 18: 8b–9a; BIRRELL 1997: 244). Also see the questions concerning *Yu's* success in the *Chuci.* "Lord *Yu* issued from *Gun's* belly. How did he [*Gun*] metamorphose? *Yu* inherited his predecessor's great task and he went on to complete his late father's achievements. How did he continue the task that earlier been in progress, and in what way was his project different? The flooding springs at their lowest deeps – how did he fill them in? The corners of the earth nine fathoms deep – how did he bank them up? Responding Dragon of the rivers and seas, what limits did he reach and where did he pass? What plan did *Gun* devise, and how did *Yu* succeed?" (*Tianwen* 3: 6b–7b; BIRRELL 1997: 242).

Taoism remebers history ultimately to forget it in the absolute freedom of the Tao."[141]

While discussing J. LEGGE's attitude towards Chinese mythology, A. BIRRELL remarks that the Confucian tradition (in this case the *Shundian* chapter of the *Shujing*) consciously humanizes and historicizes the gods and other spiritual beings of the ancient Chinese pantheon. "In each case, the mythical figure of other classical texts undergoes a transformative process, becoming at once humanized and historicized. At the same time, each mythical figure is demoted from his or her divine status in the other classical pantheons and is relegated to an inferior position to *Yao* and *Shun*."[142] Despite this kind of historization process, however, D.L. PORKERT claims that the original mythical and cosmological structure of the *Gun* and *Yu* myths can be demonstrated.[143]

---

[141] GIRARDOT 1983: 139. The same difference in attitude has already been stressed by W. BOLTZ: "For it is precisely the Confucianists, who, more than any other school of thought, were historically minded. (...) Their shy humanism tended to make them either indifferent toward supernatural matters, or to seek to explain them in purely rationalistic terms. The results have been disastrous for the preservation of early Chinese mythology..." (BOLTZ 1981: 372).

[142] BIRRELL 1999a: 346–348. HENRICKS also approves of the Confucian origin of *Shun*. *Shun* "was largely a Confucian creation" (HENRICKS 1996: 272), He even asserts that "the 'story' of *Shun* (...) is a wonderful tale produced by zealous Confucians" (HENRICKS 1996: 291). Moreover, BIRRELL provides an overview of the original functions of certain gods (*Yao, Gonggong, Gun, Shun, Yu, Houji, Kui*, etc.) appearing in two chapters (*Yaodian, Shundian*) of the *Shujing*, one of the most honoured Confucian classics (BIRRELL 1999a: 348). On the artificial character of the *Yaodian* chapter see D. HAWKES' opinion: "*Yaodian* is a fable or allegory in which the language of mythology is used in a very late and sophisticated manner" (HAWKES 1983: 19). On the general historization of myths see A. L. Ch. LO's opinion: "The inclusion of mythological material in historical writings is certainly not a peculiarly Chinese phenomenon, but the degree and extent to which myth has been incorporated into history in China hardly find any parallel in other ancient cultures. [...] their [scholars of the *Gushibian* school, G. K.] basic assumption that the early Chinese historians have as a rule drawn heavily on a variety of legendary and mythological lore is beyond all doubt. In such ancient texts as the *Shujing, Zuozhuan* and the *Guoyu*, mythic narratives make themselves felt every now and then in what are supposed to be sober historical accounts" (LO 1995: 188).

[143] "The following analysis offers a new interpretation of the origin and significance of Chinese flood myths, especially those concerning the Great *Yu*'s control of floodwaters. Specifically, it examines the cosmogonic purpose of these myths, which, I believe, should be read as references to celestial phenomena" (PORKERT 1996: 28). On the entire analysis see PORKERT 1996: 27–56.

Hundun

The myth of *Hundun*[144] could be a good example to demonstrate the separate evolution of the southern and northern cultures and mythologies. Although the name does appear in northern sources (*Zuozhuan, Shujing*), it is obvious that in these texts he is despised and rejected as something that does not fit the accepted order of the world.[145] In the southern sources (*Shanhaijing, Zhuangzi, Huainanzi, Daodejing*[146]), however, *Hundun* is a major

---

[144] On the *Hundun* myth generally see GIRARDOT 1983. Two basic occurrences in classical texts are quoted here: "The god of the south sea was *Shu* [Brief], the god of the north sea was *Hu* [Sudden], and the god of the center was *Hun Dun* [Confused]. *Shu* and *Hu* occasionally used to go together to *Hun Dun*'s land, and *Hun Dun* received them very cordially. *Shu* and *Hu* planned how to repay his generosity. They said: 'All humans have seven openings with which to see, hear, eat, and breathe. Only this one has not got any.' So they tried chiseling him. Each day they chiseled one opening. On the seventh day, *Hun Dun* died" (*Zhuangzi* 3: 19a–b; BIRRELL 1993: 100). "Three hundred and fifty leagues farther west is called Sky Mountain. There is a lot of gold and jade, and it has green realgar. *Ying* River springs from there and then flows southwest to empty into *Tang* Valley. There is a god [*shen*] there. His appearance is like a yellow bag, and he is red like a cinnabar flame. He has six feet and four wings. *Hun Dun* has no face or eyes. This one knows how to sing and dance. He is, in fact, *Di Jiang* [God River]" (*Shanhaijing* 2: 22b–23a; BIRRELL 1993: 100).

[145] "In two other late *Zhou* works, however, *Hun Dun* is a negative figure. In *Chronicle of Zuo*, *Hun Dun* is labeled as the First of the Four Ominous Ones, along with *Qiong Qi* (Gargoyle), *Tao Wu* (the Block), and *Tao Tie* (Glutton) (KARLGREN 1946: 247). In the *Classic of History*, *Hun Dun* is one of the 'Four Evil Ones' exiled by *Shun* for being rebellious and barbarous (GIRARDOT 1983: 123)" (BIRRELL 1983: 99). Also see GIRARDOT's opinion: 'Whereas in the official version the emphasis is on the heroic triumph over a destructive chaos condition (deluge, barbarian revolt, etc.) and the reestablishment and preservation of the civilized order, the Taoist reinterpretation of similar mythic themes stresses the artificiality of the human order and the need to reidentify with the condition or creature of chaos. Furthermore, it is important to realize that in the Confucian and Taoist sinicized versions of tribal mythology the original demiurgic figure (animal ancestor) is fundamentally ambiguous with respect to the chaos condition and can be either the heroic 'tamer of the flood' or the agent responsible for, and identified with, the return of chaos" (GIRARDOT 1983: 173). Moreover, N.J. GIRARDOT (198: 138) stresses the conscious attempt to downplay the importance of *Hundun*: "There apparently was a need, therefore, to expunge the significance of a figure like *Hundun* from the official historical view of the past".

[146] As we have noted in the introduction, *Laozi* is often associated with the state of *Chu*. Moreover, linguistic evidence also suggest that the rhyme technique used in the *Daodejing* reflects the local dialect of *Chu*. The same usage can be detected in other literary products of *Chu* (*Chuci* and *Zhuangzi*) as well (BAXTER 1998: 247–248). It is to be noted that although the term *Hundun* does not occur in the *Daodejing*, there are several references to some kind of chaos which is referred to as *hun, dun* or *dundun* (BIRRELL 1994: 385). As for the ralation between *dundun* and shamanism,

and fundamental[147] figure, who has no evil associations at all. Although the southern texts do not depict him in exactly the same way, still the consensus of his/its being a "benign and neutral figure" is conspicuous (BIRRELL 1993: 99). M. KALTENMARK and N. J. GIRARDOT both agree that the myth of *Hundun* is basically of southern provenance.

"As indicated by his quotation, many of the mythic motifs uncovered by KALTENMARK are identical with the theme of chaos found in the Taoist texts. KALTENMARK's findings, therefore, support the contention that there is a special southern or 'barbaric' focus for the mythological symbolism associated with *hundun*. KALTENMARK's analysis also helps to clarify the process of 'sinicization' or the 'Chinese' reinterpretation of elements from various local cultures."[148]

Its indebtedness to southern tradition is also exemplified by the fact that *Hundun* became an integral part of later Taoist cosmogonic mythology.[149]

Pengzu[150]

The Chinese Methuselah, who was believed to live for 800 years, appears in several southern sources. In the first chapter of the *Zhuangzi*, *Zhuang Zhou* complains that *Pengzu* is given too much credit, and mentions him as a person who was not an immortal, but lived from the 26th to the 7th century (BIRRELL 1993: 187). Though in a slightly cryptic context, *Tianwen* also mentions him in clear association with longevity,[151] just like one of the

---

N. J. GIRARDOT (1993: 111) notes: "I want again to draw attention to the characteristic reduplicated use of the *hundun* terminology as seen in the *Daodejing* and in the parable of *Hongmeng*. From the standpoint of comparative linguistics the function of reduplication is often linked to the development and use of 'secret languages' that in a primitive religious context can have associations with initiation ritual in general, and more specifically, with the shaman's ability to speak the language of the ancestral spirits or divine animals."

[147] This expression can be conceived literally (and visually) as well, if we accept J. S. MAJOR's opinion which claims that at the bottom of the famous silk banner from *Mawangdui*, we can find the personification of *Hundun*, the aquatic primordial chaos (MAJOR 1999: 126).

[148] GIRARDOT 1983: 173. Also see E. PORÉE-MASPERO's theory: "I would like only to stress the relevance of PORÉE-MASPERO's thesis for suggesting a general linguistic, historical, and cultural foundation for the 'foreign' or 'barbarian' connotations associated with the *hundun* theme in Taoism" (GIRARDOT 1983: 173).

[149] On Taoist cosmogonic myths see GIRARDOT 1976, 1983; YU 1981, 1986.

[150] On *Pengzu* see YUAN 1985: 378–379; BIRRELL 1993: 187–188; TOKAREV 1988: 435.

[151] "When *Peng Geng* poured out pheasant soup, how did God enjoy his sacrificial offering? He received the gift of eternal life, so how did he achieve such longevity?" (*Tianwen* 3:

medical manuscripts (*Yangshengfang*) from *Mawangdui* (PREGADIO 1989–90: 386). Interestingly enough, the two lists of shamans in the *Shanhaijing*, quoted above, both contain a shaman *Peng*,[152] who is probably identical with *Pengzu*, who, according the *Shuowenjiezi* at least, was the first healer in the world (CHOW 1978: 70). A later source (the *Baopuzi*, attributed to GE HONG, the passionate collector of southern, in this case *Jiangnan*, sources) also contains a lengthy description of his myth, regarding him as the great-great-grandson of *Zhuanxu* whose close relationship with *Chu* was stressed above.[153] In sum, the figure of this mythic representative of longevity and immortality is probably deeply rooted in the religious context of *Chu*.[154]

Huangdi and Yandi

In the early sources *Huangdi*[155] played only a minor role, and it was only during the *Han* dynasty that a more complex mythological system was organized around him. This relatively late rise to prominence is, as noted above, a hint at his special provenance.[156] As we have mentioned, the *Chu* people regarded *Zhuanxu* (the grandson of *Huangdi*) as their ancestor. It can be assumed that the culture-bearer hero of later times might have functioned as a warrior god in *Chu*,[157] as he often appears together with gods whose indebtedness to the *Chu* culture can be easily demonstrated. In these mythic narratives he is repeatedly fighting with *Kui*,[158] *Chiyou*[159] and

---

32b; BIRRELL 1993: 188). Furthermore, even Confucius refers to him as Old *Peng* (*Lunyu* 7.1).

[152] *Shanhaijing* 11: 6a, 16: 3a. ZHANG ZHENGMING asserts that Shaman *Peng* (*Wu Peng*) was venerated in *Chu* (ZHANG 1996: 113).

[153] *Shenxianzhuan* 1: 7b–11b. (BIRRELL 1993: 188.)

[154] "A belief in immortality and in ecstatic spirit-journeys was both a characteristic and a consequence of the distinctive religious cosmology of *Qi* and *Chu* and its expression in shamanistic practices" (MAJOR 1978: 231). As noted above, the quest for immortality and longevity, probably a *Chu* heritage, was also a major concern for the subsequent *Han* emperors.

[155] On *Huangdi* se SEIDEL 1969: 34–58; LE BLANC 1986.

[156] This is the same phenomenon that we encountered in the case of *Nüwa*.

[157] An interesting hint at his *Chu* roots is the mythical tradition that one of his ministers had a typical *Chu* name. "Yuan suggests that *Huangdi* was a thunder spirit [YUAN 1985: 403] and notes that one of *Huangdi*'s ministers was a *Xiong Shi* (*Xiong* is a *Chu* surname found in the received textual tradition but not in the *Chu* bronze inscriptions), who could command *Lei Gong*" (COOK 1993: 540).

[158] *Shanhaijing* 14: 6b.

[159] On *Chiyou* see BIRRELL 1993: 50–52; LEWIS 1990; LOEWE 1990. The figure of *Chiyou*, as we have already noted, has firm relationship with shamanism and non-Chinese

Yandi. Huangdi, who appears both in the *Shanhaijing* and the *Zhuangzi*, gradually acquired a central role in the Taoism, whose roots in *Chu* culture have already been referred to.[160] Within Taoism *Huangdi* played a prominent role in the so-called *Huang-Lao* Taoism, the *Chu* (and *Qi*) background of which in particular has been emphasized by J. S. MAJOR.[161] On the other hand, *Huangdi* did certainly not originate in *Chu*, but must have been rather popular there.[162]

According to the *Xinshu*, *Huangdi* had a brother, *Yandi*;[163] thus, if we trust the mythic genealogy, *Yandi* also has to reveal some kind of affinity towards *Chu* culture. This kind of relationship of *Yandi*, featuring in the *Tianwen*, the *Huainanzi*, three times in the *Shanhaijing* and in one of the texts from *Mawangdui* (*Wuxingzhan*), was stressed by J. S. MAJOR (1999: 128). C. A. COOK has demonstrated that he was deemed as one of the founding ancestor of the *Chu* royal house;[164] furthermore he is mentioned in the *Chu*

---

barbarous cultures (LOEWE 1994: 236), and he also appears in the *Shanhaijing* (17: 60–6b). M. LEWIS notes that "*Chiyou* was perhaps the mythic projection of the rainmaking shaman or shamaness" (LEWIS 1990: 165). *Chiyou*'s shamanic feature is further confirmed by the fact that he is closely related to rain-magic, a shamanic funcion *par excellence*: "*Dong Zhongshu* (179?–104? B.C.) claimed that when seeking rain in the summer you should sacrifice to *Chiyou* and also expose to the heat mortars and pestles" (HENRICKS 1994: 79.n.56). Moreover, in an aristocratic *Chu* tomb from 185 B.C. a manuscript was found which contained a special version of the *Huangdi–Chiyou* battle (BIRRELL 1994a: 87). In a similarly odd way, the *Huangdi–Chiyou* battle was also recorded in the context of *Yijing* divination on a bamboo text from the *Chu Wangjiatai* tomb (COOK 1998: 137).

[160] An interesting detail for *Huangdi*'s Taoist roots is *SIMA GUANG*'s commentary which says that the *Shiji* passages starting the history with *Huangdi*, instead of *Yao, Shun* or *Yu*, "were written under Taoist influence" (GIRARDOT 1983: 199). On the Taoist and Confucian philosophers' different attitude towards *Huangdi* and his relation to alchemy, metal-working and the *Hundun* motif see GIRARDOT 1983: 197–202. On his identification with *Hundun* see LO 1995: 189.

[161] MAJOR 1999: 129, 135, 140–141.

[162] On *Huangdi*'s origin in *Qi* and *Qin*, both being on the edge of the Central Plain, see LEWIS 1999: 59, 69.

[163] On *Yandi* see HENRICKS 1998. During the *Han* dynasty he was, according to HENRICKS with sound reasons, identified with *Shennong*. HENRICKS stresses that while tracing "the history of the figure *Shennong*, references to drought, fire, rain, and shamans are constant" (HENRICKS 1998: 103).

[164] COOK 1994. A further evidence of his popularity in *Chu* is the bamboo text from the *Chu Wangjiatai* tomb (COOK 1998: 137). LIAN SHAOMING has suggested that the text of the *Yijing* found at *Wangjiatai* is identical with the famous *Guizang* (COOK 1998: 137); in fact, a later encyclopaedia, the *Taipingyulan* contains a citation on the *Huangdi–Chiyou* conflict in connection with *Yijing* divination: "The *Guizang* says: In antiquity, the Yellow Spirit (*Huangdi*) and the Flame Spirit (*Yandi*) battled in the fields of *Zhuolu*. When they were about to battle, they had *Wu Xian* perform stalk divination. *Wu Xian*

Silk Manuscript together with *Zhu Rong* and *Gonggong*,[165] who both have deep roots in *Chu* mythology. He is clearly associated with shamanism in

---

said: 'There will be results!, but they will be unfortunate.' (*Taipingyulan* 1:367–368)" (COOK 1998: 138.n.12). It is to be noted that *Wu Xian*, the first and most famous (mythical) shaman of China is closely related to *Chu* culture. *Wu Xian* (Shaman *Xian*) appears in the *Huainanzi* (4.8b), in the *Zhuangzi*, in the *Lisao* and in the *Jiuge* parts of the *Chuci*. Moreover, he is mentioned among the ten shamans in the *Shanhaijing* (16.3a), while the same southern source alludes to the connection between him and shamanic ascension: "Shaman *Xian* is north of Woman *Chou* Mountain. In his right hand he grasps a bluegreen snake, in his left hand he graps a vermilion snake. He dwells on *Dengbao* Mountain, where the assembled shamans ascend and descend" (*Shanhaijing* 7.3b; MAJOR 1999: 136). ZHANG ZHENGMING notes that, together with *Wu Peng*, he was venerated in *Chu* (ZHANG 1996: 113). He is most often considered to be the first shaman, while in other sources he is credited with the title of the first professional healer [a function usually (e.g. *Shuowenjiezi*) attributed to Shaman *Peng* (see *Pengzu*)] : "*Wu Xian* was King *Yao*'s minister who served *Yao* as a physician with the 'great (...) technique' (*hongshu*) [medicine]" (CHOW 1978: 71). On the other hand, the *Shiji* claims that he was the first astrologer and astronomer, while the *Lüshichunqiu* asserts that he was the first diviner; moreover, "there is still one epigraphical source, the Curses upon the state of *Chu*," which calls him "the great and splendid god (*pixian da shen*)" (CHOW 1978: 72). The *Zhunshi* chapter of the *Shujing* places him in the time of *Taiwu* of the *Shang* dynasty when "*Wu Xian* cared for the royal house" (CHOW 1978: 74), while according to the *Zuo* chapter of the *Shiben* (Roots of the generations) he was the inventor of drum (CHANG 1999: 69). In sum, *Wu Xian* possesses all the attributes of a shamanic figure. After this digression on *Wu Xian*, we must remember that another reference to the divinatory nature of *Huangdi*'s battle can be found in the *Zuozhuan* (Xi 25): *Jin Hou* employed the diviner *Yan* to read the cracks for it (...) and he said: "Auspicious. (We) encounter the omen of '*Huangdi* battling at *Panquan*.' *Jin Hou* decided that this omen was too powerful for him..." (COOK 1998: 142). This kind of recurring reference to the connection between a mythological episode and a divination method can be explained, as E. SHAUGHNESSY does, if the astronomical (astrological) nature of the myth is emphasized (SHAUGHNESSY 1997: 210, 217–218.n.29).

[165] MAJOR 1999: 128. "*Yandi* thereupon ordered *Zhu Rong* to make the four gods descend to set up the Three Heavens..." (LI – COOK 1999: 174). In N. BARNARD's translation the sentence runs as follows: "*Yandi* thence commanded *Zhu Rong* to take [=along with] the Four Gods, to descend and stabilize the Three Heavens..." (BARNARD 1973: 111). According to the *Shanhaijing*, *Yandi*, *Zhu Rong* and *Gonggong* are mythic relatives: "The wife of *Yandi*, *Ting Yao*, the daughter of the Red River, gave birth to *Yan Ju*. *Yan Ju* gave birth to *Jie Bing*. *Jie Bing* gave birth to *Xi Qi*; and *Xi Qi* gave birth to *Zhu Rong*. *Zhu Rong* came down to dwell on the *Jiang* river where he gave birth to *Gonggong*" (*Shanhaijing* 18:10; HENRICKS 1998: 117; A. BIRRELL's other translation is quoted below). HENRICKS even risks the hypothesis that *Zhu Rong* and *Yandi* are actually the same figure. "It is very likely that *Yandi* and *Zhu Rong*—who, as we have seen, is presented as *Yandi*'s assistant and *Yandi*'s descendant—were originally one and the same, or that they are different transformations of a common predecessor (...). Once again, the identity is expressed as (and obscured by) kinship connection" (HENRICKS 1998: 119).

one of the three *Shanhaijing* passages.[166] *KE AN*, one of the commentators of the *Shanhaijing* connects the conspicuously barbaric *Xingtian* myth with the figure of *Yandi*.[167] According to the *Xinshu* the two brothers (*Huangdi* and *Yandi*) shared power over the cosmos; later on, however, as the *Huainanzi*, the similarly syncretic *Lüshichunqiu* and the Taoist *Liezi* all report, they were fighting in the form of water and fire, which motif has a slight shamanic overtone.[168]

Zhu Rong

"*Zhu Rong*, who is riding on two dragons, lives in the south. His body is similar to an animal, but his face is human-like."[169] *GUO PU*, the commentator adds that this hybrid creature, appearing in the 6th chapter of the *Shanhaijing*, is the "Spirit of the Fire." *Zhu Rong* appears in several

---

[166] "There is the kingdom of the *Di* people. *Yandi's* grandson was *Ling Qi. Ling Qi* gave birth to the *Di* people. These people could ascend to and descend from Heaven" (*Shanhaijing* 16.415; HENRICKS 1998: 117). It is to be noted that the last phrase (ascend and descend) is a recurring expression in the *Shanhaijing* to refer to shamanic practice. Furthermore, the name *Ling* means magical power, and drum (HENRICKS 1998: 117; LAWTON 1991: 164). The motifs of drum, archery and music (all being related to shamanism) appear in another passage of the *Shanhaijing*. "*Yandi's* grandson was *Bo Ling. Bo Ling* committed adultery with the wife of *Wu Quan, Anü Yuan Fu. Yuan Fu* was pregnant for three years, and it was she who gave birth to *Gu* (Drum), *Yan* and *Shu. Shu* was the first to make archery targets. *Gu* and *Yan*—these were the first to make bells and compose musical airs" (*Shanhaijing* 18.464; HENRICKS 1998: 117).

[167] "*Xingtian* tried to seize the Emperor's throne. For this the Emperor cut off his head and buried him on Mount *Changyang*. Then *Xingtian* used his nipples as his eyes and his navel as his mouth, brandishing a shield and an axe"(*Shanhaijing* 7:2b; *Ding* 1992: 29).

[168] BIRRELL 1993: 131–132; Li – COOK 1999: 174. According to R. G. HENRICKS, there are two references to *Yandi* in the *Shanhaijing* (16.415–18.471) that also seem to imply some shamanic connotations: "First note that passage 1 seems to relate *Yandi* to shamans and shamanism (...) Finally, in passage 3 there is another possible tie with shamanism, in fact a connection with the *chi* rite" (HENRICKS 1998: 117–118). Moreover, in a commentary on the *Lüshichunqiu* (6.2ab), *Gaoyou* mentions that "in former times *Yandi* was *Shennong*" (HENRICKS 1998s: 105.n.19). As for *Shennong's* connection with shamanism, R. G. HENRICKS claims that "when we trace the history of the figure *Shennong*, references to drought, fire, rain and shamans are constant" (HENRICKS 1998: 103). He suggests that the the usual attributes of *Yandi* (bells and drums, the colour 'red', invocation (*zhu*), mention of fire or 'bright sun', maidens dying young) "find their sources in *Shang* shamanistic agrarian rites", which, if proves to be true, would confirm the close relationship between *Chu* and *Shang*, mentioned at the beginning of the present article.

[169] On *Zhu Rong* see TOKAREV 1988: 401; GIRARDOT 1959: 254–257, 360–361; *YUAN* 1985: 297–298; BIRRELL 1993: 72.

southern works, like the *Chuci*, the *Huainanzi*, the *Chu* Silk Manuscript[170] and twice in the *Shanhaijing*. In the description of the genealogy of the *Chu* royal house SIMA QIAN has also mentioned *Zhu Rong*; in his interpretation, however, it seems to be the title of a position, rather than a person or a spiritual being.[171] A *Guoyu* passage states that *Zhu Rong* was the first ancestor of the *Chu*;[172] moreover, a *Zuozhuan* passage relates that the king of *Chu* condemns the ruler of *Kui* (a colony of *Chu*) of neglecting the sacrifices to *Zhu Rong*.[173] The popularity of *Zhu Rong* in *Chu* has been further confirmed by a bamboo inscription from the *Baoshan* finds, which proves that the people of *Chu* considered *Zhu Rong* as their ancestor, whom they invoked during divination.[174]

---

170 "*Yandi* thereupon ordered *Zhu Rong* to make the four gods [of the four seasons] descend to set up the Three Heavens and with (...) distribute the four poles" (LI – COOK 1999: 174; COOK 1994: 2).

171 "*Zhong Li* occupied the office of Governor of Fire for *Di Ku Gao Xin* and had very great accomplishments. He was able to light and warm [*rong*] the world. *Di Ku* named him *Zhu Rong*. When *Gong Gong* rebelled, *Di Ku* sent *Zhong Li* to punish him but he [*Zhong Li*] did not complete the mission. So *Di Ku* punished *Zhong Li* on the *geng-yin* day, made his younger brother *Wu Hui* his descendant, and appointed him to the post of Governor of Fire, and he [*Wu Hui*] became *Zhu Rong*" (*Shiji* 40:7; COOK – MAJOR 1999: 211–212). It is evident from this description that for SIMA QIAN, who basically had a northern intellectual background, *Zhu Rong* is an official title, and not the name of a spirit. It is obviously not the case, however, in the southern *Shanhaijing*. "The child of Emperor *Yan*'s wife was *Yan Ju*, who begat *Jie Bing*. *Jie Bing*'s son was *Xi Qi* who begat *Zhu Rong*, who was exiled to the region of the *Jiang* River. *Zhu Rong* begat *Gonggong*" (*Shanhaijing* 18: 10). The explanation for this conspicuous difference lies probably in the different attitude. The northern sources, which applies a historical perspective, usually conceived of the originally mythical figures as titles, positions of a historical person, as it was stressed by A. BIRRELL in connection with *Gonggong* (BIRRELL 1997: 228. n.27).

172 HAWKES 1983: 12. What's more, D. HAWKES asserts that he knows the feast-day of *Zhu Rong*. "*SIMA QIAN*'s statement that the first of the two *Zhonglis* was put to death by *Gaoxin* on a *gengyin* day throws an interesting light on the second line of the *Lisao*; for *QU YUAN*, that later scion of the high lord *Gaoyang*, was born on a *gengyin* day. It was on a *gengyin* day, too, that the 'good' king of *Chu*, *Zhaowang*, whose death had been prophesied, was gathered to his fathers. I suspect that the first *gengyin* of the year—the day on which *QU YUAN* was born—was the annual feast-day of the god *Zhu Rong*" (HAWKES 1983: 17).

173 *Zuozhuan*, *Xigong*, 26th year.

174 SUKHU 1999: 212.n.55. If we accept J. S. MAJOR's hypothesis that the serpent motif in connection with a divine being is basically a *Chu* phenomenon, then it is worth citing MORI JASUTARO's linguistic analysis which concludes that the name *Zhu Rong* originally meant Fire Serpent (TOKAREV 1988: 401).

Gonggong

Gonggong,[175] who was referred to in *SIMA QIAN*'s description of the *Chu* royal house, appears in numerous southern sources; besides the *Chu* Silk Manuscript[176] he is mentioned in the *Shanhaijing* as the son of *Zhu Rong*.[177] Another southern source mentions that he fought with *Zhuanxu*,[178] another recurrent figure in *Chu* culture. The northern tradition interpreted his figure in a more historical context, and in this perspective he was a rebel[179] against the ideal emperor *Shun*.[180] He is also the protagonist in one of the four flood myths; the sources of the flood myths can be clearly divided into two kinds: the southern documents (*Tianwen, Huainanzi, Shanhaijing*), as A. BIRRELL has demonstrated, have a rather different picture on *Gonggong* than the northern ones (*Guanzi, Shujing*).[181]

Siming

Two of the poems of the 'Nine Songs' (*Jiuge*) part of the *Chuci* are dedicated to the Lord of the Fate (*Siming*),[182] the God of Death in *Chu*.[183] At the *Han*

---

[175] On *Gonggong* see TOKAREV 1988: 418; BOLTZ 1981; BIRRELL 1993: 97–98; WERNER 1986: 81–82; YUAN 1985: 145–145; GIRARDOT 1959: 240–272, 318–319, 486–487; MA 1994.I: 470–479; MA 1994.II: 170–182.

[176] MAJOR 1999: 128; LI–COOK 1999: 175.

[177] *Shanhaijing* 18:10a. "*Zhu Rong* came down to dwell on the *Jiang* river where he gave birth to *Gonggong*" (HENRICKS 1998: 117). The *Jiang* river refers to the *Yangzi*, the main river of the *Chu* kingdom.

[178] *Huainanzi* 3: 1a–b.

[179] "And as NEEDHAM points out in relation to the speculative work of GIRARDOT, the symbolism of *hundun* and the legendary rebels is almost always linked to archaic religio-cultural traditions of metallurgy and totemic shamanism" (GIRARDOT 1993: 131). Another rebel mentioned in a *Chu* context is *Chiyou* whose attributes are so strikingly similar to those of *Gonggong* that M. GIRARDOT suggested that these two figures are nearly identical (SHAUGHNESSY 1997: 218.n.29).

[180] *Hanfeizi* 24.

[181] BIRRELL 1997: 228–235. This kind of different interpretation has already been noticed in the case of *Hundun* and *Gun*. Moreover, the figure of *Gun* was directly related to *Gonggong*. "It is worth mentioning in this connexion that a number of scholars in the 1920s and 30s felt strongly, on the basis of this passage [*Guoyu* 3.5b; G. K.] and other types of evidence, that *Gun* and *Gonggong* were originally one and the same..." (HENRICKS 1994: 77; also see LO 1995: 191–193).

[182] On *Siming* see WALEY 1955: 37–43.

[183] TŐKEI 1986: 122. The Nine Songs includes a poem dedicated to another deity (*Taiyi*) who might have a close relationship with *Chu* culture. "It should not be overlooked that the deity [*Taiyi*] also has a prehistory in the ancient state of *Chu*, which may go

court during the 2nd c. B.C. rituals were performed to him by shamans from *Chu*.[184] Moreover, *Siming* also makes an appearance in a unique case. The helping spirit of shamaness *Shenjun*, whose case contains the only reference to some kind of shaman sickness in the Chinese sources, is precisely *Siming*,[185] who must have been rather popular with the inhabitants of *Chu*.

CONCLUDING REMARKS

In sum, we can conclude that shamanism and certain figures of Chinese mythology were important elements in the religious thought of the ancient Chinese state of *Chu*. Thus, the conclusions of this study are the following:

1. Several data attest to the presence of shamanic practice in *Chu* between the 7th–3rd century B.C. This seems to be one of the earliest references to shamanism supported by written documents in the world.

---

back to remote antiquity" (ANDERSEN 1989–90: 29). The *Tang* dynasty *Wenxuan* commentaries of the "Five Ministers" comment on the title of one of the *Jiuge* poems (*Donghuang Taiyi*) as follows: "*Xiang* says: *Taiyi* is the name of a star. It is the most revered Spirit of Heaven. In the East of *Chu* is is the object of sacrifices as the companion of the Emperor of the East" (Waters 1985: 44). Besides the *Chuci*, the *Huainanzi* also contains abundant information on this god: "The constellation Great Subtlety [*Taiwei*] is the *Taiyi*'s court. The constellation Imperial Palace [*Zigong*] is his dwelling. It is said that the *Taiyi* is the most highly esteemed Spirit of Heaven, the Jewel of the Dipper" (WATERS 1985: 44). Furthermore, a recent excavation, the *Guodian* cosmogonic text (*Taiyi shengshui*) confirmed ANDERSEN's statement, as it contains explicit reference to *Taiyi* as a creator god. "Until now no Chinese text depicting a creation of the cosmos and no Chinese text in which *Taiyi* appeared as a deity was known before the late third century B.C. at the earliest; for the most part we associate such texts with the *Han* period, and *Taiyi* in particular with *Han Wudi*. Now we have a very detailed and explicit late fourth century B.C. text that portrays *Taiyi* as the ultimate creator of the cosmos" (BOLTZ 1999: 605). Moreover, the *Baoshan* texts also contain several references to *Taiyi* (see CHEN 1996: 161–162; HARPER 1999: 855, 869–873). On its cult as reflected in the archaeological finds see LI 1995–96, on its role in the later religious Taoist sect (*Shangqing*) with a clear shamanic heritage see ROBINET 1993: 132–138.

184 "The *wu* of *Jing* [*Chu*] sacrificed downstairs before the hall to the ancestors of the *wu*, to the rulers of destiny [*Siming*], the bestowers of rice, and others" (*Hanshu* 24A: 14b; Groot 1982: 1200). On the other hand, another source mentions that the shamans performing this ritual came from the state of *Jin*. This apparent contradiction, however, disappears if we realize that a certain part of the state of *Jin*, nowadays covering *Shanxi*, belonged to *Chu* (WALEY 1955: 28).

185 *Hanshu* 25A: 21a.

2. *Chu* culture, which was both politically and culturally dominant between the 7th–3rd centuries, has several idiosyncratic features in the fields of religion, art and literature. Besides these features, which have been emphasized by several scholars earlier, I endeavored to demonstrate that its mythology was also rather distinctive. The majority of information on the rather fragmented Chinese mythology was mainly derived from works either written in *Chu* (*Tianwen, Shanhaijing*) or being massively influenced by the religious complex of *Chu* (*Huainanzi, Zhuangzi*). Therefore we can conclude that this southern state, compared to the rest of contemporary China at least, had a special affinity to mythic narratives.

3. There is convincing evidence to show that the origins of Chinese mythology, which became well-known in all parts of China only during the *Han* dynasty, can be traced back to various local traditions. I assumed that the myths that were popular in *Chu* or which had a special *Chu* version were foremost preserved in the *Chu* sources mentioned above. When northern equivalents were found, it could be demonstrated that the southern versions preserved the more genuine mythic material, whereas the northern sources interpreted the myth in a more historical and moral perspective.

4. As it can be proved that *Chu* (and other southern) cultures had a massive influence on the intellectual horizon of the *Han* dynasty, it was assumed that the mythic figures who acquired a dominant role during the *Han* period have a more intimate relation to *Chu* (and other southern) culture than those who had always been part of the standard mythology. Similarly, it was argued that the representative works and schools of Taoism (*Laozi, Zhuangzi, Huainanzi, Huang-Lao, Shangqing*) were firmly embedded in a southern context, therefore they were more inclined to integrate mythic material from *Chu* (e.g. *Huangdi, Xiwangmu, Hundun*).

5. These conclusions, combined with the opinions of leading sinologists (S. ALLAN, A. BIRRELL, S. CAHILL, C. A. COOK, N. J. GIRARDOT, D. HAWKES, Ch. LE BLANC, M. LOEWE, J. S. MAJOR, R. MATHIEU, J. RAWSON) encourage us to claim that certain figures of the Chinese mythic pantheon were more popular in *Chu*. According to some scholars, this kind of prominence can be best explained if we assume that these figures originated in this southern state. The *Chu* sources (*Chuci-Tianwen, Shanhaijing, Huainanzi, Zhuangzi*), and other materials related to *Chu* culture (*Guoyu, Mawangdui, Chu* Silk Manuscript, *Baoshan, Guodian, Wangjiatai*) all attest that the following mythic figures can be relatively strongly linked to *Chu* culture, either being

rather popular there and/or having a special *Chu* interpretation: *Zhuanxu, Zhong* and *Li, Xiwangmu, Kunlun, Fuxi, Nüwa, Kui, Fusang, Gun, Hundun, Pengzu, Huangdi, Yandi, Zhu Rong, Gonggong, Wu Xian, Siming, Taiyi.*

6. In many cases (*Zhong* and *Li, Xiwangmu, Kunlun, Kui, Fusang, Pengzu, Wu Xian, Siming, Taiyi*) it can be demonstrated that shamanism, which had a prominent role in the state of *Chu*, was intimately interrelated with these myths.

7. In conclusion, we can assert that the ancient Chinese state of *Chu*, similarly to its religious, artistic and literal aspects, preserved its distinctiveness in mythology as well, greatly contributing to the world of Chinese myths.

REFERENCES

ALLAN, SARAH
  1981 Sons of Suns: myth and totemism in early China. *Bulletin of the School of Oriental and African Studies* 44: 1: 290–326.
  1991 *The shape of the turtle: Myth, Ard and Cosmos in Early China.* New York: SUNY Press.
ANDERSEN, POUL
  1989–90 The Practice of *Bugang. Cahiers d'Extrême-Asie* 5: 15–53.
BAGLEY, ROBERT
  1999 Shang Archaeology. In M. LOEWE – E. L. SHAUGHNESSY (eds.) *The Cambridge History of Ancient China.* New York: CUP, 124–231.
BARNARD, NOEL
  1973 *The Ch'u Silk Manuscript: translation and commentary.* Canberra: Australian National University.
BARNARD, NOEL – FRASER, DONALD (eds.)
  1972 *Early Chinese Art and Its Possible Influence in the Pacific Basin.* 3 vols. New York: Intercultural Arts Press.
BAXTER, WILLIAM H.
  1998 Situating the Language of the Lao-tzu. In L. KOHN – M. LAFARGUE (eds.) *Lao-tzu and the Tao-te-ching.* New York: SUNY Press, 231–253.
BIRRELL, ANNE
  1993 *Chinese Mythology.* London: The Johns Hopkins University Press (rev. ed. 1999).
  1994 Studies on Chinese Myths since 1970: An Appraisal. Part I. *History of Religions* 33.2: 380–393.
  1994a Studies on Chinese Myths since 1970: An Appraisal. Part II. *History of Religions* 33.3: 70–94.

1997 The Four Flood Myth Traditions of Classical China. *T'oung Pao* 83: 213–259.

1999 *The Classic of Mountains and Seas*. London: Penguin Books.

1999a James Legge and the Chinese Mythological Tradition. *History of Religions* 38.4: 331–353.

BLAKELEY, BARRY B.

1985–87 Recent Developments in *Chu* Studies. A Bibliographical and Institutional Overview. *Early China* 11–12: 371–387.

1999 Chu Society and State: Image versus Reality. In COOK, C. A. – MAJOR, J. S. (eds.) *Defining Chu. Image and Reality in Ancient China*. Honolulu: Hawai'i University Press, 51–66.

BODDE, DEREK

1961 Myths of Ancient China. In S. N. KRAMER (ed.) *Mythologies of the Ancient World*. New York: Dombleday and Co., 369–408.

BOLTZ, WILLIAM G.

1981 Kung Kung and the flood: reverse euhemerism in the Yao tien. *T'oung Pao* 67.3–5: 141–153.

1999 The Fourth-Century B.C. *Guodiann* Manuscripts from Chuu and the Composition of the Laotzyy. *Journal of the American Oriental Society* 119.4: 590–608.

BUMBACHER, STEPHEN P.

1998 The Earliest Manuscripts of the Laozi discovered to date. *Asiatische Studien* 52: 1175–1185.

CAHILL, SUZANNE E.

1993 *Transcendence and Divine Passion: The Queen Mother of the West in Medieval China*. Stanford: Stanford University Press.

CARR, MICHAEL

1992 Shamanic Heng, 'Constancy'. *Otaru Shōka Daigaku jinbun kenkyū* 83: 93–159.

CHAN, PING-LEUNG

1962 *Chu Tz'u and Shamanism in Ancient China*. (Ph.D. diss.) Ohio State University.

CHANG, KWANG-CHIH

1968 *The Archaeology of Ancient China*. New Haven: Yale University Press.

1972 Major aspects of Ch'u archaeology. BARNARD, NOEL – FRASER, DONALD (eds.) *Early Chinese Art and Its Possible Influence in the Pacific Basin*. 3 vols. New York: Intercultural Arts Press. Vol. 1: 5–52.

1983 *Art, Myth, and Ritual*. Cambridge: Harvard University Press.

1999 China on the Eve of the Historical Period. In M. LOEWE – E. L. SHAUGHNESSY (eds.) *The Cambridge History of Ancient China*. New York: CUP, 37–73.

CHANG, I-JEN – BOLTZ, WILLIAM G. – LOEWE, MICHAEL

1993 Kuo yü. In MICHAEL LOEWE (ed.) *Early Chinese Texts: A Bibliographical Guide*. Berkeley: University of California, 263–268.

CHEN, D. T.
    1986   *The nine songs: A re-examination of shamanism in ancient China.* (Ph.D. diss.) University of Southern California.
CHEN JIANING – YANG YANG (eds.)
    1995   *Zhongguo shenhua shijie* [The world of Chinese myths]. Beijing: Beijing Language and Culture University Press.
CHEN, PEIFEN
    1997   Early Chinese Bronze Mirrors. *Orientations* 28.3: 88–93.
CHEN, WEI
    1996   *Baoshan zhujian chutan* (Preliminary Investigations of the Chu bamboo strips from Baoshan). Wuhan: Wuhan University Press.
CHILDS-JOHNSON, ELISABETH – SULLIVAN, L. R.
    1996   The Three Gorges Dam and the Fate of China's Southern Heritage. *Orientations* 27.7: 55–61.
CHOW, TSE-TSUNG
    1978   The childbirth myth and ancient Chinese medicine: a study of aspects of the wu tradition. In D. T. ROY – TSIEN, TSUEN-HSUIN (eds.) *Ancient China: Studies in Early Civilization.* Hong Kong: Chinese University Press, 43–89.
CHRISTIE, A.
    1983   *Chinese Mythology.* Feltham: Newnes Books.
COHEN, ALVIN P.
    1978   Coercing the Rain Deities in Ancient China. *History of Religions* 17: 244–265.
COOK, CONSTANCE A.
    1993   Myth and Authenticity: Deciphering the Chu Gong Ni Bell Description. *Journal of the American Oriental Society* 113.4: 539–549.
    1994   Three High Gods of Chu. *Journal of Chinese Religions* 22: 1–22.
    1998   Myth and Fragments of a Qin *Yi* Text. A Research Note and Translation. *Journal of Chinese Religions* 26: 135–143.
    2000   *Omens and Myth: Thoughts on the Guizang Manuscript.* (Conference Paper at the International Conference on Newly Excavated Bamboo and Silk Texts – Beijing University, August 18–22, 2000)
COOK, CONSTANCE A. – BLAKELEY, BARRY B.
    1999   Introduction. In COOK, CONSTANCE A. – MAJOR, JOHN S. (eds.) *Defining Chu. Image and Reality in Ancient China.* Honolulu: Hawai'i University Press, 1–5.
COOK, CONSTANCE A. – MAJOR, JOHN S.
    1999   *Defining Chu. Image and Reality in Ancient China.* Honolulu: Hawai'i University Press.
DEMATTÉ, PAOLA
    1994   Antler and Tongue. New Archaeological Evidence in the Study of the *Chu* Tomb Guardian. *East and West* 44: 353–394.

DING WANGDAO
1992 *100 Chinese Myths and Fantasies.* Beijing: Zhongguo duiwai fanyi chuban gongsi.

DU WEIMING
1979 The Thought of Huang-Lao: A Reflection on the Lao tzu and Huang Ti Texts in the Silk Manuscripts of Ma-wang-tui. *Journal of Asian Studies* 39.1: 95–110.

DUBS, HOMER H.
1942 An Ancient Chinese Mystery Cult. *Harvard Theological Review* 35: 221–246.

DUNDES, ALAN (ed.)
1988 *The Flood Myth.* Berkeley – Los Angeles – London: University of California Press.

EBERHARD, WOLFRAM
1942 *Lokalkulturen im alten China.* Vol. I. Leiden. [Supplement to T'oung Pao XXXVII] Vol. II. Peking. [Monumenta Serica Monograph 3]
1968 *The Local Cultures of South and East China.* (Trans. by A. EBERHARD) Leiden: E. J. Brill.

ECSEDY, ILDIKÓ
1980 Western Turks in Northern China in the Middle of the 7th Century. *Acta Antiqua Hung.* 28: 249–258.
1984 The new year's tree and other traces of ancient shamanistic cult in China. In MIHÁLY HOPPÁL (ed.) *Shamanism in Eurasia.* Part 1. Göttingen: Edition Herodot, 107–121.

EICHHORN, WERNER
1973 *Die Religion Chinas.* Stuttgart – Köln – Mainz.

ELIADE, MIRCEA (ed.)
1987 *The Encyclopedia of Religion.* New York: Macmillan Publishing Company.
1989 *Shamanism. Archaic Techniques of Ecstasy.* (Trans. W. R. TRASK) London: Arkana. (1st ed. 1964)

ERKES, EDUARD
1931 Spuren chinesischer Weltschöpfungs-mythen. *T'oung Pao* 28: 355–368.
1942 Ein P'an-ku-Mythe der Hsia-Zeit? *T'oung Pao* 36: 159–173.

ERKES, EDUARD – CONRADY, M.
1931 *Das älteste Dokument zur chinesischen Kunstgeschichte, T'ien-wen.* Leipzig.

FIELD, STEPHEN
1986 *T'ien Wen: A Chinese Book of Origins.* New York: New Directions.
1992 Cosmos, Cosmograph, and the Inquiring Poet. New Answers to the 'Heaven Questions'. *Early China* 17: 83–110.

FINSTERBUSCH, KÄTE
1952 *Das Verhältnis der Shan-hai-djing zur Bildenden Kunst.* Berlin Akademie-Verlag.

FINGARETTE, H.
1972 *Confucius: The Secular as Sacred.* New York: Harper and Row.

FRACASSO, RICCARDO
  1988 Holy Mothers of Ancient China. *T'oung Pao* 74.1–3: 1–46.
  1993 Shan hai ching. In MICHAEL LOEWE (ed.) *Early Chinese Texts: A Bibliographical Guide.* Berkeley: University of California, 357–367.
  1996 *Libro dei monti e dei mari (Shanhaijing).* Venezia: Marsilio.
FU, JUYOU – CHEN SONGCHANG
  1992 *Mawangdui Hanmu Wenwu* (The Cultural Relics Unearthed from the Han Tombs at *Mawangdui*). Changsha: Hunan Publishing House.
FUNG, YU-LAN
  1952 *A History of Chinese Philosophy.* Vol. I. Princeton: Princeton University Press.
GILES, HERBERT A.
  1905 Who is Si Wang Mu? *Adversaria sinica* 1: 1–9.
GIRARDOT, NORMAN J.
  1976 The Problem of Creation Mythology in the Study of Chinese Religion. *History of Religions* 15: 289–318.
  1983 *Myth and Meaning in Early Taoism: The Theme of Chaos (hun-tun).* Berkeley – Los Angeles: University of California Press.
  1987 Mythic Themes. In MIRCEA ELIADE (ed.) *The Encyclopaedia of Religion.* New York: Macmillan Publishing company. Vol. 3: 296–305.
GOEPPER, ROGER
  1996 Precursors and Early Stages of the Chinese Script. In JESSICA RAWSON (ed.) *Mysteries of Ancient China.* London: British Museum Press, 273–281.
GIRARDOT, MARCEL
  1959 *Danses et Légendes de la Chine ancienne.* Paris: Presses Universitaires de France.
GROOT, JAN JACOB MARIE DE
  1982 *The Religious System of China.* Vol. 6. Taipei: Southern Materials Center, INC. (1st repr. 1964)
HARPER, DONALD
  1999 Warring States Natural Philosophy and Occult Thought. In M. LOEWE – E. L. SHAUGHNESSY (eds.) *The Cambridge History of Ancient China.* New York: CUP, 813–885.
HARTMAN, CHARLES.
  1986 Ch'u-tz'u. In NIENHAUSER, WILLIAM. H., Jr. (ed.) *The Indiana Companion to Traditional Chinese Literature.* Bloomington – Indianapolis: Indiana University Press, 347–349.
  1986a Poetry. In NIENHAUSER, WILLIAM. H., Jr. (ed.) *The Indiana Companion to Traditional Chinese Literature.* Bloomington – Indianapolis: Indiana University Press, 59–74.
HAWKES, DAVID
  1959 *Chu Tz'u, the Song of the South.* Oxford: Clarendon Press. (2nd ed. 1985)
  1967 The Quest of the Goddess. *Asia Major* 13: 71–94.
  1974 The Quest of the Goddess. In C. BIRCH (ed.) *Studies in Chinese Literary Genres.* Berkeley: University of California Press.

1983   The Heirs of Gao-yang. *T'oung Pao* 69.1–3: 1–21.

1993   Ch'u-tz'u. In MICHAEL LOEWE (ed.) *Early Chinese Texts: A Bibliographical Guide*. Berkeley: University of California, 48–55.

HAYASHI MINAO

1972   The Twelve Gods of the Chan-Kuo Period Silk Manuscript Excavated at Ch'ang-sha. In BARNARD, NOEL – FRASER, DONALD (eds.) *Early Chinese Art and Its Possible Influence in the Pacific Basin*. New York: Intercultural Arts Press. Vol. 1.: 123–186.

HEARN, MAXWELL K.

2000   The Rise of Pictorial Representation in China: New Evidence from a Lacquer Box in The Metropolitan Museum of Art. *Orientations* 31.5: 43–49.

HENRICKS, ROBERT S.

1994   On the Whereabouts and Identity of the Place Called 'K'ung-sang' (Hollow Mulberry) in Early Chinese Mythology. *Bulletin of the School of Oriental and African Studies* 57: 69–90.

1996   The Three-Bodied Shun and the Completion of Creation. *Bulletin of the School of Oriental and African Studies* 59: 268–295.

1998   Fire and Rain: a Look at Shen Nung (The Divine Farmer) and his Ties with Yen Ti (the 'Flaming Emperor' or 'Flaming God'). *Bulletin of the School of Oriental and African Studies* 61: 102–124.

HO PING-TI

1975   *The Cradle of the East*. Hong Kong – Chicago: University of Chicago Press.

Hubeisheng bowuguan

1991   *Zeng Hou Yi mu wenwu yishu*. Wuhan: Hubei meishu chubanshe.

IZUTSU, TOSHIHIKO

1967   *The Key Philosophical Concepts in Sufism and Taoism*. 2 vols. Tokyo: Keio Institute.

JAMES, JEAN M.

1995   An Iconographic Study of *Xiwangmu* During the Han-Dynasty. *Artibus Asiae* 55: 17–41.

JANSINOJ, E. M.

1977   *Katalog gor i morej*. Moskow: Nauka.

Jingmen shi bowuguan

1998   *Guodian Chumu zhujian*. Beijing: Wenwu chubanshe.

Jingzhou dichu bowuguan

1995   Jiangling *Wangjiatai* 15 hao Qinmu. *Wenwu* 1995.1: 37–43.

KAGAN, RICHARD C.

1980   The Chinese Approach to Shamanism. *Chinese Sociology and Anthropology* 12: 3–135.

KALTENMARK, MARK

1959   La naissance du monde en Chine. In P. GARELLI – M. LEIBOVICI (eds.) *Sources orientales. La naissance du monde*. Paris: Le Seuil, 453–467.

KANE, VIGINIA

1974–75 The Independent Bronze Industries in the South of China Contemporary with the Shang and Western Chou Dynasties. *Archives of Asian Arts* 28: 77–107.

KARLGREN, BERNHARD

1941 Huai and Han. *Bulletin of the Museum of Far Eastern Antiquities* 13: 1–4.

1946 Legends and Cults of Ancient China. *Bulletin of the Museum of Far Eastern Antiquities* 18: 199–365.

KECSKÉS, LÁSZLÓNÉ

1988 Kína (China). In ISTVÁN HAHN (ed.) *Mitológiai ábécé* (The ABC of Mythology). Budapest: Gondolat, 340–354.

KEIGHTLEY, DAVID N.

1989 *Shamanism in* Guoyu? *A Tale of* Xi *and* Wu. (Paper prepared for the Center of Chinese Studies Regional Seminar, Berkeley, 7–8. Apr. 1989.)

KELLER, ANDREA

1992 Nügua als Protagonistin im Schöpfungsgeschehen nach früch-chinesischen Quellen. *Chinablätter* 19: 233–246.

KOHN, LIVIA

1995 *Laughing at the Tao.* Princeton: Princeton University Press.

KÓSA, GÁBOR

2000 'In Search of the Spirits' – Shamanism in China before the Tang Dynasty. *Shaman* 8: 2: 131–179.

2001 Open Wide, Oh, Heaven's Door! – Shamanism in China before the Tang Dynasty. *Shaman* 9: 2: 169–197.

LAWTON, THOMAS (ed.)

1991 *New Perspectives on Chu culture during the Eastern Zhou Period.* Washington: Smithsonian Institution.

LE BLANC, CHARLES

1985 *Huainanzi.* Hong Kong: Hong Kong University Press.

1986 A Re-examination of the Myth of Huangdi. In N. J. GIRARDOT – J. S. MAJOR (eds.) *Myth and Symbol in Chinese Tradition.* Boulder: Society for the Study of Chinese Religions, 45–63.

LEWIS, MARK E.

1990 *Sanctioned Violence in Early China.* New York: SUNY Press.

1999 The *feng* and *shan* sacrifices of Emperor Wu of the Han. In JOSEPH P. MCDERMOTT (ed.) *State and Court Ritual in China.* Cambridge: Cambridge University Press, 50–80.

2000 The City-State in Spring and Autumn China. In MOGENS H. HANSEN (ed.) *A Comparative Study of Thirty City-State Cultures.* Coppenhague: C. A. Reitzels Ferlag, 359–373.

LI LING

1985 *Changsha Zidanku Zhanguo Chu boshu yanjiu.* (Survey of the Warring States Period Chu Silk Manuscript from Zidanku, Changsha) Beijing: Zhonghua.

1995–96 An Archaeological Study of Taiyi (Grand One) Worship. *Early Medieval China* 2: 1–39.

LI LING – COOK, CONSTANCE A.
1999 Translation of the Chu Silk Manuscript. In COOK, CONSTANCE A. – MAJOR, JOHN S. (eds.) *Defining Chu. Image and Reality in Ancient China.* Honolulu: Hawai'i University Press, 171–176.

LO, ALLAN CHUNG HANG
1995 The Metamorphosis of Ancient Chinese Myths. *Journal of Oriental Studies* 33.2: 186–229.

LOEWE, MICHAEL
1990 The Juedi Games: A Re-enactment of the Battle between Chiyou and Xianyuan? In W. L. IDEMA – E. ZÜRCHER (eds.) *Thought and Law in Qin and Han China.* Leiden: E. J. Brill, 140–157.
1994 *Divination, mythology and monarchy in Han China.* Cambridge: Cambridge University Press.
1994a *Ways to Paradise: The Chinese Quest for Immortality.* Taipei: SMC Publishing Inc. (1st ed. 1979)

MA CHANGYI (ed.)
1994 *Zhongguo shenhuaxue wenlun xuancui.* I–II. ('Selections from essays on Chinese mythology'). Beijing: Zhongguo guangbo dianshi chubanshe.

MACKENZIE, COLIN
1987 The Chu Tradion of Wood Carving. In ROSEMARY E. SCOTT – GRAHAM HUTT (eds.) *Style in the East Asian Tradition.* London: School of Oriental and African Studies, University of London, 82–102.
1993 Meaning and Style in the Art of Chu. In RODERICK WHITFIELD (ed.) *The Problem of Meaning in Early Chinese Ritual Bronzes.* London: The Percival David Foundation of Chinese Art, School of Oriental and African Studies, University of London, 119–149.

MACKENZIE, D.A.
1994 *Myths of China and Japan.* New York: Gramercy Books.

MAIR, VICTOR H.
1998 *Wandering on the Way. Early Taoist Tales and Parables of Chuang Tzu.* Honolulu: University of Hawai'i Press.

MAJOR, JOHN S.
1978 Research priorities in the study of *Chu* religions. *History of Religions* 17: 226–243.
1993 *Heaven and Earth in Early Han Thought.* New York: SUNY Press.
1999 Characteristics of Late Chu Religion. In COOK, CONSTANCE A. – MAJOR, JOHN S. (eds.) *Defining Chu. Image and Reality in Ancient China.* Honolulu: Hawai'i University Press, 121–143.

MÄNCHEN-HELFEN, O.
1924 The later books of the Shan-hai-jing. *Asia Major* 1: 550–586.

MASPERO, HENRI
1924 Légendes mythologiques dans le *Chou King. Journal Asiatique* 204: 1–100.

1971   Le Taoïsme. In PAUL DEMIÉVILLE (ed.) *Mélanges posthumes sur les religions et l'histoire de la Chine*. Paris: Gallimard, 34–46.

MATHIEU, RÉMI

1987   Chamanes et chamanisme en Chine ancienne. *L'Homme* 27: 10–34.

1983   *Étude sur la mythologie et l'ethnologie de la Chine ancienne*. Paris: Collége de France.

1989   *Anthologie des mythes et légendes de la Chine ancienne*. Paris: Gallimard.

1992   Yu le Grand et Le Mythe du Déluge dans la Chine ancienne. *T'oung Pao* 78: 162–190.

MIYAKAWA, H. – KOLLAUTZ, A.

1966   Zur Ur- und Vorgeschichte des Schamanismus. Geweihbekrönung und Vogelkleid und ihre Beziehungen zur Magie des Totemismus. *Zeitschrift für Ethnologie* 91: 161–193.

MÜNKE, W.

1976   *Die classische chinesische Mythologie*. Stuttgart: Ernst Klett.

NAQUIN, SUSAN – CHÜN-FANG YÜ (eds.)

1992   *Pilgrims and sacred sites in China*. Berkeley – Los Angeles – Oxford: University of California Press.

NIENHAUSER, WILLIAM. H., Jr. (ed.)

1986   *The Indiana Companion to Traditional Chinese Literature*. Bloomington – Indianapolis: Indiana University Press.

NIENHAUSER, WILLIAM H., Jr. (ed.) et. al. (trans.)

1994   *The Grand Scribe's Records*. Vol. VII. Bloomington – Indianapolis: Indiana University Press.

NUMAZAWA, K.

1984   The Cultural-Historical Background of Myths on the Separation of Sky and Earth. In ALAN DUNDES (ed.) *Sacred Narrative: Readings in the Theory of Myth*. Berkeley – Los Angeles: University of California Press, 182–192.

PETERS, HEATHER

1983   *The Role of the State of Chu in Eastern Zhou Period China: A Study of Interaction and Exchange in the South*. (Ph. D. Diss.) New Haven: Yale University.

POO, MU-CHOU

1998   *In Search of Personal Welfare. A View of Ancient Chinese Religion*. New York: SUNY Press.

PORKERT, DEBORAH L.

1996   *From deluge to discourse. Myth, history, and the Generation of Chinese Fiction*. New York: SUNY Press.

PREGADIO, FABRIZIO

1980–90 The Medical Texts of Ma-wang-tui. *Cahiers d'Extrême-Asie* 5: 381–186.

RAO ZONGYI

1972   Some Aspects of the Calendar, Astrology, and Religious Concepts of the Ch'u People as Revealed in the Ch'u Silk Manuscript. In BARNARD,

NOEL – FRASER, DONALD (eds.) *Early Chinese Art and Its Possible Influence in the Pacific Basin.* New York: Intercultural Arts Press. Vol. 1.: 113–122.

RAWSON, JESSICA
    1980 *Ancient China. Art and Archaeology.* London: British Museum.
    1989 *Chu* Influence on the Development of Han bronze vessels. *Arts Asiatique* 64: 84–99.
    1996 *Mysteries of Ancient China. New Discoveries from the Early Dynasties.* London: British Museum Press.
    1996a From Ritual Vessels to Pottery Tomb Figures: Changes in Ancient Chinese Burial Practice. *Orientations* 27: 9: 42–49.
    1998 Commanding the spirits: Control Through Bronze and Jade. *Orientations* 29: 2: 33–45.

ROBINET, ISABELLE
    1993 *Taoist Meditation. The Mao-shan Tradition of Great Purity.* New York: SUNY Press.
    2000 *Shangqing* – Highest Clarity. In LIVIA KOHN (ed.) *Daoism Handbook.* Leiden: E. J. Brill, 196–224.

ROTH, HAROLD D.
    1991 Who compiled the Chuang Tzu? In HENRY ROSEMONT, JR. (ed.) *Chinese Texts and Philosophical Contexts. Essays Dedicated to Angus C. Graham.* La Salle: Open Court, 79–128.
    1992 *The Textual History of the Huai-nan tzu.* Michigan: Ann Arbor.
    1993 Chuang tzu. In MICHAEL LOEWE (ed.) *Early Chinese Texts: A Bibliographical Guide.* Berkeley: University of California, 56–66.

SALMONY, ALFRED
    1954 *Antler and Tongue, An Essay on Ancient Chinese Symbolism and Its Implications.* Ascona: Artibus Asiae Publishers. [Artibus Asiae Suppl. 13]

SANTILLANA, GIORGIO DE – DECHEND, HERTHA VON
    1995 *Hamlet malma* (Hamlet's mill). (Trans. Dr. J. VÉGVÁRI) Budapest: Pontifex Kiadó.

SCHAFER, E. H.
    1951 Ritual Exposure in Ancient China. *Harvard Journal of Asiatic Studies* 14: 130–184.

SCHIPPER, KRISTOPHER
    1993 *The Taoist Body.* Taipei: SMC Publishing INC.

SCHNEIDER, LAURENCE A.
    1980 *A Madman of Chu. The Chinese Myth of Loyalty and Dissent.* Berkeley – Los Angeles – London: University of California Press.

SEIDEL, ANNA K.
    1969 *La Divinisation de Lao tseu dans le Taoisme des Han.* Paris: École Francaise d'Extrême-Orient.

SHAUGHNESSY, EDWARD
    1997 The Composition of 'Qian' and 'Kun' Hexagrams of the Zhouyi. In *Before Confucius: Studies in the Creation of the Chinese Classics.* New York: SUNY Press, 197–219.

1999 Western Zhou History. In M. LOEWE – E.L. SHAUGHNESSY (eds.) *The Cambridge History of Ancient China*. New York: CUP, 292–351.

SO, JENNY F.

1997 Red and Black on Some Early Chinese Painted Lacquers. *Orientations* 28: 9: 60–66.

1999 Chu Art: Link between the Old and New. In COOK, CONSTANCE A. – MAJOR, JOHN S. (eds.) *Defining Chu. Image and Reality in Ancient China*. Honolulu: Hawai'i University Press, 33–47.

SUKHU, GOPAL

1999 Monkeys, Shamans, Emperors, and Poets. The Chuci and Images of Chu during the Han Dynasty. In COOK, CONSTANCE A. – MAJOR, JOHN S. (eds.) *Defining Chu. Image and Reality in Ancient China*. Honolulu: Hawai'i University Press, 145–165.

TEISER, S. F.

1985–86 Engulfing the Bounds of Order: The Myth of the Great Flood in Chinese Tradition. *Journal of Chinese Religions* 13–14: 15–43.

THEERN, K. L. ET AL.

1985 *Shan Hai Ching*. Taipei: National Institute for Compilation and Translation.

THIEL, JOSEF P.

1968 Schamanismus im Alten China. *Sinologica* 10: 149–204.

THOMPSON, STITH

1955 *Motif-Index of Folk-Literature*. Copenhagen: Rosenkilde and Bagger.

TOKAREV, SZ. A.

1988 *Mitológiai Enciklopédia*. (The Encyclopaedia of Mythologies) Vol. II. Budapest: Gondolat.

TŐKEI, FERENC

1986 *A kínai elégia születése*. (The Birth of Chinese Elegy) Budapest: Kossuth Kiadó.

WALEY, ARTHUR

1955 *The Nine Songs. A Study of Shamanism in Ancient China*. London: George Allen & Unwin.

WATERS, GEOFFREY R.

1985 *Three Elegies of Ch'u. An Introduction to the Traditional Interpretation of the Ch'u Tz'u*. Ann Arbor, Michigan: The University of Wisconsin Press.

WELD, SUSAN

1999 Chu Law in Action. Legal Documents from Tomb 2 at Baoshan. In COOK, CONSTANCE A. – MAJOR, JOHN S. (eds.) *Defining Chu. Image and Reality in Ancient China*. Honolulu: Hawai'i University Press, 77–97.

WERNER, E. T. C.

1986 *Ancient tales and folklore of China*. London: Bracken Books.

WILKINSON, ENDYMION

1998 *Chinese History: A Manual*. Cambridge: Harvard University Asia Center.

WU HUNG

1987 *Xiwangmu*, the Queen Mother of the West. *Orientations* 18: 24–33.

1992 Art in a Ritual Context. Rethinking *Mawangdui*. *Early China* 17: 111–144.

YU, D. C.

1981 The Creation Myth and its Symbolism in Classical Taoism. *Philosophy East and West* 31: 4: 479–500.

1986 The Creation Myth of Chaos in the Taoist Canon. *Journal of Oriental Studies* 24: 1–20.

YÜ YING-SHIH

1987 "O, Soul, come Back!" A Study in the Changing Conceptions of the Soul and Afterlife in Pre-Buddhist China. *Harvard Journal of Asiatic Studies* 47: 363–395.

YU WEICHAO

1995 Menschen und Götter in der Kultur von *Chu*. In ROGER GOEPPER (ed.) *Das alte China: Menschen und Götter im Reich der Mitte. 5000 v. Chr. – 220 nach Chr: Kulturstiftung Ruhr, Essen, Villa Hügel, 2. Juni 1995 – 5. November 1995.* München: Hirmer, 130–135.

YUAN KE

1985 *Zhongguo gudai shenhua* (Ancient Chinese Mythology). Shanghai: Shanghai cishu chubanshe.

1993 *Dragons and Dynasties: An Introduction to Chinese Mythology.* New York: Penguin.

ZHANG ZHENGMING

1996 *Chu wenhua shi* (The history of Chu culture). Shanghai: Shanghai Renmin chubanshe.

ZHENG DEKUN

1963 *Archaeology in China.* Vol. III. University of Toronto Press: W. Heffer and Sons Ltd.

PÉTER SIMONCSICS

Shaman as the Hero of a Kamassian Tale: a Riddle in Narration

THE TALE

There was a poor man whose name was *Tarchabərdzha*. He had a jade which was lame. He saddled her and tied a black sack and a birchbark to the saddle, then he set off. He met a bear who said to him: "Take me your companion and put me into the black sack!" He did as he was told and set off again. He met a wolf who said: "Take me your companion and put me into the black sack!" Then he met water. He scooped the water into his black sack, with a basket he scooped it, then he tied the sack to the saddle of his mare. Later he saw a village on the seashore, but he did not ride to the village. He dismounted and made a fire. He tied up his horse and sat down to wait. The Tsar came along and caught sight of him: "Who is sitting there beside his tied up horse and who is treading my green grass without asking my permission?" And he gave an order to his servant to find out what kind of a man he was who dared tread the grass of the Tsar and what did he want? The servant did as he was told and asked: "What kind of a man are you and what are you looking for here?" "I came to take the Tsar's daughter." "Go and tell him to retire while he can go back of his own will." "I will not retire." "If he does not retire willingly, I take offence. I shall release the wild horses and they will knock him down together with his mare, they will tear them apart." The Tsar let his wild horses run, but our man opened his black sack and let out the black bear. The bear followed the horses and chased them away. "Release the bulls to trample that man and his mare to death!" Our man opened the black sack and released the wolf. The wolf chased away the bulls into the forest. Then the Tsar ordered his men to arrest our man. So they surrounded him and tried to grab him. Then he opened the black sack again, checked it and poured the water onto the Tsar's men. The water kept them off from him.

"*Tartyabartya, pol bartya,* half of my cattle is yours, half of my empire is yours and my daughter is yours." "I don't want your cattle, I do not want your empire, I want only your princess-daughter." Then he took the basket and poured out the water. The Tsar gave him his daughter. He put her onto the back of the lame mare and mounting his horse they together rode off to his tent. (Translation of Tale 2 published by DONNER 1944: 88–90)

THE PLOT

The hero of narration is originally a poor man who set out to sue for the hand of the Tsar's daughter. His helpers are of three kinds: a horse which is a usual assistant of the hero in mythologies of nomadic shepherds (Turkic type), the bear and the wolf, usual assistants of shamans in hunting societies of the taiga and the tundra (Uralic type) and an element, water (universal type). It is the last of these assistants, the element water which brings final victory to the hero by sweeping away his enemies and helps him to reach his goal: to win the hand of the Tsar's daughter. Thus the story reveals also the elementary force of love through the metaphor of flood.

THE MYSTERY

The name of the hero occurs in two versions in the tale: (1) *Tarchabərdʑha* and (2) in a parallelism as *Tartyabartya pol bartya*.

Starting with the second occurrence I am trying to decipher this form. The parallelism helps us to identify constant and variable elements of the text. *tya* is a constant element which by its repeated occurrence gives the frame of the parallelism:

$$...tya\ ...tya$$
$$...\ \ ...tya$$

The element *tya* can be identified as a compound of the third person singular possessive suffix *ty* + an inetymological expletive *a*. Variables—represented by dots (...) in the scheme above—are the three one syllable word: *tar* "hair, feather", *bar* "all" and *pol* "to be immersed into a stream; to be overcome by sexual desire". Thus the meaning of this cryptic parallelism can be given as "one who is covered all over in feathers/hair is swept away by passion" or "The feathered man/hairy man is in trance". Even more surprising is the result if we consider the first occurrence and put together the variables: we get the form *tarbə* which is the etymon for "shaman" in the Kamassian lexicon. Both occurrences of the name refer to the same denotatum, but in different ways. The parallelism tells a story which, in its turn, is in congruence with the plot of the tale by describing the hero, the first occurrence tries to utter and, at the same time, also to conceal a word. Kamassian poetic speech relies on transformations at the level of morphology (break-up of the word by expletives, splitting words into constituent morphs and intermixing with inetymological phonic material etc.) just as do the northern Samoyedic traditions, Nenets and Nganasan. This tale is a good example of craftmanship of cryptic art which characterizes the language of ritual.

REFERENCES

DONNER, KAI
   1944 *Kamassisches Wörterbuch nebst Sprachproben und Hauptzügen der Grammatik, bearbeitet und herausgegeben von A. Joki.* Helsinki: Lexica Societatis Finno-Ugricae 8.
SIMONCSICS PÉTER
   1998 *Kamassian.* In ABONDOLO, DANIEL (ed.) *The Uralic Languages.* London – New York: Routledge, 580–601.

KATALIN URAY-KŐHALMI

The Myth of Nishan Shaman

The first variant of Nishan Shaman's myth was published by M. P. VOLKOVA as "Nishan Shaman's Book" (*Nišan šaman i bitxe*) with a Russian translation in 1961. It has since been translated into various foreign languages. That was the most complete version collected by the Russian researcher GREBENSČIKOV in Manchuria between 1908 and 1913. He already noted that several variants were alive among the Manchus and their neighbours. SHIROKOGOROFF also put down a variant, but it disappeared without a trace, together with the rest of his notes. Interest was kindled in this story of great cultural historical appeal after the 1960s, with several variants being published. G. STARY published it in translation and transcription, together with the other three variants collected by GREBENSCIKOV and preserved in the manuscript collection of the Oriental Institute in St. Petersburg (STARY 1985). There is hardly any difference in content between these and the variant published by VOLKOVA, but they are fragmentary at places and the versified inserts are missing, which strongly resemble shamanic rhymes both in structure, style and the use of repetitive rhythm words. STARY also included in this volume a Nishan story notated in Chinese in a Manchurian village, *Ilan boo i gasan*, in 1961, which widely differs from all the so-far known variants.

Let me tell the main episodes of the story. The story as included in the St. Petersburg manuscripts (it can be termed the basic story marked 1, 1a, 1b, 1c hereinafter) is as follows: [Episode A]: during the Ming Dynasty, there lives a wealthy high dignitary, *Baldu Bayan*, in the village of Lule, whose son died in a hunt at the age of 15. He and his wife had begged for an offspring for years, when at last a beautiful and talented boy was born to them, named *Sergudai Fiyanggo* and brought up with great care. [ep. B]: When the boy turns 15, he begs his parents to let him practice his riding and arching skills in a remote forest. The aged parents are reluctant, but eventually they comply and let him go in the company of two faithful servants. They kill a lot of game. [ep. C]: The boy suddenly falls ill and dies in no time. The two faithful servants, *Ahalji* and *Bahalji* take the body home sobbing. The desperate parents lay him out at home and prepare for the burial. [ep. D]: A ragged old beggar appears who, having seen the corpse, advises the father to urgently visit *Nishan Shaman* in a nearby village, as she is capable of bringing souls back from the realm of the dead. Stepping out of the gate, the old man disappears/flies off on a cloud of five colours. [ep. E]: The father rides into the given village, where he sees a young woman hanging out clothes to dry. He asks her about the shamaness. She sends him to the other end of the village. There he learns that the woman hanging out the clothes was the shamaness. He returns to her and begs her for help. Though reluctantly she agrees to accompany Baldu Bayan, but first she says good-bye to her old mother-in-law. [ep. F]: Received with great reverence in Baldu Bayan's house, the shamaness does not find anyone among those gathered there who could help her in the ritual. She has her tested assistant, actually her young lover, *Nari Fiyanggu*, fetched. [ep. G]: The two prepare for the ceremony: a dog born at the same time as the boy, a cock, soy cheese and sacrificial paper money are prepared. The shamaness dons the ceremonial clothes, falls into a trance to the drumming of her assistant and her soul travels to the netherworld. [ep. H]: In the company of her helping spirits in the shape of animals, she reaches a river. An ugly, bad-tempered one-armed, one-eyed ferryman with a wounded arm takes her across the river for some soy cheese and money. The ferryman tells her that Sergudai Fiyanggu was taken over by a spirit called *Monggoldai Nakču* the other day. The shamaness crosses the next river with the help of her drum. [ep. I]: First she goes to the palace of Monggoldai Nakču and learns that the boy has been received by *Ilmun khan*, the lord of the netherworld because he liked the handsome and clever boy. The shamaness cannot enter Ilmun khan's palace but she has the soul of the boy playing with other children in the courtyard kidnapped by her helping spirit appearing as an eagle. [ep. J]: Noticing the disappearance of his favourite, Ilmun khan sends Monggoldai Nakču after the shamaness. The threats do not frighten the shamaness, she offers the spirit money. The spirit wants the cock and the dog for the soul. The shamaness only gives them when she has the promise that the boy's life will be extended. After much wrangling, the shamaness earns 90 years, good health and many offspring for her protege.[1] She plays a trick on the spirit with the voices of the dog and the cock and she resumes her way. [ep. K]: A dramatic meeting between the shamaness and her dead husband. He is enraged that she freed

---

[1] Paralleled to Ath 828 and Mahabharata III. 293–99: Savitri and Yama.

someone else from the other world and wishes to throw Nishan into a cauldron of boiling oil. Although the shamaness keeps explaining that she is unable to bring a soul back to a decaying body, the husband still behaves violently. Nishan gets angry and with her helping crane spirit, she removes his soul to the city of *Fungtu* (Ch. *Fengdu*) in the world beneath from where there is no return. (This episode often follows after the crossing of the river.) [ep. L]: The shamaness Nishan arrives at the splendid palace of *Omosi Mama*. The souls of children to be born are prepared for life on earth there. Among the goddess's assistants she meets the wife of Nari Fiyanggu, who died of the plague the year before. The deity shows Nishan what punishment is imposed for what sins in hell. But she also shows the way of salvation with the help of Buddha's teaching. [ep. M]: The shamaness returns back to earth with the soul and revives the boy. Everyone celebrates her and Baldu Bayan releases her with princely presents. At home she resorts to a virtuous life, breaks her relationship with Nari Fiyanggu and lechery. [ep. N]: Her mother-in-law learns that she met her husband's spirit and did not bring him back but cast him into Fungtu. She reports on her at the town court. The case is investigated and Nishan is found guilty of casting her husband's spirit into Fungtu. For final deliberation, the case is presented to the emperor. [ep. O]: The emperor confiscates the shamaness's instruments and has them cast into a deep well so that she cannot do harm any more.

The story of the Chinese variant put down by JIN JIZONG (No. 2) is largely different from the St. Petersburg versions (STARY 1985: i–iv.). The shamaness is called *Nüdan*. She is a young widow who learns shamanistic practices to keep her old mother-in-law. She can bring souls back from death so she becomes very famous. The emperor's son falls ill and despite the cures of two lamas, he dies [=C]. Someone recommends Nüdan [=D]. The emperor sends a coach to fetch her. She is hanging out clothes. She packs the paraphernalia of shamanic work and starts [=E]. The two jealous lamas want to kill her, waiting to ambush her by the palace gate, but she senses danger and flies over the gate with the help of her drum, right into the throne-room. The emperor is a bit annoyed, but says nothing for his son's sake. He orders her to bring back his son's soul from the netherworld. The shamaness sets out and meets the spirit of her husband, and episode K takes place. Then she finds the prince's soul in a great hall playing with other children [=I]. She brings back the soul and revives the prince, the emperor is glad [=M]. The emperor now orders her to bring back his sister's soul who died three years earlier. The shamaness refuses as the body has decayed. The emperor falls in a rage, remembers that Nüdan flew over the gate, violating the laws. The two jealous lamas also fuel his wrath [ep. P]. The emperor casts the shamaness into a deep pit in iron shackles. The shamaness dies [=O]. Suddenly darkness settles on the palace. A huge bird flies over it. An arrow is shot at the bird, a huge falcon feather falls down. A counsellor of the emperor realizes that it is the helping spirit of the unjustly killed shamaness. The emperor repents his sin and orders annual offerings in honour of the shamaness and the ancestors. That is why Nüdan shamaness is regarded as the founder of shamanism [=Q].

The second variant is about a dead prince, without hunting being mentioned. It contains no bargaining for further years, or the visit to Omosi Mama's palace. Though the encounter with the husband is included, she is not punished for that but for flying over the gate and refusing to revive the emperor's sister. The shamaness's helping spirit taking a bird's shape only appears after her death, not for the liberation of the boy's spirit or for taking her husband's soul to Fungtu. A new instance is the casting of the shamaness herself into the pit, not only her tools, and her death is also new. Her innocent death turns her into the ancestor of shamans.

It is highly informative to compare these Manchu variants with versions spread among related and neighbouring peoples. From among related ethnic groups, there is a *Heẓe* variant (a Nanai dialect along the Sungari) [=3], a *Solon* variant (equestrian Tunguz people) [=4] and a *Mergen Oročon* version (a north-Manchurian Tunguz dialect) [=5]. Among their neighbours, two *Dahur* variants are known [=6, 7]. The Dahurs have been in close cultural contact with the Tunguz people of Manchuria. They hunt and cultivate gardens and fields. The mirroring of the relevant way of life is conspicuous in the variants. In the Manchu variants in St Petersburg the Chinese influence is striking: including the traditional Chinese etiquette and funeral customs in the house of Baldu Bayan and the town of Fungtu in the world beneath, derived from Taoism. The presentation of punishments in hell is a Buddhist influence. The variant notated by JIN JIZONG is entirely in a Chinese setting [2]. The Heze group live in China and prusue an ancient way of life, hunting, fishing and tilling land. In their variant, the hunt is emphasized [3] and the involvement of the shamanic spirits is more elaborate. The husband's spirit appears after the crossing of the first river, but the spirit of the shamanic drum takes him beyond the mountains in the netherworld, not to Fungtu. The shamaness receives presents at the end. She is not punished, but she does not become the ancestor of shamans, either (RICHTSFELD 1989).

Solons are Tunguz people who switched over to steppe cattle breeding in the Mongolian way back in the 15th–16th centuries. This is also verified by their story [4]. The request of the old couple is heard by the Mongol deity *Qormusda Tengri*. The lord of the netherworld is not Ilmun khan but the Turkic–Mongol *Erlik khan*. His old envoy is Mongol *Tsagan Ebügen*. Affluent *Bardu Bayan* lives in a yurt and has large studs and herds. The sacrificial animals are a dog and a goat, the soy cheese gives way to dried noodles. Upon the mother-in-law's complaint the shamaness hurles her husband into the navel of the earth, Qormusda sends 9 *Jangjun* (military dignitaries) to kill her in chains also cast into the navel of the earth. [=O]. Before she dies, the shamaness spits around and the shamans arise so [=Q]. A seemingly later moment also appears: in episode K the husband tears off the drum's half, that's why shamans have drums covered on one end only, and that is why they can no longer revive the dead but merely banish the demons. HEISSIG mentions two analogies, one Evenki and one Khorchin Mongol. In both, lamas damage the drums (HEISSIG 1997: 227–230). That suggests that these popular, rationalizing explanations were created in the 15th–16th centuries during the forced conversion to Lamaism. The cause for the one-sidedness of shaman drums is certainly different, since the Siberian shaman drums have long been one-sided. In China, on the other hand, there were drums with both ends covered, so the episode may compare the shamanic drums to these.

G. HEYNE published a Mergen Orochon (Oroqen) variant [5] of the myth of Nishan shaman (HEYNE 1999). The Mergen Orochons are Tunguz people pursuing typical nomadic hunting occupations in the taiga. The story of 'Neshun Shaman' was put down by WALTHER STÜTZNER in 1927–28. This shamaness was very powerful, she was alone capable of traversing the entire netherworld, *irmunkan*, in her lifetime. She did so when her only son *Segune Biangö* died at the age of 15 [C]. She got to the netherworld crossing a river on her drum [H], she took a hen and dog as animal sacrifices [G]. In three days she got the child's soul back from Irmunkan [I] and bargained for more years [J] as well. Hearing it, the emperor summoned Neshun to revive his dear daughter dead for three years [P]. The shamaness brought back her soul but when she saw her decayed body, she fled back to the netherworld in horror. The emperor got outraged, cast her in a deep well, with iron chains, stones and a curse on paper above her [O]. Though the shamaness died, a little bell of her clothes—her helping spirit—was freed and has lived to this day [Q]. In this variant, the husband's spirit does not appear, and Omosi Mama and the Buddhist hell are also excluded, similarly to all other Tunguz variants. No signs of Chinese or Mongolian influence can be detected.

The Dahurs have long been living near the rivers Nonni and Amur in North Manchuria, subsisting on land tillage, cattle breeding and hunting. They were long drawn under the cultural influence of the Manchus. One of

the Dahur variants was published by the Mongolian researcher
ENGKEBATU (ENGKEBATU – NAR 1985: 187–220) in Mongolian [6], the
other was recorded by CAROLINE HUMPHREY in Morin Dawaa [7]. The son
of a rich man, *Barlo Bayin, Heregdei Piayanggu* is a great hunter and also kills
roes. That is taboo to the Dahurs [B]. The spirits of the animals complain
to the lord of death, who seizes the youth's soul and he dies [C]. The
grieving old father is recommended to see *Isan Shaman / Yadgan.* From
there, the story is similar to the St. Petersburg Manchu variants, including
the hanging of the clothes [D, F, H, I, J]. The shaman's assistant is called
Narati Anggu. A limp ferryman takes the shamaness across the river. The
boy's spirit is playing ball with the son of *Irmu khan.* Isan's *Guarad*
(=Garudi) helping spirit kidnaps him. Longer life is arranged in an office in
charge of life lengths. No Monggoldai Nakču or similar spirits are included.
The shamaness meets her husband's soul [K], but sends him to Fengtu only
in version 6, and boxes his ears in version 7. Similarly to the Manchu
versions (and unlike the Nanai and Tunguz variants), *Ome* (Omosi Mama)
appears and relates the agonies of hell [L]. Isan takes the boy's soul home
and revives him. The story deviates at this point, as the Chinese emperor
summons her to revive his dead wife. She fails [P]. The outraged ruler hurls
her in a deep pit chained [O]. Before dying, Isan leaves a black glass behind
from which shamanic souls appear. In another Dahur variant [6] the
shamans arise from her scattered hair [Q]. Thus the Dahurs also venerate
her as the ancestress of shamans (HUMPHREY 1996: 306–312, 316–319).

The belief that Nishan was the first shaman and the later shamans all
derive from her is included in the Solon, Mergen Orochon and Dahur
stories [4, 5, 6, 7]. It is clear here that the myth of the first shaman was tied
to the story of Nishan shaman. LOPATIN (1922: 237–238, 1960: 134–135)
recorded and published a Nanai myth which says that *Hadau,* the world
creating Demiurge is bothered by his creations, the people getting old and
dying. He sees a spirit in his dream who orders him to become a shaman
and escort the souls of the deceased to the netherworld. To become a
shaman, he needs to seek the tree that grows drums, bells, mirrors, antlers,
spirit images and shoot as many of them with his bow as necessary. Hadau
finds the tree but shoots too many of the objects which scatter all over the
world. From them arise the shamans. The same story was also recorded by
Hungarian BENEDEK BARÁTHOSI-BALOGH from a man called *Ajdanu* in
the village of Udan in 1908–14 (BARÁTHOSI-BALOGH 1996: 72–73). All that
differs here is the spirit coming in the shape of an old man with a long
white beard and that Hadau gets the shamanic objects from a tree called
kunguru jagdi, whose bark is all reptiles and creeping beasts, the roots are
snakes, the leaves are metal mirrors, and the flowers are bells. He collects

them in a sack but when he gets them out at home, many of them fly off the smoke-hole and settle on suitable people who thus become shamans.

Let us infer some conclusions now. Studying the Nishan shaman stories one can contend that the names of the characters are essentially identical. The shamaness is called *Nišan, Nizan, Nešan, Yasen, Nüdan* in the Manchu variants (1, 1a, 1b, 2). In the Heze version (3) it is *Yi-xin* pronounced *Yisin*, in the Solon variant (4) *Esan*, in Mergen Orochon (5) *Nešun*, in the Dahur versions (6,7) *Isan*. In the Manchu and Tunguz variants the rich official is called *Baldu Bayan* (1, 4) and *Bardu Bayan* (3), in the Dahur version *Bayan Bolod* (6) and *Barlo Bayin*. The boy is called (1) *Sergudai Fiyanggo*, (1a) *Surdai Fiyanggu*, (1b) *Sergudi Fiyanggu*, (3) *Sirhude Fiyanggu*, (4) *Serwildipenku*, (5) *Sergune Biangö*, (7) *Heregdei Piyangi*—which are all identical. When the assistant is named, the name is also the same: (1) *Nari Fiyanggu*, (3) *Nalin Fiyanggu*, (4) *Narguldipenku*, (7) *Narati Anggu*. They either go back to a common Manchu source, or the Manchu story influenced the rest. It is, however, striking when one compares the variants that they divide into two major groups irrespective of cultural and linguistic environment: in a) Baldu Bayan's son dies and is resurrected (1, 1a, 1b, 3, 4, 7) and in b) the emperor himself is the bereaved. In the latter, not only the boy's soul, but also the soul of his sister, daughter, wife (2, 5, 7 cf. ep. P) must be retrieved. In the Orochon and Dahur stories, the emperor orders the shamaness to find the daughter and wife, respectively after the successful resuscitation, so here the two motifs are combined. Probably two elaborations of a basic story influenced one another or got merged. Well-meaning and rich gentlemen called *Baldu / Bardo / Pardo Bayan* also appear in other Manchu stories and myths (HEFTER 1939: 116). One may presume that the revival of the emperor's son is the older story. The skeleton is the following: a prestigeous gentleman's/emperor's young son dies. A young yet powerful shamaness brings the child's soul back. After the initial happiness, they turn against the shamaness for various reasons and even kill her.

Although not without doubts and reluctance, let me add here a presumably historical episode preserved about the Zhuan-zhuan rulers by the *Weishu* and *Beishi* (*Weishu* 103, *Beishi* 98; CSONGOR 1993: 32–3). Towards the end of the dynasty, when *Chounu* was regnant (508–521), one of his sons called Zuihu got lost. There was a *wu* or healing shamaness, *Shidouhun Diwan*, or shortly *Diwan* who behaved as if she were in contact with spirits. This shamaness said the boy was in heaven but she could bring him back. *Chounu* and the mother were overjoyed. In mid-autumn the shamaness set up a tent next to the big lake, fasted for seven days to be able to communicate with the heavenly spirits purified and after a night Zuihu was there in the tent saying he had been in heaven all the time.

Diwan was said to be a saintly woman and made katun (title of a ruler's wife). Diwan's beauty mesmerized the ruler so that he followed her advice in everything. Years later, when Zuihu grew up, he told his mother he had been in Diwan's house and not in heaven and she had taught him what to say. The mother complained to Chounu, who did not believe her. When Diwan heard it, she slandered Zuihu to the ruler and he had him killed. Thereupon Chounu's mother, Zuihu's grandmother secretly asked some people to stifle Diwan, and when Chounu returned from a campaign defeated, he and his senior advisers were also murdered upon his mother's order. The basis story can also be discerned here: the dead young prince, the beautiful shamaness who brings him back from death and who is first celebrated and then killed for her sins/failure. The Nishan Shaman story may be a very old North Manchurian tradition. Perhaps other early variants will be found.

REFERENCES

BARÁTHOSI-BALOGH, BENEDEK
  1996 *Távoli utakon (On Distant Ways)*. Budapest: Museum of Ethnography.
ČOG – ONON – NAYIDAN – MERGENBÖKE
  1988 *Evengki arad-un aman üliger*. Hailar: Öber mongol-un soyul-in keblel-ün goriya.
CSONGOR, BARNABÁS
  1993 *Kínai források az ázsiai avarokról* (Chinese Sources on the Asian Avars). Történelem és kultúra 9. Budapest: Balassi Kiadó – Orientalisztikai Munkaközösség.
ENGKEBATU – NAR
  1985 *Dagur kelen-ü üge kelelge-yin materiyal*. Kökehota.
HEFTER, JOHN
  1939 Moculin – Ein Heldenepos der Golden. *Sinica* 14: 108–150.
HEISSIG, WALTHER
  1997 Zu zwei evenkisch-daghurischen Varianten des mandschu Erzählstoffes "Nišan šaman-i bithe." *Central Asiatic Journal* 41: 200–230.
HEYNE, F. GEORG
  1999 Neshun-Saman – eine Schamanengeschichte der Mergen Oroqen. *Kleine Beiträge aus dem Staatlichen Museum für Völkerkunde Dresden* (Dresden) 17: 38–48.
HUMPHREY, CAROLINE – URGUNGE ONON
  1996 *Shamans and Elders. Experience, knowledge and power among the Daur Mongols*. Oxford: Clarendon Press.
LOPATIN, IVAN A.
  1922 *Goldy amurskie, ussurijskie i sungarijskie*. Vladivostok: OIAK.

1960 *The Cult of Dead among the Natives of the Amur Basin.* 's-Gravenhage: Mouton & Co.

NOWAK, MARGARET – DURRANT, STEPHEN
1977 *The tale of the Nishan Shamaness.* Seattle–London: University of Washington Press.

RICHTSFELD, BRUNO J.
1989 Die Mandschu-Erzählung "Nišan saman-i bithe" bei den Hezhe: *Münchener Beiträge zur Völkerkunde* 2: 117–155.

STARY, GIOVANNI
1985 *Three unedited manuscripts of the Manchu epic tale "Nišan šaman-i bithe".* Wiesbaden: Harrassowitz.

VOLKOVA, MARIJA PETROVNA
1961 *Nišan saman-i bithe (Predanie o nišanskoj šamanke)* Moskva: Nauka.

EPISODES IN NISHAN SHAMANESS

Variant:	A	B	C	D	E	F	G	H	I	J	K	L	M	N	O	P	Q
1. Mandchu (VOLKOVA – STARY)	A	B	C	D	E	F	G	H	I	J	K	L	M	N	O		
1a. – „ -- -- „ -- (VOLKOVA – STARY)			C	D	E		G	H	I								
1b. –„ -- -- „ -- (VOLKOVA – STARY)	A	B	C	D	E	F	G	H	I	J	K	L					
2. Chinese (STARY)			C	D	E				I		K		M		O	P	Q
3. Hezhe (RICHTSFELD)	A	B	C	D	E	F	G	H	I	J	K		M				
4. Solon (HEISSIG)	A	B	C	D	E	F	G	H	I	J	K		M				
5. Oroqen (HEYNE)	A		C					H	I	J			M	N	O	P	Q
6. Daghur (ENGKEBATU)		B	C				G			J	K	L	M	N	O		Q
7. Daghur (HUMPHREY)	A	B	C	D	E	F		H	I	J	K	L				P.	Q
8. Zhuan-zhuan	A		C	D			G		I				M	N	O		

Part II.

TRADITIONAL ROLES

DAGMAR EIGNER

Tamang Healing Rituals and Psychotherapy:
a Comparison

TAMANG SHAMANS IN NEPAL

The Tamang are one of the largest ethnic minorities in Nepal. They speak a Tibeto–Burmese language and originally came from Tibet. Many of the clients of the Tamang shamans, however, belong to other ethnic groups. A healer is usually chosen because of the reputation he or she enjoys and not because of having the same cultural background. In the multi-ethnic urban area of Kathmandu Valley, a shaman has to be able to deal with patients coming from a different ethnic group, having a different cultural background, speaking a different mother tongue, and living in a different social world. A healer in such an area often knows nothing about the client before the first consultation. Nepali, a language related to Hindi, is used as the *lingua franca* in Central Nepal.

Tamang shamans gain their knowledge and skills in various ways. For instance, GYANI DOLMA says that she has learnt everything in her dreams. She is in her late fifties and has been practicing as a shaman for about 20 years in Kathmandu Valley. Her father was a powerful, well-known shaman in the eastern hills of Nepal. Nine years after his death, GYANI DOLMA fell ill and remained in that condition for 14 months. Before she recovered she felt overcome by her father's spirit who announced that he would henceforth act through her. The divinities who had already lent healing power to her father would now help her in the work of healing. When her father's long-lost ritual paraphernalia were found, this was considered proof of his genuine spirit speaking through her. The spirit of GYANI DOLMA's deceased father became her teacher, coming to her in her dreams and during the healing rituals, and now gives her everything she needs. She says that in her childhood she was not allowed to attend the rituals her father performed, so she could not learn anything from him when he was still alive.

In contrast, RAM BAHADUR is a young shaman who comes from a village outside Kathmandu Valley and spends some of his time in the community where GYANI DOLMA lives, partly doing his own healing work, which has a different emphasis than that of GYANI DOLMA's work; and also partly assisting her when she wants his help or company in a long difficult night session. Many of RAM BAHADUR's elder relatives have been shamans, and he has learnt myths and ritual procedures from an early age. In his youth, the gods came over him, making him tremble—which in this context is always seen as a sign of possession—and gave him knowledge. This was considered as his calling experience, but, according to his narration, he did not suffer from an initial crisis as GYANI DOLMA did. RAM BAHADUR is a specialist for shamanic myths and tales, and for specific Tamang rituals that he only does for Tamang clients.

THERAPY METHODS

Shamanic healing incorporates a variety of features. Every good shaman has a repertoire of several different methods that he or she uses according to the needs of the specific case. Some shamans say that, first of all, short, simple, inexpensive therapies should be employed. These methods include blowing magical formulae over the patient's body, brushing out the illness with a little broom of rice-straw, chasing away the illness-causing agent with a knife, and giving the patient water mixed with ashes or rice grains, over which magical formulae have been blown, to drink. It is only when the easy and cheap methods do not work, that other rituals have to be performed. Some of them take place in the early evening and are centered around giving offerings to pacify deities and spirits. Every difficult, complicated case calls for a nocturnal healing ceremony that lasts from sunset until dawn.

POSSESSION RITUALS

One of the indications for such a night-long ritual is the patient's possession by a malevolent spirit that is under the control of a witch who has sent the spirit to cause illness. Witches are thought to be real persons motivated by envy and anger. Relatives or neighbours who play an important role in the patient's social relations and with whom the patient may have a conflict, are often accused of witchcraft. In order to appease a witch, those who are involved in the conflict have to reach a symbolic reconciliation with the witch.

Such healing rituals start with the shaman calling guardian divinities through drumming and chanting in front of a small altar table. Spiritual forces are called from outside to give their power and assist in the healing ritual. Then the shaman turns towards the patient and, still drumming and singing, challenges the possessing agent to reveal its identity, requesting it to speak through the patient's mouth. During the nocturnal ceremony, the shaman enters an altered state of consciousness and also tries to induce a similar state in the patient, facilitating this through continuous drumming and singing.

Usually the patient soon enters into an altered state of consciousness and trembles and shakes, which is seen as a sign of possession. The shaman entices the illness-causing spirit with kind empathic words, with promises of food, dress, and jewelry: "Come on, wake up, arise! Don't feel worried! Many might have hit you, many might have thrashed you, my dear child. Your heart might have been torn into shreds. Tell me who you are! You may feel hungry, you may feel thirsty. Don't be sad! I will give you food to eat and clothes to wear. My dear child, please come moving along, opening up all parts of your body. I will give you a band to tie the locks of your hair. I will give you a golden ring to be hung down from between your nostrils. You don't have to worry. My dear child, you don't have to cry. You have to talk with me, discuss things with me."

The elaborate invitations have a certain poetic quality intended to move the patient's heart so that he/she opens up and talks about worry some experiences and unresolved conflicts. The long songs of the shaman—still accompanied by drumming of 4 to 5 beats per second—help to intensify an altered state of consciousness in the patient and, to some extent, in all the people who are present.

The patient is trembling, crying, screaming, and groaning. Finally the illness-causing spirit starts speaking through the patient's mouth and says who it is. As soon as the spirit reveals the identity of its master (the witch who controls and has sent it), very often this person speaks through the patient. The witch is not present at the healing ritual—shamans say witches send "the thing that speaks" so that they can express the hurts they have experienced and talk about problems in the extended family or in the neighbourhood from their own point of view.

This middle part of the ritual is dedicated to the discussion of the interpersonal psychosocial problems. The witch—speaking through the mouth of the patient—is asked by the shaman: "Why are you so angry?

What harm has been done to you? What do you want?" Like in the psychodrama technique as practiced in modern Western psychotherapy, the patient gets into the role of the conflict-partner (the witch) and uses his/her intuition to express the feelings and needs of the conflict-partner. And, like in psychodrama, successful therapy can only be achieved if the patient acquires some understanding of the other person's situation. In possession rituals in Nepal the witch is never one who only does evil and who sends illness for no reason. In this central part of the healing session, the patient should come into inner harmony with the conflict-partner and become free of disturbing emotions and illness-causing tensions (EIGNER 1994, 1996).

The outline of the ritual drama and the standard questions (Who are you? What are your worries? Why has the illness been caused?) provide a language for expressing the problems, and a structure for personal experiences. The patient can change "roles" according to his or her needs and wants. Sometimes the patient talks out of his or her own point of view, explaining the hurts and frustrations that have been experienced, and at other times witches or also ancestor spirits speak through the mouth of the patient about their feelings and past events. The changes of "roles" occur very quickly and without announcement. Thus, different points of view of psychosocial problems are expressed, as is done in some of the techniques of modern Western psychodrama.

In an altered state of consciousness, a patient is optimally accessible to verbal and nonverbal symbolic suggestions. Due to the "possession" by a spirit, and in the protected situation of the healing ritual, the patient can talk freely and act without being held responsible and without having to fear negative consequences. This usually brings about a cathartic abreaction followed by changes of affective attitudes and perceptions. Thus, spirit possession is not only a diagnostic category, but also a therapeutic technique.

Ritual possession can be seen as a system of privileged communication. The patient is unconsciously (or half-consciously) using the possessing entity as a device to communicate personal concerns and complaints to an attentive audience. The previously chaotic and unstructured emotional behaviour is made comprehensible and assumes a socially binding form that everyone has to acknowledge. This may then lead to a resolution of hitherto unaddressed interpersonal conflicts.

In the last part of such a possession ritual the illness-causing agents have to promise to leave the patient and never come back again to cause trouble. These promises strongly suggest to the patient and his family members that with the termination of the healing ritual the patient's suffering will come to an end. Within the framework of the ritual structure the individual problems have been discussed and solutions have been found.

The illness-causing agents are offered a substitute for the patient: a clay figure is connected to the head of the patient by a five-coloured thread. Along this thread the illness-causing spirit should move to its new dwelling place. An egg or a cock also serves as a sacrificial offering to the hungry spirit and, in an indirect way, also as a sort of recompense to the witch. The sacrifice is considered accepted when the cock shakes its head as water is dripped on it. Then the shaman repeatedly hits the cock against the patient's body and moves it along the thread towards the clay figure, luring the spirit into following. The cock finally is sacrificed at the bank of a little river or at a cremation ground. Three lines of ashes are drawn between the place of offering and the house because it is thought that the spirit cannot cross those lines of ashes and so will be unable to reenter the house.

Sacrificial offerings are universally performed and have a marked anxiety- and guilt-relieving effect. Such rites are often associated with the admission of transgressions against kin and community members, which also becomes apparent during the discussion of family and neighbourhood conflicts during the shamanic possession ceremonies.

The presence of at least some family members is regarded as essential. They should hear what is said during the course of a possession ritual, and they can say what the patient does not reveal, and express their own feelings. By attending the healing ritual they get a better understanding of the conflicts in the extended family. The patient knows that ultimately he or she is not left alone with his/her problems and that the relatives, who are also involved in the conflicts in one way or another, will help make the ill family member well. In shamanic healing, Western family therapy has been practiced for thousands of years.

In these kinds of healing rituals the patient plays a very active role. The special ritual space and time, which is separated from ordinary space and time, the encouragement of the shaman and the audience, and the intensity of the whole situation make it easy for the patient to have cathartic experiences and to work through his or her psychosocial problems. It is GYANI DOLMA's special skill to relate to the individual problems of the patients (within a given ritual framework) who can then enact their personal dramas that reflect their experiences within their communities. Especially in a multi-ethnic urban environment like Kathmandu Valley is today, it seems important to place the individual problems of the patient in the context of his or her life and social network, and find suitable solutions for specific situations, rather than employ ancient myths to provide the meaning context.

RITUALS FOR THE RETRIEVAL OF LOST VITAL ENERGY

Another kind of night ritual is called the *khargo* ritual. The Nepali word *khargo* means "obstacle", a very difficult time in a person's life, and the shamans say that if it is not removed, if this is not "cut", as they express it, the person will die. The patient's apparent symptoms are mostly very unspecific. Often it is only said that the patient does not feel good and everything that he or she does, fails.

In the central part of this ritual the shaman contacts Yama Raja, the King of the Realm of the Dead. The shaman must negotiate with him in order to persuade him to give back the lost vital energy of the patient, so that the patient can continue to lead a good life, free of illness and misfortune. After successful negotiations, a sacrificial offering which substitutes for the patient must be given to Yama Raja to make him content and happy. Then a banana trunk is nailed or fastened in some other way to stand up in the room where the ritual takes place. A five-coloured thread connects the patient's head to the banana trunk. The attendants of Yama Raja should bring the lost vital energy of the patient with them and deliver it into the banana trunk. As soon as they have arrived, the vital energy is shifted back into the patient, and the banana trunk is felled, so that the vital energy cannot escape back to the Realm of the Dead.

After this, the shaman has to go on another trip to see if the transfer has been successful and everything has been done in the right way. During these journeys, which last for approximately one minute, the body of the shaman falls backwards on the floor. Neither during that time nor afterwards does he tell about his experiences on his trip. After he has sat up again, assured by his journey that everything is alright now, he only says: "It is done: the obstacle is removed."

The patient does not show much outward activity during the course of this kind of healing ritual. In one case it took me quite some time to find out who the patient was—partly due to the fact that the patient was not even present in the first hour or two of the ritual (which lasted from sunset until dawn), but was staying in another room of the house.

These healing rituals are performed by Tamang shamans for Tamang patients. Invocations are usually sung in the Tamang language, and personal stories of the shamans, like narratives of the source of power to claim one's legitimization, are replaced by culture-specific myths.

IMAGERY AND THE MAGICAL FLIGHT OF THE SHAMAN

The shaman's magical flight has been compared to techniques of modern psychotherapy, like C. G. JUNG's *active imagination* (1969), R. DESOILLE's *directed daydream* (1966), or H. LEUNER's *guided affective imagery* (1969), (for example, see PETERS 1998). In their altered states of consciousness the shamans conduct an inner dialogue with the characters appearing in their visions or they go to other places to find out more about the situations related to the illness-causing situation. The inner dialogue in an altered state of consciousness is therapeutically beneficial because the images yield knowledge and include ways of knowing that are different, yet complementary, to those in an ordinary state of consciousness. In the course of the inner dialogue, often a teacher appears in the visual imagery to provide answers to problems that cannot be solved by ordinary means.

But the magical flight of the shamans cannot be compared with the imaginary journey of the patient in modern Western psychotherapy. The altered state of consciousness and the journey of the healer may lead to a different sort of therapy than the altered state of consciousness of the patient (PRINCE 1976). The healer and the patient play distinct and separate roles in all therapeutic encounters, so the experiences of the healer should not be confused with those of the patient.

THE STRENGTH OF THE THERAPIST

Research on shamanic healing methods has primarily focused on altered states of consciousness, magical flight, and the spirit possession of the healer. In research on modern psychotherapy, the processes that go on in the patient are of main interest. Only recently have psychiatrists and psychotherapists started to reflect on the benefits of altered states of consciousness of the therapist.

BENEDETTI (1979) sees the process of identification of the therapist with the patient—in an altered state of consciousness—as a possible opportunity for a confrontation of the healer with the illness-causing forces; and this is what the shamans say their main job in a healing ritual is. The integrated, strong self of the healer has to subdue the illness-causing forces. The patient then, knowing about this process and feeling it, and in the shamanic rituals being reassured of it all the time, can participate in the strength of the psychotherapist/shaman. Thus, the integration and strengthening of the patient's self can take place, as, for example, in BENEDETTI's therapy as he describes and interprets it, or in the *khargo* rituals the Tamang shamans perform. In the possession rituals in Nepal much reassurance is given to the patient through the strength of the shaman and the assertion that the illness-causing agents will be subdued and that the psychosocial problems can be solved. In all these kinds of therapies the strength and personality characteristics of the healers are of paramount importance, a fact often overlooked in modern psychotherapy which emphasizes techniques.

Also, in the possession rituals the shamans take a very active part. Spirits and divinities speak and act through them to keep the session going, to encourage the patient, and to summarize what has been said. Shamans unite with spiritual beings and bring their power into the ritual process.

Calling on spirit helpers and tutelary divinities enables the shamans to act and to direct the healing sessions. They say that it is not they themselves who effect the cures, but the spiritual powers with whom they come into contact. According to GEMOLL (1965), the old Greek word *therapeio*'s first meaning is "to be a servant, to serve the gods", and only the second meaning is "to heal". In the development of Western medicine the spiritual dimension has been lost.

Invocations of tutelary deities also separate ordinary time and space from ritual time and space. V. TURNER (1989) talks about the liminal phase of the ritual, in which special processes can take place, apart from everyday reality. Certain qualities of the liminal phase allow a playful mixture of events—more in the sense of possible or phantasized combinations. Events that may never have happened but that fit into the symbolic language and could have taken place are narrated or acted out. In this way emotions, thoughts and impulses can be expressed in a very subtle manner. And the patients know that they cannot be made responsible for anything they say.

UNIVERSAL ASPECTS OF "SYMBOLIC HEALING"

On a surface level, the two kinds of healing rituals which have been briefly described here are quite different, and the importance of the therapeutic principles operant in these shamanic healing methods varies considerably. J. DOW (1986) postulates that there is a common structure in all kinds of symbolic healing methods regardless of the surface structure and the culture in which they occur. The term "symbolic healing" has been coined by D. E. MOERMAN (1979), implying that all kinds of Western psychotherapies, shamanic therapies, and religious healings invoke similar psychological processes. Taking a position close to that taken by

N. CHOMSKY (1965) on language, DOW says that there is a universal structure in symbolic healing that he sees as being due to a deep structure. The different cultural forms of symbolic healing and also different ·healing rituals in one culture can then be regarded as surface structures manifesting the rules set by the deep structure.

Shamans as well as psychotherapists try to redefine and restructure the problems that the patients have communicated to them. The extent of the activity of the healer and the patient is not crucial for the success of the therapy. According to DOW (1986), important elements of this universal structure are symbols shared by both healer and patient, and the redefinition of the patient's problems in terms of these symbols (like, for example, spirit possession or loss of vital energy), then the attachment of the patient's emotions to these specific symbols, and the manipulation of these symbols to help the patient to change his emotions. Regardless of the surface patterns of a healing ritual or psychotherapeutic technique, regardless of the concepts of illness employed and of the activity or passivity of the patient and the therapist during the course of a healing session, similar or "universal" processes seem to enable the transition from the state of illness to the state of health.

The meaning of the symbolic structure of possession rituals is shared by members of all ethnic groups living in Central Nepal. It is assumed that there are people who have the ability to harm others. If they wish to do so, they can send spirits, who are under their command, to give troubles to another person. The spirit as well as the witch can talk through the other person's mouth in order to tell what has happened, why that person has been harmed, and what has to be done to solve the problems. Within this surface structure patients and healers of different ethnic groups can express psychosocial conflicts and work on them. The symbols referred to during the *khargo* rituals are only familiar to the Tamang: the shaman's journey to the realm of Yama Raja, who keeps lost vital energy of people, the negotiations with him, and shifting the lost vital energy through a banana trunk and along a five-coloured thread back to the patient. This kind of healing ritual is done by Tamang shamans for Tamang patients, because the meaning of the surface structure is understood only by members of this ethnic group. The deep structures of these two kinds of rituals, however, are the same.

REFERENCES

BENEDETTI, GAETANO
  1979 Über Meditation in der Psychotherapie. *Psychotherapie und Medizinische Psychologie* 29: 95.

CHOMSKY, NOAM
  1965 *Aspects of theory of syntax.* Cambridge, MA: M.I.T. Press.

DESOILLE, ROBERT
  1966 *The directed daydream: A series of three lectures given at the Sorbonne.* New York: Psychosynthesis Research Foundation.

DOW, JAMES
  1986 Universal aspects of symbolic healing: A theoretical synthesis. *American Anthropologist* 88: 57–69.

EIGNER, DAGMAR
  1994 Schamanische Therapie in Zentral-Nepal. *Curare* 17: 2: 217–228.
  1996 Besessenheit in der schamanischen Therapie. In RENAUD VAN QUEKELBERGHE – DAGMAR EIGNER (eds.) *Jahrbuch für Transkulturelle Medizin und Psychotherapie* 1994: *Trance, Besessenheit, Heilrituale und Psychotherapie.* Berlin: Verlag für Wissenschaft und Bildung, 67–84.

GEMOLL, WILHELM
  1965 *Griechisch–deutsches Schul- und Handwörterbuch.* München: Freytag.

JUNG, CARL GUSTAV
  1969 *On the nature of the psyche.* (Collected Works, Vol. 8) Trans. By RICHARD HULL. Princeton: Bollington Foundation.

LEUNER, HANSCARL
  1969 Guided affective imagery therapy: A method of intensive therapy. *American Journal of Psychotherapy* 23: 4–22.

MOERMAN, DANIELE
  1979 Anthropology of symbolic healing. *Current Anthropology* 20: 59–80.

PETERS, LARRY
  1998 *Tamang Shamans. An Ethnopsychiatric Study of Ecstasy and Healing in Nepal.* New Delhi: Nirala.

PRINCE, RAYMOND
  1976 Psychotherapy as the manipulation of endogenous healing mechanisms: A transcultural survey. *Transcultural Psychiatric Review* 13: 115–133.

TURNER, VICTOR
  1989 *Vom Ritual zum Theater. Der Ernst des menschlichen Spiels.* Frankfurt: Qumran.

ULLA JOHANSEN

Ecstasy and Possession:
a Short Contribution to a Lengthy Discussion

THE PROBLEM: ELIADE, HULTKRANTZ AND URBAN SHAMANISM IN CONTRAST WITH LEWIS'S EARLIER WRITINGS

To demonstrate my problem, I quote the founder of modern shamanistic research, MIRCEA ELIADE, himself. Summarizing the essence of shamanism, he writes in the conclusion of his famous book *Shamanism: Archaic Techniques of Ecstasy*, "...the specific element of shamanism [is] not the incorporation of 'spirits' by the shaman, but ecstasy, which is brought about by the journey to heaven or underworld; the incorporation of spirits and possession by spirits (...) do not belong (...) to shamanism in its strict meaning" (1956: 461).

In a recent article HULTKRANTZ (1999: 6) reaffirms this position by proposing that shamanistic research should use two different categories— "shamanism" and "mediumism". The latter category refers to shamanism connected with possession at the culmination of the trance, despite the fact that most of the other characteristics of the shamans who feel possessed by their spirits may coincide with those of the shamans who experience upper world journeys.

This view of shamanism has had a decisive influence on New Age or urban shamanism, which has more or less neglected the fact that possession—the subjective experience of entry of another being into one's self—seems to be as important as ecstasy—the feeling of a person in trance that his or her self leaves the body. Since religious possession is mainly a lower-class phenomenon in the Americas and Europe, shamanism connected with a possession trance possibly would never have become the core feature of a religious movement of mostly upper middle-class people (JACOBSEN 1999: 167ff.) as New Age shamanism has. I will not discuss this attitude further, since I do not want to dwell on urban shamanism, but on classical shamanism. I call it "classical shamanism" because the denotation "traditional" in distinction from neoshamanism would imply that the latter is not based on traditions. This is not the case, however, at least in Siberia, where neoshamanism endeavours to strengthen still existing traditions or to revitalize forms of shamanism which have survived only in anthropological reports.

Opposite opinions about the essence of shamanism also exist. To characterize this I quote another, by now, famous book on shamanism, IOAN LEWIS's *Ecstatic Religion* (1971: 56): "...we are perfectly justified in applying the term shaman to mean (...) a 'master of spirits', with the implication that this inspired priest incarnates spirits, becoming possessed voluntarily...". Under the influence of ANNA-LEENA SIIKALA's fundamental treatise *The Rite Technique of the Siberian Shaman* (1978), LEWIS has mitigated this apodictic definition in the new edition of his book (1989: 32). However, his recent book, *Religion in Context. Cults and Charisma* (1986: 89ff.), shows that, for him, possession is still the essence of shamanism.

Looking at these contradictory opinions, I feel like the famous Turkish wag NASIR-ED-DIN *hoca* in one of his stories: One day the judge of the small town left for the center of the province and asked the *hoca* to act as judge in his place. Proudly NASIR-ED-DIN seated himself on the judge's chair and soon he had to adjudicate the first quarrel. The representatives of one side described their point of view very vividly. NASIR-ED-DIN was impressed and said: "Yes, you are right". Thereafter the representatives of the opposite side spoke with beautiful words and quite convincingly. The *hoca* was impressed again and said: "You are right". But from behind his chair his wife approached and whispered: "My *hoca*, you cannot say to both sides 'you are right', you should judge". Than NASIR-ED DIN turned around to her and said: "You are right too."

Thus, I shall try, if not to settle, then at least to explain, this ecstasy-possession dispute, although HUMPHREY and THOMAS (1994: 3), also referring to ELIADE and LEWIS's contradictory positions, warned: "...definitional debates over shamanism or spirit mediumship and types of possession have frustrated (...) investigation".

In our case, we also have to keep in mind that LEWIS and ELIADE acquired different experiences of what we call shamanism, and by using this single term, we are still declaring it to be a more or less homogenous phenomenon. For LEWIS, who did field research in East Africa, possession is the main characteristic of shamanism, although he is open-minded and sees that SIIKALA's other types of shamanism give alternatives to possession. On the other hand, a check of the many sources ELIADE used to compose his famous book shows that he nearly exclusively read Western

European sources, or translations of Russian works mostly in French or German. These sources did not deal with Africa or South America outside the Amazon basin. Thus, the examples he gives are mostly from the north of Eurasia and this has strongly influenced his views of shamanism. HULTKRANTZ's ample field-experiences concern the Indians of North America, who have not developed possession phenomena. Do these contradictory opinions simply reflect regional differences in shamanic séances?

APPROXIMATION OF ASPECTS BY DIFFERENTIATION OF THE CONCEPTS "SOUL JOURNEY" AND "POSSESSION" BY SIIKALA AND MERKUR

If I now try to give a short overview of more detailed interpretations of shamanic séances, I have in mind only the regular rituals of experienced shamans, not the initiations of young shamans with their extraordinary visions.

The pioneer work in this field was done by A.-L. SIIKALA, who began her penetrating analysis by elaborating the structure of shamanic séances in the different societies of Northern Siberia as described in the reports of anthropologists in the 19th and the beginning of the 20th century. She left the Turkic groups and the Kets undiscussed in her nevertheless far reaching study. Only in a later article (SIIKALA 1992: 4) does she include them in her discussion and reckons them to a southern type.

She points out that in shamanic séances the intensity of trance varies, beginning at a low level in the phases of preparation and invitations to the shaman's spirits occurring in all types of shamanism, and coming to a culmination when the shaman feels that his soul travels to another world. At the end of a séance the absorption of the shaman by role-taking (as SIIKALA puts it) usually is low again in all types of shamanic séances. By taking an overview of the details of the process of shamanic séances she derives a general model of shamanic ritual which enables her to discern three different forms of shamanic experience during the culmination of trance. Since all specialists in shamanism have read this book, which is basic for shamanistic research, I characterize them only briefly in SIIKALA's own words:

1. "The shaman identifies completely with the spirit (...) he is regarded as having changed quite concretely into a spirit";

2. "manifesting both his own role as a shaman and that of a spirit the shaman creates a dialogue situation in which the spirit is regarded as acting and speaking from outside the physical being of the shaman";

3. "the shaman is regarded as "seeing" or "hearing" the spirits during the séance". SIIKALA calls this "description of counter role" (1978: 334).

It is obvious that the experience of journeying is connected with forms 2 and 3, and possession is characterized by the first variant, although the focus of SIIKALA's book is on northern Siberia, which is not an area where possession is distributed (see p. 76, "actemes").

Seven years after SIIKALA's epochal book, D. MERKUR tried to draw an even more clearly outlined picture of shamanic trances on the basis of an analysis of reports on the classical shamanism of the Inuit. He discerns a triad of depth of shamanic trances: light, medium and deep. Most descriptions in his sources indicate light trances in MERKUR's opinion (1985: 70ff.).

Phenomena like inspirations, ventriloquism and what he calls "identification", which may happen with different spirits at the same time, are connected with "light trances". They should not be conflated with possession, in his opinion.

"Medium trances" happen only in cases of what MERKUR (1985: 94ff.) denotes as "lucid possession". These are possessions of only parts of the shaman's personality, leaving him full conscious awareness and the possibility of at least partially controlling his movements.

Deep trances occur among the Inuit in connection with soul journeys or "somnambulistic possession" as he puts it (MERKUR 1985: 98ff.). In this, he is in agreement with SIIKALA's conception, at least concerning possession, that is, the loss of control over one's body. This happens among the Inuit, however, only during the shamanic initiation period (1985: 108f. and 111), and not in the cases of professional shamanizing which we are considering here. Only one report of RASMUSSEN's, about a Copper-Inuit shaman, who, after having called the Sea Woman, became possessed by her and spoke with her deep voice, seems to indicate a full possession. Nevertheless, MERKUR does not classify this example as "somnambulistic possession", but as "lucid possession", with the argument: "His lucidity is established by his consciousness of suffering". This points up the difficulty of making clear distinctions between different forms of possession. They can be looked at, rather, as forming a long scale with possession "defined by the shaman's complete oblivion to physical reality" (MERKUR 1985: 111) at one end, and a "role taking" (SIIKALA), with a diminished focus on the spirit world, at the opposite end.

PROTOTYPES OF SOUL JOURNEYS TO THE UPPER WORLD AND POSSESSIONS

Both of these books have advanced our knowledge considerably by opening our eyes to the great variety of shamanic experiences and the forms of trance connected with them. Both colleagues and others who have written about shamanic trances agree with the point that the most significant cultural differences in the shamanic experience are manifested at the stage of deep trance (e.g. SIIKALA 1992: 11; BÄCKMAN – HULTKRANTZ 1978: 95ff.), which sets in when the shaman feels that his soul leaves his body for a journey into the world of the spirits and gods, or he feels that his body has been entered and is governed by one mighty spirit. When trying to give prototypes of these different forms of shamanic experience during the séances, I will select reports on these culminations of fully professional shamans' séances excluding, as already mentioned, the trance experiences which occur during the initiation phase of young shamans.

The experience of flight at the culmination of the séance is expressed unambiguously in the words of the shamans, and the anthropologist could often observe a loss of consciousness or at least, in SIIKALA's words (1978: 337f.), a deep identification with his role and an interruption of the connection with his audience.

VITASHEVSKY (1917–25: 179f.) gives a report of a Yakut séance of this type, which may serve as a prototype of soul journeys to the upper world. I will briefly summarize his report: The first task of the shaman was to drive out of his ill client the *abasylar* (malevolent spirits), which had intruded into his body. Thereafter he journeyed to the upper world in search of the client's soul, which had been frightened and fled. He made motions as if he hovered and travelled in a southerly direction and indicated with his arms that he was ascending higher and higher, holding presents for the spirits of the upper world in his right hand. An assistant accompanied him, imitating the movements of the shaman. They had to pass the dwelling places of nine spirits of the upper world, whom they greeted and presented with tea and vodka. The shaman repeatedly looked up and down again, because his way was steep. On his way back he had to bend forward. He had been successful in bringing back the soul of the ill person, but he became extremely tired at the end of the séance.

As a contrast to journeying to the upper world, I have selected a prototype which shows full possession, that is, possession with complete oblivion of physical reality. Examples which doubtlessly show this were described by the German psychiatrist GÜNTHER SCHÜTTLER (1971: 46ff., 68ff., 85ff.), who carried out his research together with the Mongolia specialist, SAGASTER, and the Tibet specialist, PHUKHANG (MELCHES 1990: 29ff., 48ff., 72ff.). He examined and interviewed Tibetan oracles. Like the Black-Hat magicians, who are Tibetan shamans, the oracles were able to invite tutelary deities of local Buddhism and become possessed by them. They declared that when they were dressed in their ritual costumes they felt a sort of formication and pain as if somebody were tightly pressing their body, but once the spirit had entered it, they did not feel anything, even when other people touched them. They could not control themselves, but they saw and heard what happened in the room. Though the oracles spoke, moved and drank liquids sacrificed to the tutelary god residing in their body during possession, they could not remember after the séance, which usually ended with a total collapse of the oracle immediately after they felt that the tutelary god had left them. The oracles always needed assistants for making the incantations to invite the god, for dressing them, for interpreting the sentences the god said through their mouths and to attend them when they collapsed.

Shamans of the lamaistic Buryats are possessed by spirits of bulls in a similar way (HAMAYON 1990: 672ff.) and OMAR describes in this volume how Kazakh *baksy* show by their behavior that they experience the entrance of a spirit. Again, it can be only one spirit at a time who takes control of their bodies and minds.

Obviously Korean shamanism can be cited as a further example of possession-shamanism. I have read in KISTER's book (1997: 96f.) that the shamanesses are viewed as mediums for one spirit when they are in a state of trance. They must have reached a deep stage of possession, for they stand barefooted on chopper blades without being hurt, or hold huge heavy pots filled with rice cakes with their teeth. The observations of L. KENDALL (1987: 57) and KIM HOGARTH (1998: 97) are similar. In all cases, the shamanesses were helped by assistants.

As already mentioned, however, the question of whether the observer was actually perceiving a full possession or not, could not be decided as unambiguously as questions concerning the authenticity of journeys. Obviously, a wide range of various levels of possession can be identified.

OTHER FORMS OF IDENTIFICATION WITH THE SPIRITS:
DISCOURSE AND SOUL GUIDING TO THE LOWER WORLD

SIIKALA has already stressed (1978) that neither the whole, nor every séance leads to a culmination with possession or a soul journey to the upper world. More detailed paragraphs of the observers' descriptions refer to calling the spirits and discourse with them. From some regions, e.g. the steppe area of Tyva, I could not find any reports of full possession or a journey to the upper world, though the feathers on the coats and crowns of the shamans suggest the latter tradition. MÄNCHEN-HELFEN (1931: 116ff.) reports, for example, a séance of a female shaman in western Tyva. She began with invocations of her spirits until she had assembled them in her tent. Then she sent them to the world of spirits to give her information and to help her remove an aggressive spirit from the body of an ill girl. But she did not travel there, herself, she only had the different spirits (and more than one of them) tell of their experiences during the journey through her mouth, nor did she really feel possessed by them. It was a dialogue between her and the different spirits. At the end of the séance, which lasted for hours, she did not collapse, but she was very tired. SIIKALA's analyses (1978: 78, 324ff.) have shown that séances without a dramatic culmination also often occur among Palaeo-asiatic groups in northeastern Siberia, who practice a kind of shamanism HULTKRANTZ (1999: 7) calls "democratisized shamanism".

JOCHELSON (1926: 201ff.) observed how a Yukaghirized Koryak shaman, after a preparatory phase of shamanizing, opened the door of his hut and inhaled his helping spirits (not just one spirit) with deep breaths. They spoke through his mouth. He then inhaled the spirit which had caused an illness, and for a while he behaved like this spirit and it spoke through his mouth. At the end of the séance, first he exhaled the disease spirit, and then he exhaled his helping spirits, outside of the hut. He finished the séancewithout losing consciousness. Though we can observe something like possession, there was obviously no deep trance. The shaman embodied many spirits at the same time and he had them speak in a dialogue form. VITASHEVSKY (1917–25: 173ff.) observed similar activities by a Yakut shaman. This shaman did not use a friendly manner when he invited the spirit who had caused an illness to enter him, but, instead, adopted a threatening attitude. He inhaled the spirit only for a moment, and then kept it in his drum. The window of the Yakut's house was opened, and, turning the inner side of his drum so that it faced out the window, the shaman expelled the evil spirit from the house by some heavy strokes upon his drum. KARJALAINEN (1924: 318) learned that the spirits breathed on the shaman during the séance. They "inspired" him and whispered the right words to him, but did not enter him. MERKUR (1985: 73) calls similar types of experience "incorporation" or "identification" and stresses that these should not be considered possession. As already indicated, possession cannot be looked upon as a condition, the manifestation of which could be easily perceived and affirmed or denied by a simple "yes" or "no". The question must be to what extent a person feels possessed by a spirit. It varies between strong possession and weaker forms. There are mild forms of possession, which are, rather, forms of a vivid dialogue between spirits.

Within the category of journeys to other worlds, there must also be differentiations. Possessed shamans such as, for example, the Manchu and Nanay shamans, may act as psychopomps to the lower, not the upper world, since the spirits inhabiting them do not fear malevolent spirits of the world of the deceased. They may even bring back souls of ill persons from the lower world (SHIROKOGOROFF 1935: 314, SIIKALA 1978: 260 after STERNBERG 1935).

DISTRIBUTION AND REASONS FOR THE DIFFERENTIATION OF TRANCE EXPERIENCES AT THE CULMINATION OF SÉANCES

Journeys to the upper world and full possession, however, are never practiced by shamans of the same group in Siberia. Even among groups with similar languages such as the Tungus, there must be discerned groups of the north, including Northern Transbaikal-Tungus, who practiced upper world journeys, and southern groups in Manchuria and the Amur region, whose shamans were possessed and travelled only to the lower world (DELABY 1976–77: 129f.).

Neglecting the other experiences, at the present we are looking at the distribution of journeying to the upper world and full possession at the culmination of séances. As for the context of these two phenomena, which generally exclude each other in northern Asia, a northern and a southern-southeastern area of shamanism can be discerned (cf. HULTKRANTZ 1999: 6). The map should give an initial overview of the extent of these areas. The southern one also includes the Aborigines of Taiwan (QUACK 1985: 146) and probably early Japanese village rituals, which cannot be shown here.

The main reason for these differences of trance experience is viewed by HAMAYON (1996) in terms of the differing economic bases of the Siberian ethnic groups. In her opinion, the hunters and fishers of the north developed relations to the spirits by giving and receiving. They made sacrifices and got wild animals and/or fishes in return while hunting or fishing. Such partnership-relations excluded the idea of being possessed by one of the spirits. In contrast, cattle ownership is the basis of hierarchical relations in what HAMAYON calls the "pastoral shamanism" of Central Asia. Reciprocity is developed much less in these societies and thus, possession is more common here. As a third type, HAMAYON adduces "peripheric shamanism" without explaining it further. I suppose this is shamanism with fully developed possession trances.

SIIKALA's (1992) explanations for the two "completely different" (1992: 2) areas of shamanism coincide widely with those of HAMAYON, but she stresses the influence of social factors on shamanism—the size and organization of the ethnic groups. Thus, she differentiates small-group-shamanism of the Northern peoples and clan-shamanism of "patriarchalic feudalism" of the South, including all Turkic and Mongolian groups of Siberia. The first social type has developed soul journey shamanism, the second, possession.

Again I must answer like NASIR-ED-DIN to both of these competent colleagues, "You are right". But their explanations leave many problems unsolved, e.g. why did the Yakut, mainly cattle breeders with a highly developed clan structure, display soul journey shamanism? Why do we meet among the hunters and fishermen south of the Amur basin, and neighbours of the Manchu, possession trance?

I feel we must keep in mind that all these ethnic groups have their history which, though mostly unwritten, reaches back for thousands of years, and shamanic traditions did not change as fast in the centuries before as they do now. Obviously, a center of possession shamanism blossomed in China 4000 years before our time, and influenced its minority peoples too, e.g. the Moso (MATHIEU 1998: 211), and even the Aborigines of Taiwan (QUACK 1985). In Korea and Tibet, possession shamanism is a very old tradition, too. Journey-shamanism in the far north of the continent (JOHANSEN 1999) and among Inuit and North American Indians (HULTKRANTZ 1999) had already developed. Far off from the Chinese center in the southwest of China, we also meet journey-shamanism as, for instance, in the north (FOURNIER 1977; PETERS 1982) and west of Nepal, the "Blind Land", where OPPITZ made his famous films, and in Northern Thailand (still unpublished materials of the late FRIEDHELM SCHOLZ in Heidelberg) or Malaysia (CONDOMINAS 1977) among small local groups. BASILOV supposes that in pre-Islamic times even the Kazakhs practiced journeys to the upper world instead of possession shamanism (1983: 215ff.).

It thus becomes obvious that possession shamanism has developed in the great realms of Eastern and Central Asia with their differentiated state religions as a peripheral religious complex (see LEWIS 1971: 32ff.) and was distributed to the neighbouring countries. Far from these realms, in small societies without differentiated religious structures, powerful shamans practiced journeys to the upper world as one of the central rituals of their tribes.

LEGEND

Relatively few séances are described in a way that makes it fully clear what form of experience the shaman had at the culmination of the séance. Others, e.g. the biography of a Daur who had left his country of origin relatively early, do not seem to be quite reliable. Fantastic journeys of heroes are often described in the folklore of the Siberian peoples, but these descriptions do not give reliable hints about the experiences of journeys to the upper world by the shamans of the various groups. Therefore, they are not taken into consideration here.

I could not read all sources theoretically available. I especially could not get the reports published in local Russian journals during the time I was preparing this paper, but could only know about their existence by seeing Popov's bibliography. For some groups, I could not find any reports about their shamanic experiences at all, e.g. from Enec Samoyeds, Evens or Udehe. For others, I found only hints, e.g. reports or pictures of feathers on the shaman's dress, which would seem to indicate a flight experience of the shaman at the culmination of the trance.

Some treatises on Asiatic or Inuit shamanism were especially helpful for me, because they had already analysed the older reports on shamanism. Thus, I could rely on their research. In this connection I have to name mainly HAMAYON (1990) on the Buryats, JACOBSEN (1999) and MERKUR (1985) on the different Inuit groups, KARJALAINEN (1927) on the Obugrians, and SIIKALA (1978) on most of the North Siberian groups. I add in brackets the authors whose reports I have not read in the original, but only in quotations by the forenamed colleagues. The lists of Peters and Price-Williams (1980) are mostly not based on original sources of Siberian shamanism and thus could not be used.

The abbreviations on the map indicate the different peoples. The sources I have used for them are the following:

Journey to the upper world

Possession by a spirit

Only discourse and/or journey to the world of deceased observed

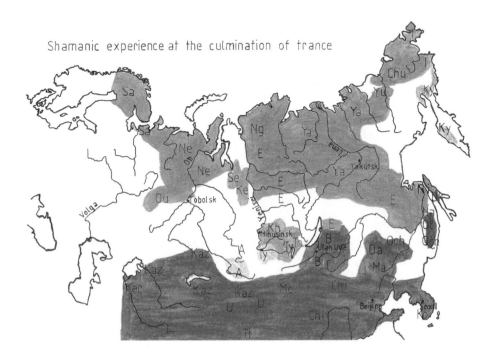

Shamanic experience at the culmination of trance

ABBREVIATIONS:

A = Altayans, especially Teleuts (POTANIN 1883; VERBITSKIY 1858, 1893; RADLOFF 1893; MALOV 1909; ANOKHIN 1924)

B = Buryats (AGAPITOV – KHANGALOV 1883; VLADIMIRTSEV 1927; HAMAYON 1990; MAZIN 1984)

Chi = Chinese (SHIROKOGOROFF 1935)

Chu = Chukchee (D'YACHKOV 1893; BOGORAS 1907; FINDEISEN 1956)

Da = Daur-Mongols (HUMPHREY – ONON 1996)

E = Evenks-Birarchen, Kumarchen and Khingan-Tungusic groups inclusive (SHIROKOGOROFF 1935; ANISIMOV 1958, 1963; VASILYEVICH 1963, DELABY 1976–77)

I = Inuit (HULTKRANTZ 1999; JACOBSEN 1999 (H. EGEDE 1741, P. EGEDE
  – N. EGEDE 1741, RASMUSSEN 1908, RÜTTEL 1917); MERKUR 1985
  (BOAS 1888; NELSON 1899; RASMUSSEN 1929, 1938; STEFANSSON 1913)
Kar = Karakalpaks (SHALEKENOV 1958)
Kaz = Kazakhs (DIVAYEV 1899; OMAR in this volume; RADLOFF 1893)
Ke = Kets (ANUCHIN 1914; DONNER 1933)
Kh = Khakas (LANKENAU 1872)
Ko = Koreans (KIM HOGARTH 1998; KENDALL 1987; KISTER 1997)
Ky = Koryak (JOCHELSON 1905-08)
Ma = Manchu (SHIROKOGOROFF 1935)
Mo = Mongols (POTANIN 1883; RUBRUCK 1253–55; VLADIMIRTSEV 1927)
Na = Nanai (LOPATIN 1940–41, 1946–49, 1960; SMOLYAK 1991;
  STERNBERG 1935)
Ne = Nenets (LEHTISALO 1924; STARTSEV 1930)
Ng = Nganasans (POPOV 1936, 1984; SIMCHENKO 1996)
Ni = Nivxi or Gilyaks (STERNBERG 1904–05)
Ol = Olchens (SMOLYAK 1991)
Och = Orochons (LOPATIN 1960; QIU PU 1983; SHIROKOGOROFF 1935)
Ok = Oroks (LOPATIN 1960)
Ou = Obugrians (KARJALAINEN [GONDATTI 1888; MUNKÁCSI 1896] 1927;
  STARTSEV 1928)
Sa = Samis (BÄCKMAN – HULTKRANTZ 1978)
Se = Selkups (DONNER 1918)
Ti = Tibetans (SCHÜTTLER 1971; MELCHES 1990)
To = Tofalar (Karagas) (CHUDINOV 1931; MEL'NIKOVA 1994)
Ty = Ethnic groups of the Tyva region (BADAMXATAN 1962; KON 1936;
  MÄNCHEN-HELFEN 1931; OLSEN 1915; OSTROVSKIKH 1898; POTANIN
  1893; VAYNSHTEYN 1961, 1996)
U = Uighurs (OMAR in this volume)
Ya = Yakuts (KSENOFONTOV 1929; PRIKLONSKIY 1890; SEROSHEVSKIY
  1896; VITASHEVSKIY 1890, 1917–25)
Yu = Yukaghirs (JOCHELSON 1926)

REFERENCES

AGAPITOV, N. N. – KHANGALOV, M. N.
1883 Shamanstvo u buryat Ir-kutskoy gubernii. *Izvestiya Vostochno-Sibirskogo Otdela Imperatorskogo Russkogo Geograficheskogo Obshchestva* 14: 1–2: 1–61.

ANISIMOV, A. F.
1958 *Religiya Evenkov v istoriko-geneticheskom izuchenii i problemy proizkhozdeniya pervobytnykh verovany*. Moscow: Leningrad.
1963 Cosmological Concepts of the Peoples of the North. In H. N. MICHAEL (ed.) *Studies in Siberian Shamanism*. University of Toronto Press, 157–229. [Translations from Russian Sources. Vol. 4.]

ANOKHIN, A. V.
1924 Materialy po shamanstvu u altaicev. *Sbornik Muzeya Antropologii i Etnografii pri Rossiyskoy Akademii Nauk* 4.2.

ANUCHIN, V. I.
1914 Ocherk shamanstva u eniseyskikh ostyakov. *Sbornik Muzeya Antropologii i Etnografii pri Rossiyskoy Akademii Nauk* 2.2.

BADAMKHATAN, S.
1962 Xövsgölyn caatan ardyn az baydyn toym. *Studia Ethnographica Instituti Historiae Academiae Scientiarum Reipublicae Populi Mongoli* 2.1.

BÄCKMAN, L. – HULTKRANTZ, Å.
1978 *Studies in Lapp Shamanism*. Stockholm: Almqvist–Wiksell.

BASILOV, V. N.
1983 Zur Erforschung der Überreste von Schamanismus in Zentralasien. In H. P. DUERR (ed.) *Sehnsucht nach dem Ursprung*. Zu MIRCEA ELIADE. Frankfurt: Syndikat, 207–225.

BOAS, F.
1907 The Central Eskimo. *Annual Report of the Bureau of American Ethnology*. Vol. 6. Washington, 399–669.

BOGORAS, W.
1907 The Chukchee-Religion. *Memoirs of the American Museum of Natural History* 11. (Leiden: Brill; New York: Stechert)

CHUDINOV, B.
1931 *Puteshestvie po Karagassii*. Leningrad: Molodaya Gvardia.

CONDOMINAS, G.
1977 Une séance de chamanisme dans une longue maison bidayuh (Sarawak, Malaisie). *L'ethnographie* (Numéro Spécial: Voyages chamaniques) Paris: Gabalda, 249–271.

DELABY, L.
1976–77 *Schamanes toungouses*. Paris: Nanterre. (Études mongoles et sibériennes 7.)

DIVAYEV, A.
1899 Iz oblasti kirgizskikh verovany. Baksy kak lekar' i koldun. *Izvestiya obshchestva arkheologii, istorii i etnografii pri Kazanskom Universitete* 15: 3: 307–341.

DONNER, K.
1918 *Bland Samojeder i Sibirien aren 1911–1913, 1914.* Stockholm: Albert Bonniers Förlag. (2nd ed.)
1933 Ethnological Notes about the Yenisey–Ostyak. *Suomalais–ugrilaisen Seuran Toimituksia* 66.

D'YACHKOV, G.
1893 *Anadyrskiykray.* Zapiski Obshchestva Izucheniya Amurskago kraya 2.

EGEDE, H.
1741 *A Description of Greenland.* London: T. & J. Allman.

EGEDE, P. – EGEDE, N.
1741 *Continuation of Hans Egedes Relationer fra Grønland.* Meddelelser om Grønland. Vol. 120.

ELIADE, M.
1956 *Schamanismus und archaische Ekstasetechnik.* Zurich – Stuttgart: Rascher Verlag.

FINDEISEN, H.
1956 W. G. Bogoras' Schilderung zweier schamanischer Séancen der Küsten-Tschuktschen (Nordostsibirien). *Abhandlungen und Aufsätze aus dem Institut für Menschen und Menschheitskunde (Augsburg)* 38.

FOURNIER, A.
1977 Note préliminaire sur le poembo de Sari. *L'Ethnographie* (Numéro Spécial: Voyages chamaniques) 239–248.

GONDATTI, N. L.
1888 *Sledy yazychestva a inorodtsev Severo-zapadnoy Sibiri.* Moscow.

HAMAYON, R.
1990 *La chasse à l'âme. Esquisse d'un théorie du chamanisme sibérien.* Nanterre: Societé d'Ethnologie.
1996 Shamanism in Siberia: From Partnership in Supernature to Counter-power in Society. In N. THOMAS – C. HUMPHREY (eds.) *Shamanism, History and the State.* Ann Arbor: Michigan University Press, 76–89.

HULTKRANTZ, ÅKE
1999 The Specific Character of North American Shamanism. *European Review of Native American Studies* 13: 2: 1–9.

HUMPHREY, C. – ONON, U.
1996 *Shamans and Elders. Experience, knowledge and power among the Daur Mongols.* Oxford: Clarendon Press.

HUMPHREY, C. – THOMAS, N.
1996 Introduction. In N. THOMAS – C. HUMPHREY (eds.) *Shamanism, History and the State.* Ann Arbor: Michigan University Press, 1–12.

JACOBSEN, M. D.
1999 *Shamanism. Traditional and Contemporary Approaches to the Mastery of Spirits and Healing.* New York – Oxford: Berghahn Books.

JOCHELSON, W.
1905–08 *The Koryak. The Jesup North Pacific Expedition.* Memoir of the American Museum of Natural History (New York) VI.

1926 *The Yukaghir and the Yukaghirized Tungus.* Memoir of the American Museum of Natural History (New York) IX.

JOHANSEN, U.

1999 Further Thoughts on the History of Shamanism. *Shaman. Journal of the International Society for Shamanistic Research* 7. 1: 40–58.

KARJALAINEN, K. F.

1927 *Die Religion der Jugra-Völker.* Vol. III. Helsinki: Suomalainen Tiedeakatemia; Porvoo: Werner Söderström osakeyhtiö. [Folklore Fellows Communications No. 63]

KENDALL, L.

1987 *Shamans, Housewives, and Other Restless Spirits. Women in Korean Ritual Life.* Honolulu: Hawaii University Press.

KIM HOGARTH – HYUN-KEY

1998 *Kut: Happiness Through Reciprocity.* Budapest: Akadémiai Kiadó.

KISTER, D.

1997 *Korean Shamanist Ritual. Symbols and Dramas of Transformation.* Budapest: Akadémiai Kiadó.

KON, N. F.

1936 *Za pyatdesyat let.* Vol. III. Moscow: Sovetskij pisatel'.

KSENOFONTOV, G. V.

1929 *Khrestes. Shamanizm i khristianstvo.* Irkutsk.

LANKENAU, H. V.

1872 Die Schamanen und das Schamanenwesen. *Globus* 22: 278–283.

LEHTISALO, T.

1924 *Entwurf einer Mythologie der Juraksamojeden.* Helsinki. (Mémoires de la Societé Finno-ougrienne LIII.)

LEWIS, I. M.

1971 *Ecstatic Religion. An Anthropological Study of Spirit Possession and Shamanism.* Harmondsworth: Penguin Books (2nd ed. London – New York: Routledge, 1989).

1983 Die Berufung des Schamanen. In H. P. DUERR (ed.) *Sehnsucht nach dem Ursprung.* Zu MIRCEA ELIADE. Frankfurt: Syndikat, 174–191.

1986 *Religion in Context. Cults and Charisma.* New York: Cambridge University Press.

LOPATIN, I. A.

1940–41 A shamanistic performance to regain the favour of the spirit. *Anthropos* 35–36: 352–355.

1946–49 A shamanistic performance for a sick boy. *Anthropos* 41–44: 365–368.

1960 The Cult of the Dead among the Natives of the Amur Basin. *Central Asiatic Studies* 6. The Hague: Mouton.

MÄNCHEN-HELFEN, O.

1931 *Reise ins asiatische Tuva.* Berlin: Der Bücherkreis.

MALOV, S.

1909 Neskol'ko slov o shamanstve u tureckogo naseleniya Kuzneckogo uyezda Tomskoy Gubernii. *Zivaya Starina* 18: 2–3: 38–41.

MATHIEU, C.
1998 The Moso Ddaba Religious Specialists. In M. OPPITZ – E. HSU (eds.)
Naxi and Moso Ethnography. Kin, Rites, Pictographs. Zurich:
Völkerkundemuseum, 109–234.

MAZIN, A. I.
1984 *Tradicionnye verovaniya i obryady evenkov orochonov (konec XIX – nachalo XX
v.).* Novosibirsk: Nauka.

MEL'NIKOVA, L. V.
1994 *Tofy.* Irkutsk: Vostochno-Sibirskoe knizhnoe Izdatel'stvo.

MELCHES, V.
1990 *Die Besessenheit tibetischer Orakelmedien. Darstellung und Vergleich von vier
Beispielen.* (Köln, M. A. Thesis)

MERKUR, D.
1985 *Becoming Half Hidden: Shamanism and Initiation Among the Inuit.* Stockholm:
Almquist – Wiksell.

MUNKÁCSI, B.
1896 *Vogul népköltési gyüjtemény.* Vol. IV. Budapest: Akadémiai Kiadó.

NELSON, E. W.
1899 *The Eskimo about Bering Street.* Washington. [Annual Report of the Bureau
of American Ethnology. Vol. 18.]

OLSEN, Ö.
1915 *Et primitivt folk. De mongolske ren-nomader.* Kristiania: J. W. Cappelens
Forlag.

OSTROVSKIKH, P. E.
1898 Kratkiy otchet o poezdke v Todzinskiy khoshun Uryankhayskoy zemli.
Izvestiya Imperatorskogo Russkogo Geograficheskogo obshchestva 34: 426–432.

PETERS, L.
1982 Trance, initiation, and psychotherapy in Tamang shamanism. *American
Ethnologist* 9: 21–46.

PETERS, L. – PRICE-WILLIAMS, D.
1980 Towards an experimental analysis of shamanism. *American Ethnologist* 7:
397–418.

POPOV, A. A.
1932 *Materialy dlya bibliografii russkoy literatury po izucheniyu shamanstva severo-
aziatskikh narodov.* Leningrad: Institut Narodov Severa.
1936 *Tavgiycy.* Moscow – Leningrad: Izdatel'stvo Akademii Nauk SSSR.
1984 *Nganasany. Social'noe ustroystvo i verovaniya.* Leningrad: Nauka.

POTANIN, G. N.
1881–1883 *Ocherki severo-zapadnoy Mongolii.* Vol. II–IV. St. Petersburg.

PRIKLONSKIY, V. L.
1890 Jakutskiya narodnyya poveriya i skazki. *Zivaya Starina* 2: 169–176.

QUACK, A.
1985 *Priesterinnen, Heilerinnen, Schamaninnen? Die póringao der Puyuma von Katipol
(Taiwan).* Berlin: Reimer. [Collectanea Instituti Anthropos, Vol. 32.]

QIU PU

1983   *The Oroqens – China's Nomadic Hunters.* Beijing: Foreign Language Press.

RADLOFF, W.

1893   *Aus Sibirien. Lose Blätter aus meinem Tagebuche.* Vol. 2. Leipzig: T. O. Weigel.

RASMUSSEN, K.

1908   *The People of the Polar North.* Ed. G. HERRING. London: Kegan Paul, Trench, Trubner & Co.

1938   *Knud Rasmussen's Posthumus Notes on the Life and Doings of the East Greenlanders in Olden Times.* Ed. H. OSTERMAN. Meddelelser im Grønland. Vol. 109.

RUBRUCK, W. V.

1934   *Reise zu den Mongolen 1253–1255.* (Ed. F. RISCH) Leipzig: A. Deichertsche Verlagsbuchhandlung D. Werner Scholl.

RÜTTEL, F. C. P.

1917   *Ti aar bland østgrønlandske Hedninger. Dagbog fra Angmagsalik* Copenhagen, Kristiania: Gyldendalske Boghandel.

SCHÜTTLER, G.

1971   *Die letzten tibetischen Orakelpriester.* Wiesbaden: Franz Steiner.

SEROSHEVSKIY, V. L.

1896   *Jakuty.* Petersburg: Imperatorskoe Russkoe Geograficheskoe Obshchestva.

SHALEKENOV, U.

1958   Byt karakalpakskogo krest'yanstva Chimbayskogo rayona v proshlom i nastoyashchem. *Materialy i issledovaniya po etnografii Karakalpakov. Trudy Khorezmskoy ekspedicii.* Vol. III. Moscow: Izdatel'stvo Akademii Nauk, 269–370.

SHIROKOGOROFF, S. M.

1935   *Psychomental Complex of the Tungus.* London: Kegan Paul, Trench, Trubner & Co. [Repr. Berlin: Reinhold Schletzer Verlag, 1999]

SIIKALA, A.-L.

1978   *The Rite Technique of the Siberian Shaman.* Helsinki: Finnish Anthropological Society. [Folklore Fellows' Communications. Vol. 220.]

1992   Siberian and Inner Asian Shamanism. In A.-L. SIIKALA – M. HOPPÁL *Studies on Shamanism.* Helsinki – Budapest: Akadémiai Kiadó, 1–14.

SIMCHENKO, Y. B.

1996   *Tradicionnye verovaniya nganasan.* 2 vols. Moscow: Institut Ethnologii i Antropologii Rossiyskoy Akademii Nauk.

SMOLYAK, A. V.

1991   *Shaman: lichnost', funkcii, mirovozzrenie (narody Nizhnego Amura).* Moscow: Nauka.

STARTSEV, G.

1928   *Ostyaki. Social'no-etnografichesiy ocherk.* Leningrad: Priboy.

1930   *Samoedy (Nencha). Istoriko-etnograficheskoe issledovanie.* Leningrad: Institut Narodov Severa.

STEFANSSON, V.
1913 *My Life with the Eskimo*. New York: Macmillan Company.
STERNBERG, L.
1904–05 Die Religion der Giljaken. *Archiv für Religionswissenschaft* 8: 1–2: 244–274; 456–473.
1935 Die Auserwählung im sibirischen Schamanismus. *Zeitschrift für Missionskunde und Religionswissenschaft* (Berlin) 50: 229–252.
VASILYEVICH, G. M.
1963 Early Concepts about the Universe among the Evenks. In H. N. MICHAEL (ed.) *Studies in Siberian Shamanism*. Toronto: University of Toronto Press, 46–83. [Translations from Russian Sources, Vol. 4.]
VAYNSHTEYN, S. I.
1961 *Tuvintsy-Todzintsy. Istoriko-etnograficheskiye ocherki*. Moscow: Izdatel'stvo Vostochnoy Literatury.
1996 *Die Welt der Nomaden im Zentrum Asiens*. Berlin: Reinhold Schletzer-Verlag.
VERBITSKIY, V.
1858 Zametki kochevogo altaytsa. *Vestnik Russkogo Geograficheskogo Obshchestva* 24: 77–109.
1893 *Altayskie inorodcy*. Moscow: Imperatorskoe Obshchestvo Lubiteley Estestvo znaniya, Antropologii i Etnografii.
VITASHEVSKIY, N. A.
1890 Materialy dlya izucheniya shamanstva u yakutov. *Zapiski vostochno-sibirskogo otdela Imperatorskogo Russkogo Geografichekogo obshchestva po otd. etnografii* 2: 2: 36–48.
1917–25 Iz nablyudeniy nad yakutskimi shamanskimi deystviyami. In *Sbornik Muzeya Antropologii i Etnografii* 5: 1: 165–188.
VLADIMIRTSEV, B. Y.
1927 *Etnologo-lingvisticheskie issledovaniya v Urge, Urginskom i Kenteyskom rayonakh*. Leningrad: Izdatel'stvo Akademii Nauk. [Severnaya Mongoliya vol. II. 1–42.]

CLIFFORD SATHER

The Shaman as Preserver and Undoer of Life: The Role of the Shaman in Saribas Iban Death Rituals

INTRODUCTION

The Iban describe their shamans as "healers" or "preservers of life". Yet, the Iban shaman or *manang* is also an undoer of life, who, as part of the ritual role he performs, also effects a final symbolic separation of the living from the dead. My purpose in this paper is to explore this seeming paradox by examining the role of the *manang* in the *beserara' bunga*, a rite constituting a major part of the traditional Iban funerary cycle.[1]

MIRCEA ELIADE (1964: 508–509), in the Epilogue to *Shamanism: Archaic Techniques of Ecstasy*, characterizes shamans as "antidemonic champions", who

> In a general way, ...defend[ ] life, health, ...and the world of "light", against death, disease, ... disasters, and the world of "darkness".

The Iban often describe their *manang* in quite similar terms. Thus, it is said that the "*manang* preserves the life of human beings by performing rituals" (*manang tu' ngidup ka orang ngena' jalai pelian*) or that the "*manang* performs rituals in order that the sick may be made well" (*manang belian ngasuh orang ke sakit suman*).

Yet, the Iban shaman may also be described as an undoer of life. In the *pelian beserara' bunga*, one of the most important rituals in his repertoire, the *manang* acts as an arbitrator of the final separation of the living from the

---

1 SATHER 2003. An earlier version of this paper was presented at the symposium "Discovery of Shamanic Heritage" held in Budapest in April 2000. Here, I wish to thank MIHÁLY HOPPÁL, the symposium organizer, and the other participants for their comments. I thank also LOUISE KLEMPERER and REED WADLEY for their critical readings and helpful suggestions in preparing the present version.

dead. This he does at the conclusion of the mourning period by severing a plant stalk representing an aspect of the newly dead person's self, an aspect that symbolizes, as an otherwise invisible plant image, an individual's global state of mortality and wellbeing in the material world. At the same time, in a narrative song that immediately precedes this act, the shaman relates a symbolic division of family food crops and household wealth in which half of these things is retained by the living in this world, while the other half is taken by the spirits of the dead for their use in the otherworld. Through this division, the *manang* undoes the material ties that formerly connected the deceased with the members of his or her household and so removes the former's presence from the material fabric of the living social world. At the same time, this act has also a deeper meaning. The share taken by the dead also represents, in a more tangible sense, the corporeal presence of the deceased, his or her flesh and blood, which the spirits of the dead return to the earth (*tanah*),[2] thereby making possible, as we shall see, the regeneration of new life and its continuance in this world through the medium of cultivated crops and tangible household wealth. My object in this paper is to explore the seemingly contradictory nature of the shaman's actions in this ritual by looking at the ways in which they serve to create and recreate major eschatological ideas concerned with the nature of death, as well as underline and, in the end, give validation to the life-affirming powers of the shaman himself.

ELIADE, again, in the Epilogue to *Shamanism*, takes up, near its conclusion, the same issue: namely, the association of shamanism with eschatology. Essentially, ELIADE argues that the shaman, because of his ability to travel between seen and unseen worlds, is thereby "able to contribute decisively to the *knowledge of death*" (emphasis in the original) (1964: 509; see also ELIADE 1987: 207). Thus, he writes, "The lands that the shaman sees and the personages that he meets during his ecstatic journeys in the beyond are minutely described by the shaman himself, during or after his trance". Consequently, these experiences give substance and form to what ELIADE (1964: 509–510) aptly describes as a "funerary geography".

> The unknown and terrifying world of death assumes form, is organized in accordance with particular patterns; finally it displays a structure and, in the course of time, becomes familiar and acceptable.

---

2 The earth, identified in the songs with the "land of Selampandai" (*menua Selampandai*), is, as we shall see, the material substance from which this god is thought to fashion the human body.

As a consequence, the

> ...inhabitants of the world of death become *visible*; they show a form, display a personality, even a biography. Little by little the world of the dead becomes knowable, and death itself is evaluated primarily as a rite of passage to a spiritual mode of being.

Here, however, it is important to distinguish between narratives of travel and ecstatic experiences of spatial dislocation. ELIADE's writings tend to conflate the two, but the distinction is crucial, and needs to be maintained, if we are to understand Iban shamanism. For the Iban *manang*, ecstatic experience (or trance) is not a necessary condition for performing the ritual separation of the living from the dead. Indeed, it is not a feature of this particular ritual at all.[3] Instead, the *manang* projects his soul and relates its experiences in effecting this separation entirely through a sung narrative. It is essentially the words of this narrative that generate a realm of discourse within which death is not only rendered intelligible—i.e. made an object of "knowledge"—but is also brought within the direct sensory experiences of the shaman's audience through a dramatic ritual performance that combines words, voice, staging, and action. At the same time, the imagery of death conveyed by this performance expresses a more complex view of death, and of its connections with life, than does the dichotomous formulation of ELIADE (i.e., as a passage from a "mundane" to a "spiritual mode of being"). For the Iban, life and death are ontologically inseparable. Through the shaman's performance, death is not only constituted as a rite of passage, but, more importantly, it is portrayed as a dissolution of aspects of the individual's self that makes possible both social continuity and the regeneration of new life in the material world. Its effects thus play themselves out as much in this world as they do in the realm of death.

---

[3] This conflation, and the habit of foregrounding subjective experience, particularly in the form of trance or so-called "ecstatic" states of consciousness, has a long history and reflects in part a persistent tendency in much of the literature on shamanism to "medicalize", or even, in some cases, "pathologize", the role of the shaman at the expense of its sociological, symbolic, and religious features (cf. HAMAYON 1995). Elsewhere I have discussed the role of trance, or as the Saribas Iban describe it, "fainting" (*luput*), in relation to more general conceptual issues concerned with the analysis of shamanism (see SATHER 2001: 10–13; 183–186).

BACKGROUND

The Iban are a major indigenous population of north-western Borneo, the majority of whom, numbering just over 600,000, live in the east Malaysian state of Sarawak (cf. FREEMAN 1970, SUTLIVE 1988, SATHER 1996). Here, despite increasing urban migration, most Iban families continue to live in longhouse communities situated along the banks of rivers or smaller tributaries and cultivate rice, supplemented with cash crops, notably rubber and pepper. Among the Iban, death rituals vary notably from one region to another and are everywhere changing rapidly at present. The materials presented in this paper relate specifically to the Iban of the Paku and Rimbas Rivers in the lower Saribas District of the Sri Aman Division of Sarawak and were recorded mainly between 1977 and 1979, and in the course of briefer visits during the 1990s.[4]

As with many other Borneo peoples, Saribas Iban death rituals are elaborate (SATHER 2003; SANDIN 1980: 33–38, 51–62). Traditionally they were multi-staged and were performed in such a way as to effect a gradual transformation of self and community between what are seen as existentially distinct states of "life" (*idup*) and "death" (*mati*) (SATHER 2003). For the Saribas Iban, these rituals, at least through the 1970s, comprised a tripartite series, with each major rite conducted by a different ritual specialist. The first of these rites, called *nyenggai' antu* or *nyabak* was traditionally performed by a female soul guide or dirge singer called the *tukang sabak*. The second rite, the *pelian beserara' bunga*, was performed by a *manang*, almost always a man, and forms the principal subject of this paper; while the third, the *gawai antu*, only briefly touched on here, was conducted by a company, or, possibly, several companies, of *lemambang* or priest bards. *Nyenggai' antu* was held as a nightlong vigil immediately preceding the interment of the dead; the *pelian beserara' bunga* was held approximately three months later, at the end of mourning; while the *gawai antu* was celebrated as

[4] Fieldwork was done primarily during university holidays and here I wish to thank the School of Comparative Social Sciences, University Sains Malaysia, and the State Government of Sarawak for making this possible. I also wish to record my thanks to the late BENEDICT SANDIN, his family, and the other families of Kerangan Pinggai longhouse, Ulu Paku, for their unstinting hospitality. I was able to return to the Saribas briefly in 1991, under the auspices of the Tun Jugah Foundation, and for a somewhat longer period in 1994, while a Fulbright Fellow at the University Malaya. These latter stays, together with briefer visits since, through 1999, were made principally for the purpose of recording, transcribing, and translating Iban shamanic songs (see SATHER 2001: 18ff)

point of view of the *tukang sabak*'s soul, which acts in these dialogues and descriptive passages as the principal interlocutor and narrating voice.

The singing of the *sabak* signals the permanent separation of the "soul" (*semengat*) from the "body" (*tubuh*) and tells of the former's migration to Sebayan. At its conclusion, as soon as the *tukang sabak* finishes singing, the body is removed from the longhouse and carried to the cemetery. Here, it is buried in the earth, the earth being the element from which it was originally forged by the god Selampandai. By the time breathing ceases, the soul is thought to have already left the body. According to MANANG BANGGA, an elderly shaman of Muton Longhouse, on the Muton tributary of the Rimbas River (SATHER 2001: 55),

> When we human beings die, our soul remains alive (*enti' kitai mensia mati, semengat kitai bedau idup*). It is exactly like a chicken that has left its cage; it has only become separated from the body (*tulin-ulin baka manuk minggal ka kerungan, semina beserara' enggau tubuh*).

Thus, the soul, although disembodied, lives on. Leaving its body behind in this world and journeying to Sebayan, here it is thought to undergo a series of further lives, deaths, and rebirths, some say seven in all. After its seventh death, the soul is then transubstantiated and returns to the material world in the form of a watery mist which condenses, especially in the early morning hours when the temperature is at its lowest, and so falls to earth as "dew" (*ambun*). It is as dew that the transformed soul stuff is taken up and nourishes, in turn, the growing rice plants by which the material life of human beings is sustained in this world. Hence, rice is identified by the Saribas Iban, in a literal sense, with the ancestral dead (see SATHER 1994b: 130). Transubstantiated, the soul returns from Sebayan and, through the medium of rice, is consumed by living human beings, with the result that, not only are rice and human existence linked, but the states of life and death are, themselves conjoined in a single ontological cycle (see SATHER 1994b: 129–30; 2001: 54–58). In this way, neither the living individual nor his or her soul is immortal. Rather, the finite existence and the ultimate transformation of the one presupposes that of the other. While the soul outlives the body, in the end, it dissolves into mist and in this form returns to the living world. By the same token, it ceases to exist in Sebayan. This transubstantiation, and the soul's return and incorporation in the family's rice crop, thus make possible the reproduction and continued existence of human life in the material world. The body, in a similar way, although more directly, is also thought to return to the earth. This takes place through the agency of the god Selampandai, and more concretely, as we shall see, through the actions of his ritual surrogate, the shaman.

BESERARA' BUNGA

Death is typically followed by a three-month mourning period called *ulit*. During this time, out of respect for the bereaved family, other longhouse members are not permitted to hold a *gawai*, sing or play musical instruments, laugh or talk loudly inside the longhouse, or wear jewelry. The *pelian beserara' bunga* is normally performed immediately after *ngetas ulit*, a brief rite that marks the conclusion of the *ulit* mourning period (cf. GANA NGADI 1998: 54ff; SANDIN 1980: 37–38).

Like the singing of the *sabak*, the *pelian beserara' bunga* is performed at night, after the conclusion of *ngetas ulit*, on the deceased's family's gallery and similarly takes place before an audience of family mourners, neighbors, and invited visitors coming from other longhouses. *Beserara'* means, literally, "to cut away" or "separate". In contrast to the singing of the *sabak*, the rite of *beserara' bunga* is performed not for the soul of the newly dead, but for his or her *bunga* (or *bungai*). In ordinary speech *bunga* means "flower", but here it refers to the deceased's plant image or plant counterpart. As a plant image, the *bunga*, which is believed to be ordinarily invisible, is conceived of as a component of the self that grows separately from the body, but which precisely mirrors the latter's state of this-worldly health, vitality, infirmity, or death, that is to say, its global state of this-worldly mortality and wellbeing (for further details, see SATHER 2001: 58–65).

In appearance, the *bunga* is likened to a bamboo plant (*buluh*) and is said to spring, together with the plants belonging to each of the other members of the same family, from a common "source" (*pun*) or "rootstock" (*pugu*).[7] While a component of the self, the plant image thus emphasizes what might be called the social or collective side of selfhood. Individual *bunga* grow together in a clump (*begumpul*), with each clump representing a single longhouse family. These clumps are thought to grow in a large garden in the invisible world where they are looked after by the ancestral shamans (*petara manang*), including the chief of these shamanic deities, Menjaya

---

[7] Here I have considerably simplified Iban ideas. In the context of Iban shamanic ritual, there are, in fact, two aspects of this plant image that are frequently distinguished: one called the *ayu* and the other the *bunga* (for an extended discussion, see SATHER 2001: 54ff). While, the *bunga* tends to be associated with life in a mortal sense, and hence with death, the *ayu* is associated more generally with life in the sense of long life, longevity, and with fertility and reproduction.

"Lord of Shamans" (*Menjaya Raja Manang*), and are weeded and otherwise tended by the souls of human shamans who are thought to repeatedly journey to this garden during healing rituals.[8]

In addition, the *manang* sometimes describe these clumps of plants as the "house of the souls" (*rumah semengat*), that is to say, the secure place where, in good health, the souls of family members remain gathered together, like the embodied human beings who, in this world, collectively dwell together inside a longhouse (*rumah*). By contrast, the souls of those who are ill, or in mortal danger, are said to have strayed from this clump. In doing so, they characteristically become disengaged from the others, perhaps even turning anti-social. Avoiding the company of the other souls, they live in the wild, often in solitude deep in the forest, where they are believed to run the certain risk of being hunted down and captured by malevolent spirits, or of becoming lost, or even of migrating prematurely to the otherworld. In this state, separated from the "flower source" (*pun bunga*) and isolated from the souls of other family members, the wandering, disembodied soul is prone to illness and disaster and so is said to place its owner in grave mortal danger (cf. SATHER 1978, 2001: 53–55). Hence, a final task performed by the *manang* at the conclusion of the *pelian beserara' bunga* is to re-aggregate the souls of the surviving family members whose connection with the flower source has been disrupted by the death of one of their members.

The *bunga* symbolizes, above all, the mortal aspect of each person's state of being in the visible, materially embodied world. Thus, at birth, a new *bunga* is said to sprout from the common rootstock and in health it grows and flourishes, like a healthy young plant. In illness, however, or in old age, the *bunga* is said to "wither" (*layu*), and in death, to "die" (*parai*), or to "fall from [its stalk]" (*gugur*). However, the rootstock, or flower source, lives on. With regard to the family, the *bunga* is thus also an image of social continuity. At death, the *manang* must therefore cut away the dead and withered *bunga* in order to protect the family's rootstock as a whole and to make room for potential new shoots.

In performing the *pelian beserara' bunga*, the shaman modifies his shrine, or *pagar api* (literally, "fence of fire"), so that it consists primarily of a freshly-cut stalk of bamboo representing, among other things, the family's *bunga*. This is fastened to an upright spear, the blade of which is attached to a traverse pole that runs between two house pillars at the center of the gallery, while the base of the spear shaft is set in an earthenware jar, the latter representing the *pugu' bunga* or "rootstock of the flower". The spear is

---

[8] The chief ritual performed to clear around and free the plant image from weeds is called the *pelian mensiang bunga,* "rite to clear around the flower".

likened to a "path" or *jalai*, along which the spirits and souls are said to move during the ritual's performance.

Branches of the stalk that face to the "west", or in the direction of the family apartments (in ritual contexts, this direction [*ka mata ari padam*] is associated with death) are said to face Sebayan.[9] One of these branches is chosen by the shaman to represent the *bunga* of the deceased, and it is this branch that the shaman severs at the climax of the *beserara' bunga* rite. To confirm its identification with the de-

Picture 1. The *manang*, draped in a ritual ikat cloth, circumambulates the *pagar api* (shrine) as he chants the *beserara' bunga* chant

ceased, the *manang* usually fastens to it a bead and a shell armlet, both traditional items of personal adornment (*Picture 1*).

Having completed these preparations, the shaman sits beside the *pagar api*, at the precise center of the family's gallery, with his audience seated mainly facing him along the upper gallery. After all is ready, he begins to sing. The opening stanzas of the *pelian beserara' bunga* are similarly set, like those of the *sabak*, inside the longhouse interior and tell of how the spirits of the dead (*antu Sebayan*) have assembled just outside the longhouse entranceway. Entering the house, they ask to sever the *bunga* in order that they might take the newly dead's portion of it with them to Sebayan. But, the god Selampandai intervenes. Significantly, Selampandai is the god of iron smithing who is thought to create each living person's body at his forge at the time of conception. He is also the creator of the first human

---

[9] See SATHER 1993: 79 for a discussion of the ritual orientation of a Saribas Iban longhouse.

being. Hence, Selampandai is the principal Iban life-giver.[10] However, Selampandai has two aspects, sometimes referred to in the songs as *Selampandai Idup,* "Selampandai of the Living", and *Selampandai Mati,* "Selampandai of the Dead". In the latter aspect, Selampandai determines the length of each person's life span or "breath of life" (*seput* or *nyawa*). As *Selampandai Mati,* he is therefore the principal life-taker, and, as a god is believed to set the finite limits to each person's allotted life span in this world.

During the *pelian beserara' bunga,* the shaman assumes the part of Selampandai, acting in both these capacities, as life-giver and life-taker, as *Selampandai Idup* and *Selampandai Mati.* In this dual persona, the shaman's soul tells the spirits of the dead that they must not take the *bunga* for themselves, but, rather, they must allow him, as Selampandai the life-taker, to divide it for them. Thus, in the words of the *pelian beserara' bunga* (SATHER 2001: 330–333):

Lalu angkat laki Indai Bilai,	Then the husband of Indai Bilai rises up,
Tuai orang di Gensarai Redak Tenchang,	Chief of the Gensarai Redak Tenchang people [the dead].
Engkanjung Raja Menggung nyintak perapang pedang bejengkung,	And together with Raja Menggung they draw their swords, gripping their curved handles.
Deka' nyarau dan limau bunga belitung,	They wish to cut off the branch of a lime tree, a *belitung* flower.
Tang kena' rara Selampandai, Manang Empung.	But they are prevented by Selampandai, by Shaman Empung.
"Enda' nuan tau' ngambi' kediri',	"You must not take it alone,
Enti' aku enda' magi panggung, enda' ngitung,	But let me divide it for you, and so present you with your share.
Peda' nuan dan ujang kena' pasung tedung, ditanchang kendawang."	For behold, the tip of its branch is bound by a cobra, encircled by a coral snake."

Both these snakes are highly venomous. Indai Bilai is a goddess of Sebayan who is said to have long, pendulous breasts, which she uses to nurse the *anak lulus,* the stillborn and dead motherless infants in the otherworld.[11] She appears often in songs describing Sebayan, while Raja Menggung and her husband are leaders of the ancestral dead (see SATHER 2001: 387fn).

---

[10] He is not, however, an ancestral shaman, nor is he represented, among the other deities in the upper world, as a shaman.

[11] For more on the *anak lulus,* see SATHER (1978: 326).

But, first, before making this division of the *bunga*, the shaman, again as Selampandai, must divide the family's food crops and household property, separating everything, in the words of the song, into two equal shares (SATHER 2001: 334–335).

Nya' baru sua'-sua' nyabau muda',	Now, in an instant,
Selampandai beguai magi ia dua.	Selampandai hurries to divide it in two.
Bedua' enggau sida' ke idup,	He divides it between those who are alive,
Enggau sida' sebayan ke danjan dulu' lela'.	And those who are dead.
Bedua' bela' bebagi barang.	He divides everything into two equal shares.
Bedua' perengka sida' ke idup,	He divides the possessions between the living,
Enggau sida' ke lama' udah laya.	And those who have long been dead.
Bebagi semua, anang kurang.	Both shares must be equal, neither more nor less than the other.

During this symbolic division, the dead are given plates, cups, saucers, and other household goods, and the various seeds and cuttings of the family's cultivated crops, including Job's tears, long-beans, gourds, pumpkins, hill and swamp rice, glutinous rice, mustard, fruit trees, and even rubber gardens.

The dead, the narrative relates, will take their share to Sebayan, while the living will use theirs in this world, where, the song relates, they will prosper. For example (SATHER 2001: 334–335):

Bedua' singkap pinggai pemakai sida' ke idup,	He divides the plates between the living
Enggau sida' ke lama' udah parai,	And those who have long been dead.
Enggi' ia dibai' ia laya sulai,	The deceased takes his share with him to die,
Ngagai sungai Mandai Awai,	Bearing it away to the Mandai Awai stream,
Dibai' pulai lubah singkang.	Traveling there with slow steps.
Enggi' sida' ke idup taruh teguh simpan lalai,	The share of those who are alive is kept hidden, concealed for safekeeping
Enti' maya sida' begawai besai,	Until such a time as they hold a great *gawai*,
Dikena' sida' nyambut Sigai,	Using [the plates] to receive Sigai,
Anak tuai Raja Simpulang Gana.	The eldest son of Raja Simpulang Gana.

Raja Simpulang Gana is the Iban god of agriculture and Sigai (or Sigi) is his son. The reference is to the invocation of these deities that occurs during major agricultural rituals, with the imagery here, and in the other stanzas, indicating the family's future prosperity. After the family's household items have been divided, Selampandai divides its food crops, including, for example, the family's hill rice seeds (SATHER 2001: 342–345). Here, he momentarily assumes the voice of the deceased:

Bedua' sempuli padi bukit.

Untung enggi' aku penuh sintung
  panggung sesupit,

Ke dibai' aku pulai ka menua kami

Di Bukit Tambit Selabit, Seladan Jarang.

Enggi' sida' ditanam ba' emperan
  tanah bukit.

Ngambika ia memadang kedil pisit,

Baka pemansang padi bangang.

Nya' ke di-inang anak bujang
  Lemambang Bejit,

Ngasuh ia betangkai balat nyelulai
  kelalu rapit,

Teda empa' sida' pedua' enggau
  Dayak bansa Kelabit,

Laban sida' beruntung panggung benasit,

Berega ka duit ringgit gudang.

Divide the hill rice seeds.

My share fills a *sintung* covered by
  a *supit* basket.

These I carry, as I return to our country

At Pack-Strap Hill; at Basket- Fastening
  Mountain [otherworld landmarks].

Theirs they plant on a hilltop plain.

Here it covers the land, growing close
  together,

Luxuriant like *bangang* padi.

It is nurtured by the leaf-monkey bard

So that its heavy panicles hang down thickly.

Any leftover grain that cannot be eaten is
  shared with the Kelabit Dayaks,

Because they are lucky and prosper,

Earning dollar coins.

After all of these objects have been divided, the dead, in return, announce the various charms and medicines that they intend to leave behind for the living. Again, these gifts are typically catalogued in great detail in the shaman's narrative. For example (SATHER 2001: 352–353):

"Uji sambut nuan enggau kukut jari kanan

Taring uting babi dupan enggau batu
  tanduk rusa' ngulam,

Enggau batu ai' ulih ngambi' di kaki
  kerangan,

Ditambah enggau batu gumbang ke
  besegang ngalun kerangan.

Tu' batu buah pauh laba berendam
  dikemeran ka ikan bam,

Kena' nuan nyeridi ka simpuli padi rutan

Ngambika belayan ia kedil jampat
  mansang.

Agi' ga' ditambah aku enggau batu
  engkenyang tanam.

Kena' nuan nyeridi ka simpuli padi
  engkanan,

Ngambika belayan iya berat tetensam
  magang-magang.

Tu' batu letan beri' Gepi Ini Andan,

Taruh nuan dalam serangan kena' nuan
  besimpan mali puang."

"Try to receive with the nails of your
  right hand

The rooting tusk of a pig and the petrified
  antler of a grazing sambur deer,

Together with a water-stone charm found at
  the foot of a gravel bed,

And a petrified wave that dashed against the
  shingle.

This is the petrified *pauh laba* fruit taken
  from beneath the sea where it was
  guarded by a whale.

Use it to tend your *rutan* rice,

And the crop will be abundant and grow
  quickly.

Again, I add to it a petrified *engkenyang*
  plant.

Use it to tend your *engkanan* rice,

And the crop will be heavily laden, bending
  down its stalks.

This is the stone *letan* rod given by Ini' Andan,

Keep it safely for use when you store your
  rice, and your rice bins will never be empty."

In part, the first half of the *pelian beserara' bunga* is structured around a symbolic division of material goods and food crops. Exchange also constitutes an important element of the *sabak* narrative (cf. SATHER 2003). However, the division of goods that takes place during the *pelian beserara' bunga* is, in a sense, the opposite, a negation of the possibility of future exchange. Through this division, a shared family estate is dissolved and from it, each of the parties to this division is furnished with the material necessities—the household utensils, seeds, and plant cuttings—by which its members may fashion for themselves a separate existence, without the future necessity of calling upon the resources of the others. Hence, as a result of this division, the living and the dead, ideally at least, become self-sufficient, and the dead, in particular, are no longer required to draw upon the labor and material possessions of their living kin.[12] Before leaving the longhouse, the dead complete this separation by bestowing charms and medicines which act to prolong the lives of their living kin in this world. The transfer of healing powers represented by these gifts is also consistent, of course, with the *manang's* role as a curer and preserver of life, and also as an intercessor between the living and the dead.

The *manang's* soul next announces that the time has come to sever the *bunga*. First, however, the shaman, in a series of self-reflexive lines, expresses his reluctance to do so and describes the grief that the soul of the newly dead experiences in taking final leave of its loved ones. For the mourners, particularly for the members of the bereaved family, this is a climactic moment of great sorrow (SATHER 2001: 356–359).[13]

---

12 The spirits of the dead are often depicted as greedy; hence, family members who fail to do their share, and live off of the labor of others, are sometimes likened to the *antu Sebayan*.

13 The precise wording, of course, varies from one singer to another as well as by performance. The mark of a skillful singer is his ability to compose the wording in such a way as to make it particularly appropriate to each occasion. The text cited here was recorded during a performance of the *pelian beserara' bunga* that took place on 28th October 1977 at Tanjong Longhouse in the Ulu Paku (see SATHER 2001 for the full Iban text and translation). This particular performance was sung by two *manang*, both of whom are, regrettably, now dead, but who were at the time famous local singers, MANANG ENTERI of Suri Baroh and MANANG MERAMAT of Nanga Deit, Rimbas (SATHER 2001: 326).

Nya' baru tebang kepapa' ruyak di janga'.
Naka' pengelembau ati kami Menani kaju'
  jari main beserara',
Deka' nyerara' enggau sida' ke lela'
  dulu' midang.

Now fell the *kepapa'* tree, splitting its fork.
How reluctant we *Menani* are to perform with
  our hands the *beserara'* rite,
To part with those who are dead.

Tak duduk dugau-dugau sida' ke lela'
  dulu' lenyau,
Ba' pun rengun bunga tawai.
Ai' mata iya balat nyaya labuh keberai,
Jari iya bepaut ba' nanyi bunga tawai,
Jari ngengkang enggi' sida' ke midang,
Bepaut ba' gagang megai tangkai.

And now the Dead One sits deep in thought,

At the base of a fragrant *tawai* flower.
His tears spill heavily,
His hands draw closer the *nanyi tawai* flower.
With all the fingers of their hands,
Those who have died draw towards them
  the flowering stalk.

"Naka' meh pengenggai aku serara'
  deh Nyara', bali' Gendai,
Aku ga' agi' belala' ngulih ka utai
  macham bebarang.
Peda' duduk besila sida' ke lenyau dulu'
  laya ba' pun rengun bunga,
Jari bepaut ba' lenggi' dan dua.
Jari ngengkang bepaut ba' takang
  bunga kenanga.

"How reluctant I am to be severed by *Nyara'*,
  the transformed *Gendai* [the shaman],
For I still wish to seek riches in this world."

Behold the dead are sitting with their knees
  folded at the base of a fragrant flower,
Their hands hold the top of two branches.
All the fingers of their hands draw towards
  them the stalk of the *kenanga* flower.[14]

"Naka' meh pengenggai aku tu' serara'
  enggau lantang bujang melisa,
Aku ga' belala' ngila' ka sida' ke biak
  benung reremba..."

"How unwilling I am to part from the happy,
  daring bachelors,
For I should dearly like to watch over them
  in their youth..."

The *manang* at this point, still singing, rises, and circling the shrine, he cuts the branch facing "westward", toward the family apartments (SATHER 2001: 358–359) (*Picture 2*):

Lalu bejaku' Lansu, Manang Usam,
"Kati ku' aku enda' nyerara' magi nuan?
Nuan ga' udah lesi bebadi laya danjan,
Laban petara nadai agi' ngemata ngintu
  nuan,

Then speaks *Lansu'*, Shaman *Usam*,
"How can I not separate you?
For you have died
Because the gods no longer watch over you.

Nya' alai tingkil ga' nuan baka selinggir
  ujung dan."

Therefore I break you off like a twig from
  the end of a main branch."

---

14 *Kenang* in Iban means "remembrance". Here, in these lines, the *bunga* is represented by actual flowers, in this instance by different types of flowers, known as *bunga tanam*, which Iban farmers interplant with rice.

Picture 2. At the climax of the chant, the *manang* severs the *bunga* representing the plant image of the deceased whose portrait appears at the base of the shrine (note the armshell and beads)

Severing the *bunga* thus parts the living from the dead, removing the deceased's presence from the living world as symbolized by this material representation of his or her invisible "flower" (or plant image). But, while the *bunga* of the deceased is carried to Sebayan, and so removed from the living world, the "main branch" or "flower source" (*pun bunga*), representing, as we have seen, the family as a whole, lives on in the material world. Hence, the imagery of the shaman's narrative, and the act of cutting itself, stress not only separation, and the mortality of the embodied self, but also affirm the social continuity of the family and its inherent capacity for renewal.

At this point, the appearance of the newly deceased is transformed into that of a spirit (*nyadi antu*), and so the deceased now appears, and is generally referred to by the living, as a "spirit of the dead" (*antu Sebayan*), losing through this transformation, in part at least, its recognizable human shape when seen by the souls of the living (SATHER 2001: 360–361):

Ke begamal rigam-rigam ke tinggi'	The Dead One, now appears huge and tall,
jam-jam,	like a tall leafy tree.
Bekaki mesai lidi...	With legs as large as laze-rods...
Bemata mesai buah terung kanggan,	Eyeballs as big as eggplants.
Sintak seput iya munyi ai' surut matak	His breathing sounds like the ebbing rush of
langan....	waves...
Nyawa iya seruran dengam-dengam.	His open mouth is forever eager to eat.
Ngeli' ka' sigi' mesai tempan.	His teeth are as large as anvils.

Expressed by this imagery is a sense of the increasing disengagement and ambivalence which the Iban feel towards the dead.[15] At the same time, accepting its fate, the spirit of the deceased now prepares to depart for Sebayan. The narrative imagery invests these preparations with an air of material factuality. It also points up, more generally, the essential inevitability of death (SATHER 2001: 360–361).

"Nadai ku' meh Lansu, Manang Sada.	"It cannot be helped, *Lansu'*, Shaman *Sada*.
'Nganti aku udah begari' masuk ka baju	Wait until I put on my collared shirt,
putung kemija,	
Masuk ka tanchut udah diterika,	Until I have donned my freshly-ironed trousers,
Nganti aku udah nanggam dekuan aku,	And have fastened around my wrist,
Enggau jam buatan China."	A wristwatch made in China."

Now, in the shaman's narrative, the spirits of the dead call for Mengalai, the chief slave and porter of Sebayan, so that he may carry the goods that they have received on their return journey (SATHER 2001: 362–363).

Nya' baru tak rengai-rengai nyawa ngumbai,	Now an incessant calling of voices is heard,
Enggi' sida' ke punggu' dulu' parai.	Made by those who have died and gone before us.
Ngangau ka Mengalai ulu' tuai sida',	They call for Mengalai, their chief slave,
Pengema' utai kalih ke belakang.	The porter who carries their goods on his back.

In departing, the shaman's soul calls upon the deceased's spirit to continue sending material blessings to those who remain in this world and continue the *bilik* household (SATHER 2001: 368–369)[16]:

---

15 It is worth noting that the term *antu Sebayan*, in the strongly dualistic language of Iban ritual, refers also, in the context of death rituals, to the actual corpse of the dead.

16 The term *bilik* (or, in Saribas dialect, *bilek*) refers to both the individual apartment within a longhouse and the family or household group whose members maintain and occupy it (cf. FREEMAN 1970: 1ff).

Diatu' kitai nyau besarara' baka ira' tabu' tali.	Now we sever our connection, like the separation of strands from a once braided cord.
Bekejang meh kitai baka batang tampung titi.	We are parted like logs once joined to form a footbridge.
Tang nuan anang enda' nganjung ka kami ubat ngasuh kaya,	But you must continue to send us charms that cause us to be rich,
Ngasuh raja, ngasuh gerai; ngasuh nyamai,	That bring us wealth, health, and happiness,
Kena' kami nampung nerujung bilik penaik nuan ke di menua tu'.	So that we who continue this household may prosper in this world.

At this point there is a break in the singing, as the shaman leads a party of family members and others to the stream or riverbank. Here they throw the severed branch and trays of food offerings in the water, the latter symbolizing the share of foodstuffs meant for the dead, and so comprised of various kinds of cultivated plants and fruits[17] (*Picture 3*).

Picture 3. Manang Digat inspects the offerings of cultivated foodstuffs to be given to the dead following the severing of the bunga.

After returning to the longhouse, the shaman moves the *kembai bunga* ("opened flowers", represented by undyed cotton cloth or yarn) and a length of ikat cloth (*pua' kumbu'*) which, at the outset, he had hung over the traverse pole, and transfers them from the side of "death" (facing the family apartments) to the side of "life" (facing the upper gallery).[18] He then resumes singing. The *manang's* soul now accompanies the spirits of the dead on their

---

[17] Alternatively, these things may be thrown beneath the longhouse floor.

[18] As will be noted presently, when he finishes singing, the shaman gathers the souls of the members of the family from the *kembai bunga*, now on the life-facing side of the shrine, and re-inserts them, one by one, into their heads.

return journey to Sebayan. The route they take is different from the one followed by the *tukang sabak*'s soul during the singing of the *sabak*. Instead of traveling from the outer threshold of the longhouse through the forest, they journey by water, normally using special boats called *bangkung*, downriver longboats, and *berangai*, coffin-shaped boats used only by the dead. They travel first downriver and then up, making a complete circuit of the riverine universe that, in Iban cosmological belief, is thought to join the living world with the Mandai River of Sebayan (cf. SATHER 1993: 80–81). There is no Bridge of Fear or Earthen Door, prominent barriers across which the deceased's soul had to pass during the *sabak* (SATHER 2003). Instead, the party enters Sebayan directly by way of the Mandai River of the Dead (*Ai' Mandai Mati*).

Having returned the spirits of the dead to Sebayan, the shaman now assembles the souls of the bereaved family, sending out his spirit guide and spirit shaman companions to help him gather them together. At the same time, he also recalls his own soul. Typically, the returning party makes the journey back to the longhouse by flying, guided by the shaman's spirit guide, spirit shaman companions, and by the sound of drumming.[19] Entering the longhouse, the song journey thus comes full-circle, returning again to where it began, in the opening lines of the song, on the longhouse gallery.

With his own soul safely back in this world, and surrounded by his human audience, the *manang* then sings a stanza disparaging Sebayan (SATHER 2001: 390–391):

Enda' nyamai tanah Mandai,	The Mandai world is unpleasant!
Enda' nyaman tanah Sebayan!	The Otherworld is tasteless!
Asi' bari' asai ke ngunyah sampi buah berangan,	Its musty rice tastes, when we chew it, like bitter chestnuts,
Lauk dipanduk asai ka ngirup ai' madu nyeruan.	Its boiled vegetables taste, when we drink them, like sour honey.
Udu kamah menua orang ke tumpah dulu' danjan!	The land of the dead is extremely dirty!
Udu jai menua orang ke rimpi' dulu' padam!	The land of those who are dead is very bad!
Rumah sida' rebah, tumbang tiang.	The houses of the dead collapse, their posts topple.
Gelegar sida' tingkar buruk papan.	The floors cave in, for their planks are rotten.

---

[19] No actual drums are beaten. Drumming plays only a slight part in Iban shamanism, and, as in this case, drums are not normally employed to initiate soul journeying, but rather as a means of guiding the shaman's soul back on its return to this world. In conversations, *manang* often say that their soul is guided to the longhouse by sound, usually by that of water flowing or, as here, of drumming.

Here the shaman's narrative incorporates a mirror-like reversal of the praise-song sung by the soul guide when she and the deceased's soul first arrive in the otherworld. By disparaging Sebayan, the *manang*, in concluding the *pelian beserara' bunga*, celebrates, in effect, the primacy of the embodied, this-worldly existence of the living over the insubstantiated, dreamlike existence of the souls and spirit dead. In addition, these words are addressed to the aggregate souls of the surviving family members which the shaman, when he finishes singing, gathers from the *kembai bunga* (or "opened flower") where they are thought to have attached themselves as he sang. He then restores them to the body of each family member by pressing the soul into the top of his or her head. This is done inside the family apartment. While the words of the *sabak* mark the migration of the deceased's soul to Sebayan, those of the *pelian beserara' bunga* are intended, instead, to reassemble the souls of the survivors by gathering them together at the "house of the souls" represented by the rootstock of the *bunga* (itself symbolized by the jar at the base of the shaman's shrine). The *manang* concludes by calling back his own soul. He then, as a final ritual act, reasserts the integrity of the living world by erecting a series of unseen barriers (*pelepa'*) at the various exit and entry points, first demarcating in this way the family apartment, then the longhouse as a whole, thereby restoring the proper separation of this world from Sebayan (see SATHER 2001: 404).

Significantly, the association of the shaman with Selampandai identifies him, at once, as both a life-giver (or preserver of life)—his usual function—and as a life-taker. As we have seen, Selampandi not only creates each person's body, but he also imparts to each embodied individual a finite life span, typically associated with the breath, which a shaman may, by interceding directly with the god, ritually lengthen or extend. In the end, however, Selampandai takes back this "breath of life". Indeed, so crucial is Selampandai in sustaining life, that, even earlier, his momentary inattentiveness may result in an individual's premature death (see SATHER n.d.).

In severing the *bunga*, the shaman acts, in effect, in the capacity of *Selampandai Mati*, and so effaces this mortal aspect of the deceased's self from the living world. Identifying himself with Selampandai, the shaman thus effects within the material world, a final separation of the living from the dead. Not only does he sever the plant stalk representing the deceased's *bunga*, but he also oversees a symbolic division of the family's food crops and household wealth, hence undoing the material ties that formerly connected the deceased with the members of his or her household. At the same time, these actions have also a deeper significance. The share taken by the dead also represents the corporeal presence of the individual which the spirits of the dead, in departing from the living world, thereby return to the earth (*tanah*), thus making possible the regeneration of new life and its continuance through the intervening media of the family's cultivated crops and tangible wealth, a share of which the living retain in this world. As Manang Bangga expressed it, when we die, "our flesh and blood, as human beings, return to the country of Selampandai, [to that] of Selampandai of the Dead...[where] our blood enters the *padi*" (SATHER 2001: 55). It is this return, above all, that the *pelian beserara' bunga* is meant to bring about.

GAWAI ANTU

The *gawai antu* is, by far, the most complex ritual in the Saribas Iban funerary cycle. In contrast to the singing of the *sabak* and the severing of the flower rite, it is concerned more with a transformation of community than it is with the fate of the individual self. This is reflected, simultaneously, at the level of both the spirits of the dead and the longhouse of the mourners. While the *sabak* concerns chiefly the soul and the *pelian beserara' bunga*, the plant image, the *gawai antu* concerns primarily the *antu Sebayan* or "spirits of the dead", particularly their reconstitution, vis-a-vis their living kin, as a separate longhouse community. Significantly, the *gawai antu* is thus described by Saribas bards and elder laymen as a rite of *berumah* or "house-building" and at its conclusion tomb huts are erected over the graves of the dead (cf. SATHER 1993: 94ff).

The *gawai antu* honors the dead and fulfils each family's final, and most onerous, obligations to its ancestors. The rite recalls, in particular, the most recent dead, and invites them into the public areas of the longhouse, and so temporarily dissolves the boundaries, reinforced at the conclusion of the *pelian beserara' bunga*, that separate the living world from that of the dead. Performing the *gawai* brings great renown upon the sponsoring longhouse, but it is also fraught with danger. With the penetration of the dead into the living world, the potential for calamity is enormous should details of the ritual be forgotten or incorrectly performed (see SATHER 1993, 2003).

As a symbolic act of house-building, the *gawai antu* effects the final ontological transformation of the dead. It also, in a parallel fashion, constitutes the sponsoring longhouse of the mourners as a discrete ritual community in relation to the longhouses of those who attend as visitors. The dead receive final memorialization for their achievements in this world and, with their return from Sebayan and reconstitution as a house group, their status is further altered and they become, in effect, sufficiently differentiated from their living kin so that they may now be received as invited ritual guests (*pengabang*), analogous to the human visitors (also called *pengabang*) coming, in the material world, from neighboring longhouse communities to attend the *gawai*. In this role, the ancestral dead now play a part, vis-a-vis the longhouse community from which they originated, similar to that of the gods (*petara* or *betara*), who, in other *gawai*, are ritually invoked by the bards, and entertained by their longhouse hosts, as temporary ritual visitors from beyond the human world.

CONCLUSION: ESCHATOLOGY AND NARRATIVES OF TRAVEL

At the core of each of these three major rituals constituting the Iban funerary cycle is a sung narrative. The words of this narrative are known as its *leka main*. Literally, *leka* means "seed" or "gist of"; *main*, "play", "entertainment", or "doing" (RICHARDS 1981: 201–2; SUTLIVE 1994: 132, 144). Taken together, *leka main* refers to ritual poetry, either sung or spoken (cf. RICHARDS 1981: 202; SATHER 2001: 1ff). Rituals performed by the *manang*, including the *beserara' bunga*, are called *pelian*. These rituals are highly diverse, but the majority are performed as healing rites. In them, the *manang* is believed to dispatch his soul (*semengat*), aided by a spirit guide (*yang*) [or guides], out into the cosmos—into the unseen dimensions of "this world" (*dunya tu'*)—or beyond them, as in the *pelian beserara' bunga*—into the land of the dead (*menua Sebayan*).

Every *pelian* narrative (its *leka main*, or, more specifically, its *leka pelian*) is composed around an ordered journey described as its *jalai*, meaning literally, its "journey" or "path". In this journey, the shaman's soul is typically accompanied by its spirit guide and additional spirit-shaman companions, and much of their travel unfolds dialogically, through encounters, greetings, and conversations. For Iban audiences, the words of the *leka main* not only describe these travels, but quite literally bring them to life. Using spoken dialogue, the *manang* assumes the different voices of the various invisible personae that his soul and its companions encounter—thereby verbally enacting these unseen meetings—while at the same time, using the representational power of verbal imagery, he depicts for his audience the invisible landscapes within which they occur. For Iban audiences, the poetic power of these ritual songs derives from the very action of traveling itself, from the paths taken, and from the places and personae met with along the way. In addition, the songs are also about the shaman's own agency and the projection of his ritual self into other worlds.

For the Iban, death and dying, as we have noted, are, in some regards, relatively familiar experiences. Thus, for example, the soul is thought to leave the body, as it does at death, when a person dreams or falls unconscious, and, from time to time, the soul of a living person may even journey to Sebayan or may encounter and converse with the spirits of Sebayan in dreams. The significance of this is far-reaching. It means that for the living, death is not entirely beyond ordinary experience. People regularly enter into temporary states that are believed to involve experiential aspects of death, such as soul loss, the withering of their plant image, or the straying of their soul from the flower source. In addition, these states, particularly soul loss, are a regular part of the shaman's ritual calling. Moreover, familiarity with aspects of death is reinforced by the repeated singing of ritual narratives in which journeys are enacted across the divisions that are otherwise believed to separate the realms of life and death.

While death may mark, in part, an end to individuality, in the sense that it implies a separation of the parts of the self that formerly made up the individual, it does not imply a total annihilation, since at least some of these parts, as in the case of the "flower source" or "spirit dead", may live on as parts of larger wholes. Here, death is not a total ending, but is seen, instead, as a stage in a long and continuous transformation of elements, one "of taking apart and putting together" (cf. BLOCH 1988: 13–14; SATHER 2003).

In the case of the *pelian beserara' bunga*, at its climax, the shaman, in the words of the narrative he sings, momentarily takes on the identity of Selampandai, the god who, at once, both forges the individual's body and, at the same time, assigns a finite life span to his or her corporeal presence, which, following death, in the form of flesh, blood, and breath, he takes back again to his own world. As Selampandai, the shaman cuts away the dead "flower" representing the life image of the deceased, thereby severing it from its family "rootstock" or "source". In the words of the song, death is portrayed as inevitable. It is not, however, a moment of complete annihilation, but marks a sequential dissolution of elements that makes possible not only new life in this world, but, ultimately, the emergence, in a realm beyond it, of a more enduring community of spirit dead.

Even the *manang*, as a sustainer of human life, cannot alter the inevitability of death. In the words of the *beserara' bunga*, following the cutting away of the flower, the newly departed soul, in acknowledgement, addresses the soul of the *manang* in the dialogic mode of the *leka main*, saying (SATHER 2001: 362–363):

"Nadai ku' meh Lansu bali' Gendai,

Laban seput aku enda' tau' idup buai Selampandai.

"It cannot be helped, *Lansu'*, transformed *Gendai*,
Because my breath [of life] is gone, thrown away by Selampandai.

Nyawa aku udah ketak petara enda' panjai,   My life has been cut short by the gods,
Uji beri' aku makai dulu' deh lantang anak   But I ask that you first give me food; my
    andai,   beloved child,
Laban aku nyau deka' pulai ngagai menua   Because presently I depart for our country
kami di Sungai Mandai Midang."   along the Mandai Midang Stream."

Here, the soul acknowledges the shaman's role, as Selampandai's surrogate. For his part, the shaman, while unable to prevent death from occurring, has nonetheless a significant life-affirming role to play all the same. This he does by attending to the grief of the living, providing guidance, and effecting and making intelligible the separation of the living from the dead, and by directing offerings to the newly deceased and so making easier his or her passage to the otherworld. Notably, all of this is done, both affirming and undoing life, through a medium of words, literally, for the Iban, "words of doing" (*leka main*).

REFERENCES

BLOCH, MAURICE
    1988 Death and the concept of person. In S. CEDERROTH – C. CORLIN – J.
          LINDSTROM (eds.) *On the Meaning of Death*. Uppsala: Uppsala Studies in
          Cultural Anthropology, No. 8: 11–29.
ELIADE, MIRCEA
    1964 *Shamanism: Archaic Techniques of Ecstasy*. Trans. WILLARD R. TRASK.
          Princeton: Princeton University Press.
    1987 Shamanism. In MIRCEA ELIADE (ed.-in-chief) *The Encyclopedia of Religion*.
          New York: Macmillan and Free Press, Vol. 13: 201–208.
FREEMAN, DEREK
    1970 *Report on the Iban*. London: Athlone Press.
GANA NGADI, HENRY
    1998 *Iban Rites of Passage and Some Related Ritual Acts*. Kuala Lumpur: Dewan
          Bahasa dan Pustaka.
HAMAYON, ROBERTE
    1995 Are "trance", "ecstasy" and similar concepts appropriate in the study of
          shamanism? In TAE-GON KIM – MIHÁLY HOPPÁL (eds.) *Shamanism in
          Performing Arts*. Budapest: Akadémiai Kiadó, 17–34.
HERTZ, ROBERT
    1960 A Contribution to the Study of the Collective Representation of Death.
          In *Death and the Right Hand*. Trans. R. and C. NEEDHAM. London:
          Cohen & West, 27–86.
RICHARDS, ANTHONY
    1981 *An Iban-English Dictionary*. Oxford: Clarendon Press.

SANDIN, BENEDICT

1968 *Leka Sabak*. Kuching: Borneo Literature Bureau.

1980 *Iban Adat and Augury*. Penang: Penerbit Universiti Sains Malaysia.

SATHER, CLIFFORD

1978 The Malevolent *Koklir*. *Bijdragen tot de Taal-, Land,-en Volkenkunde*. 134: 310–355.

1993 Posts, hearths and thresholds: the Iban longhouse as a ritual structure. In JAMES J. FOX (ed.) *Inside Austronesian Houses: Perspectives on Domestic Designs for Living*. Publication, Department of Anthropology, Research School of Pacific and Asian Studies. Canberra: The Australian National University, 65–115.

1994 One-sided-One: Iban rice myths, agricultural ritual and notions of ancestry. *Contributions to Southeast Asian Ethnography* 10: 119–150.

1996 "All Threads are White": Iban Egalitarianism Reconsidered. In JAMES J. FOX – CLIFFORD SATHER (eds.) *Origins, Ancestry and Alliance*, Publication, Department of Anthropology, Research School of Pacific and Asian Studies. Canberra: The Australian National University, 70–110.

2001 *Seeds of Play, Words of Power: an ethnographic study of Iban shamanic chants*. Kuching: Tun Jugah Foundation and the Borneo Research Council, Vol. 5. Borneo Classics Series.

2003 Transformations of Self and Community in Saribas Iban Death Rituals, In W. R. WILDER (ed.) *Journeys of the Soul: Anthropological Studies of Death, Burial, and Reburial in Borneo*. Williamsburg: Borneo Research Council, Monograph Series, No. 7.

SUTLIVE, VINSON

1988 *The Iban of Sarawak: Chronicle of a vanishing world*. Prospect Heights: Waveland Press.

1994 *Handy Reference Iban-English Dictionary*. Kuching: Tun Jugah Foundation.

DÁVID SOMFAI KARA

Living Epic Tradition
among Inner Asian Nomads

My purpose in this paper is to provide some information about the present status of epic tradition among some Inner Asian nomad groups speaking Turkic languages[1]. In the last five years, from 1995 to 1999, I have visited several parts of Inner Asia where one can still find storytellers or bards who keep alive the old tradition of storytelling. These old storytellers are the last ones who perform epics in the traditional way and there is a great fear that after they pass away this ancient art will disappear completely.

I would also like to say a few words about their former role in the nomadic society and the changes of modern times. Of course, there are many similarities, but also many differences between the former and present roles of storytellers, but one must admire the storytellers' skill at memorising thousands of lines by heart and one must acknowledge the importance of epic tradition among these Inner Asian nomads.

The first time that I ever met an epic teller was in 1995 when I met a Kyrgyz *manasčy*[2] in the village of Aral, which is in the Talas region. Asankan Zhumanaliev was born in 1945 and worked as a teacher at the local school. When I met him he had just arrived back from Bishkek where he had had some meetings with officials who were organising the so-called 1000th anniversary of the *Manas* Epic[3].

---

[1] By the term "Inner Asia", I mean the territory of Mongolia, Western China (Xinjiang), Siberia, Kazakstan and Kyrgyzstan. Thus, the nomad or semi-nomad Turkic groups we refer to are: 1) Kypchak group: Kazak, Karakalpak, Kyrgyz; 2) South Siberian Group: Tyva (Tuva), Altaj-kiži and its dialects, Aghban-tadar (Khakas) dialects; 3) Saqa (Yakut).

[2] (Manasči) *Manaschy* is the person who memorises and chants the epic *Manas*. See ABRAMSON 1990: 361, Petrosjan 1984: 426.

[3] In 1995 the new independent Kyrgyz administration organised a big celebration for the 1000th anniversary of the *Manas* epic. It does not really make sense, since Manas is an imaginary figure of Kyrgyz folklore and the epic itself was created most likely during the seventeenth and eighteenth centuries (ŽIRMUNSKIJ 1962: 296–317).

The *Manas* is a huge Kyrgyz epic, which contains more than 50,000 lines (MUSAJEV 1984: 420–442). This epic is about the land conquests of the Kyrgyz tribes. Manas is an epic hero who leads the Kyrgyz from the Altai Mountains to the *Tianshan*, or Tengir-Too,[4] driving out the Kalmaks, or Oirat Mongols[5]. Of course there is some reality in the fact that some of the Kyrgyz tribes came from the Altai, but the epic is basically about the Kyrgyz's fight for independence from the Zöün-Gar (Jungar) Empire[6], and later, from the Manchu–Chinese invasion[7]. The epic *Manas* played an important role among the Kyrgyz tribes by unifying them through giving them a common national identity.

Although Asankan was quite tired, he accepted my request and invited me to his house for the night to listen to the *Manas*. It was a wonderful night and I enjoyed the *Manas* until dawn. Before I said goodbye to the *manasčy*, I asked him some questions. Then he explained to me that in his childhood he had met an old man in the woods. The old man invited him to listen to stories and when the young boy showed interest in listening to them, he started to chant the great *Manas*. They spent more then a year together with the old man teaching the epic to Asankan, and then the old man died. Asankan has been telling the *Manas* ever since, and also has had some students learning from him (*Picture 1*).

In Kyrgyzstan the government itself encourages the young Kyrgyz generation to memorise the *Manas*. But, of course one cannot easily memorise 50,000 lines. I have realised that they have a special kind of technique: they fall into trance like a shaman, and the words come almost automatically. The *Manas* has a simple melody and is sung without any accompanying musical instrument, but the *manaschy* sometimes expresses the action very passionately with his face and arms. The *Manasč* is a

---

4   Tengir-Too is the Kyrgyz name for Tianshan, which means 'Heavenly Mountains' in Chinese. The Kyrgyz name also means the same.

5   The western Mongolian union was called "Dörben Oirad", or the "Four Oirats" founded by ESEN XAAN (1440–1455) in the fifteenth century. (See: Mongol Ugsaatnii Dzüi II 1996: 11–12). Later, they started to penetrate to the west, fighting against the Kazak and Kyrgyz tribes. The Kazak and Kyrgyz called these non-Muslim tribes "*kalmak*", which probably meant 'pagan' in Turkic (PLOSKICH 1984: 457–462).

6   Jüün-Gar, or "The Right Wing", was the name of the Oirat Mongol Empire founded by BAATAR KHUNG-TAIJI in 1635 when some of the Oirat tribes moved towards Tianshan and started to conquer Turkic territories (PLOSKICH 1984: 458).

7   The Manchu *Qing* dynasty conquered the Jüün-Gar Oirat Empire in 1755. They occupied Eastern Turkestan and tried to penetrate further to the Fregana Valley, Qoqaan, through Kyrgyz territory in the eighteenth century (PLOSKICH 1984: 483).

Picture 1. (Photo by L. KUNKOVÁCS)

person who can see and hear the spirit of *Manas baatyr*,[8] called '*arwak*'[9] in Kyrgyz.

I remember in 1994, when in Karakalpakstan,[10] I was asking around for a shaman (in Kazak, "*baksy*"[11]), and they took me to a *Karakalpak* bard also called "*baksy*". This word, which comes from old *Uigur* through Chinese, means 'a sort of teacher, teaching religion or theory' (the *Nom*[12]). The word

---

[8] The word "*baatyr*" means 'brave man', 'hero'. The nomads call their legendary forefathers and heroes "*baatyr*" (ABRAMSON 1990: 336).

[9] This word "*arwak*" comes from the Arabic word "*rūḥ*" 'spirit', plural "*arwāḥ*" (ABRAMSON 1990: 337).

[10] The Republic of Karakalpakstan is not an independent country. It is part of Özbekistan, south of the Dead Sea of the Aral, where the river Amu-darya used to reach the sea. Its capital is Nökis. The population of the Republic consists of Karakalpaks, Kazaks and Özbeks. The Karakalpaks speak a Kypchak Turkic dialect close to Kazak. They used to live under the rule of the Khaan of Khiwa. They numbered about 400,000 in 1990 in the Republic (Tishkov 1994: 182).

[11] The Ancient Uigur word "*baqšy*" comes from the Chinese word "*boshï*".

[12] The Uigur word "*nom*" comes from Greek through Sogd, and used to mean 'religion', 'theory' or 'Buddhism'. In Modern Mongolian it also means 'book' or 'prayer'.

"bakshi" in modern Mongolian simply means 'teacher', but Muslim Turks of Inner Asia use this word for either 'shaman' (Kazak, Kyrgyz, Uigur) or 'bard' (Özbek, Karakalpak). This fact also proves that there must be a strong link between the shamans and the bards.

Later this same year, during my expedition to *Altai*,[13] I was amazed by the art of the Altai-kiži[14] *kajčy*s in the Republic of Altai.[15] The greatest *kaichy*, ALEKSEI KALKIN (born in 1925) was already too old to perform the *kai* technique (PETROSJAN 1973: 439, 455). In his country he was a living legend. Local people respected him a lot and considered him not only a *kajčy*,[16] but also a *kam* (shaman)[17] who can talk with Erlik, Lord of the Lower World (*Altygy Oroon*) (POTAPOV 1991: 254–260). The *kaj* is a special technique; the singer presses the air from the lower part of his throat, and thereby makes vibrations inside his throat. This *kaj* technique can also be found among the Khakas, who call it *"xaj"* (see later), and the western Mongols (Oirat) who call it *"xäälexe"*.[18] In Western Mongolia and the Altai, a two-string instrument, the *tobšuur*, accompanies *kaj* singing (PETROSJAN 1973: 455).

I met a *kajčy* near Ongdoi[19] who could perform some short stories (*Picture 2*). He told me that longer stories were considered sacred, and only great *kajčy*s like Kalkin are able to perform them, because they have protector spirits (*eelüü*)[20] and the *kajčy*'s soul must enter the lower world to meet these spirits. He was even afraid to try to learn them.

---

[13] The Altai Mountains stretch from the west border of China and Mongolia to South Siberia. In the territory of the Russian Federation they are situated in the Altai Republic and West Tyva.

[14] Altai-kiži is the name of the biggest minority in the Altai Republic. They speak a South Siberian Turkic dialect. Other smaller groups are the Telengit, Bajat, Kumandy, Čalkandy, Tuba. Their total number was about 60,000 in 1990 (TISHKOV 1994: 82).

[15] The Republic of Altai is part of the Russian Federation in the northern part of the Altai Mountains where the borders of China, Mongolia and Kazakstan join each other. Its capital is Gorno-Altaisk (formerly Ulaluu). In addition to the Altaj-kižis, Russians and Kazaks also live in the Republic.

[16] The *kajčy* is a person who performs epic songs by singing with the *kaj* technique (Petrosjan 1973: 22).

[17] South Siberian Turks use the word *"kam"* or *"xam"* to designate a shaman (POTAPOV 1991: 116).

[18] Classical Mongolian *"qayilaqu"* is pronounced *"xääl(e)x(e)"* in the Oirat dialect. It is interesting that they only use the verb derived from the noun *"qaj"* (COLOO 1988: 413).

[19] It is one of the counties in the Altai Republic.

[20] The word *"ee"* means 'possessor'. It is also the name for the possessor-spirits, who protect nature (mountains, rivers) and other sacred things. If something has protector spirit, they call it *"eelüü"*, which means 'it has a possessor-spirit' (POTAPOV 1991: 25).

But he explained how he became a *kajčy*, hearing strange voices in the woods when he was young. Performing *kaj* singing, itself, is a sacred thing among the Altai-kiži people; you have to purify ·your instrument and the place of performance with the smoke of burning juniper (*artyš*) saying "*alas-alas*".[21]

Picture 2. (Photo by L. KUNKOVÁCS)

One of the most sacred epics (*čörčök*) is *Maadaj-Kara*.[22] In this epic, Maadaj-Kara's son Kögüdej travels to the lower world and destroys the evil Erlik, Lord of Bad Spirits. It has been greatly influenced by Buddhism, and reflects the radical changes of shamanic beliefs among the Altai-kiži minority in the last century when the "White Custom" (*Ak-Džaŋ*), also known as Burkhanism,[23] was introduced. This story is

---

21 The word "*alas*" is widespread among Inner Asian Turks (Kazak, Kyrgyz, Tyva etc.). They use this magic word to cleanse bad spirits from things. Sometimes it is connected with fire, or with smoke from burning juniper (POTAPOV 1991: 121).

22 This epic is basically about Kögüdej-Mergen, the son of the old Maadaj-Kara, but strangely, the epic is named after the father (Petrosjan 1973).

23 In 1904–1905 some religious leaders of the Altaj-kiži people decided to prohibit shamanic practices and blood sacrifices (*džükeli*) among their tribes, and they founded the so-called "White Custom" (*Ak Džaŋ* in Altai). The new "religion" is often called Burkhanism in the scientific literature, because the word "*burqan*" means 'Buddha' or 'god'. This new religion was a syncretism of Mongolian Buddhism and local shamanic beliefs. Other minorities like the Telengit, Kumandy etc. preserved their old shamanic beliefs, and the Burkhanists call this practice "*Kara Džaŋ*" (Black Custom) by (POTAPOV 1991: 92).

widespread among the Siberian nomads of the taiga region. In the Altai
language, the word for epic is *"kaj-čörčök"*. *"čörčök"* simply means 'story',
and because all the sacred stories are performed with the *kaj* singing
technique, they are referred to as *"kaj-čörčök"*.

In Inner Asia the word for "epic" usually comes from the word "story"
or from the word "song". Only the epics' length and manner of being
performed distinguish them from shorter stories or songs.

Turkic:

Kazak	*žïr*	=	long song
Kyrgyz	*džomok*	=	story
Tyva (Tuva)	*tool*	=	story or epic[24]
Altai-kiži	*(kaj) čörčök*	=	story
Agban-tadar (Khakas)	*(alïptïg) nïmax*[25]	=	story
Saqa (Yakut)	*oloŋxo*	=	song?[26]

Mongolian:

Khalka (Modern Mongolian)	*tuuli*	=	story
Buriad (Buryat)	*üliger*	=	story
Khalimag (Kalmyk)	*duun*	=	song

In 1997, during my first visit to the Saqa Republic[27] (Yakutia), I had the
opportunity to meet a so-called *oloŋxohut* who performs the *oloŋxo*,[28] a Sakha
epic song. GAVRIL KOLESOV lived in the capital of Yakutsk (Džokuuskaj)
and worked as an actor, but had learned his art of performing *olongkho* as a
child in his village. Then later, when he became an actor, he was asked to
perform the greatest Sakha epic known, the *Ñurgun Bootur* (OJUNSKIJ 1969:

---

24 The Tyva word *"tool"* comes from the Mongolian word *"tuuli"*.

25 The word *"nïmax"* comes from the Turkic word *"jomak"* > *"jïmax"*, with the initial *"j"*
becoming *"n"* because of the subsequent nasal *"m"*, according to the phonetic rules of
Khakas. See Kyrgyz *jomak* > *džomok*.

26 The origin of this word is unclear. VASILYEV, a Yakut expert, derives it from the Kazak
word *"öleŋ"* 'song' (*öleŋ* > *öleŋke** > *oloŋqo/oloŋxo*).

27 The Yakuts call themselves *"saqa"* or *"saqa-uraaŋqaj"* which probably comes from the
Mongolian *"džaqa-urianqai"* meaning 'Siberian Turks living at the edge' (*džaqa* = edge).
The Saqas fled from the Baikal probably in the 14th–15th centuries because the
Buryat–Mongol tribes of Ekhiret-Bulgat moved to the territory. In their dialect the
Saqas were called *"jaquud"*, the plural for *jaqa* > *jaq(a)*. That is the reason why the
Russians call them Yakut. Since 1992 the official name of Yakutia is Saqa Republic. It is
the biggest province of the Russian Federation (3,1 million square km) with a
population of nearly 400,000 Saqas. There are many Russians and some small minorities
like the Evenki, Even and Yukagir.

28 See Petrosjan 1985: 544. See also SEROŠEVSKIJ 1993: 589.

25–26), written down by the famous Sakha writer, PLATON OJUUNSKAJ.[29] The written version contains more than 40,000 lines. It tells the story of how Ňurgun Bootur, a divine hero, and son of the Upper World (*üehee tangaralar*), destroys the monsters of the Lower World (*abaahylar*) (OJUNSKIJ 1969: 18–19).

The Sakha *oloŋxo* is performed, like the *Manas*, without any musical instrument, but with a special technique called "*kylyhä*" which involves the singer jumping one octave up and down constantly (RESHETNIKOVA 1993: 26–69). They also have a special way of sitting on a Sakha chair (*oloppos*), crossing their legs and folding their hands on their knee (*Picture 3*).

Among the Saqas the enemy is always a monster, while in the Southern Siberian region, the hero fights some fearful emperor (*kaan*) who has magic power often connected with the Lower World (*Erlik*). The Muslim nomads who live in the steppe region, the Kazaks and Kyrgyz, do not talk about wonderful beings of other worlds in their epics. Instead, their stories are about normal human beings, heroes who defend their tribes against others, usually non-Muslim tribes (Kalmak), e.g. in the Kyrgyz *Manas*, and the Kazak epics such as Koŋyrat's *Alpamys*, Kypčak's *Koblandy* and Nogaj's *Edige* etc.[30]

Picture 3.

---

[29] See OJUNSKIJ 1969: 20. See also Pamjatniki Fol'klora Narodov Sibiri 1993: 11.

[30] The various Kazak tribes have different epic traditions. Some epics and their heroes belong to certain tribes. See (Petrosjan 1975). Also see KENŽEBEKOB (5) 1989: 70–95, and SADWAKASOV (3) 1986: 30–75.

In 1998 I had a chance to listen to the last Khakas (Tadar)[31] *xajǯy*, ORGUDAJEV, in the village of Xyzyl-Aal of the Khakas Republic.[32] The Tadars, as they call themselves, are divided into smaller groups, such as the Sagai, Xaas, Xyzyl and Šor. It is interesting that only the Khyzyl group preserved an epic tradition. Great *xajǯy-nymaxšys* like Kurbizhekov and Kadyshev were also from the Khyzyls (PETROSJAN 1988: 498–500). Many young talented Tadar men have started to learn the *xaj* technique (see footnote 17) accompanied by their national instrument called a *shatkhan* (STOJANOV 1988: 577), a sort of zither with seven strings (*Picture 4*). But

ORGUDAYEV is the last real *xajǯy*, chanting whole epics in the traditional way. He told an interesting story of how, as a child, he had met a great *xajǯy* and how he was first forced to learn singing with the *xaj* technique. Sadly, the very next day some young artists arrived in the village to popularise singing with the *xaj* technique among the young generation, but the last *xajǯy* living in the same village was not even invited.

Picture 4.

---

[31] The so-called "Khakas" people call themselves "Tadar" from the Russian term "Tatar". Before the Soviet Era the Russians called everybody "Tatar" who spoke a Turkic language. The Turkic groups around the Abakan River accepted this term as a general name for their different groups (Xaas, Xyzyl, Sagaj, Šor etc.) and called the Russians "Xazax" (Cossack) in return. The name "Khakas" comes from the Chinese pronunciation of the word "Kyrgyz", a people who ruled the territory before the Russians. See Narody Rossiji 1994: 374. Also see KYZLASOV 1993: 140.

[32] The Khakas Republic is part of the Russian Federation, and its capital is Abakan (Agban), which is named after its main river. Because of intensive Russian immigration, the Tadars (Khakas people) are only a small minority in their own republic (11% in 1989). They speak South Siberian Turkic dialects (Sagaj, Xaas, Šor etc.) closely related to Turkic dialects of the Altai Republic.

Then, on the same expedition to the Tyva Republic,[33] we visited a Tyva *tooldžu*,[34] ANDREJ ČÜLDÜM-OOL (born in 1916), living not far from Šagaan-Aryg (Pamjatniki Fol'klora 1997: 19). He lived in abysmal poverty with his son and his family. He was out on the plain looking after cows. He is one of the last *tooldžu*s singing epic songs. Unlike the Khakas or Altai-kiži, the Tyvas sing their stories with a normal voice, accompanied by a two-stringed violin-like instrument called an *igil*,[35] similar to the Mongolian *morin-xuur* (*Picture 5*).

Andrei explained to us that even though the Tyvas are masters of the throat-singing technique

Picture 5.

---

[33] The Republic of Tyva was founded by the Soviets in 1921 when Outer Mongolia became independent from China. The Tyva Republic was first nominally independent but under Russian control. Then in 1944 Stalin annexed it to the Russian Federation as an "autonomous district". It became a republic again only in the seventies. Now, besides the Tyva majority, there are Russians (30%) and some other minorities living in the Republic. Its capital is Kyzyl (earlier known as Beldir). There are some small Tyva groups in Mongolia and China as well. The Tyvas had different names: *urianxai*, *sojod* (Mongolian) and *tuvinec* (in Russian). See TISHKOV 1994: 338.

[34] The word *"tool"* means 'story'. It comes from the Mongolian word *"tuuli"*. The person who performs the *tool* is called *"tooldžu"*.

[35] The Tyva word *"igil"* can only be found in Atai Turkic *(ikili)*.

called *xöömei*, it is forbidden to sing epics with *xöömei* or *kargyraa*.[36] He said the *tool* (the Tyva word for epic song) had to be clear and simple. Other Siberian Turks express the importance of epic songs through special techniques, changing their normal voices.

The Tyva epic tradition was influenced by the Mongols; they have been living together since the Mongolian conquest[37] in 1207. Most of the Tyvas of the steppe were bilingual, speaking Turkic and Mongolian. Their heroes usually go to distant countries to get a wife, and they have the ability to transform into different creatures. This genre of epic song was completely overshadowed by the *xöömei* singing tradition in Tyva.

Then, recently, I was a guest of one of the greatest living *Manasčy* in Kyrgyzstan, living in the village of Üč-Kajnar, in the Ysyk-Köl region.[38]

During the 1000th anniversary of the *Manas* Epic in 1995, which was simply state propaganda, these *manasčy* were national heroes, but not for long. Four years after the celebrations, this old *manasčy* did not even get his pension. It was sad to see him struggling with his family. We sacrificed a sheep for the spirit of Manas and then, after the meal, he started to sing and took us to the wonderful world of the *Manas*. While he was chanting the *Manas*, he closed his eyes, falling into trance (*Picture 6*). He started with a calm pace, later he got quite excited. He even fell down from his chair and moved around the room, sitting on the floor. When he returned from trance, he asked us how he got on the floor on the other side of the room. Then he remembered how he had gotten lost in childhood, wandering in the mountains. While he was sleeping, an old man with a long white beard[39] and white clothes told him to become a *manasčy*. After that, he started to see Manas and hear voices, and when he fell into trance he did not really know what he was actually talking about.

---

[36] Tyva throat singing has three main techniques: *xöömej, sygyt* and *kargyraa*. Tyvas do not sing with the *kaj* technique. *Xöömej* is a high frequency style while *kargyraa* is low frequency. *Sygyt* is produced through the *xöömei* style, but with the tongue touching the palate.

[37] See LIGETI 1971: 239. "*Taulai džil Džočiyi baragun garun čerigüdier hoin irgentür morilagulbai.*" In the year of the Rabbit (1207) he (Chinggis Khaan) sent Jochi with his right-wing troops against the "people of the forest". "*Džoči oirad, buriad, bargun, ursud, kabkanas, kanggas, TUBA-si orogulugad, tümen kirgisud-tur kürübesü...*" Jochi conquered the Oirat, Buriad, Bargu, Ursut, Kabkanas, Kanggas and TYVA, then reached the Kyrgyz...

[38] Ysyk-Köl is the biggest lake in Kyrgyzstan. Its name means 'Hot Lake'. It is called hot because it is salty and never freezes. Actually, it is quite cold. The Russians call it Issyk-Kul'.

[39] This old white man can be found among many Inner Asian people. The Kyrgyz call them "*ooluyā*" which comes from the Arabic word "*awliyā*" meaning 'sacred man'.

Picture 6.

CONCLUSION

During my meetings with these storytellers I became more and more convinced that there was a strong link between shamans and bards. All the circumstances are the same:

1. A young child is chosen by the spirits to learn some kind of trade.[40]
2. The child gets lost, loses consciousness, and gets some sort of revelation from the spirits.
3. After that he or she must sometimes fall into trance and be in contact with these spirits.

The difference between shamans and bards is their function and role in a nomadic society. While the shamans see the future, heal people, or talk with benevolent or malevolent spirits, the bards, by telling long sacred stories, call on the spirits of their imaginary forefathers, heroes who give them power to fight and survive the struggles for power in their nomadic society. The old stories also help the nomads build up their self-awareness and pride, unifying some groups and separating others.

---

[40] HOPPÁL 1994: 24–29.

In former times these epics served as schools or books where people could learn something about their history, traditions, and beliefs, which then helped them understand the world that surrounded them. Nowadays, as the nomadic societies fall apart, the importance of the role of bards decreases, and fewer and fewer people listen to these stories. Books, radio and television are replacing them.

Who has time to listen to stories for a couple of days in our rushing era?

REFERENCES

ABRAMSON, SAUL MATVEJEVICH
1990 *Kirgizy*. Bishkek: Kyrgyzstan.
COLOO, DZH.
1988 *Oird-iin ajalguu*. [Mongol xeln-ii nutg-iin ayalguun-ii toli II], Ulaanbaatar: Uls-iin Xewlel-iin Gadzar.
BADAMKHATAN, S. (glav. red.)
1996 *Oird-iin ugsaatn-ii dzüi*. [Mongol ugsaatnii dzüi II], Ulaanbaatar: Uls-iin Xewlel-iin Gadzar.
HOPPÁL MIHÁLY
1994 *Sámánok, lelkek és jelképek*. Budapest: Helikon.
KENŻEBEKOV, O. (b. red.)
1989 *Batyrlar žyry, Kyrymnyng kyryk batyry*. (Kazak xalyk ädebijeti V), Almaty: Žazywąy, 70–95.
KYZLASOV, LEONID ROMANOVICH (otv. red.)
1993 *Istorija Khakasiji do 1917*. Moscow: Nauka.
LIGETI, LOUIS (trans.)
1971 *Histoire secrète des Mongols*. Budapest: Akadémiai Kiadó.
MUSAJEV, SAMAR MUSAJEVICH (MUSA-UULU)
1984 Kirgiz narodnyj epos "Manas". In *Epos Narodov SSSR*. Kniga I. Moscow: Nauka, 420–442.
OJUNSKIJ, PLATON ALEKSEJEVICH
1969 *Ńurgun Bootur Stremitel'nyj* (na plastinke) Annotacija: I. V. PUCHOV. St. Petersburg: Melodija, 20–39.
Pamjatniki Fol'klora Narodov Sibiri (glav. red.)
1993 *Jakutskij gerojicheskij epos "Kyys Debelije"*. Novosibirsk: Nauka.
1997 *Tuvinskije gerojičeskije skazanija*. Novosibirsk: Nauka.
PETROSJAN, AFRO AVETISOVNA (glav. red.) *Epos Narodov SSSR*. Moscow: Nauka.
1973 *Maadaj-Kara*. Moscow: Nauka.
1975 *Koblnady Batyr*. Moscow: Nauka.
1984 *Manas, kniga I*. Moscow: Nauka.
1985 *Kulun Kullustuur*. Moscow: Nauka.
1988 *Altyn Aryg*. Moscow: Nauka.
PLOSKICH, VLADIMIR MIKHAJLOVICH (glav. red.)

1984 *Istorija Kirgizkoj SSSR.* Tom 1. Frunze: Kyrgyzstan.

POTAPOV, LEONID PAVLOVICH

1991 *Altajskij šamanizm.* St. Petersburg: Nauka.

RESHETNIKOVA, A. P.

1993 Muzyka jakutskich olonkho. In *Pamjatniki Fol'klora Narodov Sibiri. Jakutskij gerojicheskij epos "Kyys Debelije".* Novosibirsk: Nauka, 26–69.

SADWAKASOV, T. (b. red.)

1986 *Batyrlar žyry.* (Kazak xalyk ädebijeti III), Almaty: Žazywąy, 30–75.

SEROSHEVSKIJ, VACLAV LEOPODOVICH (SEROSZEWSKI, WŁACŁAW)

1993 *Jakuty.* Moscow: Rossijskaja Politekhnicheskaja Enciklopedija.

STOJANOV, A. K.

1988 Iskusstvo khakaskij khajdži. In *Epos Narodov SSSR.* Altyn Aryg, Moscow: Nauka.

TISHKOV, V. A. (glav. red.)

1994 *Narody Rossii.* Moscow: Bol'shaja Rossijskaja Enciklopedija.

ŽIRMUNSKIJ, VIKTOR MAKSIMOVICH

1962 *Narodnyj geroičeskij epos.* Moscow: Nauka.

Part III.

LOCAL TRADITIONS

EUGENE HELIMSKI

Nganasan Shamanistic Tradition: Observations and Hypotheses[1]

NGANASANS AND THEIR LANGUAGE

The Nganasan language, known also as Tawgi or Tawgi-Samoyed, belongs to the Samoyedic group of the Uralic language family and forms, together with Nenets (Yurak-Samoyed) and Enets (Yenisei-Samoyed) languages, its Northern Samoyedic subgroup—an areal, and probably also genetic, unit. The immediate neighbours of Nganasans are Nenets and Enets in the west, Dolgans (formerly also Evenkis and Yakuts) in the south and south-east, in our days also Russians and other Russian-speaking migrants from other parts of the former Soviet Union.

Until recently all Nganasans—numbering now, as well as during all last decades and perhaps even centuries, about 1000 persons—led the nomadic life of tundra dwellers, with their economy based on hunting wild reindeers and breeding domesticated ones. They were the only inhabitants of the central and northern parts of the vast peninsular area of Taimyr in the extreme North of Siberia, making thus the northernmost indigenous population of Eurasia and—together with the Eskimo—of the entire world. Till 1940s and even, to a lesser extent, till 1960s they enjoyed a relative isolation from the rest of the world, at least in their everyday life (for example, as late as in 1930s Nganasan hunters were still not equipped with firearms, continuing to use spears and bows). The prolonged relative isolation in a remote area determined the formation or, in many cases, an unusually stable conservation of unique features in the Nganasan

---

[1]   The author often addressed the issues of Nganasan culture and Nganasan shamanism in his publications of 1989–1997 (partly reprinted in HELIMSKI 2000). This conference paper—with the exception of the section "Posthumous children"—is mainly a synopsis of these publications.

traditional cultures, spiritual as well as material. This circumstance has been unanimously attested and documented in the works of those researchers (mainly ethnologists) who had opportunities to conduct field work in the area during the last decades, and confirmed by the author's personal experiences.

Regretfully, the exposure to the modern world and especially the tragic consequences of the totalitarian national policy in the USSR had destructive impact on the cultural traditions and languages of many ethnic minorities in Siberia, including also the Nganasans. In 1960s most of them were compelled, by administrative measures and in the framework of an ideology-triggered campaign of settling down the Northern nomads, to move to three newly-built villages with mixed Nganasan-Dolgan (partly also Russian) population—Ust'-Avam, Volochanka and Novaya, all located on the southern outskirts of the area of their former nomadic routes. This innovation very soon put an end to the Nganasan reindeer breeding— cutting them therefore off from the hereditary hunting areas—and, together with the compulsory education of children in Russian-language boarding schools, provoked a rapid decline of the entire ethnic culture (on a line with creating for relatively few Nganasans some opportunities of entering the Russian-Soviet cultural milieu).

The language situation among the Nganasans is also quickly deteriorating (see HELIMSKI 1994, 1997). As usually, the loss of native cultural traditions moves hand in hand with the loss of the mother tongue. However, it was possible during the last decades and is possible also today to gather from the representatives of the older generations comprehensive and valuable examples of Nganasan folklore.

NGAMTUSUO (KOSTERKINS): THE NGANASAN SHAMAN DYNASTY

My own observations concerning Nganasan shamanism are essentially based on the experience of attending in 1987–1989, as a guest and a participant, several shamanic séances given by TUBIAKU KOSTERKIN (ŋamtusuə Tubiaʔku), a highly endowed and deeply impressing person who was considered to have been until his death in December 1989 the last real, "great" shaman of the Nganasans. An offspring of the famous dynasty of shamans, TUBIAKU was born and spent most of his life in the tundras of the Pyasina river basin. Many years he combined the life of an independent hunter, fisherman and reindeer breeder with an extensive shamanic practice, that he "inherited" from his father D'üpəðüʔə. This occupation brought him in late 1940s, when the Stalinist political purges reached also this northernmost corner of the Soviet Union, into prison. (It was during the years of his imprisonment that his elder brother DEMNIME (*D'emn'iʔmiǝ*), until then a layman with shamanic background, started as a practising shaman; the two brothers stayed rivals and enemies until the end of their lives.) Still later, for the last twenty years of his lifetime, TUBIAKU together with other kinsmen had to settle down in the village of Ust'-Avam.

The publications on the Nganasan shamanism mention almost invariably different representatives of the Kosterkins (*Ŋamtusuǝ*) dynasty. A. A. POPOV and B. O. DOLGIH, who lived and worked among the Nganasans in late 1920s and 1930s (B. O. DOLGIH visited them also later), had an opportunity to observe the activities of TUBIAKU's father DYUHADE (*D'üpǝδüʔǝ*) and collected from him or from his (former) audience an essential part of their information on the shamanic and religious traditions of the Nganasans. DEMNIME served as the main informer to Y. B. SIMČENKO (1960s–1970s) and, in 1977, was visited and filmed by LENNART MERI. Both Y. B. SIMČENKO and G. N. GRAČEVA had numerous opportunities to interview also TUBIAKU (see especially SIMČENKO 1996, II). There exist also numerous (and partly contradictory) legends concerning the ancestor shamans from the same family.[2] Several 20th century representatives of this dynasty—shamans and active participants of shamanic actions mentioned in this paper—are shown in the genealogical scheme below.

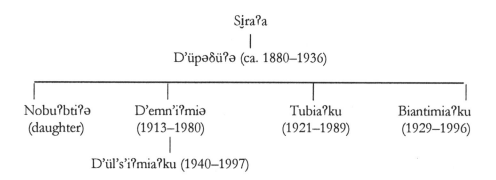

Siraʔa
|
D'üpǝδüʔǝ (ca. 1880–1936)

| Nobuʔbtiʔǝ (daughter) | D'emn'iʔmiǝ (1913–1980) | Tubiaʔku (1921–1989) | Biantimiaʔku (1929–1996) |

D'ül's'iʔmiaʔku (1940–1997)

---

[2] Latest contributions to this topic are LAMBERT 1997 and KOSTERKINA – PLUŽNIKOV 1999, as well as a comprehensive and richly illustrated Internet presentation by AADO LINTROP.

TUBIAKU KOSTERKIN'S LAST "SMALL" SÈANCES

After the death (in early 1980s) of his second wife and main assistant (*tuəbtuʔsʼi*) during the séances, TUBIAKU stopped his activities as a public servant and sold his shamanic costume to the district museum in Dudinka. This deprived him of the possibility to make distant shamanic journeys (in the altered state of mind) necessary, for example, for healing patients— which was always the dominant function of séances. Still, he asserted that his assisting spirits stayed near him and were always ready to help within the limits of their competence; besides, regular contacts were needed both by these spirits and by himself. So TUBIAKU restricted himself to smaller domestic shamanic rites, performed without a drum and with only some most essential parts of the costume (for example, a fringed horned crown *ŋojbuʔkəə*). They served the limited purposes of eliminating troubles in TUBIAKU's own family and securing the general prosperity of the participants. Otherwise, however—and, in particular, from the viewpoint of form and content of incantations performed during the rites—they were typical of Nganasan shamanism, as it could be judged from the attitudes of the shaman himself and his native audience.

Basically these smaller séances consisted of the incarnations of assisting spirits invoked by the shaman. The spirits were believed to come to the appeals and tunes produced by TUBIAKU and his audience, and to start speaking through the shaman's lips. They spoke exclusively in the form of incantations, sung to each spirit's individual, easily recognisable melody. TUBIAKU served both as the organiser of the entire rite and as the medium. His switch from one of these two functions to the other was signalled by the position of the fringe (*sʼejmiði*) of his crown: with fringe raised, he remained himself, and with fringe lowered and covering his eyes, he was undergoing the spiritual transfiguration into a visitor from the supernatural world.[3]

Due to the assistance of TUBIAKU's daughter, NADEZHDA KOSTERKINA the tape recordings from two such rites, both held in August 1989, were completely transcribed in the Nganasan language and translated into Russian (TESb 30–146). A posthumous publication by Y. B. SIMČENKO, containing the transcriptions and translations of two TUBIAKU's séances from 1976 and 1978, appeared in 1996 (SIMČENKO 1996: II: 51–145).

Of decisive importance were naturally also the comments and occasional remarks, taken during our prolonged talks with TUBIAKU as a

---

[3]   For more details see HELIMSKI – KOSTERKINA 1992.

qualified informant on most various matters of the traditional language usage, folklore, and customs of the Nganasans.

POSTHUMOUS CHILDREN: THE NGANASAN SHAMANISM OF 1990S

TUBIAKU KOSTERKIN died in December 1989—only four months after two of his small séances were recorded as well as filmed by AADO LINTROP, and having since conducted only one such séance, the last one, in November. Six years later he was followed by his younger brother and permanent assistant (*tuəbtuʔsʼi* "words-repeating-person") BORIS (*BiantimiaʔkU*), who—according to DYUHADE KOSTERKIN's prediction—was supposed to be the last custodian of Nganasan shamanism (TESb 55), though not being a shaman himself. According to the common opinion of the Nganasans, TUBIAKU's death was fatal to Nganasan shamanism; some accuse him of being too selfish and jealous of a potential rival to have prepared a successor to his art.

Most of elderly Nganasans (50 years and more) possess, due to their earlier regular participation in shamanic rites, very thorough knowledge of corresponding practices as well as of the language and vocabulary of incantations. This is true also of some representatives of the younger generation—for example, of TUBIAKU KOSTERKIN's son LEONID (*LəbtiʔmaʔkU*) and daughter NADEZHDA (*DiɲiʔmiaʔkU*). Therefore within the next few decades the continuation of field research by asking questions about Nganasan shamanism will remain possible.

However, it can be hardly expected that these people use or are going to use their knowledge as practising shamans. This reluctance is determined by internal reasons much more than by external ones (in contemporary Russia a local "revival" of shamanism would be viewed only positively, also by the authorities), and could have been only strengthened by the sad story of DYULSIMIAKU KOSTERKIN, which is universally known among the Nganasan population.

DYULSIMIAKU, the son of DEMNIME and the nephew of TUBIAKU, had a long experience of serving as an assistant to his father and later occasionally to his uncle as well as to an old Dolgan female shaman (now dead) during their rites. He also preserved, as a sacred relic, his late father's shamanic costume and accessories. Insistent demands and tempting proposals from the guests coming to Ust'-Avam and from the organisers of various festivals of native cultures, induced him—especially after 1989—to make use of this material heritage, together with the spiritual one.

Dressed and equipped like his father, he started to perform (imitate) his
father's rites and to sing his father's (or rather: his father's spirits') songs in
public, both in Ust'-Avam and far away from home; some of his brilliant
performances are recorded on CDs ("Musique du monde: Nganasan",
Buda Records 92564-2, ed. by H. LECOMTE) and in TV-films
(H. ANDERSON e.a.: "Nganasan. Ett folk i Sibirien", 1990). DYULSIMIAKU
followed the path of his father (who appears in some films by LENNART
MERI and MIHÁLY HOPPÁL) and uncle. But, unlike them, he acted like a
shaman without having ever undergone a shaman's initiation. "He is a
variety actor, not a real shaman",—the people in Ust'-Avam would repeat,
contrary to some journalists who referred to him as "the last shaman of
Taimyr" (see e.g. "Polityka", dodatek, nr. 2(4), Warszawa, 15.04.1995).
DYULSIMIAKU himself did not claim being a shaman—until 1996, when he,
according to his own confidential words (we met in August), abruptly
felt—in the age of 56!—a call of the spirits and "started to see hidden
things". The peculiar circumstances of the spirits' call—DYULSIMIAKU told
how he woke up in the middle of night and saw that a portrait of LENIN
hanging on the wall approaches and jumps on him, and heard the voices
from the other world—make me suspect that he was influenced, perhaps
subconsciously, by the above mentioned Swedish film (one of its episodes
consists in intermittent showing of shamanizing DYULSIMIAKU and of
LENIN's face). Anyhow, since then he claimed standing in immediate
contact with the world of spirits. This did not last long: early in 1997
DYULSIMIAKU, who never had any serious health problems, was chopping
firewood in his neighbours' presence, than sat down on a bench near his
house and died of a sudden heart attack. Whatever real reasons this fatal
heart attack may have had (emotional stress, hard work, or innate valvular
heart disease), its explanation along the lines of the shamanic tradition is
too obvious not to be interpreted as a message: the initiation of a shaman
is a heavy disease, and one can overcome it and find the shaman's path
only in his or her teens and only under a guidance of an experienced senior
shaman—otherwise the spirit's call means a doom.

SHAMANIC REGISTER IN THE NGANASAN LANGUAGE: METRICAL PROPERTIES OF INCANTATIONS

It appears that the linguistic properties of Nganasan shamanic texts are determined by two demands: they must be easy to understand,[4] and must not be mistaken for an ordinary discourse. (The recorded examples of Nenets shamanic songs lead to a similar conclusion.) Partly this double aim is achieved by employing certain ponderous words and especially word forms that are hardly used beyond the context of shamanic séances, but are, on the other hand, morphologically (derivationally) transparent.

Of much greater importance are, however, the metrical properties of incantations. All known examples of Northern Samoyedic sacred poetry (shamanic incantations and inviting calls addressed to spirits, songs of visiting spirits) typically consist of isosyllabic lines with 8 syllables in each, with stresses on odd-numbered syllables and with an obligatory caesura after the fourth syllable (–,´ ∪ –,´ ∪ | –,´ ∪ –,´ ∪). On the other hand, whenever a specimen of a profane lyric genre (a personal song, a sung epic, an allegoric song, or even the epic narratives describing the deeds of shamans) follows a strict metrical pattern, it is also composed of isosyllabic lines, but with only 6 syllables in each. Thus, the dichotomy *sacred: profane* is reflected in the Northern Samoyedic tradition as the opposition of two basic metrical patterns of verse – *octosyllabic: hexasyllabic*. This result, obtained due to collecting the Nganasan field materials (HELIMSKI 1989b), has been confirmed by the re-examination of the well known Nenets materials within the framework of the underlying-level phonology (HELIMSKI 1989a) and later found support also in the samples collected among both Tundra and Forest Enets in 1994–1995 (which reflect, regretfully but, due to absence of shamans among the Enets in the last decades, understandably, only profane versification).

---

[4] The *tuəbtuʔsʼi* only repeats, line by line, the spirits' incantation, but does not reformulate or explain them.

HYPOTHESES ON NGANASAN SHAMANISM AND ITS LANGUAGE

Hypotheses of Allotheism and Xenotheism

An essential feature that clearly distinguishes shamanism[5] from any mono-
or polytheistic religion consists in its being *an open system of notions, images,
symbols and texts*, always favouring any creative innovations if these prove
their efficiency. A priest of a religious community is supposed only to
recite established sacred texts and to perform prescribed acts, or to preach
and admonish within a relatively narrow framework of the corresponding
religious tradition; any radical innovation is a heresy. On the contrary, a
shaman immersed into his initiation dreams or undertaking his shamanic
journey in an altered state of consciousness (GRAČEVA 1989), as well as a
spirit who arrives to the calls of those who need his assistance, are
unrestricted in their visions and in forms of expression. They are supposed
to tell what they see, hear or otherwise experience in the supernatural
world. They are free to express their purely personal attitudes and to use
their own ways of handling any concurrent problems. A dream or a
journey may acquaint a shaman with a deity which was never known
before to his people, or bring him to a new part of the universe never
mentioned in the existing mythological cosmographies. Certainly, a shaman
mainly remains under the impact of the existing local tradition (which tells
him whom he is supposed to search and what outer lands he must visit),
and takes a great risk when deviating too far from it. But—when
possessing enough self-confidence—he is free to take this risk.

This feature determines the phenomenon of *allotheism* (variability of the
pantheon), found when studying the religious notions in many shamanic
societies and very characteristic of the Nganasans. Several scholars
attempted to get a picture of the Nganasan pantheon and to describe it, if
possible, as coherent and hierarchical.[6] However, the descriptions often
and strongly contradict each other, and the contradictions start already
with the questions whether the Nganasan have a supreme deity and what
his name is (GRAČEVA 1983: 31; 1984) or whether the pantheon is
dominated by masculine gods (ŋuə) or by feminine *n'emị* ("mothers").

---

5   At least, the shamanism in the narrow and exact sense of this term—that is, the
     Siberian shamanism. The peripheral / secondary phenomena like the Korean
     shamanism must be left apart.
6   See POPOV 1936, 1984: 41–75; DOLGIH 1960, 1968, Mscr.; SIMČENKO 1976: 239–
     278; 1996, vol. I; KORTT – SIMČENKO 1990: 31–123; GRAČEVA 1983: 21–51 and
     many other publications.

Many of the deities mentioned by the scholars who visited the Nganasans between 1920s and 1970s[7] were completely unknown to our (older) informants of 1980s and 1990s. Some other were known, but characterised in a completely different way. Interestingly and characteristically, TUBIAKU KOSTERKIN in our talks avoided answering direct questions about the deities, their relationships with each other and their domains of responsibility (sometimes he even was getting angry at our insistent questions on such topics). He would always prefer to tell about his personal encounter with a certain deity under concrete circumstances—that is, to give information that would not necessarily suggest that this deity can be always found at a given place and can be always addressed in connection with a given issue (nomadizing and retiring or retraining seem to be popular also in the supernatural world).

Allotheistic phenomena seem to result directly from the variability of religious experiences of shamans and of the audience following their stories.

A special type of allotheism consists in *xenotheism*, or admission of foreign deities to the pantheon—a phenomenon very typical of all polytheistic religions, not only in shamanic societies. The shamanic practices of the Nganasans (GRAČEVA 1979, 1984) and of TUBIAKU in particular contain some impressive examples of incorporating elements of Russian orthodoxy—and even of Soviet ideology. St. Nicholas, the holy patron of Russia, underwent a transformation into one of TUBIAKU's main assistant spirits—the Iron Horse Mikuluska, who governs "the firm passport" and has at his disposal "thousands of stone man, thousands of iron Russians, the birth of all machines". An icon with the Holy Virgin, bought in Moscow, occupied a place in the sacred sledge (with cult objects) and among the attributes of the sèances. So did also a Dolgan shamanic parka (jacket).

Only at first glance was it surprising to find numerous ideological clichés of the Soviet epoch in the incantation texts. The ideology, it turns out, was treated within a genuinely mythological framework: for example, the references to LENIN (cf. also above) as the arranger of the modern world were worded much in the same way as the myths about the arrangement of the world after the Creation and its rearrangement after the Great Flood. The Nganasan shamans and their audience obviously viewed first Christianity and later communist doctrine as the religious system of another people (the Russians), which differs from that of the

---

[7] See lists in KORTT – SIMČENKO 1990: 37–123.

Nganasans, but deserves respect and attention—and eventually also utilisation (cf. HELIMSKI 1993b).

Hypothesis of Incantations Shaping Language

The metrical pattern of the shamanic verse determines a specific distribution of words of different length in syllables, with marked preference given to disyllabic and tetrasyllabic words. According to this hypothesis, *in the course of historical development preference was given to forms fitting the metrical requirement of traditional— especially shamanic—versification.*

Taking into consideration that:

— shamanic incantations are mostly improvised at a relatively high speed (even if they include standard portions), and the quality of versification is determined by previous individual experience rather than by a special preparation of texts;
— it is expedient to a Northern Samoyedic shaman to have at his disposal as many di- and tetrasyllabic word forms as possible;
— it is necessary to be able to use traditional formulae for making whole lines or groups of lines while singing;
— a shaman, as the spiritual leader of a community, ranks as its higher authority in the issues of poetry and language,

it can be assumed that:

— shamanic activity must be an important or even determining factor in enriching Northern Samoyedic languages with di- and tetrasyllabic word forms and, consequently, with disyllabic suffixes and suffixal combinations (as long as pure stems in these languages are for the most part disyllabic).
— shamanic activity must resist trends of linguistic development which are potentially dangerous for the structural (syllabic) integrity of words and poetic formulae, especially the reductive processes.

These assumptions appear to be useful in evaluating many features of Northern Samoyedic linguistic evolution (or conservative trends), for instance:

— suffixal enlargement of personal pronouns, such as Nen. *măń(ă)* 'I', En. *mod'i* 'I', *tod'i* 'thou', Ngan. *mənə* 'I', *tənə* 'thou' (PSam. **măn, *tăn*, cf. Selkup *man, tan*);

- presence of "co-affixes" in some case suffixes, such as those of the locative: Nen. -*χǎna*, Ngan. -*tǝnu* (PUr. *-na/-nǎ*);
- abundance of disyllabic verbal suffixes, mainly of secondary origin;
- coexistence of parallel — monosyllabic and disyllabic — forms of the same suffix, that "fit" correspondingly stems with odd and even numbers of syllables, such as -*TU* and -*TUǝ* (present participle), -*Kǝ* and -*Kǝ'Tǝ* (elative) in Nganasan;
- ideal preservation of vocalic "skeletons" of words (including diphthongs) in Nganasan; the same stability is characteristic of Enets (despite the fact that this language underwent profound reductive processes in the domain of consonants) and of the language of Nenets songs as distinct from colloquial Nenets (see HELIMSKI 1989a).

Hypotheses of Connection between Shamanic and Kalevala Metrics, between Octosyllabicity and Consonant Gradation

The similarity between the metrical pattern of Northern Samoyedic shamanic verse and the metre of Kalevala (and of Baltic-Finnic traditional poetry in general) is obvious; the differences are hardly relevant or primary. Thus, the discovery of Northern Samoyedic octosyllabic verse sheds new light on the much-discussed problem of the Finno-Ugrian origin of the Kalevala metre and places this problem on the Common Uralic level[8].

In view of recent research stressing the probable shamanic background of the Kalevala, where charms as transformed shamanic incantations occupy about one fifth of a whole text (OINAS 1989: 277; PENTIKÄINEN 1989), and the role of shamans as possible creators of epics (SIIKALA 1986), a hypothesis can be suggested according to which *the metre of Kalevala was originally the metre of shamanic incantations*, distinguishing sacred language from ordinary discourse (HELIMSKI 1993a).

There are also many common features in Northern Samoyedic and Baltic-Finnic ways of adopting language to metrical requirements.[9] There is hardly any doubt that the influence of (shamanic) poetry—to put it in

---

8 The areal aspect must not however be disregarded. The same metrical pattern of shamanic verse is also found in South Siberian Turkic traditions (see KENIN-LOPSAN 1987).

9 See for example, the morphological peculiarities of Kalevala, which enlarge the share of metrically suitable word forms (EVSEEV 1960: 165–167, 285–292) or the tetrasyllabicity of the names of many epic heroes, starting with *Ilmarinen*, *Väinämöinen*, and *Lemminkäinen*.

other words, of the language of spirits—should not be disregarded when viewing the linguistic evolution in Baltic-Finnic.

A very important feature of this evolution consisted in the preservation of the Common Uralic phenomenon of consonant gradation, a phenomenon which, incidentally, is present also in Nganasan and has left very clear traces in other Northern Samoyedic languages (HELIMSKI 1995b).

It cannot be denied in connection with different manifestations of consonant gradation in Uralic, that "im Hintergrund dieser Erscheinungen steht wahrscheinlich das Streben nach einem inneren rhythmischen Gleichgewicht der Rede" (HAJDÚ 1962: 53). It is therefore tempting to assume some kind of relationship between gradation and those domains of language use where the need of rhythmic balance was always very strong— that is, with versification and singing. The inherent relationship between the octosyllabic trochaic metre and the principles of the Uralic rhythmic gradation (weakening of consonant after vowels of even, and therefore unstressed, syllables) is especially evident. It will probably be not too daring to assume that this form of *gradation originates from poetic speech, and that its generalization is due to the outstanding role played by poetic (shamanic, sacral) narrative in the traditional Uralic society.*

No less important was, as it seems, the further interaction between the morphonological phenomenon and the poetic tradition. It is difficult to distinguish here causes from consequences—but in the majority of Uralic languages, which underwent not only the loss of gradation ("de-gradation") but also the intensive reductive processes in suffixal syllables, no or only weak traces of octosyllabic versification are found. On the other hand, it can hardly be accidental that in Baltic-Finnic and Nganasan we find preserved the entire batch of related extralinguistic and linguistic phenomena: the octosyllabic poetry, the syllabic structure of words practically untouched by reductive processes, and the consonant gradation.

HYPOTHESIS OF "ICED CULTURE" AND ITS FRAGILITY

In view of the terminological opposition between a "hot" (innovation-oriented) and a "cold" (tradition-oriented) culture, the case of the Nganasans can be possibly designated as an extreme manifestation of the latter, as an "iced culture". This feature may bear responsibility for the tragically rapid decline of the Nganasan culture in the last three or four decades.

The fragility hypothesis stems basically from the author's observations concerning language skills and attitudes among the Nganasans (HELIMSKI 1995a). Every detail seems to prove that, even without literacy, this ethnic group—or rather its representatives belonging to the older generation—does have a highly developed standard literary language as the language of oral tradition and, even more, the stable habits of its cultivation. The people always attached an exclusive role to the skill and quality of shamanic narrative, to the art of recital and qualified reception of epics and legends (these used to be the main occupations during the lingering snow-storms, which means—taking the local climate into considerations—for many weeks every year), to mastering the special language of allegoric poetic improvisation (Ngan. *kəiŋəirs'ə*). It was most peculiar to come across numerous and systematic manifestations of linguistic purism. The correctness and stylistic adequacy of speech is under strict self-control, at least in non-everyday speech situations and among elderly Nganasans. Exquisite, sometimes slightly ponderous polypredicative constructions, nominal forms enriched with emphatic clitics, and otherwise rarely used verbal forms of oblique moods are given obvious preference, if a narration (for example, one's life story) has been prepared in advance. Abnormal word usage and grammatical mistakes seem to be always noticed, often corrected, and sometimes mocked at (especially if the speaker is supposed, due to his or her age, to belong to the category of language authorities).

It may seem paradoxical, but I cannot exclude that this native tradition of language cultivation could have contributed to the drastically high speed of language degradation among the younger generations of Nganasans, who—since early 1960s—were brought up in a mixed Dolgan–Nganasan–Russian language environment and educated in Russian-language kindergartens and boarding schools. The loss of the Nganasan language went so fast, that in some families monolingual Nganasan grandparents just cannot communicate with their Russian-speaking grandchildren without the assistance of the intermediate generation (which is usually bilingual, or, in the worst cases, semilingual—that is, lacking an adequate knowledge of any idiom). However, despite the evident communicative need—at least that was the case in many families that I know—neither the grandparents nor the parents would display any intention to activate the children's scanty and fragmentary Nganasan language skills, to induce them to speak Nganasan at least as their second language (with Russian as the first one). Cannot it be a conscious or subconscious manifestation of purist maximalism: "Let them better not speak our language at all than butcher it"? (This kind of apprehension appears to be completely justified: the Nganasan language is so complicated, that, without having grown up in a "pure" linguistic environment, practically nobody learns to speak it well enough. By the way, the Nganasans unanimously, and not without pride, estimate their language as being very difficult in comparison with neighbouring languages, especially with Dolgan).

The sad story of DYULSIMIAKU who attempted—or was appealed—to start shamanic activities without having the due prerequisites for this step may possibly serve as another confirmation of the fragility of an 'iced culture' and of the self-destructing charge which it contains.

REFERENCES

DOLGIH, B. O.
1960 Prinesenie v žertvu olenej u nganasan i éncev. *Kratkie soobščenija Instituta étnografii, vyp. 33*: 72–81.
1968 Matriarhal'nye čerty v verovanijah nganasan. In *Problemy antropologii i istoričeskoj étnografii Azii*. Moscow: Nauka, 214–229.
Mscr. *Veroanija nganasan* (Mscr.). 290 p.

EVSEEV, M. JA.
1960 *Istoričeskie osnovy karelo-finskogo éposa. T. 2.* Moscow – Leningrad: Izd-vo AN SSSR.

GRAČEVA, G. N.
1979 K voprosu o vlijanii hristianizacii na religioznye predstavlenija nganasan. In *Hristianstvo i lamaizm u korennogo naselenija Sibiri*. Leningrad: Nauka, 29–49.
1983 *Tradicionnoe mirovozzrenie ohotnikov Tajmyra (na materiale nganasan XIX-načala XX v.).* Leningrad: Nauka.
1984 Nganasanskie nazvanija "bogov". In *Étnografija narodov Sibiri*. Novosibirsk: Nauka, 65–69.
1989 Nganasan shamans' ways and worldview. In M. HOPPÁL – O. J. VON SADOVSZKY (eds.) *Shamanism: Past and Present, 1.* Budapest – Los Angeles: Fullerton, 145–153.

HAJDÚ, P.
1962 Die Frage des Stufenwechsels in den samojedischen Sprachen. *Ural-Altajische Jahrbücher* 34: 41–54.

HELIMSKI, E. (HELIMSKIJ, E. A.)
1989a Glubinno-fonologičeskij izosillabizm neneckogo stiha. *Journal de la Société Finno-Ougrienne* 82: 223–268.
1989b Sillabika stiha v nganasanskih inoskazatel'nyh pesnjah. In ŠEJKIN, JU. I. (otv. red.). *Muzykal'naja étnografija Severnoj Azii*. Novosibirsk, 52–76.
1990 Octosyllabic and hexasyllabic verse in Northern Samoyed. In *Congressus Septimus Internationalis Fenno-Ugristarum, 2A: Summaria dissertationum. Linguistica*. Debrecen, 75.

1993a Does the language of spirits influence the development of human language? (Evidence from Northern Samoyed). In M. HOPPÁL – K. D. HOWARD (eds.) *Shamans and Cultures*. Budapest: Akadémiai Kiadó – International Society for Trans-Oceanic Research, 210–214.

1993b Zaimstvovanija iz pravoslavnoj religii i sovetskoj ideologii v ritual'noj praktike nganasanskogo šamana. In *Tradicionnye kul'tury i sreda obitanija. I Meždunarodnaja konferencija: Tezisy*. Moscow, 98–100.

1994 Nganasanskij jazyk. In *Krasnaja kmniga jazykov narodov Rossii: Ènciklopedičeskij slovar'-spravočnik*. Moscow: Academia, 38–39.

1995a Nganasan as a literary language and further reflections on literary languages. In G. ZAICZ (Hrsg.) *Zur Frage der uralischen Schriftsprachen*. Budapest: MTA Nyelvtudományi Intézet, 149–153.

1995b Proto-Uralic gradation: Continuation and traces. In *Congressus Octavus Internationalis Fenno-Ugristarum. Pars I: Orationes plenariae et conspectus quinquennales*. Jyväskyla, 17–51.

1997 Factors of Russianisation in Siberia and linguo-ecological strategies. In H. SHOJI – J. JANHUNEN (eds.) *Northern Minority Languages: Problems of Survival*. (*Senri Ethnological Studies* no. 44.) Osaka: National Museum of Ethnology, 77–91.

2000 *Komparativistika, uralistika: Lekcii i stat'i*. Moscow: Jazyki russkoj kul'tury.

HELIMSKI, E. – KOSTERKINA, N.

1992 Petites séances d'un grand chamane nganasan. *Diogéne* 158: 37–51.

KENIN-LOPSAN M. B.

1987 *Obrjadovaja praktika i fol'klor tuvinskogo šamanstva*. Novosibirsk: Nauka.

KORTT, I. R. – SIMCENKO, JU. B.

1990 *Materialien zur geistigen und dinglichen Kultur der Nganasan–Samojeden. (Systemata mundi. Materialien. Bd. 2)*. Berlin: Systemata mundi.

KOSTERKINA, N. T. – PLUŽNIKOV, N. V.

1999 Nganasanskaja saga o šamanah. In HARITONOVA, V. I. (otv. red.). *"Izbranniki duhov" – "izbravšie duhov": tradicionnoe šamanstvo i neošamanizm. Pamjati V. N. BASILOVA (1937–1998)*. Moscow: In-t étnologii i antropologii, 154–159.

LAMBERT, J.-L.

1997 *Rapport de mission chez les nganasan* (Mscr.). Paris.

LINTROP, A.

The Incantator (WWW-pages):
http://haldjas.folklore.ee/~aado/index.html,
http://haldjas.folklore.ee/~aado/ngin.htm,
http://haldjas.folklore.ee/~aado/yuk.htm,
http://haldjas.folklore.ee/~aado/tent.htm,
http://haldjas.folklore.ee/~aado/dem.htm,
http://haldjas.folklore.ee/~aado/tub.htm,
http://haldjas.folklore.ee/~aado/song.htm,

http://haldjas.folklore.ee/folklore/nr1/pics/ngapho.htm,
http://haldjas.folklore.ee/folklore/vol2/tubinc.htm)

OINAS, F. J.
1989 Shamanistic components in the Kalevala. In M. HOPPÁL – J.
PENTIKÄINEN (eds.) *Uralic Mythology and Folklore*. Budapest – Helsinki:
Ethnohraphic Institute – Finnish Literature Society, 277–286.

PENTIKÄINEN, J.
1989 The shamanic poems of the Kalevala and their Northern Eurasian
background. In M. HOPPÁL – O. J. VON SADOVSZKY (eds.) *Shamanism:
Past and Present, 1*. Budapest – Los Angeles: Fullerton, 97–102.

POPOV, A. A.
1936 *Tavgijcy*. Moscow – Leningrad: Izd-vo AN SSSR.
1984 *Nganasany: Social'noe ustrojstvo i verovanija*. Leningrad: Nauka.

SIIKALA, A.-L.
1986 Shamanistic themes in Finnish poetry. In *Traces of the Central Asian
Culture in the North* (= *MSFOu* 194). Helsinki: Suomalais-Ugrilainen
Seura, 223–233.

SIMCENKO, J. B.
1976 *Kul'tura ohotnikov na olenej Severnoj Evrazii*. Moscow: Nauka.
1996 *Tradicionnye verovanija nganasan. I–II*. Moscow: Biblioteka rossijskogo
ètnografa.

TESb
1994 HELIMSKIJ, E. A. (red.) *Tajmyrskij ètnolingvističeskij sbornik. Vyp. 1:
Materialy po nganasanskomu šamanstvu I jazyku*. Moscow: Rossijskij gos.
Gumanitarnyj Universitet.

MIHÁLY HOPPÁL

Shamans in Buryat Sacrificial Rituals

ANIMAL SACRIFICE AMONG THE BURYAT

In June 1996 an international conference on shamanism was held in Buryatia. It was known beforehand that, beside scholars, several local Buryat shamans were also invited to the event. What is more, the organisers took care to time the conference so that it coincided with the summer sacrificial festivities in order that an animal sacrifice may be performed as part of the gathering. In the olden days the *tailga*, Buryat for this rite, meant a horse sacrifice (URBANAEVA 1997 and VAN DEUSEN 1997). It is in this sense that I had always been lead to think of it, both in the related literature, and in a film that I had seen a few years before at an ethnographic film festival. This is how I had seen it represented in old photographs in the ethnographic collections in Saint Petersburg.

Recently, when I was preparing for publication the works of an undeservedly forgotten Hungarian ethnographer and traveller, BENEDEK BARÁTHOSI-BALOGH (HOPPÁL 1999), I came across an excellent description of a Buryat horse sacrifice which he had seen in 1911.

> The next day it was still dark when they shook me awake. The baron and I travelled on a Russian type carriage for a good hour until we reached a steep, rocky stretch of shore on the Baykal. There were ten or twelve carts already standing there and at least twice as many saddled horses tied up. During this time daylight began to spread so I could take a good look at the surroundings which I had only been able to guess at in the half dark. On top of the cliff I saw a huge pile of rocks, about three metres long, a metre and a half wide and rising to the height of a table. The top was made out of flat blocks so that it created a relatively even surface. The altar stone was covered in a round shape with living branches. They stood around this altar table, on which a blazing fire had been lit, in a wide semi-circle. In the meantime they had milked a few of the mares and scattered several splashes

of the fresh milk over the fire on the altar. Two people held the long reins on either side of a horse while another four men held a long piece of rope each, with the other end tied to horse's four ankles. Now they splashed a bit of the milk between the eyes of the horse which made the animal back away and rear but the two men held it fast. At the moment when the first rays of the sun emerged from the water of the Baykal, the four young men, running all in the same direction, pulled the horse to the ground with their ropes. Some ran to their help and stretched the legs so far apart that the animal could not move at all. Then an old man, one of the baron's relatives, stepped up to the horse. Using a dagger-like, strong knife he split the abdomen and, entering through the gaping hole he most competently sought out the main artery and cut through it. This all happened in a few seconds and the animal expired without any major struggle or suffering. The men standing around it cut the animal's head off and placed it in the middle of the altar. Then they pulled the skin off with agile hands and put that on the altar as well. This was followed by the dismemberment of the body and as the legs and other parts of the animal were cut off, they were laid on the altar in their natural sequence. While this was going on, the onlooking crowd of about a hundred men, women and children softly hummed an old song which gradually grew into a loud, strong singing. I forced a promise out of the baron that he would note down for me the tune and words of this ancient, hymn like song and would even make a phonographic recording of it. He also promised to let our museum have a copy. It appears, however, that his death in the following year prevented him from fulfilling this promise to ethnographic science. During this singing they splashed fresh mare's milk on the lumps of meat on the altar.

The baron told me that the sacrifice of the horse speaks directly to the great heavenly God and is a thanksgiving for the grace of God which had supplied what is necessary for man's subsistence. The animal's soul, returning to God, carries with it man's gratitude...

... After the song ended, the profane part of the ritual followed. They lit several fires and hung immense copper cauldrons over them. They put the large lumps of meat in these, cutting off each a strip the size of a finger and throwing that into the fire. Several of the young people made wooden spikes and roasted their portion over the fire that way. A few sheep were also killed in the meantime which were, it seemed, not sacrificial animals, but a small part of their meat was also cast on the fire of the altar.

A hearty lot of eating and drinking ensued, the whole company getting into high spirits. They played music, the young people danced, ran races, played various games and ended up on a wrestling contest. Even men of the older ranks got involved in the games and a massively muscular man in his fifties knocked all the proud young lads to the ground in the wrestling. It was also on this occasion that I saw the incredible mastery with which these people handle the bow and arrow even these days. Shooting at a target the width of a man's back, they hit the middle almost without a fault and when the point of the contest was the distance to which their arrows would fly, not one of the arrows landed within two thousand paces. The feast ended at about sunset and all the people got on their horses or into their carriages to head back for their shelters. The next day I myself was sitting in the carriage drawn by the great iron horse, re-living in my dreams the excitements of the previous day, filled with tremendous pride that of all living Hungarians I was the first and only one to have seen this sacrifice. (BARÁTHOSI 1930: 148–151)

The reason why I quoted the Hungarian scholar's description at such length is because he observed such a great deal of small detail. Seeing the Russian director LEONID KUPERSCHMIDT'S ethnographic film which included a Buryat horse sacrifice, I found that a great many details agreed precisely with BARÁTHOSI'S description.

The Russian director's documentary was made in 1987 and one of its episodes was the traditional performance of the horse sacrifice. By traditional I mean that the structure of the animal sacrifice has remained old and traditional even though several elements have been incorporated which are specific to our day and age (e.g. they use a lorry to transport the sacrificial animal to the spot). This sacrifice was always performed on the sacred hill of the tribe. In the past few decades this was done in secret until a few years ago when official permission was granted or, more precisely, the ban was withdrawn. What is more, this populous feast of wide kindred relations was even visited by the local party and state leaders, since they, too, are members of the tribe (in the film we can see that they even took part in the wrestling). The even distribution of the meat was an important moment of the *tailga* which is also clearly visible in the film.

NADEZHDA STEPANOVA described the preparations for the sacrifice on the bank of the Baykal in the following fashion:

This is a sensitive world, the world of the shamans. We ourselves are protected, but if anything goes wrong, it is you others who will come to harm. We are mainly concerned about you... The ceremony begins on Sunday—a nice day. There will be three lambs sacrificed, everything will go as it should. The sacrifice will be made to the host spirit of the lake Ol'khon, to his son, and to the host spirit of the lake. Three lambs have already been prepared, these will be the sacrifice. This is a very sophisticated thing, you know, the gods teaching, men and women teaching, it all happens with the permission of the gods, as it is in their honour that the rite is performed, the sacrifice goes to them. Not everyone is allowed to come and see, because everything goes according to the rules of the rite. (1996)

The female shaman MARIA TSIBENOVA told us the following about the *tailga* and the role of women:

> The tailga is a sacrificial rite, a sacrifice to the spirit, to the host spirits of the Ol'khon, the Baykal and the hosts of the birds. To the khan, so to say, of the birds, which is for us, Buryat peoples, not the eagle but, on the maternal line, the swan. There used to be an abundance of swans in this area at one time. People believe that something evil must have happened and the swans disappeared. I think it must have been a change in the environment, in the climate. Well, and now for women. According to the tradition among our people, the shamans for such a great occasion as this were always men. The male shamans always enjoyed priority. The women shamans only ever had second place. They were the helpers. This probably survived from the time when people lived in a matriarchal system. At least that is what I think. The tradition has it that women must keep away at these times, but not only women, but all strangers as well. They must keep as far away as possible, because the Buryat say buzurte, which means that women are unclean. These days we only sacrifice sheep, not horses. First we must see what sort of an occasion it is, what is the aim of the tailga, what the gods require and that defines the sort of sacrifice we make. Thus, for example, I know that to purify the Baykal on the far side requires the sacrifice of a cow. We have to plan out well in advance what the gods want, this determines the quantity of the lambs and of the vodka but that also depends on the type of spirits we are dealing with. (1996)

The *böö* (shaman) Ochir, said the following:

> The tailga is a prayer, a religious service. The question is whether we should sacrifice a horse or a sheep. We are grateful to the elder shamans by blood, to the older generations, because when those hard times began, they reached a compromise with the heavenly gods saying that from now on we shall not be able to sacrifice a horse, we shall not be able to sacrifice a cow, let us make a deal so that we shall only be sacrificing a sheep. This contract, so to speak, has been kept to by both parties. (1996)

One of the participants of the conference was V. N. ALEXEYEV, a famous researcher of Siberian shamanism who told us in an interview, among other things, that "in the olden days they used to sacrifice, say, a red bull, to the host spirits of the Ol'khon. Among us, Yakuts, a white horse was sacrificed to the deity. Depending on the age and the possibilities, the Buryat might, for example, sacrifice a sheep. There was a *tailgan* here yesterday which usually consists of several phases as a sacrifice is shown to several deities on the same occasion. A sacrifice was performed to the host spirit of the Baykal, to the spirit of the Sky and, in the third phase, to the spirits of the Ol'khon mountains. It is also interesting that in the olden days a separate sacrifice used to be performed for the individual tribal, dynastic gods. Each tribe has its own patron spirit and it is the duty of the tribe to offer it sacrifices and beseech them to grant prosperity, health and happiness for all the members of the tribe. Thus the people who gathered here obviously performed a grand scale *tailgan* which was in many respects perfectly true to the tradition. The tradition survived in people's memories and there are individuals living who still remember everything accurately. In the recent years *tailgan* rites have again been performed regularly and it is a very important and interesting aspect of the symposium that this is the first time when researching scholars and practising shamans have made a joint effort to come to understand the nature of shamanism. There are researchers here from various countries, most of whom look on shamanism, as it were, from the outside while the shamans look on it from the inside. An alliance of these two views in the future might give us a better understanding of shamanism as a phenomenon (HOPPÁL 1996).

All these opinions and data highlight the social background to the *tailga*. Later, when we have discussed the structure of the rite, we shall also talk about the historical data. This description is not based merely on local observation and note taking. Besides several dozen photographs, it also relies on a two and a half hour video recording by cameraman LAJOS NÁDORFI. The following description is practically based on this footage as ethnographic text.

ETHNOGRAPHY OF A *TAILGAN*

(June 23 1996, Eastern bank of Lake Baykal, Buryatia) Description co-authored by ÉVA ARANYOSI.

The ritual began at 11 o'clock on Sunday morning. This is when the local people, the inhabitants of villages near and far, and the participants of the conference began to gather. The venue was a resort house in a village called Enhaluk, so by local people we mean the people from the resort house and the inhabitants of the surrounding villages—a crowd of several hundred people. The preparations were rather spectacular as several crates of vodka were unloaded from two lorries (by the afternoon a hundred bottles must have been emptied—mainly by splashing, but, naturally, the participants also drank some.)

The first interesting moment was that the participants had to go through a ritual cleansing process. The women had to step over a small fire lest their impurity should jeopardise the success of the rite. (This is an analogue of the passage between two fires that is described by Marco Polo in his famous work on the court of the grand khans of Mongolia.)

On the previous day the shamans had asked the spirits whether the strangers were allowed to shoot a film. The spirits had granted permission and we were most grateful for the opportunity.

The participating men, shamans and shamanesses were gathering on the bank. Neatly stacked piles of wood, vodka bottles and cutting instruments were lying on the spot where the ceremony was going to take place. The idyllic landscape was strewn with grazing horses and cattle, while in the background the Baykal glistened like a mirror in the bright sunshine.

The preparations began. A fire was lit, water was heated in great cauldrons and one of the shamans conducting the ceremony, with the assistance of a local helper, erected the sacrificial trees: two side by side and one more a little distance away from these.

The water was beginning to steam in the cauldrons and the shamans, some with great brass mirrors, others with drums, set out to the shore where the first lamb had now been delivered. Two people were carrying it and then they placed it under the erect sacrificial birches. A Buryat lama was playing beautiful music on his recorder and we could also hear the tinkling of some bells some distance away. Some of the local women put their hands together in prayer.

One of the leaders of the ceremony stood up before the long row of benches where the male participants sat, he raised his arms high, parted them, stood facing the lake and then a few seconds later rubbed his two palms together. Then he turned right and repeated the same motions and then to the back and finally in the fourth direction, too, he raised his arms, palms to the sky. Finally he returned to his starting point, facing the lake, where he rubbed his hands together four times and stood for many seconds with his arms apart upward toward the sky.

One of the shamans sitting among those who waited beside the steaming cauldrons dripped seven drops of his vodka to the ground, and then raised it high toward his companions before drinking it. The participants and onlookers began to taste the vodka but before each drink they spilled a few drops onto the ground and they never omitted doing this.

Another shaman, who was in charge of conducting the ceremony, held a stick, the end of which was red hot and smoking. With this red hot stick he drew four circles over the heads of the chief shaman and his helper, probably with the aim of purifying them. Then he began the singing and drumming. The shamans, shamanesses, helpers and other participants were all there on the shore, facing the lake, while two strong lads held fast onto the lamb. Those standing nearer the back sprayed vodka toward the lake from the little bowls and glasses they held in their hands and also spilled a few drops on to the ground. A few people did the same from the bottle. Beside vodka there was also milk and milky tea to drink.

The shamans stood directly next to the lamb—several of them were drumming and singing, lead by the chief shaman. They were calling up the spirits. At this point the chief shaman broke a branch off one of the sacrificial trees and laid it where the lamb was being held, more precisely, he laid it under the animal's spine. This was the sign for the killing of the lamb. The animal was laid on its back, its legs were held and an incision about two inches long was made on its abdomen. Then the man put his hand in and within an instant snapped the artery to the heart. Then they started processing the meat, but first they tied a ribbon onto one of the birches standing on the bank.

In the meantime a shaman was kneeling on the bank holding a little bowl in his hand and while he was singing, he kept lifting the bowl toward the lake and splashing vodka with his hands. Then he stood up and continued the same movements. He had a vast mirror hanging round his neck. On the bank there were men sitting on the grass, splashing the earth with vodka, some from their glasses, others from their bottle.

Three female shamans and a male shaman of about fifty years of age carried on their ritual on the beech. The Buryat shaman poured vodka into a bowl after removing the cap with his teeth. Then they parted their arms together with all the others, raised their palms toward the sky facing the lake and called the host spirit of the lake. The male shaman lit a small fire, only big enough to give smoke and he drew three circles over the smoke with his vodka bottle and then another three circles with his left hand and finally another three with his right. Then he took a few steps to the right, a few to the back and finally drew five circles over the fire with his bowl. Finally he raised the bowl to the sky and splashed six times toward the lake. Behind his back one of the shaman women lay down facing the earth, parting her arms, practically embracing the earth beneath her. Then the shaman splashed some vodka on the ground, refilled the bowl and repeated his previous motions, murmuring something. The shaman women knelt down, the shaman along with them, and they touched the earth with their heads.

In the background, men were spraying vodka on the ground from glasses and bottles. Other men washed the internal and other parts of the slaughtered lamb in large bowls. The water was steaming away in the cauldrons, they were cooking the lamb and in a separate bowl they were stuffing the intestines with blood—making genuine blood sausages. A group of men and shaman women were sitting around a fire, one of the shaman women was murmuring a long prayer while dripping thirteen drops of vodka onto the ground.

At about two o'clock in the afternoon a short break ensued—several people went off to have lunch, and the shore became somewhat less crowded. Now the women were allowed to go close to the spot where the lamb had been killed. During the break the shamans were healing and purifying local people—soothing pain, hushing crying babies, and exorcising evil spirits. The high reverence of the people toward the shamans was evident.

An hour later the men lit a new fire on the shore and carried a long wooden table over to it which held the internal parts, the liver, the heart and the lungs that had been cut up into little pieces.

The killing of the second and the third sheep took place after the same fashion as the first. After a long stretch of drumming, splashing and spraying the ground with vodka the chief shaman poured a little vodka on the lamb, broke another branch off the tree and placed it along the lamb, thus giving permission for the killing. The lamb was laid on its back, its legs held tight and the incision was made in the chest. The expert man reached in and broke the main artery within a few seconds. The lamb did not struggle long. The processing of the meat began and another ribbon, which also included some bank notes, was tied onto the sacrificial birches. The lambs were skinned within a few seconds, the offal removed, the other parts chopped up, sorted out and placed in the cauldrons.

Everyone was eating, some sitting down, others standing up. Two shaman women studied slips of paper over their meals which had been given them by some participants—they had written their own names and those of their family members, asking the shamans to beseech the gods for blessing, good luck or recovery during the ceremony.

Beside the birches that had been stood on the bank, a fire was crackling and the lamb skins had been prepared next to them ready to be burned so that the sacrifice may rise to the sky with the smoke of the fire.

The meal was followed by drumming and everybody went down to the shore. They offered more vodka and also some food as sacrifice to the water and the earth. The sheep skins were thrown onto the fire. Several people knelt and touched the ground with their heads, others gave deep bows, and a shaman splashed a whole bottle of vodka about the burning skins. Although it had grown late in the afternoon, the sun was still in the sky, shining with a velvety warmth and gulls were circling over the lake.

One of the conducting shamans clapped his hands twice, first with his back to the lake and then facing it—with this gesture he symbolically declared the event concluded.

T. M. MIKHAILOV, a leading authority in the study of Buryat shamanism, pointed out in his preface to the latest edition of Buryat shaman songs the social significance of the *tailgan* rituals.

> Shamanic rites and ritual actions are very rich in their contents and formal repertoire, and their elements have a set order. We may divide sacrificial rites according to the degree to which they are compulsory and to their prescribed frequency into compulsory and non-compulsory, regular and irregular rituals. From the point of view of the aim and function of the rite, and from the point of view of participation, we may divide them into communal-collective and family/individual rites.
>
> One of the communal-collective rites was known among the Buryat as tailgan. Its main function is to beseech the heavenly being to grant prosperity, a good harvest, good pastures and for the animals to breed well for the coming year, as well as for family happiness, and to keep away trouble, illness and disaster. Rituals of this kind are usually held between the end of spring (May) and autumn (October). Each administrative area has its long-established, traditional communal order for this ceremony within which they held 7, 8 or even more tailgans each year, addressing each to one particular deity. Each of these festive occasions was conducted amongst ceremonial circumstances, they were genuine feasts with the participation of the whole population and they lasted a whole day or even several days. (MIKHAILOV 1966: 11)

RITE AND MEANING

Surveying the events of this full-day event it can be ascertained that the local shamans "worked a full day", keeping the events under their control. In the first half of the day and the rite they killed one lamb and in this case all those present functioned together, as a community. By the second half of the day, roughly after two o'clock, when it came to killing the second lamb, small groups had formed, each engaged in its partial mini-ritual, such as *libation* (drink sacrifice—this is why so much vodka was consumed) and healing/purification (KISTER 1997: 142, VAN DEUSEN 1997: 8).

I use the concepts of healing and purification together because during my field work study of Siberian shamanism I found that the task of the shaman is not so much healing (at least in our day, e.g. in Tuva) but prevention. One of the chief shamans I observed by Lake Baykal treated his queuing patients by symbolically cutting round them, thus removing illness or the evil spell (?). And with his mirror he concluded the purifying rite. This is similar to the way in which women had to pass over a purifying fire at the beginning of the event. The function of purification is to ensure a healthy condition, its meaning is to secure balance. The fact that the ceremony lasts a whole day is not the result or development of some sort of a crisis situation but a regularly repeated, consciously festive occasion during which the people express their respect before the local spirits and the host spirits of the lake.

To return to the time structure of the rite, the first half of the morning is dominated by the killing of the animals while the second half by the cooking of the meat. To speak the language of the well-known semiotic oppositions, the raw becomes cooked, the natural condition is transformed into culture. It is this transformation that the participants unconsciously experience during the rite by the fact that everybody partakes of the meat, particularly of the internal parts. These were cut into very small pieces since this impresses all participants with the notion of equality.

Repetition is another important significant element of ritual behaviour as it ensures the effect of the actions. The animals that are sacrificed, the drink that is splashed, the clapping of the hands are all organised by sacred numbers: 3, 7, 9, 13. I must note here that not even the most unfailing attention, neither counting nor note taking enable the observer to record all details properly—only a video recording can assure this during the slow motion replay in the editing room. We have defined video cameras as the greatest new opportunity in ethnographic description (HOPPÁL 1997).

An important meaning was carried and a central role played within the context of the rite by the fact, that only men were allowed to stay in the direct closeness of the animal sacrifice while women stayed in the background where they performed their own prayer service (van DEUSEN 1996: 8). The separation of men and women is a very important meaningful opposition within the structure of rituals, the typological analogues of which may be found all over Siberia among the Turkic peoples just as well as among the Finno-Ugrians.

In one of his earliest essays PÉTER VERES describes his collecting trip as a member of the ethnographic expeditions of Moscow University, when, in the summer of 1965, he, too, saw some animal sacrifices being performed among the Votyaks. Amongst this Finno-Ugric people, distantly related to Hungarians, men were associated with horse sacrifices and women with cow sacrifices. This division is a typical example of the workings of semiotic oppositions, of which he wrote in another excellent article (VERES 1975) as it was a central organising principle among the Ob Ugrian peoples.

REFERENCES (AND FURTHER READINGS ON SACRIFICE)

BARÁTHOSI-BALOGH, BENEDEK
1930 *Mongolok–Burjátok (Mongolians and Buryats)*. Budapest: Baráthosi Turáni könyvei XI. (Baráthosi's Turan Books No. XI).
1996 *Távoli utakon (Distant Journeys)*, selected and with an afterword by MIHÁLY HOPPÁL. Budapest: Museum of Ethnography.

BESE, LAJOS
1987 Egy sámánszertartás a mongolok titkos történetében (A shamanic ritual in the secret history of the Mongolians). In LAJOS BOGLÁR – MÁRIA FERENCZY (eds.) *Történelem és kultúra. Tanulmányok (History and Culture. Essays)* 3: 7–13. Budapest: Hungarian Academy of Sciences, Oriental Studies Team.

CHAKRABARTI, SHAMIRAN CHANDRA
1989 A study of the Pariplava. *Indo-Iranian Journal* 32: 4: 255–268.

EVANS-PRITCHARD, E. E.
1954 The Meaning of Sacrifice Among the Nuer. *The Journal of the Royal Anthropological Institute of Great Britain and Ireland* 83: 21–34.
1956 *Nuer Religion*. Oxford: Clarendon Press.

FIRTH, RAYMOND
1963 Offering and Sacrifice: Problems of Organisation. *The Journal of the Royal Anthropological Institute of Great Britain and Ireland* 93: I: 12–24.

GÖRMANN, MARIANN
1993 Influences from the Huns on Scandinavian Sacrificial Customs during 300–500 AD. In AHLBÄCK, TORE (ed.) *The Problem of Ritual*. Åbo: Donnerska Institutet, 275–298.

HAMAYON, ROBERTE
1978 Marchandage d'âmes entre vivants et morts. In *Le sacrifice* II, cahier 3: 151–179.

HANGALOV, M. N.
1909 Burját állatáldozatok (Buryat animal sacrifice) Hungarian translation by ZOLTÁN KOVÁCS. In *A samanizmus anyagainak jegyzetfüzete* (A notebook on the materials of shamanism). MS.

HERODOTUS
1980 *A görög–perzsa háború* (The Greco–Persian War – Hungarian translation by GYULA MURAKÖZI). Budapest: Európa.

HOPPÁL, MIHÁLY
1990 Distribution and Equality: The Hidden Channels of Communication within a Community. *Acta Ethnographica* 33: 1–4: 165–180.
1996 MS interview texts with Buryat, Mongolian, Khakas and Tuva shamans. (Hungarian translation by ZOLTÁN KOVÁCS)
1997 A video mint etnográfiai szöveg (Video as ethnographic text). *Néprajzi Értesítő* LXXIX: 203–206.

1999　The Life and Works of BENEDEK BARÁTHOSI-BALOGH, a Hungarian Researcher of Manchu–Tunguz Shamanism. *Shaman* 7: 1: 3–23.

HOROSIH, P. P.

1969　Iz shamanskyh vozzreniy irkutskih Buryat. *Etnographichesky Sbornik* 5: 252–255.

HUBERT, H. – MAUSS, H.

1899　Essai sur la nature et la fonction du sacrifice. *L'Année sociologique* II: 29–139.

1964　*Sacrifice: Its Nature and Function.* London: Cohen and West.

HULTKRANZ, ÅKE

1965　Anthropology as a Goal of Research: Some Reflections. *Folk* 7: 5–22. (Copenhagen)

HUMPHREY, CAROLINE

1983　*Karl Marx Collective: Economy, Society and Religion in a Siberian Collective Farm.* Cambridge: Cambridge University Press.

IPOLYI, ARNOLD

1854　*Magyar Mythológia (Hungarian Mythology).* Pest: Heckenast.

IVANOV, V. V.

1984　A ló és a fa – Kísérlet ősi indiai rituális és mitológiai jelképek megfejtésére (The Horse and the Tree – An attempt at deciphering certain ritual and mythological symbols). In IVANOV, V.V. *Nyelv, mítosz, kultúra (Language, Myth, Culture).* 167–212, Budapest: Gondolat.

KÁLLAY, FERENC

1861　*A pogány magyarok vallása (The religion of the pagan Hungarians)* Az áldozatokról (hús áldozat) (On Sacrifices – meat sacrifice) 96–105. Pest: Lauffer and Stolp.

KISTER, DANIEL

1997　*Korean Shamanist Ritual.* Budapest: Akadémiai Kiadó. (Bibliotheca Shamanistica vol. 5.)

KONAGAYA, YUKI

1995　Mongolian Perspective to Animal Resources: Analysing the Ritual of Slaughter. Paper for the conference on animism in Sapporo. MS.

LOT-FALCK, EVELINE

1977　Koca-Kan, rituel érotique altaien. *Etudes Mongoles et Sibériennes* 8: 733–108.

MAYNAGASHEV, S. D.

1914　Otchot o poezdke k turetskim plemenam minusinskovo i o chinskovo uyezdov letom 1914 g. In *Izvestiya Russkovo Komiteta dlja izucheniya Sredney i Vostochnoy Azii* IInd series, No. 3. St. Petersburg.

MÉSZÁROS, GYULA

1909　*A csuvas ősvallás emlékei (Remnants of the ancient religion of the Chuvash).* Budapest: Hungarian Academy of Sciences.

MIKHAILOV, T. M.

1966 *Huhe Munke Tengeri* (Preface: On Buryat shaman belief and shamanic poetry) (Hungarian translation by ZOLTÁN KOVÁCS). Ulan-Ude: Respoublikanskaya Typografiya.

OPPITZ, MICHAEL

1993 On Sacrifice. In TOFFIN, GÉRARD (ed.) *Nepal, Past and Present.* (Proceedings of the Franco-German conference Arc-et-Senans, June 1990) 99–116. Paris: CNRS Éditions.

RADLOFF, WILHELM

1885 *Aus Siberien.* Leipzig.

SLAVNIN, V. D.

1994 Zhertoprinosheniy Konya Duhu-Pokrovitlyn roda u verhnin kumandintsev. In FUNK, D. A. (ed.) *Problemi etnicheskoy istorii i kulturi Turko-Mongolskih narodov Yuzhno Sibirii i sopredelnih teritoriy.* 57–73. Moscow.

SPERBER, DAN

1985 Interpretive Ethnography and Theoretical Anthropology. In *On Anthropological Knowledge,* 9–34. Cambridge – Paris: Cambridge University Press – Édition de la Maison des Sciences de l'Homme.

TYLOR, E. B.

1871 *Primitive Culture: Research into the development of mythology, philosophy, religion, language, art and custom, 2 vol.* London.

URBANAEVA, IRINA S.

1997 Of Miracles and Shamans in Buryatia. The 1996 Shamanism Symposium. *Shamanism* (Journal of the Foundation for Shamanic Studies) 10: 1: 4–7.

VAN DEUSEN, KIRA

1997 Buryat Shamans and Their Stories. *Shamanism* (Journal of the Foundation for Shamanic Studies) 10: 1: 7–11.

VERES, PÉTER

1975 Jobb: bal – férfi: nő (Right: left – man: woman). In VILMOS VOIGT – GYÖRGY SZÉPE – ISTVÁN SZERDAHELYI (eds.) *Jel és közösség (Sign and community)* 83–92. Budapest: Akadémiai Kiadó.

Picture 1. Tajlagan – sacrificial ritual performed by Buryats (Irkutsk region) in 1930-ies.

Picture 2. Tajlagan – preparation of the ritual meal. (Photo by P. P. Khoroshikh, 1922)

Picture 3. Horse sacrifice.
(Watercolour by
A. VORONINA,
cc. 1920-ies)

Picture 4. Sacred place with remnants of a horse sacrifice.
(Watercolour by A. VORONINA, cc. 1920-ies)

Picture 5. Animal sacrifice on the shore of Lake Baykal. (Photo by M. HOPPÁL, 1996)

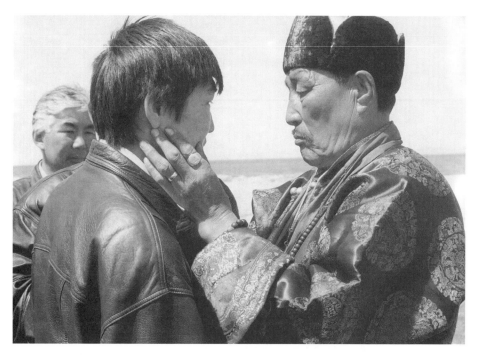

Picture 6. Buryat shaman performs a purification ritual (Photo by L. NÁDORFI, 1996)

DILMURAT OMAR

Modern Kazakh Shamanism

INTRODUCTION

As an ancient cultural phenomenon, shamanism is now studied not only in the West and in Russia, but has become an important theme for modern Chinese anthropologists as well. New editions of the early Chinese sources, that is reports from the 2nd century BC up to the Manchu period, shed light on shamanism mainly among the *xiongnu*, the early Turks, the Kao-che, the Khitan, Mongols, Manchu, and Tungus. In this connection one should refer particularly to the new editions of the writings of SIMA QIAN (2nd century BC), CHEN SHOU (2nd century AD), FAN YE (4th century AD) and the Chinese editions of the reports of medieval European and Oriental sources like MARCO POLO, RUBRUCK and RASHID-ED-DĪN.[1]

When dealing with shamanism I take it as a religious phenomenon tightly interwoven with other cultural elements such as customs, dress and adornment, folk music and dance, folk literature, especially magic and healing of the peoples who believe in the abilities of shamans.

My regional specialization has been peoples speaking Altaic languages in the People's Republic of China and their religions (OMAR 1996). I carried out fieldwork among the Uygur and my own people, the Kazakhs—a nation of about 11 million—who are distributed mainly in the Republic of Kazakhstan and the People's Republics of China and Mongolia. The conventional picture of the Kazakhs is that they are nomadic cattle-breeders, but today they are engaged in agriculture and urban professions as well.

---

[1] *Shiji* 110, *Sanguozhi* 30, *Hou Hanshu* 120, CHEN 1981; RUBRUCK 1983; ED-DĪN 1986.

SOME REMARKS ON THE HISTORY OF KAZAKH SHAMANISM

When dealing with modern Kazakh shamanism we have to keep in mind the manifold religious influences they have been exposed to during their history. In the time of the Old Turkic Empire the Turks still had their own religion, which could be characterized as veneration of heaven and earth, souls and spirits. The central figure was the shaman. But soon world religions spread into Kazakh territories. Buddhism became influential in the culture of the Old Turks, and later on Nestorianism and Manichaeism. The decisive event in the cultural history of the region, however, was the spread of Islam, beginning with the 9th century. Already by the 13th century the population of this territory can be regarded as having been islamized. But does this mean that all the older religious elements had become extinct? This was by no means the case. On the contrary, the Kazakhs developed their particular style of Islam, in which many older religious traits were preserved under the cloak of Folk-Islam (Kazakh Academy of Sciences 1989).

Shamanism, especially, showed a tough vitality. The dissemination of world religions could not banish it. Thus a combination of Muslim and shamanic elements arose. Each form of religion used the other for its own ends. Thus on one hand Islamic *moldas* took up some shamanic elements to achieve a rapid and successful dissemination of their religion, and Kazakh Islam was infiltrated by shamanism. On the other hand shamans became converts to Islam in order to survive and continue their religious practices.

The fight to promote the supremacy of ideological socialism in the Soviet Union, China and Mongolia led to even more violence against shamanism than Islamic opposition. Thus in the time after World War II shamanism seemed to have been extinguished among the Kazakhs of the Soviet Union. But this was only on the surface. Underground, the Kazakhs, who are tightly connected by a common network of relatives, still practiced shamanism in a new and silent form.

The situation among the Kazakhs of China was somewhat different. Shamans were prosecuted there too, publicly criticized and even very severely punished. Waves of atheistic education came one after the other— the most radical during Cultural Revolution. But in contrast to the situation in the Soviet Union, many shamans were able to obtain an official niche. They appeared as folk doctors, whose work was highly esteemed at the time when the Chinese medical system was still being established in the countryside. Those shamans did not make their real identity publicly known, but continued to heal in a shamanic way, while people still believed in their power. Thus shamanism has been carried on up to the present.

After the heavy suppression of shamanism in the socialist countries, which lasted until the end of the seventies, a change in the political situation occurred in the eighties, especially in the Soviet Union under GORBACHEV. The new attitude towards shamanism implied that the skills of the shamans were no longer denied, but newly interpreted with a vocabulary better adapted to the modern school education of the population as "biological", "extraordinary", or "extrasensory power".

Public advertisements of performances and treatments by persons who were regarded as possessing these powers became common. State-run theatres and gymnasia were placed at these person's disposal (ABILKHANOV 1993). In the general search for new spiritual orientation shamanism gained ground again, even in the capital Alma-Ata, and identified with a new belief in esoteric powers. At the end of the 80s even Russians became clients of modern Kazakh shamans.

After the disintegration of the Soviet Union the Kazakhs, in parallel with many other former Soviet Republics, freed themselves from Russian colonial domination. In the Kazakh Republic the restoration and development of national culture have been unfolding rapidly. The resumption of prohibited religions and the further development of national languages are among the most important ideas of this movement. Thus resuming and improving Kazakh folk medical knowledge and techniques— the traditional alternative to Western medicine—also became part of the agenda of the government. A Center of Folk Medicine was set up with the ratification of the Ministry of Public Health in 1991 in Alma-Ata.

FIELDWORK CONDITIONS

In 1995, 1996 and 1997 I carried out religious-anthropological field research in Alma-Ata for periods of one month at a time. The Center just mentioned attracted my attention and turned out to be the focus of my work.

According to the director of this center its main tasks are: 1. identifying folk physicians, 2. study of their techniques of treatment, 3. training courses in modern medicine for these folk physicians, 4. examinations and the issue of physician's licenses. The detailed sequence of operations is as follows: first, the Center looks for the folk physicians (actually, they come of their own accord). When a candidate presents himself, doctors trained in Western medicine are invited to examine the folk physician's experiences and his technique of treatment. After this inspection the folk physician is engaged to practice in the Center and his patients are subsequently reexamined by the doctors of the Western medicine as a measure of control. (The Center carried out this procedure strictly at the beginning, but later became less formal.) When the center feels satisfied with the folk physician's technique of treatment and his medical ability, it offers him a two-month-training in Western medicine. At the same time, a series of mental and psychological examinations are carried out on the folk physician. At the end of these the license is issued: this is valid for three years. At the end of this period, the process of examinations is repeated and the license renewed accordingly. In cases of ineffective treatment or unethical behaviour or fraudulent practice, the license will be revoked and the person will be forbidden to practice.

This Center of Folk Medicine is located in a small street in Alma-Ata. In the entrance hall photos with information on the medical specialties of the physicians hang on the wall. Thus the patients can choose the physician according to their ailment. Costs at the center are much lower than in the normal hospitals. Usually there are one or two folk physicians in each room. Their equipment looks simple: a bed, a desk, and two or three chairs. Instead having a stethoscope and sphygmomanometer or other medical instruments on their desks, they have a *Qu'rān*, an Islamic rosary (*tisvi*), a horsewhip (*khamchy*)[2]; a knife (*pyshaq*), water, matches and *khumalaq*, the 40 sheep ossicles used for divination. Nowadays little stones or fruit-stones are used instead.[3] On the walls of these consulting rooms hang quotations from the *Qu'rān* in beautiful script and pictures of the Holy Kaaba in Mecca. I got permission to take photos and video-films in this center and to interview not only the physicians but also the patients. I thank all these informants for their friendly cooperation.

According to my inquiries there are 30 folk physicians in this center, 20 of them women. All declared that they cure people with their "biological powers". In the rooms of some of them the Diagram of the Supreme Ultimate of Taoism also hangs on the wall. They all acknowledge that they are shamans (*bakhshy*) and that they receive their abilities from the spirits of their ancestors (*arvaq*) and by Allah as well. Their experiences of vocation, which were an essential step to become a shaman, and an elementary condition to becoming a folk physician, sounded somewhat similar.

In Xinjiang there is not yet any comparable public acknowledgment of modern shamanism by state-run centers, but shamans are not prosecuted either. They work privately in their houses. Many of them have other

---

[2] The rod of this horsewhip is about 33 cm in length. It is made of a piece of Chinese Tamarisk wood and covered with leather. The lash is also made of leather and has the same length. It is said that horsewhips made of wolfskin are most efficient.

[3] It is said that fruit-stones brought from Mecca are most efficient.

professions too, and their being shamans is known only to certain groups of the population. Therefore I had to make appointments with each of them and observed them in their private houses. This is the reason why I do not mention the smaller town of Xinjiang, where my main fieldwork was done in July 1999, and I have changed the names of the shamans who were kind enough to allow me to make photos and video-films of their work and to answer to my questions with great patience. I am very thankful to them.

THE CASES

During my fieldwork I observed and interviewed many shamans and was allowed to make 18 videos of their activities. I have selected from this material four cases about which I shall give short reports on different forms of shamanizing.

The Shamaness Mrs. KARLIGASH and her Ritual

Mrs. KARLIGASH, aged 37 (in 1996), is married and has three sons. She was born in Semey state in Kazakhstan and belongs to the Nayman tribe. She finished college and thereafter worked as high school teacher. Her father is a pious Muslim, who performs his five prayers every day. He used to work as an accountant. Mrs. KARLIGASH got her shamanic ability from her grandfather. She told me of her extreme need to read the *Qu'rān*. "The *Qu'rān* is as important to me as air to other people." At the time of her shamanic vocation she dreamt frequently of patients with various diseases. Some of them could be cured, others not. "Of course all these dreams were sent to me by almighty Allah. From 1987 to 1991 I had these dreams frequently. In 1991 at last the desire to cure people became very strong and I started my work as a physician. In the same year I came to this medical center."

Her paraphernalia are a *Qu'rān*, a rosary, a horsewhip, a knife, a matchbox and a bottle of water. She believes, as most Kazakhs do, that among the most important causes of sickness are the "evil eye" and "malicious tongue"—the language of witchcraft. They cause all sorts of diseases. Western medicine is not able to explain or cure these diseases. Only the shamans, who are helped by the spirits of their ancestors and have the support of Allah, are able to expel the effects of "evil eye" and "malicious tongue".

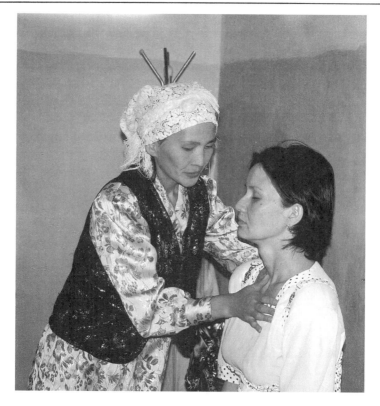

Picture 1. The shaman stretches her fingers and moves them
up and down on the patient's body.

I now give my observations of the healing of a 32 year old Kazakh woman, a nurse, married to a Russian. Her symptoms were the following: for the six months after the delivery of her child she felt aches all over and could not help slobbering. She had already seen many doctors in different hospitals and had been hospitalized. But her condition did not improve. Finally her father brought her to Mrs. KARLIGHASH two days before I met her, and her condition had improved a little. I observed the second treatment of her nine séances.

At the beginning of the ritual Mrs. KARLIGASH felt the pulse in the patient's palm, but not on the wrist as most of Kazakh folk physicians do. Then she asked the patient to stand relaxed in the middle of the room while she read aloud some paragraphs from *Qu'rān*. She stretched her hands and moved them up and down on the patient's body (*Picture 1*). She exhaled: "süf – süf." Then she pushed the patient on the bed and moved her hand up and down the patient's body several times. She took the horsewhip, acted as if she whipped the person and cried "Ket! Ket!"

(meaning Go away! Go away! in Kazakh). She whipped the demon which caused the sickness of the woman. Thereafter Mrs. KARLIGASH sat on the chair behind the desk reading aloud some passages from Qur'an and turning the rosary in her hands. She then lifted the rosary over the patient's head, turned it while she exhaled, and asked the patient to get up. She blew several times into the water-bottle and kept water in her mouth. Suddenly she spurted the water on the patient. The woman shivered. Again she read aloud some passages from the *Qu'rān* and hummed a sad Kazakh folk-song. At the end of the ritual she crossed her hand on her chest while praying for the woman. The patient stood opposite to her and did the same thing.

The Shaman Mr. TATAR and his Ritual

Mr. TATAR is a tall robust man aged 65 (1996), born in Alma-Ata. He is not only a *bakhshy* (shaman) but also a *molda* (Islamic clergyman), educated in the Islamic Seminary in Bukhara, the only one kept open during Soviet time. After his graduation he worked as an *imam*. In 1991 he gave up this position and began work in the Medical Center as a folk physician.

His apparatus comprises a *Qu'rān*, a rosary, a horsewhip, and a knife. His medicines are fresh fruits, tea, salt, sugar, and water on which he exhales giving them his "bio-energy". He owns a simple instrument, which he calls a "Measuring Instrument for Bio-energy". With it he measures the patient's "bio-energy" before and after the treatments. He also has a sketch of the passages through which vital energy circulates in human body. On this sketch the six most important acupoints are noted: *dantian* (the pubic region), *tianmu* (the Heaven Eye in the middle of the forehead) and *jigu* (the vertebrae). Many pictures of the *Qu'rān* and holy places in Mecca are fastened to the walls.

He believes that diseases and bad luck are brought by *khara kush* (black powers). These demonic powers are evil spirits that are most afraid of the holy *Qu'rān*. They also fear the shaman's horsewhip because it can turn out to be a huge python. Thus the whip is a successful tool for driving demons out of the patients' bodies. He calls his mode of treatment *dinî tazalav* (religious cleaning). A patient's spiritual dirt is cleaned by recitations of the *Qu'rān*. The shaman was dressed in white trousers and a fresh white shirt.

I now give my observations of the healing of AYGUL, a woman aged 29. She was an economist and convinced that she was suffering from the evil eye. Her symptoms were nervousness, dizziness, weakness, and insomnia.

He asked her to sit on the chair while he himself stood in front of her and read the *Qu'rān* aloud for about ten minutes. While continuing to read he took his rosary and walked around for five minutes. Then, walking and reciting the *Qu'rān* he whipped the patient mostly on her back (*Picture 2*). Placing the *Qu'rān* on her head he exhaled at her after each passage (*Picture 3*). Thereafter he asked her to hold a bottle of water in front of her chest and he exhaled into the bottle. Then he instructed her to drink the water. Taking the rosary he went on to recite the *Qu'rān* while turning the rosary over her head. Then he asked her to repeat the following words: "The disease is gone. The evil eyes and the malicious tongues are gone. Thank Allah! Thank arvaq!" He crossed his hand on his chest and prayed, then wrapped the food which she had brought, and urged her to eat it for nine days. The skin of the fruits should not be thrown away. Instead she should put it on her navel and then wrap and bury it at a place where people would not tread. Thus the ritual ended.

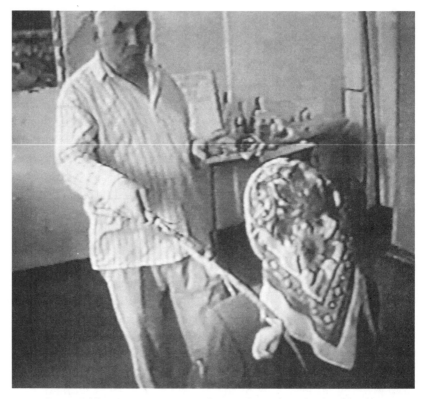

Picture 2. The shaman, concentrating on the patients back, whips her.

Picture 3. The shaman puts the Koran on the patient's head.

The Shaman Mr. BAYQUT and his Ritual

Mr. BAYQUT is a Kazakh aged 38 who lives in a small town in the Xinjiang Uygur Autonomous Region of China. His rituals usually take place in his private ten-bed hospital. He is married and has one child. His mother's father was a *bakhshy*.

Period of development: He was a civil servant, but in his youth he acquired bad habits. The worst of all was that he got drunk frequently and was quarrelsome in these situations. He turned a deaf ear to his mother's admonitions. Once, after having drunk only one glass of alcohol he fell down and lost consciousness: he could neither talk nor move. His friends carried him home and he stayed in bed unconscious for seven days. His legs and feet swelled up so badly that his mother had to cut his trousers to take them off. On the seventh day his mother asked his friends to wash him, because he looked as if he were dead. On the ninth day, however, he regained consciousness and asked for the *Qu'rān*. Then he locked himself in the room and began to read although he had never read *Qu'rān* before and did not know Arabic. After this incident he acquired the ability of a *bakhshy*. He went to study with a famous master shaman named Jumabay and worked as his assistant for three years. By 1999 Mr. BAYQUT was working independently.

His instruments are a pair of fire tongs, a *ketman*—a hoe-like farm implement, bamboo chopsticks and a bowl filled with water. He has five *arvaq* (spirits): the spirit of his grandfather, an eagle-spirit, a raven-spirit, an ape-spirit, and a snake-spirit. Under the protection of Allah and his spirits he is able to handle fire without being burned. Since the demons which cause diseases are afraid of fire, he can drive them away.

Picture 4. The shaman was possessed by his ape-sprit.

I give a report of a ritual which I observed when a patient who suffered from claustrophobia visited Mr. BAYQUT. He began about five o'clock in the afternoon. At first he felt the patient's pulse, then he slaughtered a sheep as sacrifice. While the meat was cooking, he began to invite the spirits. The snake spirit arrived and got into his body. He shivered, his arms moved like snakes, and his voice changed into the snake's voice. After the spirit left him he was possessed by each of his other spirits in succession. When the eagle-spirit entered he spread his arms as if "flying." When the ape-spirit entered he jumped, scratched, clapped his hands, and laughed like a monkey (*Picture 4*). His eyes opened widely and gave him a horrible expression.

After all his spirits had paid their visits he asked one of his assistants to put the fire-tongs and the *ketman* into the fire until they turned red. He asked the patient to lay down on the ground, took the *ketman* out of the fire saying: "ta, ta, ta, ta." Barefooted he stepped on it and pressed the patient's body slightly with his feet. The patient cried for pain because of the heat, but the shaman's feet were not burned at all. Then he took the red hot fire-tongs out of the fire and licked them (*Picture 5*). He took water into his mouth and spurted it on the patient several times. Meanwhile it was ten o'clock at night and the meat was cooked. Everybody sat down and enjoyed the meal after which he invited his spirits once more. The patient sat opposite to him. When each of the spirits entered he once again moved in a way appropriate to the animal. At one point he even leapt up and hit the patient. After each of his four animal-spirits had visited him he sat down murmuring. Than he blew the water in the bowl and asked the patient to drink it. It was now nearly midnight and his ritual was over.

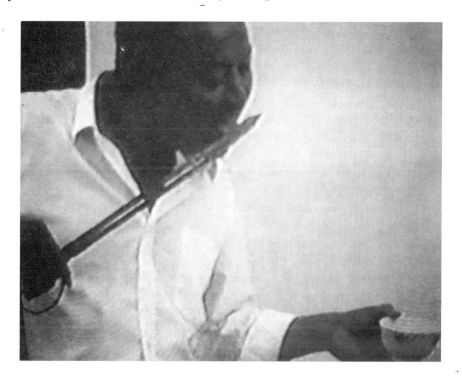

Picture 5. The shaman takes the fire-tongs out of the fire and licks it.

The Shaman Mr. AHMET and his Ritual

Mr. AHMET is a Kazakh aged of 44 (in 1999). He is married and has one son and one daughter. They live in a small town in the Xinjiang Uygur Autonomous Region. He used to be a tractor driver and later on he worked as a chauffeur. He likes wrestling and horse racing. At the beginning of the eighties Mr. AHMET suffered from a swollen leg. He tried many treatments to cure it, but all failed. Finally he felt so depressed that he did not want to leave his home. One day at noon a little cloud passed over his house and he heard a voice asking him to come out. He did so. Thereafter the cloud came very often and he could not help leaving the house as soon as the voice called him. He was tied to the bed to keep him calm, but the bed shook madly each time when he heard the voice. The spirit who called him had a human body but an eagle's head. At last he decided to leave his home and wander around. He tried various herbs and found the medicine to cure his leg himself. After a year he returned home, in his right mind again. Although he sometimes still heard the voice, he was not frightened or nervous any longer. He tried with success to treat sick livestock by setting broken bones or making up prescriptions. He then joined the master shaman JUMABAY to study his ritual knowledge. In 1999 he himself had already become a famous folk physician who could heal various diseases. Among his patients were many Mongols, Uygurs, and even Chinese too.

Mr. AHMET does not own paraphernalia except the *Qu'rān*. When treating a person he shuts his eyes tightly while feeling the patient's pulse. Then his spirit appears and tells him the cause of the disease and how to treat it. With its help he usually draws different magic figures and prescriptions for his patients. They do not have to buy medicine, however, because the prescriptions themselves are the medicines. The pieces of paper are folded and secret symbols are written on them. He tells the patients that they have to roll the prescription into a small ball, fasten a line to it and pour boiled water on the ball and then drink this water. He also tells them how frequently they have to take it. He gets his help from Allah, who is the most powerful support.

I made the observations reported here in July 1999 with three patients from the countryside. They were cattle-breeders: a mother with her adult daughter and son. Another patient, who could not come himself, had asked them to bring him medicine too. All of them had earlier obtained the help of this shaman and were quite satisfied with the curative effects of his treatment. The mother suffered from severe headaches, the daughter was very weak, and the son had fallen from a horse and broken his collarbone and wrist. Mr. AHMET felt their pulses one after the other and shut his eyes.

He wore a very thoughtful expression. Then he began to write the prescriptions for each of them and instructed them how to take the medicine. He wrapped the young man's neck and wrist with plain white cloth and then he wrote the prescription for the patient who could not appear personally. As for the costs—this is quite informal. No fixed prices exist and patients may pay in cash or in kind.

SUMMARY: CHARACTERISTICS OF MODERN KAZAKH SHAMANISM

Kazakh shamanism today can be characterized as follows:
1. Shamanism is still alive among the Kazakhs. The shamans and their patients believe in magic and in spirits, which the shamans are able to master. After the experience of vocation and a period of disease in their earlier life these shamans are able to call them and may feel possessed by them. This gives them the power of healing people. They usually fulfil this task in an altered state of consciousness, which can either be a fully developed possession trance in the evening or at night, or hardly discernible in the daytime. The old Kazakh name of the shaman bakhshy has also survived.
2. Shamanism and Islam are tightly interwoven. Shamans are pious Muslims as well, for whom Allah is the mightiest and the principal source of their shamanic abilities. They dress conservatively and most of their shamanic paraphernalia are Islamic religious objects; the most important of them are a *Qu'rān* and a rosary. The same person may be both shaman and molda—an Islamic clergyman.
3. Shamanism is strongly influenced by Western ideas as well, especially in the Kazakh Republic. Shamans work in an urban center with rooms similar to those of medical practices, obtain government licenses and behave like doctors. It has become their habit to feel the pulse of the patient at first. American and European, including Russian esoteric movements have also become influential in Kazakh shamanism, especially in the Kazakh Republic. The shamans themselves speak of their shamanic abilities as "bio-energy", "extraordinary powers", or "extrasensory abilities".
4. There are considerable differences between the shamanism of the Kazakh Republic and the Xinjiang Uygur Autonomous Region. The influence of Islam and the esoteric movements is less dominant in Xinjiang. That means that shamanic rituals are more traditional and the altered state of consciousness is more intensive. Shamanism in the Kazakh Republic is often practiced with official agreement in

rooms owned by the government, while shamanism in Xinjiang takes place by appointment with the shaman in private surroundings.[4]

REFERENCES

ABILKHANOV, ERASIL
    1993 *Folk Physicians in Kazakhstan*. Alma-Ata: Astana.
CHEN SHOU
    1959 *Sanguozhi* (History of the Three Kingdoms). Beijing: Zhonghua shuju.
OMAR, DILMURAT
    1996 *A'ertai yuxi zhuminzu samanjiao yanjiu*. (Researches on the Shamanism in Various Nations of the Altaic Language Family). Urumchi: Xinjiang renmin chubanshe.
ED-DĪN, RASHID
    1986 *Records of History (Shiji)*. Beijing: Shangwu xingshuguan.
FAN YE
    1965 *Hou Hanshu* (History of the Later Han). Beijing: Zhonghua shuju.
CHEN KAIJUN (ed.)
    1981 *Make Boluo youji* (Travels of Marco Polo). Beijing: Fujian keji chubanshe.
Kazakh Academy of Sciences (eds.)
    1994 *History of Kazakhstan*. Alma-Ata: Devir.
RUBRUCK, GULIELMUS DE
    1983 *Chushi Mengu ji* (As an Envoy in Mongolia). Beijing: Zhongguo shehui kexue chubanshe.
SIMA QIAN
    1959 *Shiji* (Records of the Historian). Beijing: Zhonghua shuju.
SU, BEIHAI
    1989 *Hasakezu wenhua shi* (Cultural History of the Kazakh Nationality). Urumchi: Xinjiang daxue chubanshe.

---

[4] I am grateful to Prof. ULLA JOHANSEN and Dr. PETER ANDREWS for their revision of my manuscript.

BARBARA WILHELMI

The Prophetic Performance and the Shamanic Ritual: Shamanism in the Bible

In the past one had only talked about shamanism in the Siberian and inner Asian regions. We now discover shamanistic features in other cultures and religions. Shamanistic thinking and acting is not a religion of its own but rather appears in different religions (SIIKALA 1992: 1).

Now we shall examine the question whether phenomena can be discovered in Ancient Israel, as well as later in the Babylonian exile which can be compared to shamanic occurrences. The basis of this research is various texts from the Hebraic Bible which reports from periods of the early kingdom around 1000 B.C. and from the time of exile at around 587 B.C.

MIRCEA ELIADE defined the basic characteristics of shamanism to be techniques of ecstasy and the ascent of souls. Later on additional characteristics of shamanistic behavior were added. In this context I will not go into a detailed description and definition of the individual shamanistic traits and will focus this research on the following aspects:

- — What is the importance of ecstasy?
- — Does the tambourine take a special function and are there hints in regard to shaman dresses?
- — Does the phenomena of "ascent" or "journey" exist?
- — Does communication with the "other-world" take place?
- — Are there reports from rituals as performances?

ECSTASY

States of ecstasy are found with male or female prophets in the Hebraic Bible. According to WEIPPERT a prophet is "male or female person who is ordered by the respective divinity or god to communicate a revelation in verbal or meta-verbal form to the intended receivers (...) these revelations are received by the prophets through a cognitive experience, a vision, an audition, a dream, or a divine revelation" (WEIPPERT 1988: 289).

The prophets can have very different ways of living. Some prophets are grouped around superior being, like for example Eliza (2King 2,3ff) or Miriam (Ex 15,20ff). Others hold a position as Cult-prophets at a sanctuary. They live in houses of prophets (1Sam 19,20ff) or they live alone and they may live in one place or move about.

Rarely they are described with the words "roae" for seer (1Sam 9.9), "ish elohim" for man of god and "ishah elohim" for woman of god, or "hosae". By far the most common expression is "nabi" for the male prophet and "ishah nebiah" for the female prophet. This word is related to the Akkadian verb "nabu" which means to call or proclaim. It is important that "nabi" is not understood as nomen agentis, but rather as nomen rei acti. In other words, the "nabi" is the one who is called upon to act and express himself as the chosen one. In the Hebraic Bible the word "nabi" is mentioned a total of 309 times. We also find it in the scriptures from the time of the prophets as well as during the early time of the kings in ancient Israel (COENEN – BEYREUTHER – BIETENHARD 1993: 1018).

In the books of Samuel we read about prophets that joined together to form groups. They were filled with the spirit of Yahweh, played trance-inducing music, and fell into states of ecstasy. Saul was enraptured as a prophet and laid naked on the ground (1Sam 10, 6.10,11,6; 1Sam 19,20f). The influence of the spirit is described as an irresistible force which suppresses and transforms one's will, leading the individual into the prophetic state of ecstasy.

While the traditional interpretation sees a uniqueness in the scriptures of the prophets, we now see this slowly giving way to more differentiated perceptions. There are "nebiim" with ethical pathos and there are the prophets from the scriptures with ecstatic experiences. This means, we can imagine ecstatic experiences when "ruah" as the spirit of God is using utterances of someone in ecstasy (as with the "nebiim" with Saul as well as Isaiah) like "qaw-laqaw saw-lasaw" in an onomatopoetic way (Isaiah 28, 13). Also in Ezekiel we see additional aspects of shamanic features: He lays there for a while as if he were dead (Eze 4, 1f) and he flies to other places (Ezekiel 3,12; 8,3; 11,1). It is interesting that the same expression "nebiim" is used for those acting in the name of Yahweh as well as those criticized for being false prophets. Therefore the false prophets cannot be recognized strictly based upon the existence of these states of ecstasy.

It can be concluded that ecstasy is part of being a prophet. The word itself makes this apparent. The word for "falling into a state of ecstasy" contains the same letters that are used for the word "prophet."

The suggestion by KAPELRUD that the "nabi" phenomenon in Israel is of a purely Canaan origin is doubtful. Besides the complete rejection of many practices, there are also some clearly positive statements in Biblical texts. As is told in the stories of Moses and Joshua (Num 11.10f), seventy elders fell into states of ecstasy. Joshua criticized this while Moses responded, "Let Yahweh turn all people into prophets! So that Yahweh can put his spirit on to them!" Even when one is of the same opinion as the "Elohist" writer, who is trying to introduce some foreign element into the Mosaic tradition, the abundance of conflicting opinions and representations with respect to ecstasy does not support the proposition of a singular Canaan origin of the "nabi" phenomena.

The conflicting points of view regarding ecstatic prophecy may have their roots in the original Israelitic Nabitum, or in the critical attitude of people in exile in Babylon (in 600 B.C) against the ruling kingdom. Furthermore, the majority of the scriptures originating from this time were summarized in a larger compilation of traditional texts. These exiled people considered the rising kingdoms to be the primary source of the decline of the country. In contrast, it appeared to them that the spontaneous appearance of the spirit seemed closer to the original relationship with God. Around the time of the exodus, there were increasing occurrences of prophetic phenomena.

THE TAMBOURINE AND THE SPECIAL SHAMAN CLOTHING

In the stories of Saul and David musical instruments are often mentioned, for example in 1Sam. 10,5 the harp, the drums, the flutes and the lute. David is shown as the one who plays music or he dances while others are playing the drums. Especially in these stories, there is an association with the instruments and the trance. In particular, we see that the tambourine "top" is mentioned several times in connection with the male prophets. Oftentimes the details are not too specific and it is not easy to determine if the groups are strictly made up of men or if they are mixed.

In comparison, the tambourine is often closely associated with the female prophets. In Exodus 15, 20 for example the female prophets surrounded Miriam and in 1Sam 18,6 the young women. In Psalms 68,26 there is a musical parade with "the singers up front, followed by the strings, in the middle the Virgins who play the tambourine." The religious metaphor "virgin" is associated with the tambourine. We see this in Jer 31,4: "Again I will build you up (...) Virgin Israel. And again you will decorate yourself with your tambourine."

Iconographic artifacts also speak for the strong relationship between women and the tambourine. Figurines dating back to around 900 B.C. were found holding round disks either in front of their breasts or at their sides. This raises the question about the meaning or identity of these round disks (KEEL – UEHLINGER 1993: 187f). It is difficult to determine what it actually should portray without knowing the original intention. Some suggest they depict a cake or an offering; this is based on the passage in Jer 7, 18 where it says "Cake for the heavenly queen."

In contrast to the iconographic context in the Syrio-Phoenician region it seems that the depiction often does indeed represent a tambourine. For example, "in processions, in which often a woman appears who is playing a tambourine." Also there is a new Assyrian seal dating back to approximately 800 or 900 B.C. on which the goddess Ishtar is depicted as she joyfully plays the tambourine welcoming the weather god (KEEL – UEHLINGER 1993: 188).

Based on iconographic evidence KEEL and UEHLINGER conclude that during the course of time the tambourine was used increasingly for rituals and cult worship. These were played by people and not by goddesses. In my opinion, even if people were playing the tambourine, they may have been in a relationship with the goddess.

When examining the literature it becomes apparent that various musical instruments (strings, cymbals, wind instruments, tambourine) play an integral part in prophetic and cult worship. According to the Hebraic Bible, musical instruments serve two purposes. One is to beautify life- named Jubal's music (Genesis 4,21). The second is to use music as a vessel for the gospel of God which means music is commanded by God (Num 10,2f., Ex 19, 16–19, Deut 31, 19; OSTERLOH – ENGELLAND 1959: 405f). Therefore people often have revelations or experience a closeness with God through musical expression. This is why Elisha has a lyre musician come to play before he can begin his prophesizing (2Kings 3, 15).

In comparison to the other instruments one could conclude that the tambourine itself has no specific function for an ecstatic experience because it is often mentioned with other instruments. Nevertheless, the tambourine has earned a specific role because it is often mentioned in connection with women and female prophets.

Additionally it becomes evident, that the Hebraic word "top" for the tambourine with its two letters "t" and "p" are also included in the word "tepilah" which stands for prayer (and also "fright" and "fear"). In the

Hebraic language this is important because single letters have a meaning on their own. During the development of the Hebraic language the radical, how the letters are pronounced, had a basic meaning which can still be found in its original form today. Aleph, the first letter of the Hebrew alphabet, represents an ox, while beth, the second one, symbolizes a house. Although the language has developed further there are still related letter compounds evident. The identified relationship of "T" and "I" the word "tepliah" suggests that there is a special relationship between the drumming and the praying.

Furthermore in two passages in the text of Ezekiel (Ez 13,10. 14.18) prophets are initially criticized for an action which is described with the word "tapel". The suggested translation assumes that this has to do with a "hapax legomenon" which means a unique word that is only appearing in that specific context with a poorly understood meaning. In comparison a connection with the more frequently used word for "prayer" (using a tambourine) appears to be much more reasonable.

In the following paragraph (Ez 13, 18) one could pose the same question regarding "metaprot" (from "tapar"). The translation "sewing" is confirmed at two additional points in the paragraph. Indeed, this could mean that "sewing" therefore has a religious and magical meaning (GESENIUS 1962: 887). This passage in the book of Ezekiel is also of great interest for the question in regard to the description of shamanistic clothing.

The text describes how God ordered the prophet Ezekiel to turn against the "daughters" of his own people. These daughters appear as female prophets from their own revelation. He criticizes the sewing of "kessatot" (hapax legomenon) and headdresses of all sizes. The Septuaginta translated "kessatot" as pillow. Luther and others followed this translation. In this version it could mean a kind of feather object. Gesenius sees a parallel with the Akkadian word "kasu" – "to tie" or "to bind". "Kessatot" could then be understood as "ribbons".

This translation gains plausibility when we include the information concerning where these ties and ribbons should be fastened, namely alongside the arms. This reminds us of the shamanic dress and not only from the inner Eurasian region.

During the exile, there were new influences on the rituals due to the contact with the Babylonian and other cultures. RENATE JOST points out an increased activity of prophets in Juda and during the exile (JOST 1995: 189). In contrast ARVID KAPELRUD supposes that "shamanistic features had receded into the background after the fall of Jerusalem in 567 B.C.

(KAPELRUD 1967: 96). Although we cannot discuss the details, we conclude that there had been a change in the ritual activity.

THE JOURNEY – THE ASCENT

The idea of soul hunting is well-known in the context of shamanism (HAMAYON 1990). There are some similarities to the prophet Ezekiel accusing his people's prophetic women of hunting souls by means of their handmade dresses. This concept of the soul seems to be unimaginable in the context of Ancient Israel. "Nefesh" the soul means the breath, which makes alive and gives vitality an energy. The idea of "nefesh" was not considered to be separate from the body. Nevertheless, there were terms like "spirit" and "ghost", which refer to entities that are able to move to other places. MARIE-THERES WACKER points out that Ezekiel himself has shamanic features. He had experienced trances and traveled through the sky (WACKER 1997: 20; SIIKALA 1992: 1).

Ezekiel 3,12–14 describes how the prophet Ezekiel had been raised and carried away by the spirit. We can think of this journey as a flight because wings were mentioned several times before. Moreover the prophet described experiencing different states of consciousness and visions, and being accompanied by helping spirits. This seems to be characteristic of shamanic systems (HORWITZ 1991: 40).

THE COMMUNICATION WITH THE OTHERWORLD.
THE CONJURATION OF THE DEAD.

The traditional cult allowed a person to get in contact with the divine world and even to seek advice from oracles such as the well-known oracle Urim a Tummim. However, there were many prohibited activities mentioned in the prohibitions and commandments of the Pentateuch. The quantity and the distinction of the prohibitions show that the people seemed to practice divination frequently, they walked over burning coals or cut themselves in ritual mourning; they visited sooth-sayers, sorcerers, augurs, wizards or used other divination methods (Lev 19, 31; 20,6; Deut 18,10–14, 2Kings 21,6; WACKER 1997: 13). There was no doubt about the powerful effect of those prohibited rituals.

These prohibitions were addressed to both men and women. Some of them, however, are explicitly against women whose activities carried the penalty of death. See for example Exodus 22, 17–18: "do not allow a sorceress ('mekassepah') to live!"

I do not want to start a detailed discussion of whether the undue hardship is related to the presumed responsibility of women within the cult of the dead. This assumption, however, becomes evident in the narrative of King Saul who visited the woman in Endor. Saul, at the end of his reign, displaced or destroyed the sooth-sayers and mediums in some kind of witch hunt. Nevertheless, in this story Saul ordered his servants to look for a woman who is able to come in contact with the spirits of the dead.

In this narrative, however, the woman of Endor is not referred to as a witch. The Hebrew word "isha" means just "woman". Presumably the intention of that narrative was to integrate opposite aspects of rituals activities and cults. There is no other narrative in the Bible about conjuring the dead.

Before visiting the woman of Endor King Saul "tried in vain to get divine guidance" by Yahweh. But "it was completely useless through dreams, through the oracles Urim and Tummim, and through prophets. Then he was asked by a spirit to practice "ba ob", in order to get in contact with the dead seer Samuel" (KAPELRUD 1967: 94). Some consider the word 'ob' to mean a tool or a method that the woman might have used (KAPELRUD 1967: 94). GESENIUS associates "ob" with "bag of goatskin" used in former times to keep liquids (GESENIUS 1962: 14–15). Perhaps the word refers to the liquid, gas, or steam used within the procedure.

An interesting detail is the disguise Saul wears in order to remain unrecognised by the woman. On the other hand FOHRER points out that the disguise is part of the mourning cult; it is important to disguise one's self in order to avoid being caught by the fatal power of the dead (FOHRER 1953: 11).

The recalled soul of Samuel could be seen exclusively by the woman. Saul asked: "What do you see?" The woman replied: "I see 'Elohim' coming up out of the ground" (1Sam 28,13). The word "elohim" usually is translated with "god" although the plural "gods" would be the correct translation, but in this context it is probably "a ghost" or "a being." The recalled soul seems to have a body; he is even dressed in the coat he wore when he was alive. The woman's description of the coat identifies for Saul the entity as Samuel. We find another hint of a shamanic feature in the narrative which tells us that Saul let himself fall down to the ground. We can presume that the woman faced the recalled soul. Perhaps she is in the same position as TAE-GON KIM describes: "the shaman normally prays to the spirits, while facing them" (KIM 1995: 7). Unable though to see him, Saul heard his voice: "Why have you disturbed me by bringing me up?".

Finally he gives the answer by repeating what he had already said before his death.

The ritual involves lying on the ground. It is interpreted as a reaction to the terrible news or a collapse from exhaustion because Saul did not eat during that day and night. This gives the reason for the woman's activity to slaughter of a calf and baking of unleavened bread. Finally she urged Saul to eat. The word "t macher" emphasizes the sequences of the procedure. In another context this word points out the importance of the exact moment, for instance the "following" new moon. Therefore the meal seems to be a constituent part of the ritual.

The duration of the ritual was "one night" excluding Saul's fasting period. This is similar to TAE-GON KIM's information about the time of the shamanic rituals. "It can be said that the time of rituals is basically night-time" (KIM 1995: 7). In those days the calf was the offering in Israel and in other cultures too, while the unleavened bread was part of the religion only in Israel. This combination of foods was either entirely possible at the time or else it was only brought into this context at a later date. In either case, it would mean that the "world of the spirits of the dead" already was or would later become "integrated into the belief in the Israelite God" (WACKER 1997: 20). This also strengthens the use of the word "isha" to describe the woman of Endor, who was described as a "witch" only in later translations of the Bible.

I agree here with MARIE-THERES WACKER, who claims that "the story shows that when the woman of Endor urges and ultimately compels King Saul to eat before he leaves her home and continues his journey, she plays a role for King Saul which is quite closely similar to the role played by a shamanic healer" (WACKER 1997: 20).

THE PROPHETIC RITUAL AS PERFORMANCE

Thus far, mention has been made of only a few of the rituals which were common during this era. A large number of such rituals must remain unconsidered. Within the scope of this paper, I would like to look more closely at only one peculiarity among the Biblical prophets. It has been said of them that they were principally effective through their announcing the Word of God. It has also been said, however, that they performed symbolic or sign-related actions: e.g. Isaiah walked naked and barefoot (Isaiah 20), Jeremiah hid a girdle "in a hole of the rock" at Euphrates (Jeremiah 20) and Ezekiel dug through a wall (Ezekiel 12).

Sign-related or symbolic acts are "closely connected to magical acts that can be encountered everywhere", whereby the symbolic element is independent of the magical element (FOHRER 1953: 10–11; 14). They are also distinct from repeated rituals because symbolic acts are discrete actions which are performed only once. FOHRER therefore suggests that they contain "a mysterious power" which "transforms itself into reality" in order to "achieve its fulfillment" (FOHRER 1953: 9).

Although each prophet sometimes performs various unique acts which are distinctly his or her own and which are not intended to be repeated either in their theme or in their expression, these acts nonetheless share certain traits in common.

In most cases, an action or a movement is performed with material that is used in a symbolical manner; furthermore, the action or movement is performed at a particular time, in a particular space or place, and by one person. The action has an underlying concept. It is important to note that each act is a unique, one-time-only performance which must be separated from the verbal explanation of its meaning. The act can be understood without the subsequent verbal explanation, which is offered to emphasize the fact that the preceding action was performed in fulfillment of a divine command. The direct oral statement acquires importance of its own because of its relationship to the preceding corporeal performance with its materials and symbols. The action evokes new experiences in its beholders. Furthermore, it is also important that the announcement occurs in front of an audience and that it has a form.

The scheme can be summarized in the following six points: 1. A person receives a "commission" from God or God's spirit; 2. The act is performed in front of an audience; 3. At a particular place; 4. During a specified period of time; 5. With special materials or in a special manner (e.g. naked); 6. Something is done.

TAE-GON KIM identifies five features which characterize the shamanic ritual: "a) taboos and purification of the space used for the rituals, b) ritual time/selection of time; c) offerings: water, slain animals; d) the shaman's performance (song/dance as the other-man); e) the break rite" (KIM 1995: 5).

These features can be readily compared with the ones listed in my scheme. The time factor plays an important role in both forms of action: in the ritual time at the correct moment (kairos) as well as in the available passing time (chronos) and in the relationship to the "eternal space of time". The prophet's performances, however, are not solely restricted to night-time hours. They can take place either by day or by night. The offerings are related to the "materials" used in the prophet's actions.

The concept of "the other-man" who, as shaman, performs the action through singing or dancing, occurs in TAE-GON KIM's paradigm (KIM 1995: 5). In the symbolic action, this "being other" happens through the divine command as well as in the special, individual action itself. TAE-GON KIM juxtaposes the shamanic ritual with the art-performance and discovers a shared pattern here too: e.g. both forms of action have a concept, an audience and a "stage" (KIM 1995: 5).

The "faithful" in the shamanic ritual correspond to the "audience members" in the art-performance. In my opinion, the prophet's symbolic action has both. On the one hand, the prophet's action is embedded within the context of the faith; its concept, however, primarily involves provocation and criticism. It is directed towards an audience which "accidentally" happens to be present at the site.

As already mentioned, the symbolic action also has a concept and an intention (namely, the desire to change the situation). The prophet's action, however, does not lead along a direct path to the desired improvement, but usually begins by shaking up and confronting the members of the audience. Afterwards, it is hoped, the audience members will themselves modify their behavior accordingly.

I have staged some of these prophetic, sign-related actions in artistic performances in front of an audience and have been able to experience many of the aforementioned features firsthand. I deliberately chose not to design this "reconstruction" in the sense of a "planned and rehearsed" theatrical presentation but staged it instead as an art-performance. In so doing, it was important for me to consider the provocative element as well as the immediately present factors of place, material, time, and a witnessing audience.

CONCLUSIONS

Inquiry into the shamanic phenomenon in the Hebrew Bible disclosed a great abundance of material which cannot be fully discussed here. Nonetheless, the following can be said about the existence of shamanic forms:

1. Shamanic phenomena are present with various degrees of frequency and significance. There were permissible as well as forbidden rituals.
2. The most frequent mention is made of ecstasy, although the importance accorded to this phenomenon varies from century to century. Ecstatic states were also welcomed as late as the era of the Pauline texts. This can be inferred from our knowledge of the fact

that Paul ranked glossolalia (the gift of tongues) and the prophetic state of being among the charisms (free gifts of grace). However, Paul discriminates (e.g. for the Corinthian congregation) between these acts depending upon whether they are engaged in by men or women.

3. This raises the question of when the gender-specific discrimination in relation to shamanic forms first arose, because this differentiation is also present in the Hebrew Bible. It remains unclear in which context we should understand the refusal to accept women's shamanic acts and the devaluation of cultic practices performed by women.

4. It would also be interesting to directly compare this with concrete descriptions of rituals from other cultures. The categories of research could be defined more precisely because many shamanic actions are still not identified as such and can only be recognized as shamanic from this new vantage point: e.g. Moses' removal of his shoes before the burning thorn bush can be understood as his entering the "stage" (cf. TAE-GON KIM).

5. These concluding remarks about the prophetic, sign-related action in comparison to shamanic and artistic forms have revealed certain shared features as well as certain differences between the several forms. The important insight is that, through contemporary art, the present-day forms are indeed closely related to the "ancient" expressive forms. Although the sign-related actions performed by the scriptural prophets convey primal thoughts as well as "arche-patterns", these acts were directly related to the concrete political situations of their day. The following questions remain to be answered: Is this combination found solely among the scriptural prophets? What social contexts and political intentions may also have accompanied the fundamental patterns which characterize other (ritual) performances? In this inquiry too, we have seen that the ritualized practices had political consequences, e.g., women who engaged in ritual practices were viewed and at times persecuted according to different standards than were applied to men who performed similar acts.

6. The task of preserving the heritage, as the Symposium on "Discovery of Shamanic Heritage" points out, will always also include the question of social and political consequences. Looking to the future, the task will not merely be to view and elucidate testimony from ancient times or from nearby or more distant geographical regions of far greater importance; there is also the need to discover the roots

and a new vantage point from which these connections can be viewed and fruitfully used.

This includes avoiding the word "shamanism", because this term suggests standardization and it is a depreciating expression-see the final syllable: "ism". I agree with MIHÁLY HOPPÁL, who proposes to speak about "shamanic phenomena" or "shamanhood".

REFERENCES

Die Bibel, Die Heilige Schrift des Alten und Neuen Bundes, Deutsche Ausgabe mit den Erläuterungen der Jerusalemer Bibel. ARENHOEVEL, DIEGO – DEISSLER, ALFONS – VÖGTLE, ANTON (eds.) 1968 (7th ed.), Freiburg: Herder.

COENEN, LOTHAR – BEYREUTHER, ERICH – BIETENHARD, HANS (eds.)
1993 *Theologisches Begriffslexikon zum Neuen Testament.* Budapest: Brockhaus.

FOHRER, GEORG
1953 *Die symbolischen Handlungen der Propheten.* Zurich: Zwingli Verlag.

GESENIUS, WILHELM
1962 *Hebräisches und Aramäisches Handwörterbuch.* Berlin: Springer (17th ed.)

HAMAYON, ROBERTE
1990 *La chasse á l'âme. Esquisse d'une théorie du chamanisme sibérien.* Nanterre: Société d'ethnologie.

HORWITZ, JONATHAN
1991 Shamanic Rites seen from an Shamanic Perspective. In TORE AHLBÄCK (ed.) *The Problem of Ritual.* Åbo – Stockholm: Almqvist & Wiskell, 39–52. (Scripta Instituti Donneriani Aboensis, Vol. 15)

JOST, RENATE
1995 *Frauen, Männer und die Himmelskönigin, Exegetische Studien.* Gütersloh: Chr. Kaiser.

KAPELRUD, ARVIN S.
1967 Shamanistic Features in the Old Testament. In C.-M. EDSMAN (ed.) *Studies on Shamanism.* Uppsala: Almqvist & Wiksell, 90–96.

KEEL, OTHMAR – UEHLINGER, CHRISTOPH
1993 *Göttinnen, Götter und Gottessymbole, Neue Erkenntnisse zur Religionsgeschichte Kanaans und Israels aufgrund bislang unerschlossener ikonographischer Quellen.* Freiburg: Herder. (2nd ed.)

KIM, TAE-GON
1995 The symbolic Ur-meaning of Shamanism and Performing Arts. In MIHÁLY HOPPÁL – TAE-GON KIM (eds.) *Shamanism in Performing Arts.* Budapest: Akadémiai Kiadó, 1–16.

OSTERLOH, EDO – ENGELLAND, HANS (eds.)
1959 *Biblisch-Theologisches Handwörterbuch.* Göttingen: Vandenhoeck–Ruprecht.

RINGGREN, HELMER
  1982 *Israelitische Religion.* Stuttgart: Kohlhammer. [CHRISTEL MATTHIAS
       SCHRÖDER (ed.) Die Religionen der Menschheit. Bd 26.]
SIIKALA, ANNA-LEENA
  1992 Siberian and Inner Asian Shamanism. In ANNA-LEENA SIIKALA –
       MIHÁLY HOPPÁL (eds.) *Studies on Shamanism.* Helsinki – Budapest:
       Finnish Anthropological Society – Akadémiai Kiadó, 1–14. [Ethnologica
       Uralica 2.]
TROMNAN, GERNOT – LÖFFLER, RUTH (eds.)
  1991 *Schamanen – Mittler zwischen Menschen und Geister.* Begleitband zur
       Ausstellung im Kultur- und Stadthistorischen Museum Duisburg
       14.04.1991 – 30.06.1991.
WACKER, MARIE-THERES
  1997 Schamaninnen in der Welt der Bibel? *Schlangenbrut* 57: 17–22.
WEIPPERT, MANFRED
  1988 Aspekte israelitischer Prophetie im Lichte verwandter Erscheinungen im
       Alten Orient. In GERLINDE MAUER – URSULA MAGEN (eds.) *Ad bene et
       fideliter seminandum. Festschrift für K. Deller.* Neukirchen – Vluyn, 287–319.

YEE-HEUM YOON

The Diversity and Continuity of Shamanism in Korean Religious History[*]

INTRODUCTION: KOREAN SHAMANISM TODAY

It is well known that shamanism is the oldest religious tradition in Korea. The oriental religions of Confucianism, Buddhism, and Taoism were introduced much later. Confucianism and Buddhism tried to suppress the shamanic worldview. While Buddhism adopted a more tolerant approach than Confucianism its rigid attitude toward realizing the ideal of enlightenment required that one discard all profane desires including fortunetelling. Intellectualism was further re-enforced after the introduction of Western culture including Christianity and modern science.

Today, while shamans outnumber ministers of protestant churches, which are currently the most active religious organizations, foreigners find it difficult to meet shamans or even to see them perform. Nevertheless, shamanism is a dominant value in everyday life. Many businessmen, politicians, military personnel, government officials and others go to shamans for fortune telling. During the opening celebrations for new businesses, for example, the owners often observe a shamanic ritual named *gosa* which includes the smiling head of a dead pig and rice wine.

Shamanic traditions are handed down from one generation to the next in the traditional arts: songs and dances dramas, folk tales and epics, folk paintings and sculptures. This tells us that Koreans express their artistic drives through their own shamanic archetype. It is noteworthy that the majority of participants and winners of national folkloric contests today are shamans and their disciples.

---

[*] The unabridged version of this article is accessible at the following site www.culturelink.or.kr/archives.html.

SHAMANISM AS A DISTINCTIVE RELIGIOUS TRADITION

Shamanism is so complex that scholars have found it difficult to share a common definition. This disagreement originates from the various points of view scholars bring to the topic. Some see shamanism in terms of folklore, others in terms of cultural norms or indigenous social structure, spiritual ethos or the magical-religious context of a given culture.

There is no doubt that shamanism is a religious practice closely related to the shaman's spiritual experience—just as Buddhism is related to the Buddha's teachings. A shaman is a religious professional who has direct experiences of possession or ecstasy. For an outsider the shaman's experience can be called a mystic experience. The term "mystic" has two meanings. One points to what is unable to be explained by the commonsense logic of everyday life: the other points to a state of ecstasy, that is the state of being absent of self-consciousness during which one experiences trance or possession. In other words, trance and possession are two sides of the same coin, ecstasy.

While direct personal experience of the divine is not among the fundamental tenets of either Confucianism or Buddhism they both show some degree of such experience since they have intermingled with shamanism. Taoism on the other hand, although it shares its cosmological and metaphysical system with Confucianism, has more extensively adopted elements of shamanism. Christianity, however, has maintained the fundamental tenet of monotheism: opposition to a personal experience of the divine.

It is in the dualism of body and soul that shamanism differentiates itself from other religious belief systems. According to Korean custom if the face of a sleeping person is painted, he has died. This implies that sleeping is a state when one's spirit flies out from the body, dreams reflect what the soul experienced during its flight, and if the soul cannot return to its body, death occurs. For the same reason souls of different individuals can be interchanged. Possession also shows the same principle of dualism that a soul or deity can come into a person's body. No other religion, including Taoism, fully accepts this dualism.

Shamanism fulfills the practical needs of everyday life. People engage the services of a shaman to promote conception, restore or enhance health, and acquire wealth or power. These practices are called *kibog*, which literally means "praying for the blessed conditions of everyday life". When earthly needs are fulfilled people should be content; thus, the locus of their happiness is in this-worldly life.

By way of comparison to other religions, the Buddha was equipped with the ideal conditions for earthly life, but he left this behind and took up an ascetic way of life in order to achieve Enlightenment. Confucius pursued a dream of making the ideal society morally ordered by means of cultivating kings. After realizing the impossibility of this task he devoted his life to handing down his ideals to the next generations by means of educating his disciples. Jesus performed miracles as a token of love but never did anything related to earthly desires. These comparisons reveal that shamanism is more heavily engaged with worldly desires. After the introduction of these other religions shamanism became a latent religion, or spirituality, and its belief system pervaded the cultural ethos of Korea.

The mystical nature of shamanism expresses itself within such spiritual dimensions in artistic practices. Art parallels religion especially in the case of traditional and folk arts because artistic practices convey something profound in situations unexplainable by everyday logic, thus they are basically spiritual. Since shamanism also provides the matrix for pursuing worldly desires it extends its influences into various social dimensions including folklore and even economic and political activities. There is no doubt that its uncountable manifestations and extensions make shamanism confusing. Here we see that we need to distinguish shamanism as a distinctive religious tradition from shamanism as a latent cultural tradition.

A HISTORICAL REVIEW OF SPECIFIC TOPICS

Korean history had two major cultural shocks. The first arose when Confucianism, Buddhism, and Taoism were introduced during the Three Kingdoms Era. At the end of this period (from the Koryo Dynasty to the beginning of the Yi Dynasty) the mainstream of Korean culture was established in the classic religions. The second shock began in the late-18th century with the mutual interactions between these religions. To illustrate this we will discuss the myths of founders of kingdoms; ancient celestial observers; cosmological fate determinism; and rain-making rituals.

Myths of the Founder Kings

Myths of founder kings of ancient Korean kingdoms emphasize the founder's sacred blood lineage and his extraordinary birth. These mythic stories consecrate the hero's sacred power. This can be seen in the myths of Tan'gun, the founder of Kochoson; Chumong, the founder of Koguryŏ;

and Sogtalhae, the founder of Shilla. It is a well known story that Chachaung an ancient king of Shilla, was believed to also be a shaman and a blacksmith named *Alchi*. It was during the Bronze Age that the new technology of alchemy and blacksmithing made a certain group able to have new weapons to conquer other groups and create a kingdom. In this respect, we believe that archaic kingship was created by three forces: the technology of alchemical blacksmithing, the shaman-priest, and political power groups. A mythic hero who is said to be the founder of an archaic kingdom was not an individual person, and the king himself was neither a shaman nor a blacksmith, but rather the symbol of all three social powers combined.

By all accounts shamanism had a decisive function in both forming and governing ancient kingdoms. When Anshisung, an ancient Koguryŏ city was attacked and almost defeated they offered a beautiful woman to the shrine of the founder, Chumong. They believed that the deity would be pleased by the offering and would save the city from the crisis. Thus we see that this ancient kingdom used distinctive shamanic beliefs including spiritual dualism in order to overcome a national crisis. The same types of accounts can be found in numerous ancient documents.

The Celestial Observer

Humans are eager to see the future events of the world as well as those of their own lives. When they come face to face with their own helplessness they eventually get in touch with a secret way of predicting the future, that is, fatalism. There are two forms of fatalism. In the first one fate is determined by capricious deities. This might be called theistic fatalism. The second one finds that fate is determined by a cosmic law or principle by which all things in the world including them are destined. This is cosmological fatalism. Shamanism is the most distinctive theistic tradition while astrology and meteorology are central to the cosmological tradition. The latter is revealed in the practices of ancient observers of celestial events. The regular changes of celestial bodies and natural phenomena reflect a principle by which all things come into being. Therefore, celestial observers were regarded as more rational and scientific than shamans.

In the era of Yejong (Koryo Dynasty) there were some serious conflicts between shamans and celestial observers. During the Koryo Dynasty celestial observers, or Ilkwans, enjoyed authority over shamans. During the Yi Dynasty celestial observers were given the official title Kwansanggam. Their job was to observe celestial changes and to interpret the Law of

Change. Because they were trained in the cosmological and metaphysical theories of classical Confucianism they looked down on shamans who had no such training.

To illustrate this process we mention two myths: the Ch'ŏyong narrative of Shilla and the Pari Kogju of today. Ch'ŏyong became a deity in order to expel evil spirits and demons. King Hŏn'gang asked the celestial observer about the future of his trip. This implies that even in the Shilla period, celestial observances seemed more reasonable than shamans' divination. Later this trend became enforced during the Yi Dynasty. In the myth of the abandoned princess, Pari Kongju, the first shaman, reveals this in an interesting way. The king and the queen wanted to have a prince and asked the celestial observers rather than shamans to divine about the pregnancy. (It seems reasonable that the king's request was made before the existence of the first shaman.) However the shamanic myth was plotted on the basis of a non-shamanic worldview.

The same ambivalence is shown in the cases of shaman-medical doctors. Bureaucrats despised shamanism but when the government became helpless against wide-spread infectious diseases, it sent shamans to heal the sick. Although Confucian officials looked down on shamans they nonetheless used their mystic capacity.

Cosmological Fatalism

During the era of King Ŭija, the last king of Paekche Dynasty, the king dreamed that Paekche was a full moon and Shilla was a new moon. A shaman interpreted his dream in such a way that the full moon implies that Paekche Dynasty was declining and the new moon implies that Shilla Dynasty is rising. The king became angry and punished the shaman. Then he found a celestial observer to interpret the dream in the opposite way. Celestial observers were clearly more supportive of royal power than shamans. This demonstrates that celestial observers and shamans had the same job but were in a competitive relation. Their antagonistic attitude was derived from the differences in their belief systems.

Celestial observers were educated in the classics and their knowledge was respected while shamanism, since it was based on oral tradition, was marginalized. Cosmological fatalism was represented by Taoism which shared the Chinese classic cosmological worldview with Confucianism. The difference between them lies in the fact that Confucianism suppresses fatalism in practice, while Taoism accepts fatalistic practices and transforms them into occult rituals. Thus, Confucianism is more akin to Taoism in terms of its cosmological viewpoint than to shamanism, which has an entirely different worldview.

An interesting event happened in the 16th century when King Chungjong of the Yi Dynasty abolished Sokyugso, the most distinctive Taoist shrine that had been run by royal courts. The Yi Dynasty intended to establish a classical society on the ground of the Confucian worldview and it set about oppressing Buddhism, Taoism, and shamanism.

They sent out shaman-doctors to abolish Taoist shrines and care for sick persons. Women of royal families during the Yi Dynasty were the ardent patrons of shamanism while their husbands tried to suppress shamanism in their offices and schools. It was through such processes that Korean shamanism changed. For instance after the 16th century (after King Chungjong and before the Japanese Invasion War) new kinds of shamans appeared. They conducted their rituals by chanting sacred scriptures while sitting on the floor. As a result they were called *anzen mudang*, meaning "sitting shaman". Sitting shamans are those who became shamans by learning the shamans' practices from a teacher. As a result they were called "learned shamans". They were the opposite of *sun mudang*, signifying a "standing shaman". Standing shamans are those who became shamans by possession or shaman illness.

The visible difference between these two types of shamans can be seen in the way they perform their rituals. Sitting shamans chant sacred scriptures while sitting and standing shamans perform dances and music while conducting rituals Here we see that shamanism took over the empty space that Taoism left in the middle of the Yi Dynasty. It adopted Taoist chanting of sacred scriptures and gave birth to the practice of sitting shamans. Standing shamans were dispersed to the north and sitting shamans to the south of the Han River.

In the 12th century a famous scholar, Yi Kyubo, of the Koryo Dynasty recorded that he saw the sacred paintings of Ch'ilsŏng and the Triple Buddha Jesuk, which were displayed in a shaman's shrine. Ch'ilsŏng, "the seven stars" was the major symbol of Taoism. The Triple Buddha Jesuk indicated the Buddhist concept of The Key Being. Consequently, we see that shamanism had already accepted elements of Taoism as well as Buddhism to a considerable extent. Shamanism accepted Taoist cosmological fatalism which was alien to the archaic belief system of shamanism and finally gave birth to the hybrid form of sitting shamanism.

Rituals for Rain

Agricultural societies universally develop rain rituals. Korean society has maintained plentiful rain-bringing rituals from archaic times until now. The historical process reveals how interrelations between shamanism and kingship took place.

According to the records of the Three Kingdoms rain rituals were conducted by the king himself. Some kings of Koguryŏ conducted rain rituals for the Mountain-River Deity and the kings of Shilla and other kingdoms performed rain rituals at the tomb of the founder of the dynasty. Rituals for the founder signify paying homage to the origin of their own community, and the conduct of rituals by the king himself signifies the enforcement of communal identity and the requirement for communal loyalty. One cannot find any record that shamans conducted rain rituals in the age of Unified Shilla. Thus, we draw the conclusion that until the Unified Shilla period kings were the main conductors of rain rituals.

Fortunately young students of mine have discovered materials concerning rain rituals in Koryo and Chosŏn Dynasty. These records show that during the reign of King Hyŏnjong (11th century), shamans began to perform rain rituals. Approximately two to three hundred shamans were gathered in one place in order to endure the heat of the sun. This was done after the Chinese model of using shamans' secret rainmaking powers. This cruel treatment of shamans lasted until the reign of the Great King Sejong when Confucian officials determined to stop this policy towards shamans. The reason for stopping it seems to be derived from the fact that Confucian leaders began to have political control of the dynasty.

Fortunetelling Altars

It was during the initial appearance of Western culture that Korean shamanism faced its most serious trial. Nevertheless, shamanism survived in modern industrial society as a form of pursuing earthly desires. Shamanistic practices continue within the protestant movement in the form of *Kajong-jedan*, literally, "family altars". These altars represent a new trend in Korean protestant movements which started in 1970s with a family oriented faith movement. This movement which was organized outside church congregations constituted a para-church. It explosively expanded in the 1990s when many congregations became more secularized.

Fortunetelling altars are used mainly for curing and bringing good luck. The nature of these activities is more like traditional *kibog*, rather than the belief system of Christianity. The main difference is that the diviner uses the bible as a tool for prognostication: opening it at random and predicting the future from the first sentence that he reads. Fortunetellers are generally pious lay-persons without theological background. They initiate a fortunetelling altar for their own family and make themselves into the altar governor or priest. This priesthood persists even after the altar grows to have hundreds or even thousands of participants. The altar is not an organization within an established religion but an irregular group of voluntary participants loosely connected to various churches.

The movement reveals its affinity to shamanism in two ways. The motivation of the participants' activities and beliefs reflect that of shamanism. And the organizational characteristics of the movement are also the same as that of shamanism. Diviners make interpretations based on their own personal religious experiences. These interpretations tend to be anti-doctrinal and anti-intellectual. The spirit and attitude of this movement, then, is not born from mainstream Christianity but rather from the ethos of *kibog*.

Even though the movement has roots in shamanism it actually arose after Pentecostalism was introduced to Korea from America. So, Pentecostal emotionalism constitutes another root. Activities such as fortunetelling, curing diseases, and praying for good luck are characterized by activities like *kibog*. Thus the fortunetelling altar is a hybrid movement born out of a shamanic worldview dressed up in a Pentecostal costume.

CONCLUSION

Shamanism has a long history in Korea beginning with the myths of the founders of archaic kingdoms and continuing with the Christian faith-movements of today. Almost all of the arts, customs, and ways of thinking have been grounded in shamanism in such a way that it serves as the matrix for Korean popular culture. Given this connection we propose a descriptive definition of shamanism as a religion closely related to shamans' spiritual experiences which are essentially mystic.

Besides the systematic logic of scientific thought human beings also embrace many emotions including joys, fears, and hopes. Over the years the dreams of Koreans have been expressed in diverse traditional arts and ways of pursuing earthly desires. Korean popular culture was formed on the ground of shamanism which constitutes the archetype of mystic sensibility. The integrity of this archetype today is historically maintained within shamanic religious practice.

When we discuss shamanism in Korea we deal with two layers. The first is a distinctive religious tradition represented by the lineage of shamanic religious professionals. The second is a latent tradition reflecting a deep sense of mystic experiences in popular culture. These two layers are interdependent and interactions between them are deeply layered in historical processes. Because shamanism was in a marginal state for more than a millennium few written records are available to us today. However, there are other resources revealing latent shamanism scattered throughout Korean history. We should try to gather them together in order to reconstruct the full picture.

Part IV.

SHAMANISM AND THE MODERN WORLD

MAJAN GARLINSKI

Video-Ethnography and Shamanic Rituals

"A five minute film, shot in
Athens in the 5th century,
would change profoundly the
image which historians draw
us of that period."
Claude Lévi-Strauss

I am not an expert in shamanism. My knowledge of shamanic rituals and
shamanism is based on my video-ethnographic field studies in East Nepal
during 1987–88. There I had the chance, together with my partner ALBIN
BIERI, to participate in a common project with the ethnographer MARTIN
GAENSZLE to document audio-visually different shamanic rituals and
ancestral cults. One of the results of that collaboration is "Deva and Cinta"
(1990), an ethnographic video of a ritual cycle celebrated among the
Mewahang and Kulunge Rai. I also had the pleasure to work until 1998 as
an assistant of MICHAEL OPPITZ at the Ethnographic Museum of Zurich
University. There I established, in close collaboration with my mentor, not
only a Collection of Moving Images with special regard for audio-visual
documents on shamanic topics but also video productions to complement
exhibitions such as "A Shaman's Gear from the Himalayas" (1997) and
"Naxi: Pieces, Myths and Pictographs" (1998).

Since 1999 I have been engaged as a curator for the department of
visual anthropology at the Ethnographic Museum in Geneva. Recently we
were looking for rushes that document different museum activities. Our
discovery was disillusioning: while we hold numerous recordings from the
time before the eighties, we have hardly any useful contemporary audio-
visual documents. Worldwide one notices a similar phenomenon: there are
only a few audio-visual records of shamanic rituals that can serve as
secondary source material.

From this perspective the title of this conference, "Discovery Shamanic Heritage" (Budapest, April 1–4 2000) gets a slight shift of accent: heritage should not only be a question of something that has been passed down from preceding generations, but, as a constant process, it should be also understood as something that will be passed down to future generations. If one agrees that traditional forms of shamanic rituals are vanishing with a growing speed then one cannot simply lay back, satisfied with the important, mostly written accounts done so far, but one has to intensify the research as soon as possible. There is an urgent need for a common, concentrated effort.

In the following I will try, from the point of view of someone who has gained, over the last fifteen years, experience in the field of visual anthropology, to reflect on that situation and sketch out some possibilities that may lead to satisfactory solutions in the near future.

A shamanic ritual can be understood as a performance. Even if written words remain the usual form of communicating scientific knowledge, it is not necessarily the most appropriate way to produce ethnographic documents. This is true especially regarding pre-interpreted domains with a strong momentum like many aspects of the material culture, rituals, or ethnomusicology. In these cases the complementary use of tape recorders, photo, film or video cameras permit not only a more direct recording but also analysis and representation. JAY RUBY, one of the specialists in visual anthropology has clearly pointed out that:

> "If one regards filming and the resultant product, film, in a manner analogous to the way in that one regards writing and its various products, as a medium and technology of communication, then, the ethnographer simply selects the most appropriate modes and codes for communicating ethnography" (RUBY 1975: 105).

For many years ethnographers recorded oral traditions on audio tapes that then were transcribed, analyzed and published as written texts. Very seldom did they regard their audio-recordings as a value in itself. A similar situation concerns ethnographic photos. These stills usually fulfill an auxiliary function as illustrations of the texts. If already audio recordings and still pictures fulfil only auxiliary functions then why should it be different with audio-visual tools like film or video? The answer is as simple as it is disturbing. Regardless of the current overflow of pictures that mimic reality and the importance of visual media in everyday life, academics do not consider it worthy of their own systematic interest. Or as PAUL HENLEY, director of the British Granada Center, has put it crudely: "Many

British anthropologists would see a film as a useful hook to bring in the punters, but not as something you would spend much time on once you had got them inside" (1993: 74). One of the reasons for this strange attitude may be that only a few anthropologists are willing or able to read pictures, even less to read them as an interplay of form and content. Therefore they remain on the surface and gather only a small part of what they see. The American film theoretician JAMES MONACO refers on that problem in his book *How to Read a Film* (1981) when he writes:

"Is it necessary, really, to learn how to read a film? Obviously, anyone of minimal intelligence over the age of four can, more or less, grasp the basic content of a film (...) without any special training. Yet precisely because the media so very closely mimic reality, we apprehend them much more easily than we comprehend them. (...) yet we all too naturally accept the vast amounts of information they convey to us in massive doses without questioning how they tell us what they tell" (MONACO 1981: vii).

This innocence of not looking at films as a question of content and form is quite common not only on the side by the recipients but, astonishingly, also on the side by ethnographers using the video tools in their scientific fieldwork.

"You press the button, we do the rest", was the famous Kodak slogan in the twenties, to promote their still picture cameras. One can find many analogous statements in current advertisements for video cameras. They suggest that anyone can take good pictures if they have the right camcorder. Does that mean that everyone can be a film- or video-maker? Potentially, yes, if the person is willing and able to learn how to tell a story with pictures and sound. Though, the reality is slightly different. Anyone, who once had the doubtful pleasure to assist in screenings of family tapes, will know that there is a big gap between taking pictures and the quality of the final product. Most well-equipped amateurs are so emphatically concentrated on their subjects that they neglect formal aspects. They easily forget that shooting is always an interplay between form and content. To play this game well one has to be skilled. Most ethnographers understand themselves as specialists in their profession. Film- and video-makers are professionals on their part. If one tries to work as a video-ethnographer, one combines therefore two independent professions to merge into a third one, that is not a simple addition but the synthesis of both, respecting cinematographic and ethnographic demands. Unfortunately, only a few ethnographers equipped with video tools for their fieldwork, seem to be aware of that professional intersection. This may be one of the reasons why many rituals shot and presented by ethnographers are penurious. The other reason may be the idea of taking field-note record footage. If one shoots shamanic rituals exclusively for conservation and research purposes, then one of the most appropriate ways would be to use infinite sequences with long and medium shots only; with an inevitably tedious result. This marks one pole.

The other pole is, in general, a little annoying. In the seventies some ethnographers started to collaborate with TV crews. Their technically clean, beautiful pictures are often sterile, undifferentiated and cannot tell the story they should in an intelligent montage. While the visuals are often flat, the sound track is overloaded by pleasing music and a too-present voice-over. Both attempt to glue the story together as if there were neither any direct cinema, nor any ethnographic films where the subjects had the ability to speak for themselves. Announced euphemistically as TV documentaries they show strange people and their customs mostly in the form of a restless travelogue: the exotic still attracts the public. Such productions present at best only glimpses of rituals. This is not astonishing if one looks more closely at the conditions of production. Most of the television crews spend less than one month in the field; nevertheless they are expected to bring something extraordinary home. But before the biases they have brought with them can be confronted with the reality that might lead to new conclusions and to a different perception, they have already left. Therefore most broadcast documentation tells us more about their makers and the society to which they belong than about their subjects. Finally they resemble one another formally, irrespective of the country in which they were produced, as each television company tries to sell its products all over the world. Therefore their applied audio-visual language has to be international.

There do exist documentaries that take the challenge more seriously, at least in comparison with the one mentioned above. In the famous "Disappearing World" series made by Granada Television or the BBC series "Under the Sun", ethnographers were directly involved as consultants. Although those series have permitted "a mutually beneficial synthesis of skills and ideas" as PAUL HENLEY (1993: 75) notes, "there have been some tensions in the relationship between director and consultant since they are working to different audiences and different agendas". With the New Economy that was introduced in the nineties one can take it for granted that the influence of the ethnographic consultant will be reduced, as "it is widely believed that the overall effect of this new environment will be a progressive lowering of standards in the independent sector as companies find themselves obliged to seek the maximum number of viewers for the minimum cost" (HENLEY 1993: 77).

Ethnographers who are interested in analyzing shamanic séances by means of audio-visual documents find themselves in a dilemma: there are only a few that can serve as secondary source material. The field-note recordings of ethnographers are rarely published and the TV documentaries show at best only glimpses of rituals. But, the ethnographic work is also jeopardized from within, what JEAN ROUCH, one of the great ethnographic filmmakers, has formulated as follows:

> "The ethnography has been practically eliminated on the profit of ethnology. So how can one make a theory of a practice one does not know?" (ROUCH 1991: 277)

I read his rhetorical question not as a farewell to ethnography but, on the contrary and in respect of his own *œuvre*, as a provocation to continue ethnographic fieldwork with all senses and necessary tools, including writing and improved audio-visual skills. If we do not shoot shamanic rituals in an intelligent manner today, the future generations of researchers will find a big gap or at best only 'incomplete' images of those rituals. But how should it be done?

It is not my intention to speak in detail about how one should record and edit a film or video since there are already many articles and books written on that subject. *Cross-cultural Film-making: A Handbook for Making Documentary and Ethnographic Films and Videos* (1997) is one of them. The authors ILISA BARBASH and LUCIEN TAYLOR, provide a step-by-step guide to film- and video-making, from research and funding to distribution, confronting the reader with ethical and aesthetic reflections enriched with advice from leading filmmakers. If one wishes to work ethnographically with audio-visual tools but has only a broad idea of film- and video-making then such books can be very helpful. Beyond reading books it is good to watch, analyze, and discuss films, especially those the books cited. Even better, of course, is to combine book knowledge with film shooting practice.

As every ritual performance is an original, one cannot count on a manual, except what the ritual itself offers. Therefore one should try to find the appropriate answer and in respect to the concrete circumstances, the best possible solution. Nevertheless there is hardly any reason to shy away from recording a ceremony audio-visually. While the act of performing the ritual presents the invisible to the visible world, the video ethnographer only has to follow this process with eyes and ears wide open. That was what we, ALBIN BIERI and I, tried when we worked as videographers together with the German ethnographer MARTIN GAENSZLE.

The basic idea of that collaboration was to obtain, for further research purposes, audio-visual documents of different shamanic rituals and ancestral cults among the Mewahang and Kulunge Rai of the Sankhuwa Valley in Eastern Nepal. Therefore the shooting should have been done in such a clear and detailed way that MARTIN GAENSZLE could carefully analyze the rituals as form of 'darkroom ethnography' during his field studies and later on at home. Without neglecting the ethnographer's needs for source material, we had in mind to edit at least one of the rituals for public screenings outside academic circles.

These antagonistic approaches caused many intensive discussions. While one asks for the audio-visual totality with uninterrupted long sequences, the other demands to take advantage of the full range of possible shot compositions. The two approaches conflict with one another since one involves the inclusion of material that the other excludes. However, neglecting cinematographic aspects does not necessarily result in a more adequate representation of the perceived reality. If the conflict between form and content is understood as a challenge, than it can provoke creative solutions where the form supports the demands of a holistic ethnographic research in a subtle way. Out of various recorded rites we decided to concentrate for the editing on the double ritual of *deva* and *cinta*. The *deva* consists of a ritual journey and a blood sacrifice to the *dewas*, ancestral deities who are linked with the territory and are responsible for the prosperity of the household. This ritual, that takes place in the afternoon in the courtyard of the client's house, has to be celebrated at least twice a year in combination with a *cinta*, a shamanic séance that lasts through the night. Although we observed and in a way also participated from the early beginning till the end we recorded out of these eighteen hours of ritual performance ten hours and condensed these rituals through editing, by fully respecting the sequential chronology, to approximately one hundred minutes.

Both rituals are dense with symbolism on various levels: artifacts, gestures, interaction, rhythm, and language. The recitations during the *dewa* are exclusively in Rai ritual language, whereas the *jhakri*-like shaman partly chants in Nepali and partly in Rai. In the ethnographic video-documentation "Deva and Cinta" we tried to convey the atmosphere and 'meaning' of these multi-layered performances with only the necessary minimum of verbal interpretations and explanations, so that the visual and auditive events may be comprehended in their own right. This ethnographic documentation was shown at different festivals, including the film "Himalaya Festival in Kathmandu" in 1994, where it received a warm reception, especially from the Rai people. Unfortunately "Deva and Cinta" was never screened for the people at the location of shooting, at least as far as I know. So I cannot refer to their feedback; but I received not only insight into the living tradition of the eastern Himalayan form of shamanic practice but also glimpses of 'the beauty of exactitude.'

With the expression of 'the beauty of exactitude' I pay respect to one of the most outstanding films on shamanic rituals ever made: "Shamans of the Blind Country" (1980) directed by the ethnographer MICHAEL OPPITZ. His first film and epic-long documentary on magical healing in the Himalayas— as preserved in the secluded society of the Northern Magar in Central West Nepal—he dedicated to MAYA DEREN. She began as an experimental filmmaker and ended as a documentarist and writer. Concerning this professional transformation MAYA DEREN said:

> "I had begun as an artist, as someone who manipulates the elements of a reality in the image of his creative integrity and transposes this into a work of art; I end by recording, as modestly and exactly as possible, the logic of a reality that forced me to recognize its own integrity and to surrender my manipulations" (OPPITZ 1982: 26).

The documentary "Shamans of the Blind Country" goes far beyond simple ethnographic documentation of shamanic rituals. While our audio-visual recording of the double ritual of *deva* and *cinta* includes three thematic blocks—the introduction, the ritual of *deva*, and that of *cinta*— OPPITZ' film has a holistic approach, presenting Magar shamanism as a total social fact. This means presentation of an overview and, as he explained it to students at New York University "in Magar shamanism the spheres of the religious and the profane are interwoven in such a way that they take place on the same plane (…) we attempted to express this close connection between sacred and profane in our cutting as well" (OPPITZ 1982: 18). Thematic blocks are simple documentary units that he describes as "units of meaning, or units of a subject matter with the totality of possible subjects (...)" (OPPITZ 1988: 307). While it is relatively easy to record a ritual with modern video cameras it is a real challenge to create a thick interwoven documentary on shamanic practices. In a long conservation with the Persian film scholar AHMED ALASTI, OPPITZ circumscribed the tasks of making visual connections "between interrelated thematic blocks. To do that, you must first know the relationships. It is (...) an intellectual necessity (...), because there is a connection that the people themselves make. In making such connections of 'necessary relations' you acquire a more and more holistic attitude toward the society in front of your camera. (...) As an ethnographer, you will also end up as a bridge

maker because the people you study are themselves fanatic bridge makers"
(OPPITZ 1988: 308ff).

It was obvious that he, who said, "over the centuries the visual and the
verbal or textual anthropology were without any discussions accepted as
equal partners in establishing a descriptive ethnography", would adopt in
his ethnographic work on shamanism different forms of expression. His
Magar collection consists, besides his published written work and the
feature long documentary "Shamans of the Blind Country", of thirty-four
hours uncut married prints that were made in connection with this
outstanding ethnographic documentary, seventy-five hours of. audio
recordings of ritual chants, twenty handwritten journals and nearly five-
thousand stills. He developed, at the Ethnographic Museum in Zurich, a
special archival system based on the one the curators of the Musée de
l'Homme in Paris used for their collection. The idea was to glue the paper
prints together with their captions, registration numbers, etc. on a
pasteboard. Unfortunately these conservators were not aware that it would
deteriorate over time since it was not stored on non-acid archival material.
His idea was to remake a new paper print that combined on one and the
same page the original picture and a description together with technical
information, like author, location, number of trip, film and picture etc. as
shown below.

15.11.1978   **3/6:35**
Taka NW Nepal   Foto: M. Oppitz

Nächtliche Séance wider den kindermordenden
Geist *rā* mit Man Bahadur, Beth Bahadur, Jaibir
und Bhimsen.

Man Bahadur hat seine Trommel in eine hori-
zontale Position gebracht und auf ihr ein paar
Stoffkügelchen, *ri*, deponiert, die aus dem Be-
sitz der Patientin stammen. Diese Kügelchen
werden durch sanftes Anschlagen der Trommel
in Vibration gebracht und auf der Membrane
fortbewegt. Dies ist eine Divinationsmethode: je
nachdem, wo die Stoffkügelchen von dem Rah-
men der Trommel fallen, dementsprechend sind
die Zukunftsaussichten für die Patientin.

Picture 1. [Illustration Taka (15.11.1978; 3/6: 35)] (© Voelkerkundemuseum Zurich;
original photo MICHAEL OPPITZ; archival photo ERICH FREI)
Man Bahadur has set his drum horizontally. He has placed some pellets (*ri*) from the
clothing belonging to the patient on it. The pellets will be moved on the drum-skin by
the vibration of gentle drumbeats. This is a method of divination: the future prospects of
the patient depend on where the clothing pellets fall from the edge of the drum.

Out of the total number of five-thousand Magar positives, three thousand, dealing directly with different aspects of shamanism, have been treated in the above mentioned manner. Each twice: one for present researchers and one for future students. A CD-ROM version of the Magar pictures is also planned. This would not be a difficult task, because the texts are already stored in a separate text file on computer. Reading the description one notes immediately the quality of the text that adds information we cannot derive directly from the picture and which at the same time refers to the pictorial content. The latter is very important if one thinks about the functioning of digital retrieval systems. Therefore it is indispensable to describe or index each picture as exactly as possible so that the text refers to the invisible and the visible aspects of it without duplicating the picture's content verbally. The way the Magar pictures are archived and classified can be taken as a model.

If the remaining two-thousand pictures are treated as thoroughly as those mentioned above, then one would need only a small step to present them in a digitalized form. In this way the material would be accessible for research from various perspectives. For example it might be presented in combination with software that would allow iconographic identification of the picture's content and then published on CD-ROM as well as the Internet. It would open efficient access to a revealing source of material. If one were to work in a similar way also on the other parts (diaries, sound recordings and film), something that would involve a huge amount of work and require substantial financial support, then one could consider the possibility of an "Ethnographic Encyclopedia on the Magar". Such a precise, densely interwoven, multimedia presentation of the sources would not only reflect various dimensions of their cultural life, but would be an extraordinary treasure for research by future generations of social scientists when the Magar have replaced the naked flame with the electric light.

The project outlined above may seem to be old-fashioned, especially at a time when only the very latest things count, where money is scarce and where cultural projects are financed only when the sponsor derives a social benefit from it. On the other hand, one should learn from mistakes made in the past and collections should be developed in as detailed a way as necessary and made as clear as possible, in order to be more accessible and usable than at present. The envisaged project of a digitalized, ethnographic Magar Encyclopaedia aims in this direction. At the same time one should not forget, that an archive is finally only a means and not an end in itself. On the way to new insights it corresponds to a bridge between the sources and their users. The modern technique allows the latter to consult various archives in a short time without having to travel. There is, however, the danger that the sensuality of the photography as well as of the quest falls by the wayside.

This brings us back to our main problem: there will be no further archives on "shamanhood" if we do not continue to do fieldwork and to document as ethnographers shamanic rituals with all possible tools, of course including pictures and sound. As MICHAEL OPPITZ said: "Theory and practice in ethnography are in an eternal dialectical movement" (1998: 308).

REFERENCES

BARBASH, ILISA – TAYLOR, LUCIEN
1993 *Cross-Cultural Filmmaking – A Handbook for Making Documentary and Ethnographic Films and Videos.* Berkeley – Los Angeles – London: University of California Press.
HENLEY, PAUL
1993 The Future of Ethnographic Film-making in Britain. In PETER I. CRAWFORD (ed.) *The Nordic Eye – Proceedings from NAFA 1.* Hojbjerg: Intervention Press.
MONACO, JAMES
1981 *How to Read a Film.* London – New York: Oxford University Press.
OPPITZ, MICHAEL
1982 *Materials on the Making of an Ethnographic Film.* New Delhi: Goethe Institute.
1988 Shooting Shamans. *Visual Anthropology* 1: 305–315.
1989 *Kunst der Genauigkeit. Wort und Bild in der Ethnographie.* München: Trickster Verlag.
ROUCH, JEAN
1991 Le feed-back dans l'anthropologie visuelle: entretien avec Jean Rouch. In D. DALL'AGNOLO – B. ETTERICH et al. (eds.) *Ethnofilm. Katalog, Beiträge, Interviews.* Berlin: Dietrich Reimer Verlag, 271–277.
RUBY, JAY
1975 Is an Ethnographic Film a Filmic Ethnography? *Studies in the Anthropology of Visual Communication* 2.2: 104–111.

FILMOGRAPHY

BIERI, ALBIN – GARLINSKI, MAJAN – GAENSZLE, MARTIN

    1990 Deva and Cinta—An Ethnographic Documentation of a Ritual Cycle Celebrated Among the Mewahang and Kulunge Rai of East Nepal, Switzerland/FRG/Nepal, 127'.

GARLINSKI, MAJAN

    1997 Eine Schamanenruestung aus dem Himalaya: Eins – Auspacken der Ruestung im Museum; Zwei – Die Trommeln und ihr Spiel (A Shaman's Gear from the Himalayas: One – Out Packing of the Gear in the Museum; Two – The Drums and Theirs Play), Switzerland, 44'.

GARLINSKI, MAJAN – OPPITZ, MICHAEL

    1998 Naxi – Pieces, Myths and Pictographs – Exhibition Trailer, Switzerland, 16'.

OPPITZ, MICHAEL

    1980 Shamans of the Blind Country, FRG/USA/Nepal, 223'.

SEONG-NAE KIM

Korean Shamanic Heritage in Cyber Culture

CYBORG MUDANG "CYSHA" ABORTED

In September 1998 the appearance of cyborg mudang 'Cysha', whose character was invented by a Korean internet service company, drew wide attention from the mass media.[1] One of the major internet service providers in Korea, LG Internet, announced that cyborg mudang 'Cysha' would go down a mountain after apprenticeship and be active on its internet service, Channel *i*, by the end of this month. The name, Cysha, was rendered by combining the first syllables of the words "cyber" and "shaman". Cysha takes the form of a ten-year-old cyborg, named Child Spirit (Agi Tongja) of indistinct gender. The rationale of this· virtual creation of cyborg shaman lay in the 'redemptive' role of Cysha who would help suffering Web users or *netizens* eradicate computer viruses and noxious pornographic sites.[2] Cysha would also instruct them how to use shamanic talisman (*bujok*) and provide fortunetelling. In its service ("Do you believe in talismans?"), anyone could download talismans for personal use and also use talismans as screen savers. The birth of cyborg mudang Cysha forecast the virtualization of shamanic practices.

But within a matter of weeks after Cysha was introduced to the public, LG Internet was forced to abandon its plans when faced by intense public opposition. Some netizens opposed the idea of a cyborg shaman because they believed that, such a superstitious character was an anachronistic throwback and had no place in cyberspace during the high technology era.

---

1 Here 'mudang' is a Korean translation of the term, 'shaman.' 'Cyborg' indicates a cybernetical invention, a machine with a human character. Supposedly it has an artificial intelligence and a virtual body. Thus a cyborg represents itself embodied virtuality (HAYLES 1999: xii).

2 In Korea, the Web users are often referred to 'netizens', literally meaning 'citizens of internet world'. This popular usage implies the principally democratic environment in cyberspace.

Others were worried about cyber mysticism. But there were also other netizens who supported this idea for its novelty. Those supportive netizens said that such 'digital' talismans could substitute the traditional function of old-type 'analog' talismans made by real shamans in prayer, and if even virtual talismans could comfort suffering hearts of netizens, the efficacy of a cyborg shaman would be sufficiently acceptable.

Although the birth of cyborg shaman 'Cysha' was aborted due to public accusation of the superstitious practice, actual Korean shamans are now already active in cyberspace. Presently, twenty internet Web sites of Korean shamans are open under the address of "shaman" or "mudang". In comparison to a cyborg shaman, Cysha, I call these shamans having Web sites "cyberspace shamans or mudangs" or "internet shamans". It is predicted that the number of cyberspace mudangs' sites will quickly expand as more of the general Korean public goes online. Instead of disappearing into the backyard of high media technology and information society, Korean shamanic heritage is indeed surviving in the cyber world and undergoing significant transformation even though it is still in its incipient stage.

Despite materialistic prosperity and technological progress, the human search for an ultimate answer for anxiety and uncertainty of life remains the same. In the age of information technology, religious imagination continues to feed human desire to seek for moving out of reality—that is, virtual reality which is constructed by means of electronic communication and hyper-mediated environment such as World Wide Web or internet world in general sense. This phenomenon is characterized by new terms such as "techgnosis" (DAVIS 1998), "electronic LSD" (RHEINGOLD 1991: 353) or "electronic ecstasy" (BAUDRILLARD 1983).

Although Korean shamans' activities in cyberspace are presently small in scale and neglected by main-line traditional shamans and shamanistic researchers, it will be worth exploring the emerging new phenomena that have occurred in light of Korean shamanic heritage. In this paper, I examine the contemporary transitions which Korean shamanic heritage is undergoing in cyberspace and explore the impact of this transformation on shamanic heritage itself. First of all, I will examine the types and features of current cyberspace shamanic practices through case studies. Next, I will discuss the nature of virtual religiosity and suggest future visions for the virtual transformation of Korean shamanic heritage. Perhaps, the era of cyborg Cysha has not come yet but it is anticipated in the new environment of life—that is, hyper-mediated cyber culture.

Types of Cyberspace Shamanic Practices

The cyberspace shamanic practices in Korea, following the trends of internet business and personal use of computer, have grown rapidly since 1996. The first mudang to open an internet home page in 1996 was PUCHE TOSA, a forty-year-old male shaman. His home page received 163,000 hits in Feb. 2000 alone. The popularity of internet shamanic sites has turned explosive in 1998 during the crisis of IMF when young Koreans lived under the anxiety of bankruptcy and unemployment. The internet shamans who opened home pages are mostly twenty and thirty year olds who are already accustomed to electronic communication and immersed in cyber life-style. For them, online internet contact with clients seems to be more natural and preferred to old-fashioned face-to-face consultation.

Cyberspace mudangs' Web sites are divided into two types: informative and commercial. The informative sites mainly focus on providing general information about the history and religious tradition of Korean shamanism. These sites are usually run by shamans designated as living cultural treasure and by the national association of shamans. But the majority of cyberspace shamanic practices belong to the commercial type, selling online talismans or running fee-based email divination, which is referred to as email counseling or consultation. Although some shamanic Web sites often combine these two types of practices, there are still clear distinctions between the two.

The Informative Site: General Information about Korean Shamanism

The informative type of shamanic sites usually specifies its objectives as providing general information about Korean shamanism, which may not be easily accessible to the public, particularly younger generations of netizens, and also to correct public misconceptions of shamanism as superstition or pseudo-religion. The typical informative site is Kyunggi Province Todang Kut site (http://www.mudang.com). This site is run by the Preservation Association of Invisible Cultural Treasure, Todang Kut (Shamanic Rite for Village). In this site, there is a detailed description of the Todang Kut ritual performance and also the life history of the living cultural treasure Master O. SUBOK, who is in charge of preservation and regular public performance of Todang Kut. This site provides a reference menu of shamanism-related terminology and also English descriptions for non-Korean visitors.

Another informative site is "Korean Shamanism" (http://shamanism. view.co.kr), which is a kind of portal site.[3] This site is run by National Association of Indigenous Religion. This site has two parts: "the World of Korean shamanism, seeking harmony and ecstasy of *kut*" and "Famous Shamans in Korea". The part of "the World of Korean Shamanism" has four sections, the history of Korean shamanism, the structure of *kut*, the various genres of *kut*, and shamanic deities. This part provides a general knowledge of Korean shamanism in a rather academic style. The other part, entitled "Famous Shamans in Korea", introduces personal profiles and specificity of shamans, mainly members of the National Association of Indigenous Religions.

In the section of "Famous Shamans in Korea" hundreds of shamans' names are introduced in order of location of their shrines and offices. They are carefully selected according to qualification standards regarding priestly virtues such as personal character, spiritual capacity, social service, and artistic talent. In each individual mudang's home page, there are information menus such as personal life history, specialty, and map of location. The web site manager runs BBS, where the mudang announces the time schedule of the *kut* performance, and also replies to on-line questions about shamanism. Any visitor can ask questions and discuss relevant issues with the site manager. The number of visitors on Dec 4th of last year was 9,524 and the rate of these hits is now increasing as the site manager continually adds more new participating shamans.

It must be noted that the informative type of site contains a section which provides the background story and original rationale for opening the site. The common theme of such narratives is how deeply the shamans lament for the social prejudice against their practices. The story expresses their assertion that shamanism is the Korean indigenous religion and traditional culture. Also in the case of commercial-type sites, they include some mention of similar narratives of resentment toward social prejudice as well as general information on Korean shamanism.

---

[3] There is another portal site on Korean shamanism, http://www.shaman.co.kr. This site is run by a weekly newspaper company, Segye Musok Shinmun, literally meaning World Shamanism Newspaper. This site provides daily fortunetelling and basic knowledge about Korean shamanism.

THE COMMERCIAL SITE: SHAMANIC TALISMAN SALES AND COUNSELING

The commercial type of shamanic practices consists of talisman sales and fee-based counseling service. These commercial sites are more popular than the informative ones. Because of its direct pricing method, this type is often suspected of pseudo-shamanic practices and thus became target for a self-purification campaign by the leading shamans. In spite of these negative preconceptions, however, the shamanic talisman sales and counseling service in cyberspace became a common method of publicizing shamanic activities. Here are typical examples.

Case 1. Dolmani's House

"Here are lucky talismans. You must think this is something strange to see in the modern world. But who knows, if your present bad luck would turn into good luck? Please select talismans according to your age. In addition, Dolmani offers various kinds of talismans for everyday use. If you need it, please send an email or leave your name in the visitor's room.

Everyday use talismans: 30 luck talismans useful from the first day to the thirtieth of the month. 18 talismans useful for moving, college entrance examination, marriage, romance, new furniture, new clothing, new car, new job, promotion, friendship, birth, travel, business, school examination, birthday, wealth, school grade, etc.

Price: 4,800 won for all 48 kinds of talismans."

Case 2. Paekamkwan House

"Please click the talismans if you want to know about details.

First, select the desirable item. Check on the item box. If you click, you can see the talisman ahead. Before your payment, you would see the invoice ahead.

Wish Fulfillment Talisman Price: 10,000 won (=US$ 9)

Three Misfortune Avoidance Talisman Price: 10,000 won

Good Luck Talisman Price: 10,000 won

Besides, there are counseling services: personal lot (fee: 5,000 won), marital affinity (fee: 10,000 won), naming (fee: 50,000 won), etc.

Second, pay online to the account suggested below. After checking the receipt of money, detailed counseling will be sent."

These two cases are typical examples of cyber transaction of shamanic talismans and counseling. If you send personal information about four columns of your birthday (year, month, day, time), pay online to the account of the shaman counselor, and click on the desirable talisman item at the Web site, the talisman will appear on the computer base screen whenever you open the computer.

There are indeed other kinds of cyber divination services which follow the principles of Chinese philosophy such as I-ching. It is no longer unusual to find the computer machines at department stores and amusement parks. Computer divination has been extensively used in popular places, but its capacity is expanded drastically on behalf of the power of internet. In cyberspace, realtime divination became available, and people can visit divination sites by accident or for curiosity while navigating in the cyberspace. Because diviners' sites are open to any visitors and also free from social prejudices against shamanic practices, it is highly likely that cyber talisman sales and counseling by shamans will increase further.

PERSONAL MOTIVE OF CYBERSPACE MUDANG: A CASE STUDY

Online shamanic practices develop rapidly because it became easy and cheap in terms of personnel and equipment for the shamans to open an internet site. The first cyber shaman to take advantage of the possibilities of the internet for both informative and commercial purposes was PUCHE TOSA (Fan Taoist Hermit), whose personal name is KIM KWANGSU. He set up his internet home page (http://members.iworld. net/moodang) in 1996. He is a forty year old male shaman. Before he became a mudang, he worked briefly as a dietitian at a small company. He had to quit his job when he became seriously ill after a hallucinatory dream. In his dream, an old man appeared and asked him to go up the mountain, and then the shamanic deities and family ancestors appeared to him. His mother, also a shaman who knows the difficult life of shamans, finally accepted his fate of becoming a shaman, and helped prepare his initiation rite. After his initiation, his life was turned upside down. He became isolated from society. If he came home after a light drink or meeting people, his guardian spirit Grandfather Spirit would scold him harshly. So he stopped going out. He was still young and interested in romance too. But every secular interest and emotion was prohibited. So in solitude of the night, he took up computers and Web-surfing as a pastime. It was a time of the early media hype about the future expansion of the internet.

He explains his personal motive for opening his own internet website: "Once I visited a religion site by accident. I could not find any information about shamanism, only Christianity, Buddhism, United Church, and other religions. So I decided to open a site that could help people understand what shamanism is."

Immediately, his internet site had to face deeply rooted social prejudice against shamanism. He was blamed for deluding the world and deceiving the people by means of modern conveniences. Despite initial negative reactions, however, his internet site has become popular among the Korean netizens. Within three months after the opening, his site received over ten thousand hits. Once he became famous in the internet world, weekly journals and monthly magazines competed to report about his personal history and online divination practices. His Web site home-page was modelled by following internet shamans.

PUCHE TOSA describes that the initial motive was to provide correct information about shamanism. The second purpose was to change the religious communities' prejudice against shamanism and persuade them to be open-minded toward religions other than their own. In short, he started his internet service with expectations of religious dialogue with the wide public. He emphasizes the chief function of mudang as a soul counselor to help people overcome their daily difficulties, and to teach them to understand shamanism as a religion of harmony.

His internet site is divided into six menus: email counseling ("soul counseling"), Korean musok (shamanic folklore), mystic talismans, Korean folk culture, and newspaper articles. All the menu except for the talismans menu and email consultation are composed of general information. The mystic talismans menu is only for display and not for downloading or sales. If anyone needs a specific talisman, he/she could consult with PUCHE TOSA via the email-counseling menu.

The email-counseling menu has four items which range from individual- and family-relationship problems to business investments and commercial transaction problems related to real estate sales and purchases. A special item is concerned with counseling about shamanic ritual and prayer. In this case, the price of counseling is not specified. In fact, there must be off-line contact between PUCHE TOSA and clients. For the first two years of internet service, PUCHE TOSA offered free counseling for the sake of publicity. Once his site became famous, however, he changed his mind and charged a fee for counseling. The price ranges from 20,000 to 50,000 won depending on the case.

In his "soul counseling", he consults with clients by combining online and off-line communication. If clients send personal messages about their problems, he replies in a long letter according to instant inspiration that strikes him at the moment of reading the messages. At first he himself wondered how email divination without face-to-face meeting could be possible. He was not quite sure because there are no shamanic spirits with typing skills. But he soon came to know that his hesitation and suspicion was wrong. Whenever he receives the email message, his guardian spirit inspires him instantly with a right divination. Once he consulted with a man who stood at a crossroads regarding whether or not he should better quit his job and go abroad for graduate study. At the moment he read the email message, he received an inspiration that the man should better stay in the country.

In this case of PUCHE TOSA's cyberspace activities, we could see the continuity of ordinary shamanic practices outside cyberspace. PUCHE TOSA's site does not go beyond the conventions of Korean shamanic practices. He seems to prefer more personal contact with clients and reject the idea of on-line talisman sales because cyber talismans are only pseudo-talismans without spiritual power. He insists that shamanic talismans can be effective only when they are made of proper yellow paper and red letters during the shaman's prayer. He said cyber talismans were indeed fake. Therefore, when he suggested to the site users to download 70 different kinds of cyber talismans for screen savers, it sounds like a joke. He occasionally makes new talismans and gives them for free. According to him, cyber talismans are only means to satisfy people's curiosities, not for sale. They might have the effect of advertising actual shamanic talismans. He specifies his intention of image-only pseudo-talismans as instrumental in that they express hospitality to the site users and promote general understanding about shamanism per se.

NEO-SHAMANIC FEATURES

As far as the shamanic counseling and talismans sales are concerned, there seems little difference between internet shamans and real shamans. Their common features are commercial practices. The commercialization of shamanic practices has been widespread since the off-the-site consultation such as telephone counseling became popular earlier in the 1980s, and also individual shamans began to publicize their activities through popular magazines. The religious sector was not an exception in the milieu of consumer culture where anything could be valued and exchanged as a commodity. Under the titles such as "Today's Fortune" "Oriental Philosophy", "Tojong Pikyul (Prophetic Secret Text according to Tojong, who invented popular divination text on the basis of simplified version of I-ching in the 17th century during Chosun dynasty), "Astrological Fortune" "Love Marriage Matching" "Fortune Philosophy" etc., telephone fortune-telling services, indicated by the area code 700, were widely used at home or at business offices. But these telephone fortune-telling services have been rapidly replaced by internet service as the internet-user population have grown. Probably, in the beginning of internet shamanic service, the internet sites were used originally for the extensive religious service by shamans, but soon concentrated on cyber counseling.

The emergence of cyberspace mudangs envisages the virtual transformation of shamanic heritage and requires a new paradigm of shamanistic studies. Growing shamanic practices in cyberspace have resulted in the transformation of shamanic heritage from the inside. The shamanic practices are inclined to individual ecstatic power acquisition and psychological counseling rather than religious ritual service. This trend of neo-shamanism, to borrow MICHAEL HARNER's terminology, is replacing traditional Korean shamanism.[4] I would characterize those Korean cyber-space mudangs as a type of neo-shaman.

Mostly the cyber neo-shamans tend to follow the conventional way of forced initiation and related psychic syndromes, such as *sinbyung*, against their will. However, the next phase of career building process is individual-oriented. According to self-portraits described on their internet sites, neo-shamans tend to build their career by learning from all kinds of popular psychology and religious literature by themselves, rather than by following classical way of long-term discipleship under the guidance of teacher shamans or spiritual parents. Thus most of the neo-shamans are not knowledgeable of or skillful in shamanic ritual performance, *kut*. They prefer calling their central work as 'soul counseling'.[5] Moreover, the shamanic clients also prefer this counseling practice to religious ritual because the counseling and talisman purchase cost much less than ritual

---

4 MICHAEL HARNER (1980) was the first scholar who prophesied the revival of shamanism in the highly technological Western societies and named this phenomenon as neo-shamanism. Neo-shamanism has become accepted as a sort of new age spirituality. This trend of synthesizing other spiritual traditions and also healing practices has produced various manual-type books for personal ecstatic experiences. See DOORE (1988) and TOWNSEND (1988) for an anthropological analysis of this phenomenon.

5 A female shaman of 35 year old age, YOO MYUNG-OK makes very clear about her identity as a soul counselor and a neo-shaman in her autobiography, *Mudang without a Shrine* (2000). Despite the fact that she had passed initiation rite at a prominent traditional shaman, she refused to learn singing and dancing necessary for shamanic ritual performance, and instead concentrated on counseling and fortune-telling.

performance. Compare 30,000 won for counseling fee with 3,000,000 won at minimum for ritual performance!

Neo-shamans tend to hold their specialty which is highly individualized, for example, specialty of luck talisman or talisman of health or love-finding talisman. This kind of specialization of practice means a much easier and convenient access to consultation with individual clients. Traditional shamans meet a specific group and character of clients at their private office or shrine. Their major group of clients were usually housewives and low-middle class people whose interests are focused on the personal or family affairs. Recently businessmen constitute a significant percentage of their clients. But neo-shamans can encounter a much wider range of clients of various social economic backgrounds not restricted by age, gender, occupation, or religious faith. A neo-shamanic client can be basically *anyone* who navigates cyberspace. Therefore, the shaman-client online relationship is arranged *anytime,* instantly and conveniently. In some cases, online shamanic service could be extended to off-line direct personal contact, but the main emphasis is on the on-line counseling in this cyber neo-shamanic practice.

SOCIAL IMPLICATIONS OF VIRTUALIZATION

The popularity of internet shamanic practices can be attributed to the genuine characteristics of cyberspace: virtualization and deterritorialization. By definition, "cyberspace" indicates the artificial and virtual space which is constituted by digital information and maintained by electronic, globally networked communication.[6] In cyberspace, human emotions and experience are transformed into information which is accessible to participants from any direction. Hence the virtualization of real time and space, real human subject and material object occurs here. Virtualization means "becoming other" and deterritorialization "spatio-temporal phenomenon" associated with it (LEVY 1998: 17). Cyberspace exteriorizes interior reality of experience and interiorizes exterior reality. In this displacement of reality and experience, cyberspace opens a window to the cosmic flux of information, blurring the notions of unity, identity, and location, which entail deterritorialization.

---

[6] The cyberspace is in a narrow sense a communication space newly created in the computer mediated communication environment. But its implication extends to the whole range of everyday life style medicated by internet. See DAVID HAKEN (1999: 2) and MIKE FEATHERSTONE & ROGER BURROWS (1995: 5–7).

Virtualization and deterritorialization in cyberspace sets forth a paradigm shift in human consciousness and life style. Cyber culture does not simply indicate a localized territorial culture in cyberspace; it envisages a totally new paradigm of life style which is trans-territorial and transcendental in terms of time and space. Conventional barriers of communication disappear. Anyone can have access to all information anytime. As one clicks into the computer network and navigates through cyberspace, one can collect and use information for individual purposes. Internet navigators are both information transmitters and receivers. There is no original place of information. The equalizing effects of interactive information exchange result in an endless array of informational linkages where the origin becomes the copy, and vice versa. The boundary of center and margin is blurred and then mutually interpenetrable.

In relation to Korean cyberspace shamanic practices, the significant impact of virtualization lies in the fact that cyberspace gives rise to a democratic environment that fosters the growth of marginal groups and minor religions. In terms of information processing speed and its expansive capacity, internet is superior to any other media such as newspaper and television. Cyber-media is much more efficient in the formation of public opinion on behalf of real-time feedback process. In cyberspace, there is the convenience of immediate question-and-answer communication. In the real world, due to limits of time and place and concerns for the sake of appearance, Koreans usually hesitate to visit shamans directly. But in the cyberworld, these kinds of limitations and hesitations are not a problem. Physical and moral barriers collapse in cyberspace. In the same manner, cyberspace shamans also respond to visiting clients with greater ease and free from social prejudice.

A typical Korean cyberspace shaman, PUCHE TOSA seems well aware of the social efficiency of interactive communication in cyberspace. He does not insist on the authenticity of shamanism *per se*. Instead, in a rather modest light-hearted voice, he expresses more or less a balanced view of religion. On the screen, he describes the purpose of his internet site as follows:

"By means of a civilized instrument, I wanted to correct the prejudice against *musok* (shamanic folk practice) and spread proper understanding of our folk culture. I thought this (internet service) the most efficient method to teach people who are not knowledgeable about what *musok* is. And my project has been successful so far. (Laugh)

I trust you would help my rather absurd project. It might be individual freedom of thought to despise *musok* as superstition or peudo-religion. But please do not neglect forcibly the fact that *musok* is a living religious phenomenon and also elementary religious belief which is alive vividly in the veins of Korean people. Although we are living in the world dominated by science, there exists a mystical area beside *musok* which scientific logic does not explain. I am sincerely asking people of other religions to stop denigrating *musok*! It might be fine with me if you just come by my site light-heartedly and acknowledge its place. I hope that you open your mind and cast off your prejudices."

His appeal to the general internet public is not assertive or forceful but rather apologetic and modest. He tries to convince the visiting clients to accept the shamanic presence in the cyber world, and furthermore to justify his own philosophy of shamanic divination as follows:

"Cyber divination is not just fun or curiosity. Our life is so precious and thus not replaceable by anything else in the world. Even though our fate is fixed, we must put it in tune and try to improve it. Depending on our efforts, our fate could be changeable. Please do not compare my email divination to other fortunetelling services in cyberspace which are based on the Chinese philosophy of the I-ching. Internet PUCHE TOSA is not a fortuneteller but an 'ecstatic shaman'. PUCHE TOSA's counseling is equipped with a sense of responsibility, and it would help change your fate and improve your life."

In this context, PUCHE TOSA stresses his identity as an ecstatic shaman with a moralistic sensibility. He establishes for himself authenticity of his cyber divination while rebuking or neglecting the spiritual effects of talismans that are sold and bought directly in cyberspace. But he is also in the practice of selling talismans even though it is only a minor part of his internet service. Literally differentiating his off-line talisman sales from the on-line sales, he seems to cling to probably the last bulwark of traditional shamanism: "commercialism is not the true character of Korean shamanism." Nevertheless, PUCHE TOSA's internet practice is located on the verge of self-transformation of Korean shamanism into virtual shamanism.

NATURE OF VIRTUAL RELIGIOSITY

The virtual transformation of shamanic practice can be attributed to the nature of cyberspace and virtual religiosity. In cyberspace there is no hegemony of "real reality", but virtual reality reigns. The virtual world remains terra incognita for people who stand hesitantly at a crossroads, holding the value system of "real reality". Virtual reality does not only expand our consciousness but also transforms fundamentally our understanding of person and world. Internet information servers and consumers are indeed transformed into a *cyborg*, an amalgam and combination of physically human being and artificial intelligence. Cyborg is an intelligent machine or "a cybernetic posthuman" which is not easily divisible on the basis of the dichotomy of body and soul, humans and robots, and humans and supernatural beings (HAYLES 1999: 2). This is a different construction of human subjectivity. Once information has lost its body, "embodiment has been downplayed or erased in the cybernetic construction of the posthuman" (HAYLES 1999: 5). In the flux of continuity and discontinuity between a natural self and a cybernetic posthuman, the liberal human subject can be articulated within a context of virtual reality. The netizens who inhabit cyberspace all become cyborgs (TAYLOR 1999: 132).

Given the ambiguity of personal and social identity (gender, age, race, nationality, locality, community) or religious faith, the cyborg netizens can enjoy efficiency and pleasure of virtual communication. *Everyone* can have access to all information *everywhere*. When everyone is everywhere, this is a dream of virtual reality. The achievement of omnipotence and omniscience is not to be nowhere but to be everywhere at once. The all-at-oneness of the internet is, as RHEINGOLD (1991: 256) insists, "a form of out-of-body-experience" or "telepresence". Telepresence as a communication medium which was primarily invented for remote-sensing medical operation exemplifies the typical communication system in cyberspace and virtual reality. Telepresence as an experience of being present in a remote location creates a sense of the technical sublime, the moment that BAUDRILLARD (1983) describes as "the ecstasy of communication". By the ecstasy of communication, BAUDRILLARD means a mode of disppearance, a passage into the dissolution and the transcendence of a form. Ecstasy is then not simply a real form of religious experience but the genuine property of virtual religiosity.[7]

First spiritual cyborgs were probably shamans, those ecstatic technicians of the sacred (DAVIS 1998: 132). Following ELIADE's elegant definition of shamanism as the archaic technique of ecstasy, shamanism consists of virtual reality *per se* and thus readily enters into the realm of cyber culture. Comparing it with the shamanic ecstasy that undergoes painful physical transformation, RHEINGOLD insists the sheer pleasure of cyberspace ecstasy as follows: "Virtual reality might become the first wholesome, integrating, *nonpathological form of ecstasy* capable of liberating *safely* the long-

---

[7] For an ecstatic interpretation of the posthuman cyborg, see HALBERSTAM — LIVINGSTON 1995.

repressed Dionysian energies of our heavenly Apollonian civilization."
(RHEINGOLD 1991: 356, my emphasis)

Cyber culture wherein virtual reality reigns is essentially shamanistic.
Virtual reality breaks the frames of everyday reality. People use cyberspace
to get out of their minds as well as out of their bodies. The world of
objects and information in cyberspace forms a "technocosmos", universal
computational networks created by information technology, a navigable
and transparent communication space centered on the flow of information
(LEVY 1998: 60). In technocosmos, all previous categories of barriers and
boundaries collapse and new categories constantly appear and disappear,
thus opening onto a boundless sea of virtual beings-information.
Techonocosmos grows like a dialectic of being, creating an open and plural
culture. Individual cybernauts in the sea of virtual reality are constituted as
multiple identities and subjectivities.

In respect to religious activities in cyberspace, hierarchical relationship
between priest and common believer, between socially dominant religion
and marginal religion is no longer exclusively applied. The spirit of equality
prevails over conventional structure of inequality in every sphere of life.
Because a single cybernaut plays the dual role of information server and
receiver in cyberspace, no religious master of internet site can insist on
superior status over the clients. The religious master must be sensitive to
this democratic environment of the cyber world. The religious master's
esoteric knowledge about the spiritual world could remain intact. But it is
destined for constant modification through "the ecstasy of virtual
communication" in which things and events are continually surpassing
themselves, growing and expanding in power.

Moreover, the horizontal information network envisions the
synchronous plural matrix of real religion and virtual religion. In the
incipient stage of cyberspace religious practices, cyberspace has been
utilized mainly as the supplement to regular religious service and extensive
mission work. However, cyber religion could bring about fundamental
transformations of the existing religions on the inside and the outside.
Because of convenient accessibility to information in cyberspace, people
can have much more freedom of religion and choice among all kinds of
religions which are exhibited on the web sites. Cyberspace would accelerate
religious pluralism in terms of faith principles and practices. Specific
religious doctrines and faiths are transformed into information, which
could be accessible to and utilized by anyone regardless of religious
affiliation. New forms of religions would be created easily by a
combination of such various sources of information. Religious conversion
could occur more easily, free from conflict with church and priest

structure, because religious faith is conveniently formed and discarded on an individual basis. In cyberspace, cyber Buddhists could easily become cyber "shamanists" or Christians simultaneously, and vice versa. Erasure of embodiment and identification among cyber religious helps the construction of "the liberatory potential of *a dispersed subjectivity* distributed among diverse desiring machines" GILLES DELUEZE and FELIX GUATTARI call "body without organs" (1983, cited in HAYLES 1999: 4). The tenor of religious pluralism and the dream of religious unity could be accomplished in the liberatory potential of plural matrix of cyberspace.

VISION OF VIRTUAL KOREAN SHAMANISM

Going back to the episode illustrated in the beginning of this paper, in comparison with the case of aborted cyborg shaman Cysha, if cyborg Christ or Buddha appear on the internet service, could people express directly such outcries of abhorrence? In fact, there have already appeared several cyber Buddhist temples and Christian churches active in cyberspace. The Buddhist netizens can worship cyborg Buddha and attend Buddha's Birthday religious rites. If tenacious distrust of shamanism as a religion were to diminish, and shamanic practice tolerated just as one of many cyber religions, there could appear cyborg shamans like "Cysha" and cyber shamanic shrines.

The cyber culture would promote plural religious matrix and virtualization of shamanic faith. Cyberspace shamanism would have fundamentally different features than real shamanism. However, real shamanism as substances would never be disassociated from the virtual reality of cyberspace shamanism. Through the information processing management, the virtual serves to link the threads of multitude subjective realms of real experience and emotion and explore new frames of truth and aesthetic dimensions. A sculptor of the virtual, the cyborg shaman could coordinate variegated life events in a vast sea of information linkage, the immense hypertext as known the World Wide Web. The cyborg shaman could be a new type of artist who provides a new form of hospitality to help individual cybernaut appropriate information without fear and resentment of proselytism. Of course, the cyborg shaman would never be the substitution for the actual shaman. Though given a human name and clothed in human character, cyborg shaman is an imitation or simulation of the real shaman. But it is a harmless virtual entity in the true sense.

Therefore, in this context, Korean netizens' accusations of cyborg shaman "Cysha" for superstition prove to be unjustifiable. Their misconception of Cysha as a sort of real shaman is rooted historically in the general contemptuous treatment of Korean shamans and shamanism. The controversy over the emergence of cyborg mudang Cysha suggests where Korean shamanic heritage should be located in the rapidly computerizing public culture. Korean shamanic heritage is officially valued as a cultural treasure to be preserved and transmitted to the next generation. Several shamans actually are appointed by the government as living human treasures, and they are respected as cultural artists. However, with the exception of those few shamans designated as living cultural treasures, Korean shamans in general are still perceived on the popular level as charlatans, and their shamanic practices as superstitions. The general public considers shamanic heritage as the pre-modern tradition which the usual practice is permeated deeply in everyday life but ultimately bound to be abandoned. For this reason, people secretively seek shamans for advice or divine solutions in case of urgent problems. It is believed that shamanic heritage remains in the clandestine domain of contemporary Korean life. This is the cultural background why the appearance of cyborg shaman Cysha brought about such an outraged response from many Korean netizens.

Even though the space of the internet is currently used by a few shamans for limited purposes such as talisman sales and email counseling, Korean shamanic tradition can benefit from cyberspace practices because of the genuine nature of virtual religiosity as illustrated above. Together with cyborg shaman like "Cysha", actual cyberspace shamans could reach a much wider potential clientele and more netizens if they realize their proper position in the virtual reality. Especially, confronting deep-rooted social prejudices, the Korean shamanic tradition could be more effectively publicized to the public by means of open and democratized practices in cyberspace. The readiness of Korean shamans to adapt themselves to the virtual environment, which means when Korean shamans dare become cyborgs, will determine the future direction of Korean shamanic heritage.

REFERENCES

BAUDRILLARD, JEAN
　　1983　The Ecstasy of Communication. In HAL FOSTER (ed.) *The Anti-aesthetic: Essays on Postmodern Culture.* (Trans. JOHN JOHNSTON.) Seattle, Washington: Bay Press, 126–134.

DAVIS, ERIC
　　1998　*Techgnosis: myth, magic + mysticism in the age of information.* New York: Three Rivers Press.

DELUEZE, GILLES – GUATTARI, FELIX
　　1983　*Anti-Oedipus: Capitalism and Schizophrenia.* Minneapolis: University of Minnesota Press.

DOOR, GARY (ed.)
　　1988　*Shaman's Path: healing, personal growth, & empowerment.* Boston – London: Shambhala.

FEATHERSTONE, MIKE – BURROWS, ROGER
　　1995　*cyberspace, cyberbodies, cyberpunk.* London: Sage.

HAKEN, DAVID
　　1999　*CYBORGS@CYBERSPACE.* New York: Routledge.

HALBERSTAM, JUDITH – LIVINGSTON, IRA (eds.)
　　1995　*Posthuman Bodies.* Bloomington: Indiana University Press.

HARNER, MICHAEL
　　1980　*The Way of the Shaman: A Guide to Power and Healing.* New York: Bantham New Age.

HAYLES, N. KATHERINE
　　1999　*How We Became Posthuman: virtual bodies in cybernetics, literature, and informatics.* Chicago: The University of Chicago Press.

LEVY, PIERRE
　　1998　*Becoming Virtual: Reality in the Digital Age.* (Trans. by ROBERT BONONNO) New York: Plenum Press.

RHEINGOLD, HOWARD
　　1991　*Virtual Reality.* New York: A Touchstone Book.

TAYLOR, MARK C.
　　1999　*About religion: economies of faith in virtual culture.* Chicago: The University of Chicago Press.

TOWNSEND, JOAN
　　1988　Neo-Shamanism and the Modern Mystical Movement. In GARY DOOR (ed.) *Shaman's Path.* Boston: Shambhala, 73–83.

YOO, MYUNG-OK
　　2000　*Chip up nun mudang* (Mudang without a Shrine). Seoul: Saeroun Saramdul (New People).

BARBARA TEDLOCK

Recognizing & Celebrating
the Feminine in Shamanic Heritage

Early explorers, travellers, and scholars described shamanism as a spiritual tradition that took essentially the same form everywhere on earth. In the Americas they used the words "shaman" and "medicine man" interchangeably for practitioners of shamanism. Since very few of these explorers talked with women there are only a small number of historical records mentioning women shamans or "medicine women". In one late-nineteenth-century account the author noted in passing that in a number of Canadian aboriginal groups medicine women were feared because of their enormous power. Among the Plains Cree, a traveller in the early years of the twentieth century described the performance of a woman shaman: "As her husband beat the drum she blew all over a young man who was sick. She reached into the fire and removed two pieces of metal then stood away from the patient and sucked. The young man had to be held down, so powerful was her sucking" (MCLEAN 1889: 27; MANDELBAUM 1979).

Whenever individuals of both sexes who shared shamanic knowledge were organized into groups, early observers used terms like "fraternity", regardless of the actual membership. The EARL OF SOUTHESK wrote that among the Ojibwa of Canada, certain herbs were "known only to the medicine men, who are a sort of Masonic brotherhood, consisting of women as well as men" (SOUTHESK 1875: 329). Although he mentioned the existence of female members of the Great Medicine Society or Midewiwin, he implied that they were merely subsets of, or auxiliaries to, their masculine counterparts.

A nineteenth-century woman explorer by the name of MATILDA COXE STEVENSON, who lived in the American Southwest, also called the shamanic societies with both female and male members "fraternities". However, she noted that each of these societies had a woman leader known as the Great Mother. In November of 1891 she documented an all-night curing séance at Zuni Pueblo in which the healers became possessed by bears and other dangerous animals (STEVENSON 1904: 490–501).

> "The female theurgists wear their conventional dress and red-colored, fluffy eagle plumes attached to the forelock; their feet and legs halfway to the knee, and hands and arms midway to the elbow, are painted white. The altar and the floor before it are white with meal, sprinkled by the members of the fraternity, and a line of meal crossed four times extends from the altar to the ladder. The Beast Gods pass over this line to be present, for the time being, in the bodies of the theurgists. The animal fetishes by the altar influence the spiritual presence of the Beast Gods. When a dozen or more theurgists are on the floor, their bodies thrown forward until they appear like the animals they impersonate, growling and wrangling with one another, the scene is weird and impressive. As the night wanes and the floor became more crowded the scene grows more and more wild and weird and the excitement is intense. The women appeared even more excited than the men."

The lesson here is that while women shamans were present in a number of societies we know so little about them because male explorers and scientists were not interested in describing the women they met in anything but the stereotypic roles of "wife" and "mother". This erasure of women from shamanism was reinforced because it tends to run in families so that most women shamans were also the wives and mothers of shamans. There is evidence that from the earliest times in Siberia, as well as inner and central Asia, that the spouses of shamans were trained and initiated with their partners in a parallel or dual shamanic practice. Wherever women and men worked together as spiritual healing partners, there existed an egalitarian relationship between the sexes predicated on the cooperation of autonomous, but nonetheless connected, individuals. This type of joint practice implies that the sexes were socially linked rather than hierarchically ranked. As a result, women and men were involved in complementary roles.

The arctic explorer KNUD RASMUSSEN recorded in the early years of the twentieth century an Iglulik Inuit séance. He arranged the performance for his party shortly before they departed on a long and dangerous sledge journey. It was conducted on the western coast of northern Hudson Bay by a husband-and-wife team. Although he perceived the woman's role as that of "an assistant" helping her husband, the shaman, it is clear from his account that this couple was an interdependent team in which both parties were equally necessary for the success of the ritual (RASMUSSEN 1929: 38–39.).

"All was dark and we could only wait for what was to come. For a long time not a sound was heard, but the waiting only increased our anticipation. At last we heard a scraping of heavy claws and a deep growling. "Here it comes", whispered Tuglik [the shaman's wife and assistant]. But nothing happened, except the same scraping and growling mingled with deep, frightened groans; then came a fierce growl, followed by a wild shriek, and at the same moment, Tuglik dashed forward ... and began talking to the spirits. She spoke in her own particular spirit language.

The spirits spoke now in deep chest notes, now in a high treble. We could hear, in between the words, sounds like those of trickling water, the rushing of wind, a stormy sea, the snuffling of walrus, the growling of bear...

This sitting lasted about an hour, and when all was quiet once more, Tuglik informed us that her husband, in the shape of a fabulous bear, had been out exploring the route we were to follow on our long journey. All obstacles had been swept aside, accident, sickness, and death were rendered powerless, and we should all return in safety to our house the following summer. All this had been communicated in the special language of the spirits, which she translated for us."

At the opening of the séance the arrival of the bear spirit was announced with a dramatic enactment. The bear, however, was reluctant and scratched and growled for some time. The man groaned, as the bear possessed him. Then letting out a wild shriek the woman rushed forward to interpret for her husband who now could speak only in the esoteric language of the spirits. She was able to share in the spirit journey, both understanding the spirit language and interpreting the meanings for the audience. She spoke with and understood the spirits while remaining intellectually alert and interactive with both the spirits and the audience. Her husband as a bear-possessed spirit medium, however, withdrew into himself becoming passive and loosing his ability to communicate with the audience.

In 1951 the novelist and historian of religion MIRCEA ELIADE wrote his classic book, *Le chamanisme et les techniques archaïques de l'extase*. In this encyclopedic work he set out a dichotomy between controlled "soul flight" as shamanic and uncontrolled "trance possession" as spirit possession. This division was strongly sexed in that shamans, who are nearly all male in his book, differed from possessed persons (read women) because shamans are said to control their spirits while possessed persons become the instruments of spirits. He arrived at this description by ignoring the evidence for women's ecstatic soul flights and by not citing key feminine deities in Asian shamanism: the Womb Goddess in the Sky and the Three

Goddess Midwives (HUMPHREY – ONON 1995: 286–301). In a later essay he described the predominance of female shamans in Korea as a form of "deterioration in traditional shamanism" and he trivialized the form of shamanism practiced by women in Japan as "a technique of possession by ghosts" (ELIADE 1961: 180).

ÅKE HULTKRANTZ who conducted ethnographic fieldwork in Montana among the Shoshone Indians described only the practices of "medicine men". He did remark, in passing, that he had met "two medicine women, both very capable", however he noted that although "there are medicine women who have passed the menopause, but they are few, and their powers are not as great as the powers of their male colleagues". That this dismissive statement may reflect gender bias rather than the actual situation among the Shoshone is indicated by the fact that he attempted to generalize it when he described medicine women in other cultures. For example, he noted that "in Puget Sound (and perhaps elsewhere) female shamans are rare, and their powers are inferior to those of male shamans". Elsewhere he said, "among the Eskimos some women occasionally perform as shamans, but it is testified that only with difficulty do they achieve the same magical effects as their male colleagues" (HULTKRANTZ 1987: 57; 1992: 83; 1967: 93).

In each of these cases he offers nothing but his own say-so, ignoring all evidence to the contrary. Other ethnographers documented the fact that not only the Shoshone but also their neighbors—Ute, Paiute, and Washo nations—had an equal proportion of powerful female and male shamans. As for the indigenous peoples of Puget Sound, a missionary who lived with them for many years reported that there were four prominent women shamans among the Klallams. More generally on the Northwest Pacific Coast, a visionary power that allows a person to perceive events happening at a distance, or in the future, is usually given at birth to women rather than to men. And finally, the Icelandic explorer VILHJALMUR STEFÁNSSON noted that shamans in Canada "may be male or female and in fact some of the greatest shamans known to me are women".[1]

Unfortunately ELIADE'S and HULTKRANTZ'S descriptions have gained the status of a doctrine repeated over and over again in secondary sources.

---

[1] RUBY – BROWN 1976; MALOUF – HULTKRANTZ 1974: 56; CALLAWAY – JANETSKI – STEWART 1986; AMOSS 1978; GILL – SULLIVAN 1992. A study of all the published ethnographic materials on Inuit society reveals "a kind of gender equality", and that "women were equal in their access to the religious sphere" ACKERMAN 1990: 218–219. Other explorers and ethnographers noted that both female and male shamans cured the sick and took leading ceremonial roles at religious festivals. NELSON 1899: 427; ZAGOSKIN 1967: 122. The quotation here is from STEFÁNSSON 1922: 392.

It was their version of an old story: the removal of women from major roles in the monotheistic world religions—Judaism, Christianity, Islam—and in the East Asian philosophical traditions of Taoism and Confucianism. What they did, in effect, was to project this story backward into societies that had resisted this displacement of the feminine.[2]

Even when scholars mention that there were a large number of women shamans in a particular society and that they were very powerful the feminine presence and role may be diminished by others who simply assert that these women were either outside of, or on the margin of the shamanic tradition. Thus, even though the famous ethnographer ALFRED KROEBER reported that nearly all of the shamans in northwestern California were women, ROBERT TORRANCE asserted that these women's shamanic practices were less important, meaningful, and powerful than those of men. Without carefully reading the available historical and ethnographic sketches, biographies, and autobiographies of women shamans, or undertaking any new research, he described the form of shamanism practiced by the Yurok, Karok, Hupa as a mere "vestige of the quest for transcendent knowledge and power that had been among the hallmarks of Eurasian–American shamanism from Lapland to Puget Sound".[3]

There were materials that could have been used to construct a picture of shamanism that included women and the feminine. Early in the twentieth century a Russian author made the following general statement about shamanism: "In all the Tungus languages the term shaman refers to persons of both sexes who have mastered spirits, who at their will can introduce these spirits into themselves and use their power over the spirits in their own interests, particularly helping other people who suffer from the spirits". Another Russian ethnographer, however, carefully distinguished between persons possessed by spirits and spirits possessed by shamans, but he did not assign women to one of these dimensions and men to the other. "No one is considered a shaman", he said, "unless that female or male person can control the spirits: take them into the body or expel them at will". He noted that in Siberia, as well as in most other areas, shamans of both sexes combine trance mediumship with ecstatic soul flight (SHIROKOGOROFF 1935: 271; BASILOV 1976: 149).

A lack of control is often described as feminine in character and as one way that women can achieve social prestige. In the 1970s The British

---

[2] In Taoism women are not so much removed but rather neutered. They must stop their menstruation in order to achieve sagehood. See AMES 1981 and ZITO – BARLOW 1994: 280–281.

[3] TORRANCE 1994 and KROEBER 1925 discussed women shamans in northern California.

anthropologist IOAN LEWIS described what he saw as a worldwide pattern of "possession cults" in which people practice trance mediumship functioning as a form of indirect social and religious protest by women. More recently, however, he backed away from this interpretation and noted that spirit possession and ecstatic flight of the soul are serial phases in the assumption of the shamanic career.[4]

Ironically, even an avowed feminist embraced the division of spiritual labor between male shamans (ecstatic out-of-body soul flights) and female mediums (bodily possession by alien spirits). SUSAN SERED, in her otherwise excellent book *Priestess, Mother, Sacred Sister: Religions Dominated by Women* (1994), described soul flight as a masculine adventure and argued that religious specialists in what she called "female-dominated religions" consistently opted for possession rather than ecstatic flight. Accepting the dichotomy between flight and "indwelling", as possession is called, or, between transcendence and immanence, she reified it as a rigid separation. According to this essentialist scheme, there is a purely masculine spiritual pole that involves leaving one's body and a purely feminine spiritual pole that involves sharing one's body. This view seems to be based on sexual practices in which a masculine partner enters a feminine partner who shares her own body with him. The spiritual reality here, however, is far more complex.[5]

In séances, whether what happens is described as possession or not, the real issue is whether the trance was *sought* or not. If the trance is sought, then the question of "control" or "possession" is a matter of ideology, technique, theatrics, or audience perception. To assimilate spirit mediumship to unsought possessions, except perhaps as the initial shamanic calling, is inaccurate and misleading. In the majority of shamanic traditions possession is neither excluded by, nor opposed to, shamanic soul flight. They exist together within the same spiritual traditions and even within the same event. Thus, any descriptions of out-of-body celestial travel as "masculine" and trance possession or mediumship as "feminine",

---

[4] In the 1940s ethnographers began to discuss the idea that ritualized possession states were a way for women to achieve social prestige (PRINCE 1977: xi; IOAN LEWIS 1971; 1986).

[5] This dichotomy between transcendence, as beyond experience, outside oneself and thereby unknowable, and its opposite of immanence, as that which is experiential, present, or indwelling in form, is from the philosopher IMMANUEL KANT. The literature describes the prominence of women worldwide in "possession cults". HOGBIN (1934) notes how women are usually the mediums consulted for those diseases ascribed to possession by the spirits of ancestors. FORTUNE (1953: 95) insisted that among the Manus of New Guinea, while women may be spiritually disenfranchised with the paternal "Sir Ghost Cult", they are spiritually enfranchised in possession cults.

seriously misrepresent the complex and ambiguously gendered nature of shamanism. In Southeast Asia and South America, for example, there are shamanic traditions in which out-of-body soul flight is considered a feminine action and possession a masculine one, but both are experienced by shamans regardless of sex. This happens because shamans shape shift not only between the human and animal realms, but also between genders in such a way that each one manifests a partly feminine and partly masculine, or co-gendered personality.[6]

GENDER IN SHAMANISM

Gender is a system of meaning pertaining to the differences and similarities between women and men as they are lived and interpreted within particular historical and geographical contexts. In contemporary society many individuals understand sex as signifying gender and thus gender identity is assumed to be "natural": that is someone can "feel like a woman", or "feel like a man". As a result what are regarded as the quintessential insignias of sex have little stability either historically or comparatively. This has important implications for understanding how gender-variant identities are contextually situated within a broader system of meanings associated with femaleness and maleness worldwide. These properties are viewed in a number of societies as complementary rather than hierarchical and thus the practice of shamanism offers a context in which the outlines of self and other, female and male, define one another through interaction. Social identity is multiple, shifting, constantly being created, erased, and re-created in interaction between self and other. Thus, one can view oneself, or can oneself be viewed, as bounded and essential, boundless and contextual, or in fluid transition between these poles.

Societies that exist outside of, or on the edges of, Western biomedical and religious cultures construct multiple non-stigmatized gender statuses for individuals who do not behave according to the biological sex ascribed to them at birth. In a number of these traditions gender is united at the highest cosmic level with either the image of a non-gendered androgynous deity, or a co-gendered creator deity or culture hero. The gender crossing and gender bending of ritual specialists during shamanic séances and other

---

[6] That spirit possession and ecstatic soul flight might be serial phases in the assumption of a shamanic career was also noted by IOAN LEWIS 1986; NELSON 1995; BACIGALUPO 1998.

community-wide rituals enables them to manipulate these potent cosmic powers (NELSON 1995).

The social construction of gender combines an understanding of what is possible, proper, and perverse in gender-linked behavior with a set of values. More than two genders can be created by separating gender tasks and social roles from sexual morphology. As a result many Amerindian cultures traditionally recognized, and in some cases still recognize four genders: woman, man, woman-man, and man-woman (CALLENDER – KOCHEMS 1983; ROSCOE 1998).

It has been suggested that the figure of the shaman serves as a "third gender" mediator (SALADIN 1986; 1988; 1993). While this idea is intriguing, it represents a static description of what is in fact an extremely fluid situation in shamanic cultures. It is not membership within any one of these gender categories per se but rather the *transformation* of gender, or frequent *gender-switching, bending, blending,* or *reversing* that is directly linked with the process of coming closer to the sacred. The theme of .gender reversals and mediation frequently occurs in mythology and rituals but the significance attached to it varies greatly, depending on the form of the reversal, the context, and the specific gender culture. Some of the most diverse variations on the theme of gender flexibility are reflected in beliefs about shamans, animal spirits, and the manipulation of their sexual organs and energies.

Messages about gender within shamanic rituals range from the enforcement of difference, to the encouragement of ambiguity and the acceptance of partial or total transformation. One code through which these messages are made manifest is crossdressing. In Siberia, during the early years of the twentieth century, shamans often wore women's clothing during their séances, whether or not they were transgendered or what were called locally "soft men" in their everyday lives. Some male Chukchi shamans in northeastern Siberia identified with their female spirits so strongly that they dressed as women, did women's work, and used the special language spoken only by women. Others combined male with female features or acted out a female role without crossdressing. For example, across the Bering Strait in Alaska, an Eskimo shaman by the name of Asatchq performed a birthing ritual. While someone drummed he rubbed his belly until it swelled then, removing his pants, he knelt in the traditional birthing position and pulled blood from between his legs, followed by his shamanic icon (BALZER 1996; VITEBSKY 1995).

Birth and death provide key actions and metaphors within shamanic systems, traditions, and cultures. In many societies shamans are said "to be born" or "to die" into the profession and in their subsequent practices they may assist at actual births and deaths. A number of scholars of shamanism have focused on illness, death, dismemberment, and skeletalization leading to rebirth as shamans (ELIADE 1951; FURST 1977). What they have missed is the other side of the life-death continuum where shamans are birthed into the profession and become midwives for others.

Shamanism is a fluid gendered practice, a reflexive and highly contextualized discourse on femininity and masculinity as well as a mutually constituting dialogue between women and men. For the Kulina of Brazil, while it is not necessary to become a shaman in order to be an adult man, only shamans—in their practice as masters of game animals as well as village protectors and leaders—achieve the full potential of maleness. Similarly, among the Yurok of northern California, while it is not necessary to become a shaman in order to be an adult woman, only shamans—in their practice as sucking doctors, midwives, and village protectors—achieve the full potential of femaleness (POLLOCK 1992; THOMPSON 1991; BUCKLEY 1992).

Femininity and masculinity are not opposite ends of a single sex or gender spectrum with women on one side, men on the other, and shamans in between. Rather femininity and masculinity are terms of an unstable difference/similarity, interlocking, though contradictory, aspects or modalities of personhood. Instead of possessing exclusively feminine or exclusively masculine characteristics, people following shamanic paths include feminine and masculine characteristics within their performances. When individuals are initiated into these traditions they are trained to avoid choosing, negating, or destroying either of the binary pairs. Instead, they are encouraged to an ironic manipulation of both sides of the polarity in which the contradictions rarely resolve, not even dialectally, into larger wholes. Shamanic performance can be viewed as a type of serious play involving the tension of holding incompatible things together because they are necessary and in some sense "true".

Diviners and healing shamans within the Mazatec tradition of Mexico practice within a domestic context primarily in the areas of human reproduction and agricultural production. They search, question, untie and disentangle the internal origins of human misfortune. Depending upon their training and sexual orientation these shamans are distinctive in their healing behaviors and chants. Those traveling a strongly masculine path battle with external political and social causes of illness; their words flash forth with the terrible force of a thunderbolt. Shamans following a more feminine path find and release illnesses. These gender differences have emerged in the context of family shamanism. Here spouses commonly shamanize together as a team within a family setting. Over the years children learn how to experience and talk about healing by picking up a combination of same-sex and opposite-sex symbols, rituals, and bodily responses. As a result, some women in this tradition work with masculine spiritual energies, or powers, while others embody feminine sources of energy. Likewise males can work with either masculine or feminine powers. But the most powerful shamans of all combine an unstable mixture from each of these traditions (MUNN 1973; FEINBERG 1997).

In Chile most Mapuche shamans are biologically female. As midwives and mothers they are conceived as "givers of life" who obtain powers from the moon in order to bring fertility to land, animals, and people. While they identify themselves as women they, unlike most local women, are household heads whose families perform domestic chores for them. These women shamans make their own decisions independently from their men, traveling as they please and influencing community decisions. During public rituals they use feminine integrative symbols and actions as well as masculine exorcising or warring symbols and actions. Female symbols, like women, are called on to nurture, heal the body and integrate the self. Male symbols, like men, are called on to exorcise, defeat, and kill the outside other. Shamans in this tradition dramatically weave together these seemingly incommensurable nurturing and warrior themes and in so doing embody multiple genders during their performance of healing (BACIGALUPO 1998).

HISTORICAL EVIDENCE FOR WOMEN IN SHAMANISM

Women have been practicing as shamans for at least as long as men, if not longer. Among the Gao-ghoui peoples, nomads of the Thele confederation inhabiting central Asia from the fourth through the sixth centuries AD, there are written sources that indicate women were the original shamans. There is also evidence that Yakut and Altayan shamans, both males and females, wore women's dresses, women's decorations, jewelry, and long hair to perform shamanic rituals. In this and other contexts women were considered to be stronger, more powerful, and more accomplished than men as shamans.[7]

While some historians push shamanism back to the Neolithic period in Korea, others suggest that it evolved from the animistic beliefs of Mumun people, makers of pottery without surface designs who lived during the

---

[7] DIAKONOVA in a 1994 essay hypothesized that women rather than men were the earliest shamans.

Bronze Age. There is also evidence that female shamans took an active role in the defense of the Koguryŏ Dynasty (37 BC–AD 668) against the Sui and Tang Dynasties of China. Later, when Buddhism became the official state religion women shamans were retained in the palace as sacred healers and diviners with important official roles and titles (CHANG 1988).

A woman was the main character of the earliest known epic celebrating the life of a shaman. The Manchurian epic, called *Wubuxiben Mama*, began as an oral narrative sometime during the Jin and Yuan dynasties, lasting from 1115 to 1271. The central character, Wubuxiben, was a famous female khan, or clan leader, who devoted her entire life to using her shamanic abilities to protect her large family. The epic portrays how she went about courageously unifying and governing seven hundred tribes in the Donghai region. In the course of her nation building she discovered and developed maritime trade routes across the Sea of Japan to Kamchatka and the Aleutian Islands. The only other early Manchurian epic, called *The Tale of the Nishan Shamaness,* also featured a woman as the main character. The woman, whose name was Teteke was the first clan shaman. The mention of the Ming dynasty (1368–1644 AD) and the DAIZONG Emperor (who ruled from 1626 to 1643 AD) seems to peg the time of composition of the epic to the late-seventeenth century. The most recent translators and interpreters of the tale, however, believe that since the epic is a product of a much earlier oral folk tradition, the historical references were added much later when it was first taken down in writing.[8]

From the twelfth through the fourteenth centuries there is evidence of women as either the only, or the most numerous, shamans in central and inner Asia. In Mongolia and the Mongol areas of China and the Caucasus, and among the Abkhazians and other Caucasian peoples, women shamans and prophets were numerous and considered more powerful than men shamans (BANZAROV 1980; JOHANSONS 1972).

When we look for the earliest use of a word like "shaman", we find it in a twelfth-century Chinese Song Dynasty printing of XU MENGSHEN's historical text, *Sanchao beimeng huibian.* It discusses the practices of healers called "shanman", who were all women. In China the twelfth-century word "shanman" was replaced by the closely related terms: sama, chama, saman, and shaman. The last of which was widely adopted beginning in the Qing Dynasty. However, because these early observations of shamanic practice were fragmentary the Chinese language did not serve as the medium for the passage of the term shaman into European languages. Instead it was from

---

[8] FU 1993; SCHAFER 1973; NOWAK – DURRANT 1977. For more details about the worldview and history of Manchu shamanism see WU 1989; GUO 1995; KISTER 1999.

the seventeenth-century reports of Russian explorers in Siberia and inner Asia that the word "shaman" was borrowed into English. In the Tungus family of languages the verb stem *šam-*, meaning "to know", was combined with the suffix *-án*, "one who", to form the word *šam-án*, "one who knows". It referred to persons of either sex who knew how to see, hear, feel, embody, and control spirits in order to help themselves, their families, and other people in need (SHI 1989 and WU 1989).

Because of the profound but subtle links between language, consciousness, and those systems of ideas or beliefs we call ideology, the final syllable of the word shaman was heard not as the original *-án*, but as *-man*, as in Englishman. Just as in the conventional use of the pair of terms "man" and "woman", there is an implicit hierarchy in which man is the encompassing term that stands for the entire species. In turn the species category "man" includes the gendered division man versus woman, with woman as the supplemental term. Thus males were soon privileged as the shamanic norm.

While many linguists have argued that grammatical gender is arbitrary, independent of all sexual denotations and connotations, this is untrue, at least in the case of Indo-European languages. For centuries, there has been a tendency to valorize what is masculine in these languages, and to devalorize what is feminine. Although the feminine was originally simply different, it came to be assimilated to the non-masculine. In this way being a woman was equated with *not* being a man. Women lost their access to subjectivity and selfhood of the same value as masculine subjectivity and selfhood (IRIGARAY 1993).

The fate of the discourse on shamanism in the West is deeply ironic, since Chinese, Mongol, and Russian authors had been telling a very different story from the time of their earliest Siberian contacts. Not only did they report that women shamans existed in nearly every community they visited, but among a number of these groups they discovered that women were in the majority. In some cases women were the *only* shamans. Historical sources dating back to at least the beginning of the fourth century indicate that in northeastern Siberia—among the Koryak, Yakut, and other Altayan peoples such as the Manchu—women were the original shamanic practitioners.

Many historical forces have shaped shamanism. During the seventeenth and eighteenth centuries, in Siberia and central Asia, there was a gradual but widespread displacement of women's spiritual knowledge and power to men, who set up and controlled politically powerful centralized governments and religious cults. In some areas there was only occasional sporadic contact but wherever indigenous Siberian and central Asian peoples came into daily contact with the teachings of the so-called "great traditions", or proselytizing world religions, shamanism slowly evolved into a "little tradition", or woman's religion. Women became its experts, its practitioners, and its supporters, while the dominating intrusive religious system was in the hands of men (BASILOV 1997).

LINGUISTIC EVIDENCE FOR WOMEN SHAMANS

The ethnographer NORA CHADWICK found that Mongol, Buryat, Yakut, Tuvan, and Altayan peoples all use the same word "udagan", for a female shaman whereas there are multiple terms in these languages for male shamans. She pointed out that this philological evidence is significant for the study of the history and nature of shamanism in that it suggests that the original shamans were women rather than men. Likewise, the social anthropologist CAROLINE HUMPHREY found that the term *udagan*, and variants including *yadgan* in Daur, were used by Mongols, Buryats, Bargas, and Yakuts for female shamans while the term for a male shaman in Buryat and Halh Mongol is *böö* and in the Altai and Tuva *kam*. Today the term *yadgan*, which originates with the word for female shaman, is widely used among Mongol–Turkic peoples in North Asia for both female and male shamans (CHADWICK 1936: 81; HUMPHREY – ONON 1995: 74n, 251n).

In Australia the native word for shaman is *putari*. However for many years it was defined in a negative gender exclusive manner as an older man or "witch doctor" claiming to have special, usually malevolent powers. It was not until the 1980s that the husband-and-wife team, CATHERINE and ROBERT BERNDT discovered that there even were female *putari*. They discovered these women had special expertise in midwifery and menstruation, as well as contraceptive measures. Then, in the 1990s DIANE BELL recognized that women *putari* just like men were herbalists and traditional spiritual healers with clearly shamanic powers (BERNDT – BERNDT – STANTON 1993: 193; BELL 1998: 342–343).

Another example of gender bias is found in the ethnographic work of NORMAN WHITTEN. He translated the South American Quichua word *yachaj*, literally meaning "one who knows", as "powerful shaman" when he referred to males and as "master potter" when he referred to females (WHITTEN 1976: 116–120). What results from this seemingly simple act of translation is a misrepresentation in which women are removed from spirituality and placed in what are generally considered secular feminine roles within North American society.

What has also not been well understood is that in many traditions there is a feminine path undertaken primarily by women. This path among the Huichol of west-central Mexico, for example, focuses on weaving. The process of learning to weave, which entails the ability to access the spirit world in order to create new designs, is a feminine spiritual discipline that parallels and merges with masculine shamanic practices in such a way that a truly expert woman weaver is also an expert shaman. Women on the shamanic weaving path seek out special animal allies: a female boa constrictor, beaded lizard (a member of the Gila monster family), or horned toad (SCHAEFER 1989).

Huichol shamanism runs in families, as in the case of the well-known shaman RAMÓN MEDINA SILVA. His mother, sister, and wife were all mara'akame or "singing shamans". His shamanic teacher was his mother who instructed him in the practical and esoteric lore of animals, birds, and weather. She taught him history and myth, sang song cycles, and described esoteric details of the spiritual environment. His wife, GUADALUPE, helped him in his healing practice and after his death became an important curer, singer, and family leader. While RAMÓN's peyote-inspired yarn paintings have been widely exhibited and illustrated, only a handful of GUADALUPE's have been collected by museums or photographed.[9] He has been quoted at length but her verbal wisdom and healing knowledge have yet to be recorded and made available.

The examples abound. For example, it was not until quite recently that DIANA RIBOLI discovered that there were a number of powerful women shamans in Nepal although all previous studies had denied their existence. One of these was a woman who was the spiritual guide of nine Chepang villages. It was her special duty to initiate young men, as well as young women, into shamanism. But because her husband and nephew were also shamans she was ignored (RIBOLI 1995; NEBESKY – WOJKOWITZ 1956).

Today the importance of women shamans and feminine forms of shamanic practice can no longer be dismissed. Women are writing ethnographies centering on their first-hand experiences with sacred healing. For example, BONNIE GLASS-COFFIN's ethnography *The Gift of Life: Female Spirituality and Healing in Northern Peru* (1998) accurately portrays shamanic healing in Peru. By carefully distinguishing between masculine and feminine shamanic "styles" she shows that shamanic combat and confrontational curing techniques used by men are not central to the practice of female

---

[9] For illustrations of GUADALUPE's yarn paintings see BERRIN 1978.

shamans.[10] Instead, women often practice shamanism in teams, using supportive and sympathetic techniques rather than directly confronting or competing with one another.

CONCLUSION

The shamanic heritage is not a single, uniform, ahistorical practice but rather a group of distinctive historically sensitive practices and ideologies. These regional and historical differences in shamanic practice depend on a number of issues, most importantly the gender of the practitioner. When we pay attention to gender we recognize the feminine dimension of healing as distinct from the masculine. In so doing we return women to the shamanic heritage where they have always rightfully belonged.

REFERENCES

ACKERMAN, LILLIAN
    1990   Gender status in Yup'ik society. *Études Inuit Studies* 14: 209–221.
AMES, ROGER
    1981   Taoism and the androgynous ideal. *Women in China: Current Directions in Historical Scholarship*. Chicago: University of Chicago Press, 124–147.
AMOSS, PAMELA
    1978   *Coast Salish Spirit Dancing: The Survival of an Ancestral Religion*. Seattle: University of Washington Press.
BACIGALUPO, ANA MARIELLA
    1998   The exorcising sounds of warfare: The performance of shamanic healing and the struggle to remain Mapuche. *Anthropology of Consciousness* 9: 2–3: 1–16.
BALZER, MARJORIE
    1996   Sacred genders in Siberia: Shamans, bear festivals, and androgyny. In SABRIA PETRA RAMET (ed.) *Gender Reversals and Gender Cultures*. London: Routledge, 164–182.
BANZAROV, DORJI
    1980   The Black Faith, or Shamanism among the Mongols. *Mongolian Studies* 6: 53–91.
BASILOV, VLADIMIR
    1976   Shamanism in Central Asia. In AGEHANANDA BHARATI (ed.) *The Realm of the Extra-Human: Agents and Audiences*. The Hague: Mouton, 149–157.

---

[10] For a description of the Peruvian masculine healing path see SHARON 1978; JORALEMON – SHARON 1993.

1997 Chosen by the Spirits. In MARJORIE BALZER (ed.) *Shamanic Worlds*. Armonk, New York: North Castle Books, 3–48.

BELL, DIANE
1998 *Ngarrindjeri Wurruwarrin: A World That Is, Was, and Will Be*. North Melbourne: Spinifex.

BERRIN, KATHLEEN
1978 *Art of the Huichol Indians*. New York: Abrams.

BERNDT, CATHERINE – BERNDT, ROBERT – STANTON, JOHN
1993 *A World That Was: The Yaruldi of the Murray River and the Lakes, South Australia*. Sydney: Angus & Robertson.

BUCKLEY, THOMAS
1992 Yurok doctors and the concept of shamanism. In LOWELL, JOHN BEAN (ed.) *California Indian Shamanism*. Menlo Park, CA: Ballena Press, 117–161.

CALLANDER, CHARLES – KOCHEMS, LEE
1983 The North American *berdache*. *Current Anthropology* 24: 443–470.

CALLAWAY, DONALD – JANETSKI, JOEL – STEWART, OMER
1986 Ute. In WARREN D'AZEVEDO (ed.) *Handbook of North American Indians: Great Basin*. Washington, D.C.: Smithsonian Institution, 336–337.

CHADWICK, NORA
1936 Shamanism among the Tatars of Central Asia. *The Journal of the Royal Anthropological Institute of Great Britain and Ireland* 66: 75–112.

CHANG, CHU-KUN
1988 An introduction to Korean shamanism. In RICHARD GUISSO – CBAI-SHIN YU (eds.) *Shamanism: The Spirit World of Korea*. Berkeley: Asian Humanities Press, 30–51.

DIAKONOVA, VERA
1994 Shamans in traditional Tuvinian society. In GARY SEAMAN – JANE DAY (eds.) *Shamanism in Central Asia and the Americas*. Niwot: University Press of Colorado, 245–256.

ELIADE, MIRCEA
1951 *Le Chamanisme et les techniques archaïques de l'extase*. Paris: Librairie Payot.
1961 Recent works on shamanism: A review article. *History of Religions* 1: 152–186.

FEINBERG, BENJAMIN
1997 Three Mazatec wise ones and their books. *Critique of Anthropology* 17: 4: 411–437.

FORTUNE, REO
1953 *Manus Religion*. Philadelphia: American Philosophical Society.

FU, YUGUANG
1993 The worldview of the Manchu shamanism. In HOPPÁL, MIHÁLY– HOWARD, K. D. (eds.) *Shamans and Cultures*. Budapest: Akadémiai Kiadó, 240–248.

FURST, PETER
1977 The roots and continuities of shamanism. In BRODZKY, ANNE – DANESEWICH, ROSE – JOHNSON, NICK (eds.) *Stones, Bones and Skin: Ritual and Shamanic Art.* Toronto: Arts Canada, 1–28.

GILL, SAM – SULLIVAN, IRENE
1992 *Dictionary of Native American Mythology.* Oxford: Oxford University Press.

GLASS-COFFIN, BONNIE
1998 *The Gift of Life: Female Spirituality and Healing in Northern Peru.* Albuquerque: University of New Mexico Press.

GUO, SHUYUN
1995 On the main characteristics of the Manchu shamanic dance. In KIM, TAE-GON – HOPPÁL, MIHÁLY (eds.) *Shamanism in Performing Arts.* Budapest: Akadémiai Kiadó, 57–61.

HOBGIN, IAN
1934 *Law and Order in Polynesia.* London: Christopher's.

HOSKINS, JANET
1990 Doubling deities, descent, and personhood: An exploration of Kodi gender categories. In ATKINSON, JANE – ERRINGTON, SHELLY (eds.) *Power and Difference: Gender in Island Southeast Asia.* Stanford: Stanford University Press, 273–306.

HULTKRANTZ, ÅKE
1967 *The Religions of the American Indians.* Berkeley: University of California Press.
1987 *Native Religions of North America: The Power of Visions and Fertility.* San Francisco: Harper Collins.
1992 *Shamanic Healing and Ritual Drama.* San Francisco: Harper Collins.

HUMPHREY, CAROLINE – ONON, URGUNGE
1996 *Shamans and Elders: Experience, Knowledge and Power Among the Daur Mongols.* Oxford: Clarendon Press.

IRIGARAY, LUCE
1993 *Je, tu, nous: Toward a Culture of Difference.* New York: Routledge.

JOHANSONS, ANDREJS
1972 The shamaness of the Abkhazians. *History of Religions* 11: 3: 251–256.

JORALEMON, DONALD – SHARON, DOUGLAS
1993 *Sorcery and Shamanism: Curanderos and Clients in Northern Peru.* Salt Lake City: University of Utah Press.

KISTER, DANIEL
1999 Modern shamanistic rites and an ancient northeastern China rite. In: *Central Asian Shamanism, Shamanic Cosmology and Shamanism in Transition.*

KROEBER, ALFRED
1925 The Yurok Religion. In KROEBER, ALFRED (ed.) *Handbook of the Indians of California.* Washington D.C.: Bureau of American Ethnology Bulletin (78), 53–75.

LAKE, TELA STAR HAWK
1996 *Hawk Woman Dancing with the Moon.* New York: M. Evans & Company.

LEWIS, IOAN
  1971 *Ecstatic Religion: An Anthropological Study of Spirit Possession and Shamanism.*
         Middlesex, England: Penguin.
  1986 *Religion in Context: Cults and Charisma.* Cambridge: Cambridge University
         Press.
LÓPEZ AUSTIN, ALFRED
  1996 *The Rabbit on the Face of the Moon: Mythology in the Mesoamerican tradition.* Salt
         Lake City: University of Utah Press.
MALOUF, CARLING – HULTKRANTZ, ÅKE
  1974 *The Gosiute Indians. The Shoshone Indians: Commission Findings.* New York:
         Garland.
MANDELBAUM, D. G.
  1979 *The Plains Cree: An Ethnographic, Historical, and Comparative Study.* Regina:
         Canadian Plains Research Center.
MCLEAN, JOHN
  1889 *The Indians of Canada: Their Manners and Customs.* Toronto: William Briggs.
MUNN, HENRY
  1973 The mushrooms of language. In HARNER, MICHAEL (ed.) *Hallucinogens
         and Shamanism.* New York: Oxford University Press, 86–122.
NEBESKY-WOJKOWITZ, RENÉ DE
  1956 *Where the Gods are Mountains: Three Years among the People of the Himalayas.*
         London: Weidenfeld & Nicholson.
NELSON, EDWARD
  1899 *The Eskimo about Bering Strait.* Washington D.C.: Annual Report of the
         Bureau of American Ethnology.
NELSON, ENID
  1995 Gendered possession and communication among the Rejang of
         Sumatra. *Indonesia Circle* 67: 199–215.
NOWAK, MARGARET – DURRANT, STEPHEN
  1977 *The Tale of the Nishan Shamaness: A Manchu Folk Epic.* Seattle: University
         of Washington Press.
POLLOCK, DONALD
  1992 Culina shamanism: Gender, power, and knowledge. In LANGDON, E.
         JEAN – BAER, GERHARD (eds.) *Portals of Power: Shamanism in South
         America.* Albuquerque: University of New Mexico Press, 25–40.
PRINCE, RAYMOND
  1977 Foreword. In CRAPANZANO, VINCENT – GARRISON, VIVIAN (eds.)
         Case Studies in Spirit Possession. New York: John Wiley & Sons, xi–xvi.
RASMUSSEN, KNUD
  1929 *Intellectual Culture of the Iglulik Eskimos.* Copenhagen: Gyldendalske
         Boghandel, Nordisk Forlag.
RIBOLI, DIANA
  1995 Shamanic visual art in Nepal. In KIM, TAE-GON – HOPPÁL, MIHÁLY
         (eds.) *Shamanism in Performing Arts.* Budapest: Akadémiai Kiadó.

ROSCOE, WILL
  1998 *Changing Ones: Third and Fourth Genders in Native North America*. New York: St. Martin's Press.
RUBY, ROBERT – BROWN, JOHN
  1976 *Myron Eells and the Puget Sound Indians*. Seattle: Superior Publishing.
SALADIN D'ANGLURE, BERNARD
  1986 Du foetus au chamane: la construction d'un troisième sexe. *Études Inuit Studies* 10: 25–113.
  1988 Penser le "feminine" chamanique, ou le "tiers-sexe" des chamanes inuit. *Recherches amérindiennes au Québec* 19: 2–3: 19–50.
  1993 The shaman's share, or Inuit sexual communism in the Canadian central arctic. *Anthropologica* 35: 59–103.
SCHAFER, EDWARD
  1973 *The Divine Woman: Dragon Ladies and Rain Maidens in T'ang Literature*. Berkeley: University of California Press.
SCHAEFER, STACY
  1989 Huichol weaving: A preliminary report. In SUSAN BERNSTEIN (ed.) *Mirrors of the Gods*. San Diego: San Diego Museum of Man, 33–39.
SERED, SUSAN
  1994 *Priestess Mother Sacred Sister: Religions Dominated by Women*. New York: Oxford University Press.
SHARON, DOUGLAS
  1978 *Wizard of the Four Winds: A Shaman's Story*. New York: Free Press.
SHI, KUN
  1989 Shamanic practices among the minorities of south-west China. In HOPPÁL, MIHÁLY – VON SADOVSZKY, O. J. (eds.) *Shamanism: Past and Present*. Budapest: Ethnographic Institute of Hungarian Academy of Sciences, 145–153.
SHIROKOGOROFF, SERGEI
  1935 *Psychomental Complex of the Tungus*. London: Kegan Paul.
SOUTHESK, EARL OF
  1875 *Saskatchewan and the Rocky Mountains: A Diary and Narrative of Travel, Sport, and Adventure During a Journey through the Hudson's Bay Company's Territories, in 1859–1960*. Toronto: James Campbell & Son.
STEFANSSON, VILHJALMUR
  1922 *My Life With the Eskimo*. New York: Macmillan.
STEVENSON, MATILDA COXE
  1904 *The Zuñi Indians: Their Mythology, Esoteric Fraternities, and Ceremonies*. Twenty-third Annual Report of the Bureau of American Ethnology for the Years 1901–1902. Washington, D.C.: U.S. Government Printing Office.
THOMPSON, LUCY
  1991 The training and practices of Yurok female spiritual doctors. *Shaman's Drum* 26: 32–35.

TORRANCE, ROBERT
    1994 *The Spiritual Quest: Transcendence in Myth, Religion, and Science.* Berkeley: University of California Press.

VITEBSKY, PIERS
    1995 *The Shaman: Voyages of the Soul, Trance, Ecstasy and Healing from Siberia to the Amazon.* Boston: Little, Brown & Co.

WAIDA, MANABU
    1976 Conceptions of state and kingship in early Japan. *Zeitschrift für Religions- und Geistesgeschichte* 28: 2: 97–112.

WHITTEN, NORMAN
    1976 *Sicuanga Runa: Ethnicity and Adaptation of Ecuadorian Jungle Quichua.* Chicago: University of Illinois Press.

WU, BING-AN
    1989 Shamans in Manchuria. In HOPPÁL, MIHÁLY – VON SADOVSZKY, OTTO (eds.) *Shamanism Past and Present.* Budapest: Ethnographic Institute of Hungarian Academy of Sciences, 263–269.

ZAGOSKIN, LAVRENTIY
    1967 *Lieutenant Zagoskin's Travels in Russian America: The First Ethnographic and Geographic Investigations on the Yukon and Kuskokwim Valley of Alaska.* Toronto: University of Toronto Press.

ZITO, ANGELA – BARLOW, TANI
    1994 *Body, Subject & Power in China.* Chicago: University of Chicago Press.

JOAN B. TOWNSEND

Western Core and Neo-Shamanism: Trends and Relations with Indigenous Societies

In the last thirty years or so there has been a resurgence of interest in shamanism both by indigenous people and westerners. Although shamanism persists in some indigenous societies, in others it is disappearing or lost. Some indigenous people hope to rekindle it and with it a strong sense of ethnic identity and pride. Westerners have become enamored with the idea of shamanism as part of a larger search for new paradigms for belief, existential meaning, and guidance on how to live better, more satisfying lives.

INDIVIDUALIST NEW RELIGIOUS MOVEMENTS

Westerners' search for new paradigms is clearly an *Individualist* New Religious Movement in contrast to *Group* organized movements in which people subordinate themselves to the group's doctrine. Individualist movements are structured as networks. Individuals create their own meaning system by synthesizing a range of beliefs, both traditional, and newly invented.

Individualist Movements *do differ* from earlier movements. In the past, people whose beliefs differed from society's majority developed and maintained them by affiliation with a reference group of local like-minded people. Today such beliefs can be sustained through the plethora of workshops, books and specialty book stores, magazines, and radio and television shows. Face-to-face encounters are not essential; the reference group is maintained and spread through these media. Consequently, Individualist Movements are expanding at an exponential rate that is intensified now by the internet. This fluid network is becoming global. The

Individualist Movements are quintessential media-oriented movements [Townsend 1988, 1997a, 1997b, 1999c, In press].

Examples of Individualist Movements include:

1. "New Age" with its focus on astrology, trance channeling, tarot, and so on.
2. Neopaganism and Witchcraft/Wicca—including feminist Witchcraft, Goddess, and Gaia interests.
3. Modern Shamanic Spirituality: Core and Neo-shamanism—dealt with in this paper

It is a mistake to include Core and Neo-shamanism within Neopaganism or New Age although they may overlap somewhat in personnel and beliefs. To merge these in research seriously obscures what is happening within each of these separate systems (Townsend 1999c).

Modern Shamanic Spirituality: Core and Neo-Shamanism

Because shamanism is experiential and provides direct contact with the spirit world, it is especially popular. People who lack a recent shamanic tradition are trying to go back to an assumed "ancient shamanic tradition" by borrowing elements from a range of shamanic traditions and mythology, and inventing the rest. The result is not a "traditional" shamanism, but reconstructed generic shamanic elements or recent inventions.

The two distinct manifestations of western "shamanic" activity rose from similar bases but have evolved different approaches and goals to both shamanism and spirituality (Townsend 1988, 1999c, In press).

Core Shamanism

Core shamanism was created by Michael Harner (1980) based on his years of anthropological research. He isolated a limited number of core elements which he maintains are shared by shamans universally. He then tailored the resulting collage into a *method* to access spirit reality for contemporary westerners searching for meaning (Harner 1980; Townsend 1988, 1999c, In press). The method is disseminated mainly through workshops led by Harner or a few select people whom he certifies to teach. People then attempt to create a personal shamanic tradition for spiritual purposes that is close in some aspects to parts of living shamanic traditions.

Neo- (or pseudo) Shamanism

Neo-shamanism is an eclectic collection of beliefs and activities drawn from literature, workshops, and the internet. It is an *invented* tradition of practices and beliefs based on a constructed metaphorical, romanticized "ideal" shaman concept which often differs considerably from traditional shamans. Neo-shamanism seems to have a larger following than "pure" Core shamanism.

Both Core and Neo-shamanism are leaderless. Some people who get their introduction to shamanism by taking HARNER's workshops may remain close to his basic teachings and try to develop their abilities to journey into spiritual reality and to heal. Most, I suggest, become involved in a range of other activities and move toward a more generalized Neo-shamanism. So, for many, HARNER's *method* becomes merely one of many elements employed.

People in Neo-shamanism have been influenced by a range of sources such as the very questionable writings of CARLOS CASTANEDA. Others have taken workshops given by a variety of people or have gained their information from media such as books and the internet.

For many, "becoming a shaman" involves merely learning to enter an alternate state of consciousness to journey into spirit reality, and performing some rituals. Many, especially in Neo-shamanism, believe they are shamans and a few may actually become "shamans" in the traditional sense. Nevertheless, I suggest that for most this is merely a wish and an illusion. It is unlikely that most undergo the long apprenticeships, privations, struggles, and dangers that most traditional shamans endure.

There is, then, a continuum within Modern Shamanic Spirituality which runs from the deeply sincere who try to follow a semi-traditional "general"[1] shamanism to those who play with the newest esoteric fad [TOWNSEND In press]. *Traditionalists* adhere to HARNER's core approach or to similar

---

[1] By "general" shamanism, I mean something akin to HARNER's core shamanism. It implies an adherence to beliefs and behaviors generally thought to be traditional shamanic, but is derivative of no specific cultural system in which shamanism occurs.

My working definition of a traditional or "classic" shaman is a person who maintains direct communication with spirits, controls spirits and altered states of consciousness, and takes soul (magical) flights to the spirit world. Spirits may be allowed to enter the shaman's body and speak through him, and he can call spirits to be present at a ceremony. He usually remembers at least some of a soul journey, and normally is a healer. The shaman has a this-material-world focus rather than a goal of personal enlightenment. Shamanism is not "a religion" it is not a homogeneous or static phenomenon (TOWNSEND 1997a, 1999b).

methods gained elsewhere with only minor borrowings from anthropological and other studies.

Modernists use the basic methods and goals of Traditionalist shamanism and elaborate those with input from, for example, curanderos, other healers, and spiritual practitioners who are not, technically, shamans. They use an idealized version of shamanism in their lives and in psychotherapeutic applications. There is less interest in how real (indigenous) traditional shamans function than in how modern western "shamans" use the usually invented "shamanism" in their daily lives.

At the opposite end of the spectrum are *Eclectics* who glorify an idealized shaman concept. These include "wantabes" who attempt to become "Indian" or "native", try to involve themselves in indigenous cultures and rituals, and may make a show of being "a shaman". A person, such as a poet or artist, might even discover he/she is a shaman without being aware of it previously.[2] Beliefs and rituals come from extensive borrowings from a wide range of sources and inventions. They tend to be more involved with the overall New Age and neopagan movements than are Traditionalists or Modernists (cf. STEVENS – STEVENS 1988; SWIFTDEER 1988, n.d.; VILLOLDO et. al. 1991; WADELL 1993). Shamanism becomes mainly a method for personal development rather than a direct intervention with the spirit world to help other people.

Regardless of how "pure" the shamanic genre and the distinctions between Core and Neo-shamanism or individual practitioners, there seems to be a basic set of beliefs that are shared by almost all to a greater or lesser degree.

BELIEFS AND VALUES[3]

The metaphysical position within Shamanic Spirituality is not completely consistent. In spite of beliefs in an interconnectedness of all things, traditional shamanism is dualistic in that humans and deities or spirits are independent entities. Core shamanism seems to agree generally with this position. This contrasts with Neo-shamanic eclecticism which stresses a pantheistic or monistic approach to reality.

---

[2] FLAHERTY (1992: 3–6) lists a number of people who claim or are claimed by others to be shamans or neo-shamans. These include performers MICHAEL JACKSON, SHIRLEY MACLAINE, LIBERACE, performance artist JOSEPH BEUYS, the poet RAINER MARIA RILKE, Dadists, and many others.

[3] TOWNSEND 1998, 1999c, 1999d, In press.

Regardless of the degree of purity of the shamanic genre and the differences between core and neo-shamanism as well as individual practitioners, there is a basic set of beliefs which almost all share to a greater or lesser degree.

Fundamental is a belief that the world is not only material; there is also a "real" or literal spirit world. It can be accessed by living humans using altered states of consciousness and journeying into that reality to enlist the assistance of spirits. This is its essence. Nevertheless, Neo-shamanism does not seem to have fully dealt with the relationship of this to a pantheistic or monistic stance.

Further, the universe is powerful and interrelated. Harmony, unity, and tolerance rather than fragmentation and attitudes of ethnocentric exclusivity are stressed (cf. LYONS 1993). Spirit is in all things: animal, vegetable, and mineral; consequently we must honor and care for the whole environment.

Spirit reality is seen, generally, as good or at least benign. Evil is not considered, in contrast to traditional shamanic world views.

There are clear nativistic, millennial, and apocalyptic sub-themes in Modern Shamanic Spirituality, as in New Age: the glorification of the past, modern decline of spiritual values, and a hoped for revival of past glory (TOWNSEND 1984, 1998). The earth and humans are in grave danger. Corrupt societies pollute the earth. The reason for the impending doom is the loss of transcendent awareness by the west. Connection with the earth and with spirit has been lost, but adherents maintain that it has been retained by shamanic cultures such as Australian Aborigines and Native Americans (PETERS – GRAY 1990). The overarching theme, therefore, is spiritual transformation and the need to rely on the aid of the spirit world to deal with modern crises being faced by individuals, societies, and the earth.

Part of the mission of both Core and Neo-shamanism is to prevent this destruction by enlisting the help of the spirit world. This requires enhanced contact with indigenous peoples who are seen as a source of spiritual information and guidance, a template for the proper way to live in harmony with the earth to save it from destruction. This impacts on the relationship of core and neo-shamanism with indigenous people.

AUTHENTICITY – VALIDITY – VALUE

There is, then, a growing interpenetration of western core and neo-shamanism with native interests. I will explore three examples within the context of:

   a) authenticity—did the activity/belief come from persons, places, and procedures it describes, (DE MILLE 1990).
   b) validity—does the activity/belief correspond to our knowledge of what might be expected, (DE MILLE 1990),—does it agree with what we think we know, (DE MILLE 1980).
   c) the value of the movement to the individuals involved, whether authentic, valid or not. The activity/belief may approximate "practical" or "folk religion" focusing on practical problems and results that produce desired transformations in people's lives rather than on existential and transcendent issues (CARTER 1996; LEATHAM 1996).

"What matters in religious life is not so much what the belief asserts, but the consequences involved for those individuals who are concerned about the beliefs (whether they 'believe' in them fully or not)" (BUCHDAHL 1977: 402, italics original, discussing SMART 1973).

INTENTIONAL DISSEMINATION OF CORE SHAMANISM TO INDIGENOUS PEOPLE TO FACILITATE SHAMANISM PRESERVATION

HARNER's professional anthropological orientation and belief in the value of shamanism led him to establish the nonprofit educational Foundation for Shamanic Studies to sponsor basic and applied research (Foundation for Shamanic Studies n.d.). Because shamanism is disappearing from many traditional societies, some people have asked the Foundation to show them Core methods so they can enhance their own efforts to restore shamanism and healing to their societies (Foundation for Shamanic Studies n.d.; HORWITZ 1992–3; *Newsletter* 1991; *Shamanism* 1994). In response, the Foundation formed the Urgent Tribal Assistance Program.

The Soviets made great efforts to eradicate shamanism but Tyvan shamanism was not totally destroyed. After the Soviet Union breakup, religious control relaxed. Upon learning that a number of Tyvans wanted to restore or develop their shamanism, the Foundation with the Republic of Tyva sponsored a 10 day conference in 1993, to help in the rehabilitation of shamanism (HARNER 1994). Foundation members, researchers, and Tyvan shamans participated. Formal papers were presented, HARNER's method was demonstrated to those who wished it, and healing journeys were undertaken for people in need. The workshops were said to help identify potential shamans and teach a technique to facilitate spirit world contact (BRUNTON 1994). The Foundation's objective was one of support and encouragement for the shamans and to emphasize to them that theirs was a respected system to be maintained. After the conference, Foundation members met with the president of the Tyvan Republic regarding the relative roles of shamanism and Buddhism. Subsequently, he made a public declaration that hereafter both would be equally respected the republic (Shamanism 1994: 2).

Some Native Americans are also taking opportunities to potentially discover, revive, or enhance their shamanism. The Foundation's program has provided partial tuition rebates to individuals in 42 North American native societies so far (Shamanism 1999). LESLIE CONTON (1998) reports that she has had a number of Native Americans from the Pacific Northwest in her workshops. They say that Core shamanism helped them to get in touch with their heritage. Some have begun Core shamanic healing of others.

The introduction of the Core shamanism system to indigenous people is provocative. In some societies, much shamanic knowledge has been lost; few shamans survived. Now, those aspiring to become shamans may face a dilemma: there are so few "old-style" shamans with a broad knowledge of traditions that this generation may not be able to train enough young ones to replace themselves (BRUNTON 1994). Core shamanism may be employed to help compensate for that loss.

Nevertheless, Core shamanism is a distillation of shamanism; it is not, nor was it intended to be, traditional Tyvan, Northwest Coast, or any other society's shamanism. As a result, the kind of shamanism practiced in the future could be a syncretism of Core shamanism method and salvaged bits of indigenous traditions. We may then see an evolution of shamanic traditions which might more clearly resemble the synthesis being disseminated globally.

Within the provisos and parameters set forth overtly by HARNER, I would consider Core shamanism both authentic and valid. Perhaps more important, if it succeeds in helping revive even parts of traditional shamanic systems and enhance ethnic pride, then it is of great value to the people participating.

LESS INTENTIONAL DISSEMINATION OF NEO-SHAMANISM
AND INVENTIONS

Notwithstanding protests of the more politically oriented Native Americans, the Shamanic Spirituality movement is having an influence on Native American people. This is propagated by both natives and non-natives.

One example of an invented tradition taken up by Native Americans and also westerners as a genuine and widespread ancient traditional ritual/belief system is the Medicine Wheel which often has tangential shamanic themes. As far as I can determine, it was invented about the same time, in the late 1960s and early 1970s, by three people. Those people credited with it are: SUN BEAR (VINCENT LA DUKE, of Chippewa and mixed European descent), ELIZABETH EATON who late in life discovered she was "part Indian", and HYEMEYOHSTS STORM, a self-proclaimed Cheyenne and Crow, with some German ancestry. SUN BEAR (SUN BEAR and Wabun 1980; SUN BEAR et.al. 1983) states that his system is not traditional; it came to him in visions. EATON (1978, 1982) said she learned the system from a Paiute "Medicine Man". STORM's book, *Seven Arrows,* (1972) supposedly describes the ancient traditional religion of Cheyenne, Sioux and Crow. Nevertheless, the Northern Cheyenne Tribal Council condemned it. One Council member described it as "complete B.S. from cover to cover" (MOORE 1973).

Following the 1970s invention, many versions of the "Medicine Wheel" have emerged and a growing collection of popular books are published on the subject. Today, the Medicine Wheel, particularly for Neo-shamanism, is a mixture of miscellaneous Native American symbols as well as astrology, ersatz "shamanism", New Age, Christianity, Buddhism, Hinduism, and other elements (e.g., MEADOWS 1992, 1996).

It is also becoming a major ritual and teaching symbol within a growing number of Native American groups. For Native Americans it is sometimes seen as "Native spirituality for indigenous people all over the Americas and the world" and designed to instill "traditional values" in order to transform native societies and help heal the planet (BOPP et.al. 1984: back cover). It is often a valuable tool in alcohol and drug rehabilitation. Generally it emphasizes positive beliefs, behaviors, and values and contributes to ethnic pride.

In my opinion, both the authenticity and validity of the Medicine Wheel system in terms of traditional indigenous spirituality, is extremely questionable. Nevertheless, for native people its value as part of an evolving folk or "practical" religion shows great potential to have a positive and transformative effect on lives.

INTERACTIONS BETWEEN CORE/NEO-SHAMANS AND INDIGENOUS PEOPLES

Because many Neo-shamans glorify indigenous people as pure "noble savages", many feel they should live and practice the illusionary native spiritual life. This creates major conflicts. Indigenous "Exclusivists" maintain that their rituals, beliefs, and even shamanism *per se* are exclusively "their" property and intensely object to the "white man" "stealing" their cultural and spiritual property. In contrast, some indigenous and non-indigenous "Universalists" argue that shamanism and spirituality in general are the heritage of all humans. Consequently, some indigenous and pseudo-indigenous "medicine men", spiritual leaders, and "shamans" conduct workshops and pilgrimages, "initiate" all who wish into shamanism, and teach what I suggest is often totally invented traditions.

At its simplest, people interested in "Natives" and North American "Indians" sometimes invade native areas. For example, BRANT SEGUNDA made the Huichol shaman Don JOSÉ MATSUA famous. Subsequently, various people set up package tours to the Huichol's Sierra Madre[4] homeland so that outsiders could participate in the annual peyote hunt that is central to Huichol religion. Although poverty-stricken Huichol profit by the influx of tourism, it is also disruptive to their society (BROWN 1997: 162; see tour ads: *Shaman's Drum* 1986: 10, 13–14; 1987: 67).

INDIGENOUS PEOPLE PENETRATING INTO NEO-SHAMANISM: PSEUDO-SHAMANS TEACHING WESTERNERS

The themes of noble savage and romanticization of indigenous peoples are further exemplified by the growing neo-shamanic interest in indigenous South, Central, and North American cultures. Much of the neo-shamanic literature, including the primary journal *Shaman's Drum*, focuses on these groups.

---

[4] The Huichol, who numbered about 10,000 in the 1970s, live in five communities in the Mexican states of Jalisco, Nayarit, Zacatecas, and Durango in the remote regions of the Sierra Madre Occidental mountains (MYERHOFF 1970).

Interest in South American "shamanism" began to grow with ALBERTO VILLOLDO, a humanistic psychologist, and EDUARDO CALDERON, a Peruvian curandero. They took seekers on pilgrimages to the Nasca desert drawings and Andean Inca ruins and initiated them into "shamanism". Rituals included meditation while sitting on the Nasca drawings, walking naked in a spiral drawn on the ground, and jumping into an Andean lake (VILLOLDO 1984). Today, advertisements in *Shaman's Drum* are proliferating for Amazonian and Andean pilgrimages/workshops/tours led by people claiming to be "master shamans".

The Amazonian/Andean pilgrimages heavily stress hallucinogens, especially ayahuasca (yajé), for spiritual development, and more important, self healing. One writer recounts how he confronted "a lifetime's accumulation of emotional blocks and wounds" (WEISKOPH 1995). Another described her search to "understand and unbind the psycho-spiritual roots of an epileptic disorder" she had since childhood. After trying amanita muscaria mushrooms, she went to Central America, Colombia and then to Quito, Ecuador where she met a supposed Latino shaman, CELSO FIALLO, whom Ecuadorian shamans repudiate (ALULEMA 1996: 13). Mixing cannabis, San Pedro cactus (mescaline-containing Trichocereus pachanoi), and ayahuasca (Banisteriopsis Caapi "visionary" vine) (cf. FURST 1976) she was "cured" and now brings curanderos from South America to teach traditional use of plant hallucinogens to the larger community presumably in Santa Fe New Mexico where she lives (RUMLAND 1994). Whether the focus on hallucinogens will bring neo-shamans into direct conflict with the narcotics laws remains to be seen.[5]

The sudden popularity of ayahuasca and other hallucinogens, and the growing number of Amazonian tours, caused the editor of *Shaman's Drum* (WHITE 1996) to warn of potentially serious dangers of these drugs especially in the hands of uninformed counterfeit shamans. WILLIAMS (1998) warns of other dangers to Amazonian pilgrims such as extreme humid heat, parasites, malaria and dengue fever, fungal rashes, insect bites, and violence from bandits and narcotics traffickers.

In apparent response to the burst of tours and pseudo-shamans leading pilgrimages, some Ecuadorian and Colombian practitioners are creating organizations to counteract this trend in the exploitation of their beliefs (ALULEMA 1996; Yurayaco Declaration 1999). Siberian Buryat shamans of Ulan-Ude also created a professional organization to set themselves apart from a range of pseudo-shamans and healers (HUMPHREY 1999).

---

[5] See Yurayaco Declaration 1999 for indications of governmental repression of native ayahuasca use.

In my opinion, most adventures led by questionable "shamanic authorities" lack authenticity or validity as presented even though they may use fragments of various traditional shamanic systems. They might provide some positive results in addressing immediate practical problems of participants, but I fear there is little ultimate value in terms of long-lasting transformations in people's lives.

TRENDS, VALUE AND MEANING FOR CORE AND NEO-SHAMAN PEOPLE

The recent interest in "European" shamanism has spawned Celtic, Norse, Teutonic, and Slavic movements with much invention. These can be seen partly as a search for a unique western spiritual "ethnic identity" and partly as a response to attacks by some indigenous people that the "white man" is "stealing" their beliefs. It is here particularly that we see a tendency to merge with the larger neopagan movement (e.g., WESTWIND 1996).

We need to distinguish the *value* of core/neo-shamanism to westerners who are searching and participating in it from the implications of their contact with indigenous peoples and from our academic concern with the purity of the item being transmitted (its validity and authenticity). I have few qualms about teaching various techniques, be they yoga, Spiritualism mediumship, therapeutic touch, core/neo-shamanism, or other systems to people so long as the teacher is honest and people are informed about what he/she is teaching rather than maintaining something is valid and authentic when it is partly or wholly invented.

My research (TOWNSEND 1988, In press) has indicated that the effect on people participating in the movement is, overall, positive. It gives people meaning, purpose, and a greater sense of significance to their lives. The value conforms to practical or folk religion. Focus is on not only existential and transcendent issues, but also on practical problems and this appears to produce desired transformations in people's lives.

CONCLUSIONS

Modern Shamanic Spirituality, especially Core shamanism, sometimes feeds back to people who requesting it and are trying to regain their vanishing shamanic traditions. The result may be a reconfigured shamanism, but presumably approximate the traditional shamanism of earlier years. Reconfigured and invented traditions can also move from the western and native "Universalists" inventors into indigenous societies where they may be used for political as well as spiritual purposes.

Cultures do change and, of course, shamanism of indigenous peoples also changes. The shamanism of the 21st century will differ from that of the 18th and 19th. What might result over time, as noted above, for a society is a reconfiguration that has the remnants of its specific traditions, but incorporates parts of the invented traditions. There is a risk, however, that "new shamanism" may be taken to be *identical* with the traditional shamanic system. This is occurring, for example, with the Native American reconfiguration in use and meaning of the traditional sweat lodge as well as the invention of the medicine wheel. These are being put forth as traditions with great time depth.

A problem exists not only for indigenous people but also for researchers when natives and westerners believe that new inventions do reflect valid, ancient traditions, and they become imbedded in the cultures. Then we risk fallacies becoming "Truth" for future generations and distorting or obscuring the real historic traditions.

Authenticity and validity are important for sacred traditions. A laxity of rigor in these elements may be overlooked if the invented traditions have a positive affect in people's lives. After all, all traditions ultimately are invented. We may be moving, then, into a situation where value, rather than authenticity and validity, is the touchtone; where a practical/folk religion focusing on results leading to desired transformations in people's lives is paramount rather than ultimate metaphysical concerns.

I have several suggestions for future work in shamanism.

First, we must clarify and agree upon a clear-cut definition of shamanism. Otherwise, we will include every spiritual activity from traditional shamanism through various spiritual practitioners and healers to the Christian faith healers, evangelists, and the Charismatic Christianity movement that is rapidly spreading globally now (TOWNSEND 1997a, 1999a).

Second, we need ethnohistoric and comparative studies as well as ethnographic research:

1. to help preserve at least the memory of the "real" shamanic traditions in the face of contamination of some systems by input from neo-shamanic, media, and other influences.
2. to better delineate the evolution of shamanism in specific societies under various influences including:
   – prehistoric and historic sedentarization from the invention of herding and cultivation to the present,

— more recent political attacks and influences by universalist religions (Christian, Buddhist, Moslem, etc.)
— industrialization,
— influences of western medicine,
— modern technology including such forces as more travel by shamans and indigenous peoples, tourism or travel by westerners to indigenous peoples, internet in particular societies, and so on.

With regard to the Core and Neo-shaman movements, we need to not only delineate their impact on indigenous peoples, but also their impact on western society and their value in providing the searched-for meaning and transcendence which is the raison d' être for their quest.

ACKNOWLEDGEMENTS

I wish to sincerely thank the Faculty of Arts Endowment Fund, the Faculty of Arts Dean's Office Funding, and the Department of Anthropology for their support in making my participation here possible.

REFERENCES

ALULEMA, JOSÉ
    1996   Rymland's sources challenged. *Shaman's Drum* #41. Spring: 13.
BOPP, JULIE – BOPP, MICHAEL – BROWN, LEE – LANE, PHIL
    1984   *The Sacred Tree: Reflections on Native American Spirituality.* (Four Worlds Development Project) Lethbridge, Alberta: University of Lethbridge.
BROWN, MICHAEL F.
    1997   *The Channeling Zone: American Spirituality in an Anxious Age.* Cambridge: Harvard University Press.
BRUNTON, BILL
    1994   Tyva: land of eagles. *Shamanism* 7: 1: 3–20.
BUCHDAHL, DAVID A.
    1977   The science of religion (and the religion of science). *American Anthropologist* 79: 397–413.
CARTER, LEWIS F.
    1996   Introduction to the issue of authenticity. In LEWIS F. CARTER (ed.) *The Issue of Authenticity in the Study of Religions.* Volume 6: *Religion and the Social Order.* [Series editor: DAVID G. BROMLEY]. Greenwich, CT: JAI Press Inc., ix-xvi.

CONTON, LESLIE
  1998 *Neo-shamanism, Core shamanism, or shamanism? Reflections on contemporary shamanic practices in the Pacific Northwest.* (Paper presented at Conference on Shamanism in Contemporary Society, Univ. of Newcastle-Upon-Tyne, England)
DE MILLE, RICHARD
  1990 Validity is not authenticity: distinguishing two components of truth. In JAMES A. CLIFTON (ed.) *The Invented Indian: Cultural Fictions and Government Policies.* New Brunswick, New Jersey: Transaction Publishers, 227–253.
DE MILLE, RICHARD (ed.)
  1980 *The Don Juan Papers: Further CASTANEDA Controversies.* Santa Barbara, CA: Ross-Erikson Publishers.
EATON, EVELYN
  1978 *I Send A Voice.* Wheaton, IL: Quest Book. (Theosophical Publishing House)
  1982 *The Shaman and the Medicine Wheel.* Wheaton, IL: Quest Book (Theosophical Publishing House)
Foundation for Shamanic Studies
  n.d. *Brochure.* Norwalk, CT: Foundation for Shamanic Studies.
FLAHERTY, GLORIA
  1992 *Shamanism and the Eighteenth Century.* Princeton: Princeton University Press.
FURST, PETER T.
  1976 *Hallucinogens and Culture.* San Francisco: Chandler and Sharp Publishers.
HARNER, MICHAEL
  1980 *The Way of the Shaman.* New York: Harper and Row
  1994 The Foundation's expedition to Tyva. *Shamanism.* Spring. 7: 1: 1–2.
HORWITZ, JONATHAN
  1992–1993 Reawakening Shamanism in Sami (Russian Samiland). *Shamanism.* Winter. 5: 3: 1–5. Norwalk, CT: Foundation for Shamanic Studies.
HUMPHREY, CAROLINE
  1999 Shamans in the city. *Anthropology Today* 15: 3: 3–10.
LEATHAM, MIGUEL C.
  1996 Practical religion and peasant recruitment to non-Catholic groups in Latin America. In LEWIS F. CARTER (ed.) *The Issue of Authenticity in the Study of Religions.* Volume 6: *Religion and the Social Order.* [Series editor: DAVID G. BROMLEY]. Greenwich, CT: JAI Press Inc., 175–190.
LYONS, DAVID
  1993 A Bit of Circus: Notes on Postmodernity and New Age. *Religion* 23: 117–126.
MEADOWS, KENNETH
  1992 *The Medicine Way: A Shamanic Path to Self-Mastery.* Shaftesbury, Dorset: Element Books.

1996 *Earth Medicine: Revealing Hidden Teachings of the Native American Medicine Wheel.* Shaftesbury, Dorset: Element Books.

MOORE, JOHN H.
1973 Review of *Seven Arrows* by Hyemeyohsts Storm. *American Anthropologist* 75: 4: 1040–1043.

MYERHOFF, BARBARA G.
1970 The Deer-Maize-Peyote symbol complex among the Huichol Indians of Mexico. *Anthropology Quarterly* 43: 64–68.

Newsletter (Foundation for Shamanic Studies)
1991 Newsletter. Foundation for Shamanic Studies 4: 1. Norwalk, CT: Foundation for Shamanic Studies.

PETERS, LARRY – GRAY, LESLIE
1990 Using Shamanism for Personal Empowerment: An Interview with Leslie Gray. *ReVision: The Journal of Consciousness and Change* 13: 2: 67–70.

RUMLAND, LIZBETH
1994 Ecstasy in Ecuador: experiences with curanderos and plant teachers. *Shaman's Drum.* #34, Spring: 38–51.

Shamanism
1994 Comment, papers. Mill Valley CA: Foundation for Shamanic Studies. 7: 1: 2–22.
1999 FSS Native American Tuition Scholarships Continue. *Shamanism* 12: 1: 26.

Shaman's Drum
1985 *Shaman's Drum: A Journal of Experiential Shamanism.* Williams, OR: Cross-Cultural Shamanism Network.
1986 *Shaman's Drum: A Journal of Experiential Shamanism and Spiritual Healing.* Cross-Cultural Shamanism Network. Williams, Oregon. #6: 10–14.
1987 *Shaman's Drum: A Journal of Experiential Shamanism and Spiritual Healing.* Cross-Cultural Shamanism Network. Williams, Oregon. #10: 67.

SMART, NINIAN
1973 *The Science of Religion and the Sociology of Knowledge.* Princeton: Princeton University Press.

STEVENS, JOSE – STEVENS, LENA S.
1988 *Secrets of Shamanism: Tapping the Spirit Power within You.* New York: Avon Books.

STORM, HYEMEYOHSTS
1972 *Seven Arrows.* New York: Ballantine.

SUN BEAR – WABUN
1980 *The Medicine Wheel: Earth Astrology.* New York: Prentice Hall Press.

SUN BEAR – WABUN – WEINSTOCK, BARRY
1983 *SUN BEAR: The Path of Power.* Spokane, Washington: Bear Tribe Publishing.

SWIFTDEER, HARLEY
1988 Advertisement for Jamaican workshop.

n.d.   typescript manual for Quodoushka, Spiritual Sexuality of the Ancient Cherokee. no publisher.

TOWNSEND, JOAN B.

1984   Anthropological Perspectives on New Religious Movements. In BETTIS, J. – JOHANNESEN, S. K. (eds.) *The Return of the Millennium*. Barrytown, N.Y: New ERA Books, 137–151.

1988   Neo-shamanism and the modern mystical movement. In GARY DOORE (ed.) *Shaman's Path: Healing, Personal Growth and Empowerment*. Boston: Shambhala Publications, 73–83.

1997a   Shamanism. In STEPHEN GLAZIER (ed.) *Anthropology of Religion: A Handbook*. Westport, Ct: Greenwood, 428–469.

1997b   *Globalization of Core and Neo-shamanism*. (Paper presented at the Society for the Scientific Study of Religion conference. San Diego, California. November)

1998   *Neo-shamanism: comments on distinctions, beliefs, issues and trends*. (Society for the Scientific Study of Religion conference. Session: religion and the Radical Right. November 1998. Montreal, Canada)

1999a   Theoretical issues in the study of shamanism. [Plenary Address] Proceedings of the International Congress: Shamanism and Other Indigenous Spiritual Beliefs and Practices. Moscow: Institute of Ethnology and Anthropology of the Russian Academy of Sciences. Vol. 5, pt. 1: 32–39.

1999b   A working definition of shamanism. Proceedings of the International Congress: Shamanism and Other Indigenous Spiritual Beliefs and Practices. Moscow: Institute of Ethnology and Anthropology of the Russian Academy of Sciences. Vol. 5, pt. 1: 177.

1999c   Western contemporary core and neo-shamanism and the interpenetration with indigenous societies. Proceedings of the International Congress: Shamanism and Other Indigenous Spiritual Beliefs and Practices. Moscow: Institute of Ethnology and Anthropology of the Russian Academy of Sciences. Vol. 5, pt. 2: 223–231.

1999d   Modern non-traditional and invented shamanism. (Paper presented at the International Symposium: Shamanism: Epics and Ecology. Tampere, Finland, January 14–16.)

In press Shamanic Spirituality: Core and Neo-shamanism in contemporary Western society. In STEPHEN GLAZIER (ed.) *Anthropology of Religion: A Handbook*. Part 2. Selected Readings. Westport, CT: Greenwood.

VILLOLDO, ALBERTO

1984   The Shaman's Journey with Alberto Villoldo, Ph.D. and Don Eduardo Calderon. (Videotape) Alhotsky Film Productions. Vienna. Director: Georg Lhotsky; executive Producer: Eva Maria Stelljes.

VILLOLDO, ALBERTO – LANGEVIN, MICHAEL PETER – DAAB, RICHARD (interviewers)
   1991   A Journey into Shamanism with Alberto Villoldo. *Magical Blend*. Issue 32: 40–46, 94–95.
WADELL, STEPHANIE
   1993   Empowerment of Spirituality through Sexuality: Introduction to Quodoushka. Part 1. *Tantra: The Magazine*. Sekhmet Issue 6: 33–34.
WEISKOPH, JIMMY
   1995   From Agony to Ecstasy: The Transformative Spirit of Yaje. *Shaman's Drum* #39. Fall: 41–47.
WESTWIND, SUE
   1996   Euro-Based Shamanism is a Solution. Letters. *Shaman's Drum* #40. Winter: 11–12.
WHITE, TIMOTHY
   1996   Not All Ayahuasca Brews are Benign. *Shaman's Drum* #41. Spring: 4: 6–7.
WILLIAMS, JAMES E.
   1998   Dangers of Selva Profunda Appreciated. *Shaman's Drum* #50. Winter: 12.
Yurayaco Declaration
   1999   Yurayaco Declaration of the Union de Medicos Indigenas Yageceros de la Amazonia Colombiana. http://www.shamanicdimensions.net/ethnosha/yurayaco.html.

DANIÈLE VAZEILLES

Revival of Lakota Sioux Shamanism

On the Sioux Reservations today, the "holy men" (*wicasa wakan*) are still the depositories of the sacred knowledge of the Spirit "Grandfathers" (*tunkashila*) and the mediums of communication between "common people" (*ikce wicasa*) and "sacred" (*wakan*) Beings. Initiation rites for medicine men and shamans as well as healing ceremonies can still be compared with those of the past. A comparative study shows the dynamics of the Lakota Sioux religion.

This paper summarizes some contemporary aspects of Lakota Sioux shamanism. It is based on a personal knowledge of the Lakota Sioux Reservations in South Dakota, USA through several long periods of fieldwork between 1969 and 1986 and shorter periods between 1990 and 1998. It makes use of specialized literature, especially the biographies of Lakota Sioux Holy Men. To inquire about such a subject has been quite hard, a lot of people do not want to talk about it—"too dangerous", they say—, some people will finally agree to speak but one should not tell their names, and most well known holy men answered my questions with "yes and no" because they were under contracts with writers and publishers.

VISION QUEST

The "holy men" (*wicasa wakan*) conduct the initiation rites for the visionaries, medicine men and holy men. Today, most holy men have undergone voluntary vision questing. This was the case for John Fire Lame Deer / Tahca Ushte, a Minnecojou Sioux holy man who went on his vision seeking quest while still a teenager (LAME DEER – ERDOES 1972).[1] Others, like Black Elk / Hehaka Sapa, the Oglala Sioux holy man and prophet (see NEIHARDT 1961), were first contacted by the Spirits at an early age. Signs

---

[1] Lame Deer was one of those who answered "yes and no".

of elections by the Spirits still exist, but at the same time, "powers" may also be inherited from a deceased relative, a former well-known shaman.

In order to obtain a vision, the candidate must accomplish the voluntary quest—*hanbelachia* "crying out for a vision"—, an ascetic retreat lasting from one to four nights and days on a high place often known to be favored by the Spirits. One such place, well known to the Sioux and others Plains Indians, is Bear Butte, in the western part of South Dakota. On this high place, the candidate seeking a vision has to pray and walk in a ceremonial way within a sacred area oriented toward the Four Corners of the Universe. Sometimes, the candidate can rest in a grave-like narrow shelter covered by a buffalo robe, if available, or a quilt blanket often decorated with the Morning Star design.[2]

SWEATLODGE

Another way to acquire help from the supernatural beings is by "doing a sweatlodge" (*inipi*) "the breathing of the universe". Twelve or sixteen white willow trees, depending on the medicine man's inspiration, form the skeleton of the somewhat beehive-shaped sweatlodges, twelve for the twelve "moons" (*wi*, "moon", "month") of the year, or sixteen for the sixteen avatars of Wakan Tanka, the Great Spirit. These conical lodges are covered nowadays with tarps, blankets or quilts. Special stones, often ones "with designs inside", are used. They are to be the messengers of the powerful spirit Grandfathers – *Tunkashila*. It must be mentioned that sweatlodges can also be done by any individual, Reservation or city Indian, who wants to purify himself and clarify his thoughts in order to be able to solve some of his personal or family problems.[3]

HEALING CEREMONIES

Healing rites are conducted by medicine men and shamans. Nowadays, it seems there are no more *wapiya* men.[4] They were healers who cured by placing their mouth directly on the patient's skin or by using a straw or a bone and then blowing or sucking out of the body the disease object that a

---

[2] Cf. VAZEILLES 1974: 450–451, 1984: 190–200, 329–348, 1985, 1986b, 1989, 1990c, d, 1991a, 1996: 125–132, 1999.
[3] Sweatlodge or inipi cf. VAZEILLES 1984: 181–190, 1986a, b, 1990c, 1991a, 1996: 117–124.
[4] Wapiya cf. VAZEILLES 1984: 103–112, 1996: 52–60.

Spirit or evil-minded person had transmitted there. Some people spoke of a technique (*wicahimunga*) consisting of "throwing some objects", feathers or stones, on the sick person's body or on a piece of cloth. Lame Deer said this technique could also be used for black magic (LAME DEER – ERDOES 1972).

Yuwipi Meetings

Today, most medicine men heal by means of sacred stones (*yuwipi*). These often transparent stones, usually found on ant hills, are used in *yuwipi* meetings or "Spirit meetings" during which a "*yuwipi* man" is tied up and then released with the help of the Spirits. The *yuwipi* stones are also called *yuwipi wasicun*. This last expression also designates one of the Powers – *Tunkan*, also called *Inyan*, "the "Rock", one of the sixteen avatars of the Great Spirit. It means that these stones, in the hands of those who have had dreams and visions, are endowed with supernatural powers.

A *yuwipi* meeting is held at night, nowadays in a log cabin or a regular house. Light pieces of furniture are put away. All shining surfaces are covered. A sacred area often spread with wild sage (*Artemisia gnaphalodes*) is delimited by pots filled up with earth and carrying flags of the four sacred colors, that of the Four Corners of the Universe, black, red, yellow and white, "for the four human races" as contemporary Lakotas explain. Strings of tobacco knots are offered to the spirit Grandfathers. Sometimes they also show the four colors. These strings often encircle the sacred area.[5]

The *yuwipi* man is bound fast hand and foot, and wrapped in a star quilt (*wicahpi sina*). He is often laid down on the middle of the sacred area. *Yuwipi* songs are sung. Sparks can be seen when the Spirits are coming, strange animal sounds are heard. Gourd rattles, containing sacred stones, are used to call the Spirits and to frighten away the evil ones. Several specialists (HULTKRANTZ 1980; JILEK 1982, etc.) have already noted that this kind of ritual, known elsewhere as the shaking tent, the conjuring lodge or the spirit lodge, is undergoing a remarkable revival. In our thirty years of going back and forth from France to South Dakota, we have witnessed this growing development, of the *yuwipi* meetings and the sweatlodges, on the Sioux Reservations and on some South Dakota University campuses.

---

[5] These tobacco knots can be of several numbers, according to the medicine man's inspiration; but I was told they can be no more than 400 or 405. In the past, the *tiyospahe*, the kinship group, was supposed to be of about 400 relatives. 405 is also the number of Frank Fools Crow's Spirit Helpers (cf. MAILS 1979).

Yuwipi rites are practiced for healing purpose and to obtain some protection for the persons asking for help. They can also be séances of clairvoyance. The *yuwipi* men are often able to see where runaway children have gone or locate the young girl who has eloped with an older man.

If the case is urgent, by day or night, depending of the condition of the sick person, some *yuwipi* men cover themselves with some pieces of dark cloth before beginning a short ceremony. This technique seems to help the holy man to get into the concentrated and exalted state of consciousness that enables him to "see".[6]

DREAMERS

In the past, all Sioux were "dreamers" – *ihanblapi kin*, that is visionaries.[7] By this, I mean they experienced at least once in their lives a light "altered state of consciousness" during which they met animal Spirits that gave them certain powers (clairvoyance, ability to make charms, arms, etc.). It seemed that the kind of animal they met during the spiritual encounter indicated what kind of *wakan* persons they were to be. Accordingly, they joined the association or society linked to the animal seen in the dream or vision. For example, the ones who dreamed about an elk joined the *Hehaka ihanblapi kin*, "those who had dreams of the elk", the Elk dreamers' Society. The wolf dreamers became members of the *Akicita okalakiciye*, that is police societies and military societies. Bear dreamers were medicine men because they had gotten great knowledge about herbal medicines from their supernatural protector, *Hunonpa Wakan*, the *Wakan* Bear, the Spirit Bear.[8] Bear medicine were also *wapiya* specialists.

Deer Woman's Dreamers

Today, such dreamer associations or "cults", as WISSLER (1912) called them, no longer exist. But some Sioux still meet Deer Woman, a beautiful woman who can turn into a deer. This Spirit is no other than Anog Ite, "Double Face", an entity who plays an important part in Sioux myths and

---

[6] Cf. VAZEILLES 1982, 1984: 117–160, 1985, 1986b, 1990c, 1996: 61–104, 1999; see also POWERS 1982.
[7] Cf. WISSLER 1912; VAZEILLES 1984: 1–432, 691–714, 1985, 1986a, b, 1990a, b, c, 1991a, b, 1996, 1997, 1998.
[8] Note that *hunonpa* also designates the two legged beings, both human and non human, cf. VAZEILLES 1984: 442–443.

legends. She was said to be the wife of Tate, the Wind, and the mother of the Four Winds. Now, however, very few Lakota people know this.

A Sioux woman who has met this Deer Woman[9] can either become an excellent manual worker, making traditional objects (beadwork, quill work, and quilts) or become a runaway teenager or a prostitute. Men who dream of, or meet Deer Woman while hunting, driving their car, or dancing at an Indian Celebration, will go out of their minds and run wild, be killed by being tramped down by deer hooves, or become *winkte*, "women-to-be", that is berdaches.[10]

Berdaches

It seems some *winkte* were truly homosexuals while others were men who dressed and behaved as women on special occasion. The *winkte* have always represented both male and female potencies. Some of the contemporary Sioux transvestites still seem to be recognized as *winkte*. I have known several young Sioux *winkte* who were asked to give surnames to some children, to ensure them good health.[11]

Dreams about Dead Persons

On Sioux Reservations today, one hears stories about people meeting dead relatives or dead friends. For example, it is said that an old woman, *Unci*, "Grandmother",[12] comes back from the Dead to bring food or beverage to a living relative. The latter must accept what is offered and by doing so, condemns him or herself to die within a year or so. Other dead relatives come back to offer help, to prevent wrong doings or to announce some danger to their living relatives or friends.

Some young and older Sioux have told me that, at times, they have some clairvoyant powers which enable them to know in advance the coming illness or death of relatives or friends. Some told me this knowledge comes

---

[9] Deer Woman cf. VAZEILLES 1974: 452–456, 1984: 277–285, 1986b, 1996: 192–200.

[10] Berdache, cf. VAZEILLES 1984: 272–277, 1986b, 1990a, b; 1991a, 1992b, 1996: 187–193, 1998, 1999.

[11] I have met and talked with several Sioux transvestites who migrated from the Sioux Reservations to Minneapolis and San Francisco. Only one of them is still alive.

[12] *Unci*, a kinship term to designate one's grandmothers but also any old lady when you want to show them friendship and respect.

with the help of a "black bird" flying around their house, even knocking at their door and windows.[13]

U.F.O.'s seers

On the Cheyenne River and Pine Ridge Reservations, I met people during my two first years of fieldwork, 1969–1971, who said they have seen U.F.O.'s above the South Dakota grassland. On the Cheyenne River Reservation, some students once saw on oblong object, "a flying saucer" they said, alight on the prairie somewhere between Faith and Dupree... Two old men told me that one evening they saw "little human-like creatures three feet tall enter into a round shining UFO which disappeared as suddenly as it had appeared..."[14]

Let us remember that, in the past, tiny creatures were connected to dreams and visions related to the Spirits of the West, especially Thunderbirds – *Wakinyan*, "winged one". People told me I could see them on the tops of South Dakota's buttes, shivering during the summer heats.[15]

Thus one can still find clairvoyants, seers, healers and visionaries among contemporary Sioux, but only those recognized as holy men can be truly considered as shamans.

SHAMANS

As far as we understand, through our discussions with Sioux specialists and after having closely studied the biographical details and the visionary experiences of Sioux medicine men recorded by anthropologists and specialists of the Plains tribes, a Sioux "holy man" is a shaman. This means he is a man who can converse with the Spirits, whose soul can depart from his body in a trance or who can summon his supernatural helpers in order to solve problems bothering members of his society and heal sick people. A medicine man is a visionary who has had light trances and has acquired some clairvoyance and powers. We see another difference between those two specialists. The holy man is a person who has had a "great vision" – *wakanyan wowanyanka*. We could say only medicine men who had such a

---

[13] Cf. VAZEILLES 1974: 441–450, 1977: 167–177, 1996: 184–186.

[14] UFO's & Sioux, cf. VAZEILLES 1977: 441–442, 1996: 184.

[15] Cf. VAZEILLES 1984: chap. VI; 1986a, 1996: chap. 4: 142. Those creatures are often contrary beings, connected with *heyoka* or ritual clowns, trickster entities.

"great vision" were truly shamans. As for nowadays shamans, we cannot be so sure as we had little confidence on such topics.

Great Visions

In this type of vision, at first anthropomorphic and/or theriomorphic spirits come to take the visionary "up there" to the "Spirit World" – *Wanagi Tamakoce*. There the shaman-to-be meets or hears the Grandfathers *Tunkashila*, the most powerful avatars of Wakan Tanka, the Powers of the Four Quarters of the Universe (the Four Winds), Grandmother Earth and Grandfather Sky. The Grandfathers consult with the shaman-to-be and give a demonstration of the powers they are going to bestow upon him. These powerful Spirits then designate the animals and plants which will be the supernatural helpers of the shaman. The visionary is then made to see the future, the past and the present of his own life and that of the Indian people. He also sees what his functions are to be and what help he will be able to give to his people. The Grandfathers bestow some of their powers on the shaman-to-be before he is carried back home, usually by the messengers who came to get him.[16]

Dreams

In contrast to great visions, the dreams and visions of common medicine men and of the dreamers (*ihanblapi*) of the past such a scenario cannot be recognized. The encounter with the Spirits is less elaborated. It happens on earth, not "up there". It seems only animal-like Spirits, which nevertheless take a human appearance at times, appear to such visionaries. Also, the message and the powers received are more specialized, restricted, and personal, and, consequently are less important for the welfare of the people.[17]

---

16 VAZEILLES 1984, 1985, 1986b, 1996: chap. 1, 2, 3 & conclusion, 1997, 1998.
17 Dreams, *ihanblapi*, cf. VAZEILLES 1984: chap. 5–6, 1986b, 1990b, 1991b, 1996: chap. 5, 1997, 1998.

Functions of the Shamans

Contemporary Sioux holy men still conduct the most important rites, including Spirit Keeping Release and Sundancing. Some of them are involved in ritualistic wars against juvenile delinquency and alcoholism. A well documented example of this is provided by the biography of the Lakota Sioux Ceremonial Chief Frank Fools Crow (Mails 1979). These modern shamans are trying to fight for the welfare of their people not only at an individual level, nor at the *tiyospahe* (community) level or even at the reservation level, but for the welfare of all Indian People and Nations. Fools Crow and a few others even say they are willing to help people of all "races" who are trying to follow the "Ways of the Grandfathers", the "Red Road" as the Oglala holy man Black Elk would say.[18]

Shamans and Tribal Elections

Because of this, some holy men play an important part in tribal elections. ROBERT BURNETTE, ex-tribal Chairman of the Rosebud Reservation, wrote about his own experience. He tells how in January 1954 an old Indian woman told him he was going to win the next elections on his reservation. The same year in June, he had a dream, repeated three times the same night, about a "bluish tiny man". Later this same month, Frank Picket Pin, a well-known Rosebud Sioux holy man, approached him about the dream. In his book, *The Tortured Americans* (1971), R. BURNETTE describes a *yuwipi* meeting conducted by F. PICKET PIN in December 1955 during which the people present prayed "the Holy Spirit" for the reelection of R. BURNETTE as their tribal leader.

The Sioux are rather discreet about the part played by medicine men in tribal elections. Nonetheless, *yuwipi* meetings are held to secure the Spirits' help for candidates in coming elections. I was even told that "tiny human-like creatures are sent against" the candidates who are not welcome. During such a *yuwipi* ceremony, the *yuwipi* man may give candidates a *wasicun tunkan*, that is a sort of protective guardian stone, which they are to wear suspended from their neck in a small leather case.[19]

Such protective stones or other tiny objects are often given to people participating in special *yuwipi* meeting. Some of the *sicunpi* (powers, guardian spirit) of the *yuwipi* man has somehow been imparted to these stones and

---

[18] Cf. VAZEILLES 1974: 457–482, 1984, 1991a, 1996, 1998, 1999.
[19] Cf. VAZEILLES 1984: 127–130, 1996: 311–312.

they are considered somewhat as supports for the *sicun*, that is the guardian spirit, the supernatural helper attributed to each human being at his birth.[20] Today, some people will rather talk about "spiritual energy", even "cosmic energy", and parts of it seem to be given to the worthy participants in about the same way.

Visionaries and Politics

Nineteenth century famous Sioux leaders were great visionaries; some were holy men (see for example Little Wound in WALKER 1980). The Hunkpapa chief Sitting Bull was a seer, and saw what was going to happen during the battle of the Little Big Horn. It is also said he possessed a strong medicine against bullets. The Oglala Sioux leader Crazy Horse was a medicine man who came from a family that contributed several holy men to its *tiyospahe* (community). Many contemporary Sioux strongly believe that the spirit of Crazy Horse still watches over the Indian people.[21]

Contemporary elected Reservation leaders do not seem to be visionaries or medicine men. But it is interesting to note that several leaders of the American Indian Movement (A.I.M.)[22] have tried to acquire supernatural help by undergoing some forms of self-torture during huge annual ceremonies called Sundances. Between 1970 and 1995, I have been able, almost every year, to visit the Sioux Reservations in order to assist to a Sundance.

Some American Indian Movement members have sundanced several times a year at ceremonies held at Crow Dog's Paradise on the Rosebud Reservation or at Green Grass on the Cheyenne River Reservation. Green Grass is a holy place for the Sioux. In this village the Holy Pipe is kept which was given to them by White Buffalo Woman or Calf Maiden, mythical daughter of Sun and Moon. After having sundanced several times, AIM leaders have conducted sweatlodges and have sponsored Sundances. The Chippewa AIM leader DENNIS BANKS did so at Deganawidah-Quetzalcoatl University at Davis in California. Several AIM leaders have had visionary experiences at Sundances under the tutoring of some well known holy men, Franck Fools Crow, Lame Deer and Leonard Crow Dog, a Rosebud holy man. The last two holy men have been strong supporters of the American Indian Movement.[23]

---

[20] Cf. VAZEILLES 1982, 1984; see also WALKER 1917.
[21] CRAZY HORSE, cf. VAZEILLES 1974: 562–569.
[22] Cf. VAZEILLES 1974: Part 6 "Red Power" 548–585.
[23] Cf. VAZEILLES 1984: 539–549, 1996: 311–312.

Up to now, it was believed that only holy men (*wicasa wakan*) could conduct a Sundance. However, some contemporary Indians think that by doing four or five times the Sundance, one becomes a religious leader of the Indian people, a medicine man. Quite a lot of Sioux traditionalists call these new kinds of Spirits' specialists, "instant medicine men".

SUNDANCING

Participation in Sundances was in the "80's" the thing to do if one wanted to be and to prove he was a "real Indian", a traditionalist. The Sundance is a collective celebration which gives an opportunity to some of the "Sundancers" to communicate with the Spirits. Since I first saw this important annual ceremony of the Plains Indians, it has changed in an extraordinary way.[24] In 1969, on the Sioux Reservations there was but one Sundance, that of the Pine Ridge Oglala Sioux. In 1973, after the occupation of Wounded Knee on the same Reservation by AIM members and Chicano friends, each Sioux Reservation decided to hold one Sundance every summer. During the 1978 Sundance at Pine Ridge, there were four sundancers. Ever since, sundancers have become more and more numerous. In 1980, at the Green Grass Sundance, there were 140 dancers, some 95 male dancers, more than in Sitting Bull's time. For 15 years now or so, each traditional community on the Cheyenne River Sioux Reservation has been having a Sundance, with more than twenty sundancers at each celebration.

During this ceremony, the Sundancers undergo some sort of self-torture. They fast all along and drink very little (sage tea). They fasten to their chest by the means of bear or eagle claws or wooden pegs, a rawhide rope which is connected to the central post, the Sunpole. (The Sunpole represents the means of communication with the Great Spirit through the intercedings of *Wi* – Sun, *Tatanka* – Buffalo Bull and *Wakinyan* – Thunderbird.) Others will try to suspend themselves from the Sunpole by shorter thongs tied up in their chests or back skins. Others have vowed to pull behind them around the Sundance bowery several buffalo skulls connected to their chest skin with raw hide thongs and claws. Some others choose to be tied up between four poles, by two skewers dug in their shoulders and two others in their chest. Enduring their awful pains, they will pray for the welfare of their relatives, of the Indian Nations, and for

---

[24] VAZEILLES 1974: 508–547, 1977: 151–165, 1984: 2 chap. on Sundance 13–14, 585–690, 1986b, 1991c.

"all men of good will". Then, they will fight to get free, a wild and painful dance against ignorance, illness and poverty.

Sundancing has become a reenactment of positive ethnic identity and serves to transmit pride in native life. More and more young Indians participate actively in the Sundance, taking their share in the self-sacrificing practices. The Pine Ridge, Rosebud and Green Grass Sundances have been intertribal ceremonies with participants coming from other reservations, and from out of state; quite many sundancers are urban Indians. Some belong to revival groups of Eastern Indians who are trying to revive ancient rituals and come to see how Sioux people are doing in order to adapt tribal rites and beliefs from another tribe.

To most Sundancers, participation in these rituals is an important political statement. It seems that, for most of the dancers, their involvement is more emotional and cultural than theological. Few dancers seem to be ready to examine deeply their own religious and philosophical motivations. Nonetheless, some sundancers think sundancing is a powerful means of solving the awful problems, especially alcoholism and youth delinquency, engendered by living within dual societies.

REVIVAL, CONFLICTS

A revival of traditional activities, spiritual concepts and practices has been observed in North America during the last thirty/forty years among American Indians. Hundreds of young Indians join the Sundances and other shamanic ceremonies. It is very hard to give a quantitative analysis of this topic.

Indian Way and Young Indians

On one hand, more and more young people participate in powwows.[25] Those "Indian Celebrations" are social meetings and feasts which include religious activities and give-aways. The traditional dancing outfits that dancers proudly wear are becoming more and more "traditional", i.e. made of natural materials. Powwows are held year around on reservations and in the "Indian Centers" in urban areas. Traditional songs and dances are heard and performed but new songs and steps are eagerly recorded and greatly appreciated by Indian dancers, musicians and their relatives and friends.

---

[25] Powwows, cf. VAZEILLES 1974: 392–440, 1977: chap. 6: 121–138.

On the other hand, a lot of Indian teenagers no longer want to be members of traditional Indian ceremonies and the same thing can be said as far as Christian rites are concerned. For example, according to the Catholic priest and nuns in Eagle Butte, main town of the Cheyenne River Sioux Indian Reservation (around 5000 inhabitants in 1990's), only about a dozen or so youngsters take part in Christian activities and ceremonies. Having flunked out of high school and having nothing to do, they roam around doing mischief in rural communities and towns. Unfortunately, for the last 10 years they have been organized into quarrelsome gangs by Sioux dropouts and hooligans from urban areas[26] who had been sent back home to the reservations. As a result, juvenile delinquency and drug addicts have drastically increased. So far, reservation relatives, psychologists, police members and tribal government people are powerless.

All-Indian Way or Christian Influenced Shamanism?

Sioux people adopt whenever they can the technical and material goods of the modern world. They know the only thing that belongs to them is the Indian religion, which remains effective to combat assimilation. Indian people living more or less according to "Indian religious traditions" seem to be divided in two groups. Half of them would like to go back to "all-Indian traditions", i.e. which are not mixed with other religious practices. Their knowledge of old religious beliefs and practices go back to their grandparents who have been raised in reservation schools and so were taught to forget Indian way of life and religion.

To give just one example, a couple of years ago a group of Sioux singers and drummers at powwows and Sundances has tried to revive some old Sundance songs and prayers recorded at the turn of the century by ethnomusicologist FRANCES DENSMORE.[27] They were stopped by the Sundance's intercessor who thought those songs "too fancy". They tried to explain to the old traditionalists that F. DENSMORE recorded live shamans but to no avail.

Many Indians do not trust books written by white anthropologists and essayists, even when they are biographies of medicine men. For example, I remember one day, a Sioux "traditionalist" of forty years of age wanted to know "since when the Sioux people could talk with animals". The 75 years

---

[26] Over two third of the North American Indians live in the USA and Canadian big cities, cf. VAZEILLES 2000.

[27] Cf. DENSMORE 1918.

old holy man, who was the center of our talk on "Indian ways", answered "since Noah" and proceeded to give a Christian oriented explanation of this shamanic trend. The young man was furious: he wanted "an all-Indian answer". We became divided into two groups which hotly argued for a couple of hours, the anthropologist being asked to be a referee or to present proofs out of Sioux shamans' biographies which were, nevertheless, refused by one group of people.

Indian Traditionalists and New Agers ("Rainbow People")

As I said before, having worked in Sioux reservations in South Dakota for over 30 years, I have observed a surge of interest on the part of a large number of white people who wished to take part in Indian rituals (Sundance, sweatlodge and Vision Quest). This interest began first in the 70's and was renewed about ten years ago. Though slight at the beginning, the attendance of white people, mostly New Age devotees, at these rituals for the last ten years is tolerated less and less. Problems started at Bear Butte, a volcanic mountain East of the Black Hills where Plains Indians have always hold great religious meetings. Nowadays there is a national park on one side of which Indians have their ceremonies and, on the other side, the white New Agers. I have been told that the latter wanting "to be reconnected with the natural way" go around to the ceremonies "somewhat too naked thus embarrassing very badly" the Indian traditionalists.

NEO-SHAMANISM AND NEW AGE: LAKOTA SIOUX CONNECTIONS[28]

Today, an important question concerning some of the books about American Indians needs to be raised: who is talking about whom and about what?

One example is DOUGLAS BOYD's biography of Rolling Thunder, a Cherokee medicine man. This medicine man's reputation has rapidly spread beyond the borders of Indian reservations. His shamanic speech is filled with references to New Age beliefs and practices: for example, he often talks about the "law of karma"; he knows that a long time ago, "some of the descendents of the Ancient People escaped from the land that sank into the Pacific and landed on the West coast of North America..." (BOYD 1974: 8).

---

[28] See my paper "Shamanism and New Age: Lakota Sioux Connections", 2002.

Another author, ALLEN C. ROSS, who presents himself as being a Dakota Sioux, Doctor in Psychology, wrote his first book *Mitakuye oayasin – We are all related* in 1989. This book is full of interpretations borrowed from Western esoteric practices and beliefs all connected today with New Age, through esoteric authors like EDGAR CAYCE (1877–1945), a famous American medium in contact with "the universal memory of all times", through books about the "hemispheres of the brain" or about "Supersonics, the Science of radiational Paraphysics", through MARILYN FERGUSON'S New Age book *The Aquarian Conspiracy* and many other esoteric works.

Another writer, BARBARA MEANS ADAMS, who introduces herself as "a Makah Indian, one of the seven bands of the Oglala Sioux", is connected with New Age practices and beliefs. This Californian Sioux woman received "a crystal that changes colors" and which is supposed to be part of "a staff that was owned by a chief about 4000 B.C." She says that "pieces of this staff were revealed to several persons, and that they are waiting to be united again" (1990: 11–12). This is a theme which is a common feature to European esotericisms, legends and science fiction novels and films. Like many New Agers, ADAMS practices "automatic writing" (1990: 9) and she went through a "Near Death Experience" in a hospital, etc.

These fanciful books written by Indians, pseudo-Indians and Whites in collaboration with so-called medicine men are denounced by Reservations Indians. They also denounce the commercial exploitation of different Amerindian religions through "New Age" books, neo-shamanic training courses, and "so-called American Indian objects with divinatory powers"; to them, these practices misrepresent the North American Indians' traditional religions. American Indians consider that the mixing of religious practices derived from several Indian traditions is aiming to destroy the originality and integrity of the different Indian tribes' religious practices and beliefs. They criticize these books for their rather insulting simplification of rituals and for the reductive accounts they give of the lives and beliefs of the Indian people that are literally vampirized by these "New Age" authors and "gurus" of all kinds.

I have seen some of those fanciful books written by Sioux people on the bookcases of quite a few Indians on the Sioux reservations, together with other modern esoteric books, especially some on "Near Death Experiences". The books written by these "modern Indians seers" are appreciated. They are easy to read, being written for a general public and are even considered "marvelous because they clearly show that Sioux beliefs can be compared with Western beliefs", and because they speak about a "Mother Earth Spirituality" which speaks of "the unity of all races and all living things", and "they demonstrate that it applies Native American teachings and rituals to contemporary living".[29]

CONCLUSION

In many ways, ritual specialists seem to be winning the leadership over the civil community and reservation leaders. Such a change in the leadership system already appeared during the second part of last century when being Ghost dancers seemed to be for many Indian people the only escape from a despairing life on Reservations. Sioux Ghost Dances' leaders, men who traveled to the Nevada valley to meet Wowoka, the Païute messiah, became as famous as such historical leaders as Red Cloud, and as a result, almost half of the Sioux became Ghost Dancers.[30]

The revitalization of the traditional Sioux belief system (spirit meeting and sundancing) appears to be a powerful means of shielding the mental and physical integrity and health of Sioux People.

It is interesting to note that it is the group rituals, Sundancing, sweatlodges, Spirit meetings, directed by well known holy men, which are being revitalized. Perhaps because it seems easier for 20th century men and women to let themselves, as a group, be carried away to unearthly realms, to non-ordinary states of consciousness.

Today, only shamans-to-be go alone to communicate with the Spirits according to the ascetic rite (*hanbelachia*) performed in the past by every man at least once in his life. Calling and instruction by dream visions, guidance and teaching by a shamanic ritualist, ordeals in quest of a personal power-vision finally received in an altered state of consciousness, fasting, thirsting, pain and privation as well as high intensity rhythmic drumming, in frequencies which can be expected to evoke auditory driving responses in human brains, are the shamanic characteristic features which show the dynamics of the Sioux beliefs system.

Nowadays, they are practiced as collective activities to facilitate entry into the altered state of consciousness so important for achieving lasting personality changes. The Sioux belief system, which—as all shamanic systems—is concerned with the betterment of traditional people, tries

---

[29] See for example the essay *Rainbow Tribe. Ordinary People Journeying on the Red Road* (1992) written by ED MCGAA – Eagle Man, author also of *Mother Earth Spirituality* (1990). ED MCGAA presents himself as "an Oglala Sioux writer, lecturer, and ceremonial leader".

[30] The Ghost Dance lasted a year (1889–1890) on the Sioux Reservations, see VAZEILLES 1984: chap. 12 "The Ghost Dance": 551–584; see JAMES MOONEY's magistral study on messianic movements in North America, first published in 1896.

constantly to restructure the "cosmic harmony" between human beings and the world at large. In addition, this revivification of Sioux shamanism also appears to be a most powerful means in fighting assimilation.

What, then, is to be thought of American Indian authors, such as the Sioux A. C. ROSS and B. M. ADAMS? They "vampirize" their own culture, thus negating its originality and values since they account for it by borrowing Western esoteric values, symbolic images and beliefs. Consequently, they endanger its survival as, in doing so, they might transform parts of their culture into esoteric trivialities.

REFERENCES

ADAMS, BARBARA MEANS
    1990 *Prayers of smoke. Renewing Makaha Tribal Tradition.* Berkeley, Cal.: Celestial Arts.
BOYD, DOUG
    1974 *Rolling Thunder. A personal exploration into the secret healing powers of an American Indian medicine man.* New York: A Delta Book, Dell Publishing Co. Inc.
BURNETTE, ROBERT – KOSTER, JOHN
    1974 *The tortured Americans: an account of the American Indians' long fight against corruption, exploitation and oppression.* New Jersey: Prentice Hall Inc.
DENSMORE, FRANCES
    1918 *Teton Sioux Music.* Washington D.C.: Bulletin of the Bureau of American Ethnology, n° 61.
FERGUSON, MARILYN
    1981 *Les Enfants du Verseau, pour un nouveau paradigme.* Paris: Calmann-Lévy.
HULTKRANTZ, ÅKE
    1953 *Conception of the Soul among North American Indians.* Stockholm: The Ethnographical Museum of Sweden, Monography Series.
JILEK, WOLFGANG
    1982 *Indian healing, Shamanic ceremonialism in the Pacific Northwest today.* Surrey, B.C.: Hancock House Pub.
LAME DEER/JOHN FIRE – ERDOES, RICHARD
    1972 *Lame Deer, seeker of visions.* New York: Simon & Schuster.
McGAA, ED
    1990 *Mother Earth Spirituality: Native American Paths to Healing Ourselves and Our World.* (Illustrations by M. N. Buchfink) New York & San Francisco: Harper & Row (Native American Studies / Environmental Issues).
    1992 *Rainbow Tribe. Ordinary People Journeying on the Red Road.* New York: Harper Collins Pub. (Harper San Francisco).

MAILS, THOMAS
1979 *Fools Crow*. New York: Double day & Company.
MOONEY, JAMES
1973 *The Ghost Dance Religion and Wounded Knee*, New York: Dover Publications Inc. (1896 *The Ghost Dance Religion and Sioux Outbreak of 1890*, 14th Annual Report of the Bureau of Ethnology, Washington: Government Printing Office.)
NEIHARDT, JOHN G.
1961 *Black Elk speaks: the life story of a holy man of the Oglala Sioux*. London: Barrie & Jenkins.
ROSS, ALLEN CHUCK
1993 *Mitakuye Oyasin*. *"Nous sommes tous frères"*. Plazac-Rouffignac (24580): Editions Amrita/Arista (1989, 1990, *Mitakuye Oyasin*. *"We are all related"*, Kyle, Box 346, South Dakota: Bear Publishing).
POWERS, WILLIAM, K.
1982 *Yuwipi*. *Vision and Experience in Oglala Ritual*, Lincoln and London: University of Nebraska Press.
VAZEILLES, DANIÈLE
1974 *Interactions des Indiens et des Blancs dans la Cheyenne River Sioux Indian Reservation, S.D., USA*. (Thèse d'Ethnologie) Paris: Université de Paris-V-Sorbonne (multigraph).
1977 *Le Cercle et le Calumet*. Toulouse: Privat.
1982 Quelques aspects du chamanisme des Indiens Sioux Lakotas. *L'Ethnographie, Voyages chamaniques II*, T. 78, n° 87/88, Paris: Maisonneuve et Larose, 113–130.
1984 *Oiseau-Tonnerre et Femme Bisonne Blanche; dynamisme du chamanisme des Indiens Sioux Lakota*. (Thèse de Doctorat d'Etat dès-Lettres et Sciences humaines) Paris: Université Paris-V-Sorbonne.
1985 Chamanes et guérisseurs sioux: parenté et harmonie cosmiques. In *Anthropologie et ethnologie française: Le corps humain. Nature, culture, surnaturel. Montpellier*, 345–364.
1986a Oiseau-Tonnerre, maître des Eaux: représentations symboliques de l'eau chez les Indiens des Plaines in 111ème Congrès national des Sociétés savantes. In *Anthropologie et ethnologie français: Usages et représentations de l'eau*. Poitiers, 287–301.
1986b Communication avec les Esprits et identité culturelle: exemples sioux. *Revue languedocienne de Sociologie et Ethnologie: La communication*, Université Paul Valéry – Montpellier III, mai, 47–59.
1989 Shamans et visionnaires sioux intermédiaires entre les Esprits et les humains. In A. F. LAURENS (ed.) *Entre hommes et dieux: le convive, le héros, le prophète*, A.T.P. Les Polythéismes, Montpellier 1984–1986, Besançon: Annales Littéraires de l'université de Besançon, 169–180.
1990a Le double style de vie des berdaches, les hommes femmes amérindiens. *Revue languedocienne de Sociologie et Ethnologie: Identité et style de vie*. Université Paul Valéry – Montpellier III, 167–194.

1990b Suenos y visiones de los Sioux Lakotas. In MICHEL PERRIN (coordinator) *Anthropologia y Experiencias del Sueno*, Quito, Ecuador: Abya-Yala Ediciones (Col. 500 Anos, n° 21), 49–66.

1990c 13 notices sur les principes philosophiques des Indiens Sioux. In SYLVAIN AUROUX (ed.) *Les Notions philosophiques*. vol. 2 de *l'Encyclopédie Philosophique Universelle* (direction André Jacob) Paris: P.U.F. (*canunpa, Iktomi, inipi, hanbleceya, ihanblapi, mitakuye oyasin, Takuskanskan, ton,* sweatlodge, trickster, *wakan, Wakan Tanka, Wakanlapi, wicasa wakan, yuwipi*).

1990d Comptes rendus d'ouvrages sur les traditions, les mythes et la philosophie des Indiens Sioux. In *Les Oeuvres philosophiques*. Dirigé par JEAN-FRANCOIS MATTEI – JEAN POIRIER, vol. 3 de *l'Encyclopédie Philosophique Universelle*, Paris: PUF. (BLACK ELK & BROWN, J. E. 1953. *Les Rites Secrets des Indiens Sioux*; Densmore, Fr. 1918. *Teton Sioux Music*, DEMALLIE, R. 1985. *The Sixth Grandfather: Black Elk's Teachings given to John Neihardt*; Fire/Lame Deer (Tahca Ushte) & R. ERDOES 1972. *De mémoire indienne*; MAILS, TH. 1979. *Fools Crow*; NEIHARDT, J. & BLACK ELK (Hehaka Sapa) 1932. *Elan Noir, la vie d'un saint homme des Sioux oglala*; POWERS, M. 1986. *Oglala Women. Myth, Ritual and Reality*; POWERS, W. 1975. *Oglala Religion*; 1982. *Yuwipi, Vision and Experience in Oglala Ritual*; VAZEILLES, D. 1977. *Le cercle et le calumet*; 1984. *Oiseau-Tonnerre et Femme Bisonne Blanche. Dynamisme du chamanisme des Sioux Lakotas*; 1991. *Les chamanes, maîtres de l'Univers.*; WALKER, R. R. 1917. *The Sundance and Other Ceremonies of the Oglala Division of the Teton Dakota*; 1980. *Lakota Belief and Ritual*; 1982. *Lakota Society*; 1983. *Lakota Myth*.)

1991a *Les chamanes, maîtres de l'univers. Persistance et exportations du chamanisme.* Paris: Editions le Cerf.

1991b Rêves sioux. In *Revue Autrement: Terre indienne. Un peuple écrasé, une culture retrouvée.* Série Monde – H. S. Mai, 153–162.

1991c La danse du Soleil. In *Revue Autrement: Terre indienne. Un peuple écrasé, une culture retrouvée.* Série Monde – H. S. Mai, 163–173.

1996 *Chamanes et visionnaires sioux.* Paris: Editions Le Rocher/Le Mail.

1997 Religioni degli Indiani del Nordamerica. In FILORAMO, GIOVANNI (ed.) *Storia delle religioni. 5. Religioni dell'America precolombiana e dei popoli indigeni.* Roma–Bari: Editori Laterza (Enciclopedie del sapere), 143–168.

1999 Le Chamanisme des Amérindiens du Nord. In *Indian Summer. Les Premières Nations d'Amérique du Nord.* Bruxelles: Musées Royaux d'Art et d'Histoire, 225–237.

2000 Les Indiens des villes. In D. VAZEILLES – G. BEHLING et al. (eds.) *Identités et droits des minorités culturelles et linguistiques.* Montpellier: Université Paul Valéry – Montpellier III, 187–202.

2001 Shamanism and New Age: Lakota Sioux Connections. In HENRI-PAUL FRANCFORT – ROBERTE N. HAMAYON (in collaboration with PAUL G. BAHN (eds.) *The Concept of Shamanism: Uses and Abuses.* Budapest: Akadémiai Kiadó, 367–388.

VAZEILLES, DANIÈLE – LANIEL LE FRANCOIS, MARYSE
   1998   Les conceptions du monde des Indiens d'Amérique du Nord, In *Le discours philosophique,* Vol 4. de l'*Encyclopédie philosophique universelle.* Sous la direction de JEAN-FRANCOIS MATTEI. Paris: PUF.

WALKER, JAMES
   1917   *The Sun Dance and Other Ceremonies of the Oglala Division of the Teton Dakota in* Anthropological Papers, New York: American Museum of Natural History, Vol. 16. 2: 50–221.
   1980   *Lakota Belief and ritual.* Ed. by R. J. DE MALLIE – E. A. JAHNER. Lincoln: University of Nebraska Press, XIII–XXIX.

WISSLER, CLARK
   1912   *Societies and Ceremonial Associations in the Oglala Division of the Teton Dakota. Anthropological Papers.* New York: American Museum of Natural History, Vol. II. I: 1–99.

INDEX

aborigines of Taiwan, 83, 142–143

Allaggug, 21–24, 26–27, 30, 34

ALLAN, S. , 52, 57, 70, 76, 81–83, 96–97

allotheism, 202–203

Alma-Ata, 229–230, 233, 240

animal sacrifice, 9, 53, 117, 211, 213, 220–221, 226

Ape-spirit, 236

arwak, 181

ascent, 57, 64, 241, 246

audio-visual language, 270

baksy, 140, 147, 181, 230, 235–236, 239

Baldu Bayan, 113–116, 119

Baoshan, 67–69, 93, 95–96, 99, 107

BAUDRILLARD, J., 280, 291, 295

berdache / winkte, 312, 339, 351

Bible, 241–242, 244, 247–248, 250–251, 262

BIRRELL, A., 59, 63,–64, 70, 72–74, 76–79, 81, 84–94, 96–97,

Black Elk, 335, 342, 351

Bodhisattva, 22, 31

böö, 38–39, 41–42, 214, 309

Borneo, 156–157, 177

Buddhism, 3, 12, 16, 22–23, 26–27, 29, 31–33, 35, 38, 41, 43, 49, 140, 181, 183, 228, 255–257, 260, 285, 307, 323–324

Buryat shamans, 211, 223, 326

Buryat, 9, 140, 144–145, 147, 184, 211, 213–217, 219, 221–224, 226, 309, 326

CAHILL, S., 73–76, 96, 98

Chejudo, 27

CHEN SHOU, 227, 240

China, 2, 8–9, 13–14, 16–17, 32, 45–46, 48, 50–53, 55, 58–60, 63, 63–67, 69–70, 72–74, 78, 80, 82–84, 86, 91, 96–108, 116–117, 143, 151, 169, 179, 182, 187, 227–228, 235, 307, 311, 313, 315–316

Chinese medical system, 228

Christianity, 3, 5, 18, 26, 33, 203, 255–256, 262, 285, 301, 324, 328

Chu Silk Manuscript, 50, 53, 57, 67, 69, 77–78, 93–94, 96, 104

Chu, 45–108

co-gendered personality, 303

"cold" cultures, 206

commercialism, 290

concepts, 12, 22, 46, 49, 58, 67–69, 83, 102, 106, 133, 137, 147, 152, 157, 176, 219, 345

Confucianism, 32, 46–47, 58, 85, 255–257, 259, 301

consonant gradation, 205–206

COOK, C. A., 46, 49–50, 53, 55, 64, 67–71, 77–78, 83, 89–94, 96, 98–99, 104, 107 cosmological fatalism, 258–260

crossdressing, 304

Cultural Revolution, 228

cultural treasure, 281, 294

cyber divination service, 284

cyber neo–shamans, 287

cyber shamanic shrine, 293

cybernaut, 292–293

cybernetic posthuman, 291

cyberspace ecstasy, 291

cyberspace mudang, 280–281, 284, 287

cyberspace shaman, 280, 289, 293–294

cyberspace shamanic practices, 280–281, 289

cyborg Buddha, 293

cyborg shaman, 279–280, 293–294

David, 243

DAVIS, E., 280, 291, 295

death rituals, 153, 156, 169, 177

Deer Woman, 338–339

DELUEZE, G. and GUATTARI, F., 293, 295

deterritorialization, 288–289

Deva and Cinta, 267, 272–273, 277

directed daydream, 131, 134

DOLGIH, B. O., 197, 208

DOORE, G., 287, 332

dreamers, 338, 341

eagle-spirit, 236

ecstasy of communication, 291, 295

ecstasy, 8, 14, 18, 30, 34, 49, 75–76, 100, 134–136, 153, 176, 241–243, 250, 256, 280, 282, 291–292, 295, 316, 331, 333

electronic ecstasy, 280

ELIADE, M., 4, 7, 25, 30, 34, 47, 49, 100–101, 135–136, 147–148, 153–155, 176, 241, 291, 299–300, 305, 312

email divination, 281, 286, 290

eschatology, 26, 154, 174

etymology, 109–111

evil eye, 231, 233–234

evolution, 74, 87, 204, 206, 323, 328

Extraordinary Powers, 239

Ezekiel, 25, 242, 245–246, 248

FAN YE, 227, 240

Fengdu, 115

fire tongs, 236

folk doctors, 228

Fools Crow, 337, 342

fortunetelling altars, 261

Fusang, 81, 97

Fuxi, 76–79, 82, 97

GAENSZLE, M., 267, 271–272, 277

gender crossing, 303

gender, 13, 251, 279, 288, 291, 300, 303–306, 308–309, 311, 313–315

Girardot, N. J., 47, 49, 65, 76, 78–79, 88, 96, 101, 103,

Girimsa, 21–23, 26–27

Gonggong, 85–86, 91, 93–94, 97

Gorbachev, 229

Gračeva, G. N., 197, 202–203, 208

Gun, 73–74, 84–86, 94, 97,

Guodian, 67–69, 95–96, 102

Gwang-yu, 21–23

HARNER, M., 4, 12, 287, 295, 314, 318–319, 322–323, 330

HAWKES, D., 52–53, 60–63, 66, 83–84, 86, 93, 96, 101

HAYLES, N. K., 279, 291, 293, 295

"hot" cultures, 206

Huainanzi, 46–47, 53–54, 57, 59, 64–67, 69, 73, 78–79, 81–85, 87, 90–96, 103

Huangdi, 70, 81, 89–92, 96–97, 103

HULTKRANTZ, Å., 3, 7, 15, 135, 137, 139, 141–143, 146–148, 300, 313–314, 337, 350

Hundun, 73, 85, 87–88, 90, 94, 96–97

Iban, 153, 155–160, 162–164, 166–167, 169, 171, 173–174, 176–177

Ihanblapi (dreamers), 338, 341, 352

imam, 233

incantations, 140, 198–199, 201, 204–205

information technology, 280, 292

Internet, 197, 275, 279–281, 284–294, 317, 317, 329

interview, 43, 140, 197, 214, 221, 230–231, 276, 331, 333

Inuit, 4, 138, 143–144, 146, 150, 298, 300, 311, 315

Islam, 3, 228, 239, 301

Janγrin je, 41–43

JILEK, W., 337, 350

John Fire/Lame Deer, 335, 337, 343, 350, 352

Kalevala, 205, 210

Kalmyk, 37–43, 184

Kamassian, 109, 111

Kazakh baksy, 140

Kazakh, 140, 143, 146, 227–229, 231–233, 235, 238–240

Kazakhstan, 227, 231, 240

ketman, 236–237

Kets, 137, 146

khamchy, 230

Khitan, 227

khumalaq, 230

kibog, 256, 261–262

King Narasu, 30

King Sarasu, 21–24, 26, 30

Korea, 2, 11–12, 15–16, 21–23, 28–30, 32–35, 143, 255, 257, 262–263, 279, 281–282, 300, 306

Korean Buddhism, 22

Korean musok, 285

Korean shamanic heritage, 279–280, 294

Korean shamanism, 11–12, 15–16, 21–30, 32–33, 35, 140, 202, 255, 260–261, 281–282, 287, 290, 293, 312

Koryak, 141, 146, 148, 308

KOSTERKINS (family), 196–199, 203, 209

kui, 55, 79–80, 86, 89, 93, 97

Kunlun, 47, 73–75, 97

kut, 16, 28, 149, 281–282, 287

Lakota Sioux, 335, 342, 347, 352

language cultivation, 207

LE BLANC, CH., 66–67, 76, 79, 89, 96, 103

Leigudun, 67–68

LENIN, V. I., 200, 203

LENNART, M., 197, 200

LEVY, P., 288, 292, 295

liminal phase of the ritual, 132

LINTROP, A., 197, 199, 209

LOEWE, M., 47, 57, 63, 68, 70–71, 73, 89–90, 96–98, 101–102, 104, 106–107

loss of vital energy, 133

MAILS, TH., 337, 342, 351–352

MAJOR, J. S., 46, 48, 50–53, 55, 57, 62, 65, 69–70, 73–74, 76, 88–91, 93–94, 96, 98–99, 103–104, 107

Malaysia, 143, 156, 177

malicious tongue, 231, 234

Manchu, 8–10, 17, 113, 116–119, 121, 142–143, 146, 180, 222, 227, 307–308, 312–314

Manichaeism, 228

Mañjuśrī, 22, 31

MARCO POLO, 216, 227, 240

MATHIEU, R., 45, 47, 49, 52, 59, 63–65, 72, 77, 81, 84, 96, 105

Mawangdui, 57, 67, 77, 80–82, 88–90, 96, 101, 108

mediumship, 136, 301–302, 327

molda, 233, 239

Mongols, 15, 38, 42, 145–146, 148, 180, 182, 188, 190, 227, 238, 309, 311, 313

Muslim, 180, 182, 185, 228, 231, 239

mythosophy, 37–38

nabi, 242–243

Nanay, 8, 142

neo-shamanism, 12, 17, 287, 295, 317–322, 324–325, 327, 330, 332, 347

Nepal, 2, 125, 128, 130, 132–134, 143, 223, 267, 272–273, 277, 310, 314

Nestorianism, 228

netizen, 279–281, 285, 291, 293–294

new age spirituality, 287

New Age, 135, 287, 295, 318, 320–321, 324, 330, 347–348, 352

Ngamtusuo, 196

Nganasan(s), 111, 146, 150–151, 195–210

Nishan Shaman, 113–114, 117,121, 307, 314

Nishan Shaman's Book, 113

North American Indians, 143, 312, 346, 348, 350

Nüdan, 115–116, 119

Nüwa, 76–78, 89, 97

Obugrians, 144, 146

Octosyllabicity, 205

off-line communication, 285

Omosi Mama, 115–118

online shamanic practices, 284

online shamanic service, 288

OPPITZ, M., 10, 17, 143, 150, 223, 267, 273–274, 276–277

Paekche, 259

Pantheon, 9, 34, 58, 63, 70, 73, 86, 96, 202–203

Pari Kongju, 259

Pengzu, 88–89, 91, 97

performance, 2, 11, 30, 70, 149, 155, 157–158, 162, 166, 183, 200, 213, 229, 241, 248–251, 268, 271–272, 281–282, 287–288, 297–298, 305–306, 311, 320

poetic speech, 111, 206

POPOV, A. A., 144, 146, 150, 197, 202, 210

possession, 50, 52, 62, 126–129, 131–133, 135–145, 149, 164, 166, 239, 256, 260, 299–300, 302–303, 314

POWERS, W. K., 338, 351–352

Princess Bari, 24–25, 28

psychosynthesis, 134

Puche Tosa (Fan Taoist Hermit), 281, 284–286, 289–290

Pureland, 22, 27, 29, 33, 35

pyshaq, 230

Qu'rān, 230–235, 238–239

Queen Sŏndŏg, 29–32

raven-spirit, 236

RAWSON, J., 54, 56–58, 61, 64, 66, 96, 101, 106

realtime divination, 284

religious pluralism, 292–293

revival of shamanism, 287

RHEINGOLD, H., 280, 291–292, 295

rituals for rain, 261

RUBRUCK, W. V., 146, 151, 227, 240

Saul, 242–243, 247–248

Sergudai Fiyanggo, 113, 119

shamanic cultures, 304, 321

shamanic epidemic, 40

shamanic experience, 137, 139, 144

shamanic ritual, 2, 25, 131, 137, 160, 221, 239, 241, 248–250, 255, 267–268, 270–273, 276, 285, 287, 304, 349

shamanic trance, 138–139

Shanhaijing, 46, 53–55, 57, 59, 63–67, 69–70, 73–75, 77–79, 81–82, 84–85, 87, 89–94, 96, 101

Shilla, 21, 31–35, 258–259, 261

SIMA QIAN, 46, 53, 62, 70, 84, 93–94, 227, 240

SIMČENKO, J. B., 197–198, 202–203, 209–210

Siming, 94–95, 97

sinbyung, 287

Sioux, 324, 335–340, 342–352

snake-spirit, 236

Sŏchŏn, 23–24, 27

social prejudice, 282, 284–285, 289, 294

Socialism, 228

Sŏggamoni, 27

Solon, 116, 118–119, 121

soul counseling, 285, 287

soul flight, 299, 301–303

soul guiding, 141

Soviet Union, 5, 195, 197, 228–229, 322

spirit possession, 52, 62, 128, 131, 133, 149, 299, 302–303, 314

Sun Dance, 353

Sweatlodge, 336–337, 343, 347, 349, 352

symbolic healing, 132–134

tailgan, 214–215, 219

Taiyi, 94–95, 97, 104

talisman (bujok), 75, 279–281, 283–286, 288, 290, 294

Tamang, 125–126, 130, 132–134, 150

tambourine, 241, 243–245

Taoism, 29, 32, 46–47, 49–50, 54, 66–67, 70, 76, 85–86, 88, 90, 96, 101–102, 108, 116, 230, 255–257, 259–260, 301, 311

techgnosis, 280, 295

technocosmos, 292

telepresence, 291

Temple, 21, 31, 35, 293

Thailand, 143

Three Kingdoms, 240, 257, 261

Tianwen, 59, 61–64, 78, 83–85, 88, 90, 94, 96

Tibetan oracles, 140

tisvi, 230

Tungus, 142, 145, 149, 151, 227, 301, 308, 315

U.F.O.'s, 340

Udhn, 38

urban shamanism, 135

Uygur, 227, 235, 238–239

variants, 58, 72, 113, 116–120, 309

Veneration of Heaven and earth, 228

video-ethnography, 267

Virgil, 29, 35

virtual environment, 294

virtual reality, 280, 290–295

virtual religiosity, 280, 290–291, 294

virtual shamanism, 290

virtualization, 279, 288–289, 293

Vision Quest / Hanbelachia, 335–336, 347, 349

WALKER, J., 343, 352–353

Wangjiatai, 67–69, 77, 82–83, 90, 96, 102

White Old Man, 39–40

WISSLER, C., 338, 353

woman of Endor, 247–248

Wŏnang (Queen), 21, 23–26, 28–30

Wŏrinsŏgbo, the eighth, 26–27

Wu Xian, 64, 97

Xenotheism, 202–203

Xinjiang, 179, 230–231, 235, 238–240

xiongnu, 227

Xiwangmum 47, 73–74, 76, 96–97, 102, 108

Yakut shaman, 8, 141

Yaman ergĵana, 39

Yandi, 47, 89–93, 97

YOO MYUNG-OK, 287

Yuma-gyŏng, 33

Yuwipi meetings, 337, 342

Zhong – Li, 70–72, 93, 97

Zhu Rong, 70, 72, 78, 91–94, 97

Zhuangzi, 46–48, 54, 59, 63, 65–67, 69, 79, 84, 87–88, 90–91, 96

Zhuanxu, 70–71, 89, 94, 97